Social Work Research

An Applied Approach

Sakinah Salahu-Din

Florida Gulf Coast University

Boston   New York   San Francisco
Mexico City   Montreal   Toronto   London   Madrid   Munich   Paris
Hong Kong   Singapore   Tokyo   Cape Town   Sydney

Series Editor: *Patricia M. Quinlin*
Editorial Assistant: *Annemarie Kennedy*
Marketing Manager: *Taryn Wahlquist*
Composition and Prepress Buyer: *Linda Cox*
Illustration: *Nugraphic Design, Inc.*
Manufacturing Buyer: *JoAnne Sweeney*
Cover Administrator: *Kristina Mose-Libon*
Editorial Production Service: *Matrix Productions Inc.*
Electronic Composition: *Cabot Computer Services*

For related titles and support materials, visit our online catalog at www.ablongman.com.

Between the time Website information is gathered and then published, it is not unusual for some sites to have closed. Also, the transcription of URLs can result in unintended typographical errors. The publisher would appreciate notification where these errors occur so that they may be corrected in subsequent editions.

Library of Congress Cataloging-in-Publication Data

Salahu-Din, Sakinah N.
    Social work research : an applied approach / Sakinah N. Salahu-Din.
        p.   cm.
    Includes bibliographical references and index.
    ISBN 0-321-05722-8
        1. Social service—Research—Methodology.   I. Title.

    HV11 .S275 2003
    361.3'072—dc21   2002071199

Printed in the United States of America

10 9 8 7 6 5 4 3 2   08 07 06 05 04

Dedication

This book is dedicated to my family and a special friend. My husband Hakim gave unending help and was patient and uncomplaining while my life was consumed by "the book." I also thank my children, Maya Marlow, Abu Salahu-Din, and Ramadan Salahu-Din, and my grandchildren, Amina, Charles, and Tamari, although they sometimes asked, "Why are you writing that book?" This book is also dedicated to my sisters, Izetta Dunn of Miami, Florida, and Eleanor Bullard of Warner Robins, Georgia, who were inspiring through long-distance telephone calls, and to my brother, Robert Dunn of Atlanta, Georgia. And last, but not least, this book is dedicated to a special friend, Antoinette Mason of West Hartford, Connecticut.

This book is also dedicated to the memory of my parents, Osie and Susan Dunn, my sister, Leilia Dunn, and my brother, Ozie Dunn, who were all believers in higher education.

CONTENTS

4   Selecting a Problem for Investigation   64

PART FOUR

Qualitative Research Methods   195

10 Defining Qualitative Research   197

PREFACE

This book was written to give students a nonthreatening, step-by-step guide for learning how to conduct social work research and how to employ research methods as a basis for the evaluation of social work practice, based on my experience teaching research for more than 11 years and my 20 years of field experience as a social worker and regional social work administrator. Each chapter contains diverse generalist social work practice activities. Each also has a generalist case study at the beginning of the chapter to help students understand concepts presented, to facilitate their ability to integrate social work research theory and practice, and to provide opportunities for readers to apply the knowledge that they are acquiring. Teaching research using an experiential model taught me that this pedagogy method is less intimidating to students, who grasp concepts more quickly when opportunities are presented to practice what they are learning in a supportive environment. Thus, the hands-on instructional model is captured in this book. People reading the book can immediately apply the concepts in their educational experience, social work practice, and personal lives. Although this book was written for social work students, following a generalist model, the draft has been used with students from other disciplines, such as psychology, sociology, nutrition, education, counseling, and child study. It can also be a valuable resource for those who wish to strengthen their social research knowledge and research skills. The following section highlights some of the principal attributes of this book.

Chapter Organization

- The text emphasizes practice evaluation, with three chapters devoted to this area: practice evaluation using qualitative methods; practice evaluation using quantitative methods; and program evaluation.
- A chapter, Ethical Issues and Biases in Social Work Research, is included early to stress the significance of ethics, not only in social work practice but also in social work research.
- A chapter, Demystifying the Search for Information, is placed near the beginning of the book to emphasize the importance of learning to use the library and to access information from remote locations.
- Each chapter begins with a generalist case study to illustrate chapter concepts, which helps readers understand the topic, apply what they are learning, and integrate practice and research.
- At the beginning of each chapter, readers are greeted with a quote by a research student describing that student's feelings about a research course before taking the course, while enrolled in the course, and after completing the course. These quotes may help readers identify, in the learning process, with the first-hand experience of others.
- A Writing Strategy assignment at the end of each chapter, relating specifically to that chapter, enables students to apply concepts to generalist practice situations while improving their writing skills in research and across the curriculum.

- A Learning Activity assignment at the end of each chapter facilitates readers' understanding of information.
- An Information Technology assignment at the end of each chapter, with chapter-relevant Internet sites, gives readers an opportunity to use the Internet to search for information.
- Practice Activities throughout each chapter assist readers in focusing on specific chapter issues.
- With the long-standing emphasis on bridging the gap between research and practice, this book includes in the Appendix a paper, similar to the chapters, on creating research partnerships with child welfare agencies.
- Instructors may choose to teach from this book using the chapters consecutively or in any order that they desire.
- An *Instructor's Manual,* which includes strategies and tools for teaching social work research, such as syllabi (one syllabus is based on the book), assignments, and in-class learning activities, is available.

Acknowledgments

This book could not have been completed without the concrete and emotional support provided by family, friends, and colleagues. Catherine Posteraro, former reference librarian at Saint Joseph College and currently Executive Director of Wood Memorial Library and Museum in Connecticut, wrote Chapter 3, Demystifying the Search for Information. Professor Barbara Stuart, Yale University, provided writing strategies for each chapter and contributed to the *Instructor's Manual.*

Professors Rick Halstead and Joan Hofmann, Saint Joseph College; Professor Rob Veneziano, Western Connecticut State University, whose research classes also read the book and provided comments and suggestions; former research students, Joanne Ronalter and Donna Ward; and my husband, Dr. Hakim Salahu-Din, Central Connecticut State University, reviewed the entire book and gave invaluable comments and suggestions. Specific chapters were reviewed by Professors Ron DeGray, Saint Joseph College; Ameda A. Manetta, Winthrop University; Barbara Dicks, University of Connecticut; Virginia Rondero, Southwest Texas State University; and Lynette Warner, program supervisor, State of Connecticut Department of Children and Families. Delicia Heath, former research student, whose research paper was also used as a case example, also read selected chapters. Social research students at Saint Joseph College and Florida Gulf Coast University read the book and provided comments. Saint Joseph College administrators and social work faculty, Professors Lorrie Greenhouse Gardella, Jane Rudd, and Bob Madden and administrative assistant, Rose Meyer, and colleagues Professors Shyamala Raman, Saint Joseph College, and Barbara Dicks and Carrie J. Smith, Syracuse University, were tremendously supportive and encouraging. Dr. Johnny McGaha, Dean of the College of Professional Studies, and Dr. Patricia Washington, Chair of the Division of Social Work, both at Florida Gulf Coast University, are other advocates for this book. I am grateful to my first acquisitions editor at Allyn and Bacon, Janice Wiggins Clarke, who was motivating, had confidence in me, and was a great person with whom to work. In addition, I thank my current editor, Patricia Quinlin, for her thoughtfulness and support and for being a wonderful editor, and her editorial assistant, Annemarie Kennedy. For their helpful comments, I wish to thank the reviewers of the manuscript: Carol Boyd, Delta State University; William Cloud, University of Denver; Linda F. Crowell, University of Akron; Ameda Manetta, Winthrop University; Stephen M. Marson, University of North Carolina, Pembroke; Martha Raske, University of Southern Indiana; and Roland Wagner, San Jose State University. Last, but not least, I thank Christina Joyce at Florida Gulf Coast University for enthusiastically assisting with this project.

PART ONE

Introduction to Social Work Research

1 The Essence of Science and Social Work Research

I did not have experience with research before taking the course, except getting journals from the library for papers. I did not know what to expect because I had no knowledge about research. I was excited, however, and eager to take the class because the graduate school that I want to attend is research oriented, so I knew that I would get a good foundation before I went there.

—Junior Social Work Student

CHAPTER GOALS

Your major goals upon completion of this chapter are to:

- Understand the scientific approach to research.
- Distinguish between conventional ways of thinking and finding answers to questions and the scientific approach.
- Understand the purposes of research.
- Recognize the different approaches to research.
- Understand the relationship between research and theory.
- Understand the criteria for establishing causality.

Introduction

Research is a function that is performed by everyone regardless of educational status. Pre-school children, through curiosity about their environment, perform research. Elementary, middle, and senior high school children and youth conduct research for papers and school projects. College students write major term papers, theses, and doctoral dissertations. Social workers conduct research to find the most appropriate interventions to use with clients, to locate theories to help guide their practices, and to remain informed about issues relevant to the profession that impact clients and the social work profession in general. Some social workers use research strategies to gain understanding of clients' lives from the clients' perspective, while others perform research that will help them explain and predict clients' behavior.

People use a traditional approach to research when they search magazines, books, news-papers, journals, and the Internet to find answers to their questions about cars, appliances, televisions, lawn mowers, and other merchandise before making purchases. They apply re-search techniques when searching for information about cancer, allergies, heart disease, and other medical problems. People also find jobs, apartments, and homes by conducting research.

Why, then, does the word *research* evoke such strong feelings from students when it is such a regular part of most people's lives? On the first day in a research course, students an-swer this question in several ways. They acknowledge that they fear statistics, the detailed work involved, and the time-consuming nature of the subject. Mostly, though, they fear the unknown.

By the end of the research course, students are confident about their knowledge of re-search and its application to their personal, educational, and professional lives. When students become professional social workers, the merits of research crystallize. They use research in evaluating the effectiveness of their work with clients, families, groups, organizations, and communities and in assessing the worth of social service programs in effecting change in cli-ents' lives. And, they observe supervisors, administrators, policymakers, and legislators (whose decisions impact the lives of clients) use research in performing their individual and collective job responsibilities.

The following article summarizes one former student's feelings about research from the time that she realized that it was a required course until she was able to use her research knowl-edge and skills in her work. Students may identify with this student, and social work professors may gain a deeper understanding of students' feelings about research courses.

Persistence Pays Off

Patty McManus, BSW, Social Work Content Tutor

Since eighth grade I've wanted to be a social worker, and I always had high expectations for my future professional career. I was going to get teen runaways off the streets, be supportive of pregnant teens, and reverse the injustices of the oppressed.

After taking four years of high school courses that were of little interest to me, I entered SJC and embarked on a course of study that I actually cared about. The first shock, though, came when I saw the list of prerequisites for the social work major: Human Biology, Principles of Macroeconom-ics, and Fundamentals of Political Science. These were not my strongest subjects in high school, and

I could not imagine them being any easier at the college level. Regardless, with the support of peers and professors, I managed to make it through the first two years without incident. Then I prepared myself for the much anticipated social work curriculum.

Junior year got off to a good start. I was placed at Fred Wish School in Hartford eight hours per week. I began to learn about generalist social work practice in Methods I and about my peers' experiences in their placements in Field Practice class. Then came the second scariest moment of my undergraduate academic career, which can be summed up with two words: Research Methodology. After reading the description of this course, I was momentarily transformed into Monty Hall of the game show *Let's Make a Deal*. Maybe I can get out of taking this course if I swear on something sacred that I will *never* conduct social research of any kind, I thought. My practical side quickly accepted that escaping was not a possibility, and I tried to find something positive in the class.

I chose to study the identity formation of bi-racial teens and read voraciously on the subject. With time and patience (and a few moments of emotional instability), I managed to learn how to develop a problem statement, conduct a literature review, state a hypothesis, and collect, analyze, and report data. Overall, the semester was trying. Spring break was no break at all, but was actually spent working in the library. That semester was the only time in my undergraduate career when I actually considered dropping out to save myself the agony of completing the research paper. But the more I pressed on, the more determined I became to not only hand in a finished product, but a thoughtful one.

The hard work paid off on both academic and personal levels. I proved to myself that after this course, I could probably make it through anything at the MSW level. As a second year graduate student at UConn, I can say with confidence that this is true. So for those of you in the midst of the Social Research course or for those of you who will face the Beast in semesters to come, fear not. The concepts can be learned, and the work completed. And in the end, you will be better off for having completed the task.

For those of you who are having difficulty in this or any other Social Work course, please do not hesitate to call the ARC for an appointment.

Reprinted with permission of Dr. Judy Arzt, Director, Academic Resource Center

---

You are about to begin your journey toward understanding scientific approaches to research, which differ significantly from traditional methods. You will also learn about strategies for determining whether the services provided to clients make a difference in their lives and if agency program goals are being met. First, a case study is provided to facilitate your understanding of the concepts presented in Chapter 1. A discussion of the definition of research, making use of this example, then follows.

Generalist Case Study: Working with Baby Boomer Caregivers

Ms. Virginia Wilson is a gerontological social worker with the Department of Aging in a large metropolitan community. The agency provides and coordinates both in-home and community-based services. In-home services include case management, home delivered meals, medical transportation, respite care, home health aides, education programs, and information and referral. Coordinating long-term care, day care, and community education programs are additional community-based

(continued)

Working with Baby Boomer Caregivers   *Continued*

services the agency provides. Ms. Wilson is responsible for a caseload of 30 families that are experiencing a variety of problems ranging from needing meals at home and housekeeping services to protection from abuse and neglect.

Although a significant number of families seek services themselves, the majority are referred by other community agencies, such as hospitals, long-term care facilities, and visiting nurses. Most of the aging parents for whom services are provided are over 65 years old and represent African Americans, Caucasians, Puerto Ricans, and Jamaicans. In the last 15 years, Ms. Wilson has noted a substantial increase in clients over age 80. In this period, requests for services from children who are primary caregivers for their aging parents have increased. These requests for services are from the baby boomer generation, those born in the United States during the two decades immediately following World War II when there was a high birthrate. These baby boomers themselves expect to reach retirement age between 2010 and 2020.

The baby boomer caregivers may co-reside or live apart from their parents. Heart problems, cancer, pancreatitis, Alzheimer's, hypertension, and osteoporosis are examples of health problems facing their aging parents. Besides caring for their parents, these middle-aged children also have pre-teen and teenage children in the home who are experiencing normal pre-teen/adolescent conflicts, and the older adolescents are planning for employment or college after graduating from high school. Caregivers who co-reside with their parents provide most or all of their care, such as bathing, cooking, cleaning, and transporting for medical appointments. In some families, the adult children also take care of all of the personal needs of their parents because the parents are immobile or incontinent.

Adult children who live in separate households also provide significant amounts of care for their parents. Ordinarily these caregivers visit their parents daily, performing tasks in the parents' homes and often bringing work, such as their parents' laundry, back to their own home. Ms. Wilson noted that many of these families were experiencing role strain because of the need to help their parents, parent their children, and maintain full- or part-time employment all at once. Ms. Wilson also observed other stressors, such as conflictual relationships with other family members. Dissension often related to the refusal of sisters, brothers, aunts, uncles, nieces, and nephews to participate in the caregiving, even when they lived close by. In addition, there was the expectation that women should assume the caregiving role.

The medical system also creates frustrations for caregivers. For example, the ambulance is the only method of transporting immobile parents to medical appointments. If the visit were not an emergency, there could be an astronomical bill for ambulance services. Other complaints concern the high cost of medications not covered by Medicare, neglect while in the hospital or rehabilitation center, and long waits in doctors' offices. Some of the families considered long-term care placements for their parents. Clients of color, especially African Americans and Puerto Ricans, believed that their communities were strongly against placing aging parents in facilities. When they considered such placements, they did not follow through most of the time. Families that placed their parents felt a great sense of guilt.

Even though the care providers met with frustrations and stress, there were a number of reasons why many felt responsible for taking care of their parents. Both women and men felt obligated because of positive relationships with their parents throughout their lives. They believed that no one else was available or willing to accept the job. And, they maintained that they owed this care to their parents. As the number of requests for help are increasing, Ms. Wilson believes that she must find a way to help the baby boomer caregivers cope with these situations. She wants to know why people caring for their parents are experiencing so much stress and frustration.

> *Activity 1.* Think about experiences conducting research for personal, professional, or educational purposes. After recalling the process used, define research in your own words.

What Is Research?

Research is a way of finding answers to questions. It can be done in many ways. This chapter describes both the traditional approach and the scientific approach to doing research. This book shows you how to use a scientific method to solve problems and find answers to questions. The scientific process entails using logic, following rules, repeating steps, combining theories with facts, and using creativity, imagination, and critical thinking skills.

Regardless of your feelings about research, you are a consumer of research. In fact, you may have participated in research studies. Furthermore, most people conduct research, but do not usually consider themselves researchers. For example, before buying a car, you look for information about the reliability of the car, its price, and its rate of depreciation. To get this data, you may read *Consumer Reports* magazine, *Edmund's Car Guide* on the Internet, newspapers, and other printed materials and consider input from friends, especially those who are experts on cars. Besides conducting research to become a smart consumer, you may also carry out research on topics of a more personal nature, such as on problems that affect a friend, a family member, or you yourself. For example, if a family member is diagnosed with cancer, diabetes, or heart disease, you may search for materials to help you understand the disease and to prepare the family for meetings with the doctor. Although the research performed by most people is not scientific, it is research—an attempt to find answers to questions. Social workers who understand research are in a position to:

- Conduct research to determine how to best help clients.
- Conduct research to find answers to questions about the effectiveness of their interventions (services, therapy, programs) with clients.
- Be accountable to their clients, their agencies, the public, and funding sources by demonstrating how services and programs are making a positive difference in clients' lives.
- Be savvy consumers and help empower their clients to be smart consumers.
- Add to the knowledge base of the social work profession by producing research and sharing it with others through presentations and publications.
- Critique and understand research disseminated in journals and other professional literature.

In the case example at the beginning of this chapter, Ms. Wilson, the social worker, wants to conduct research on her new group of clients. She wants to conduct this investigation to help baby boomer clients, to be more informed herself about these caregiving arrangements, to be accountable, and to help empower her clients to take advantage of available resources and be capable of advocating for their parents. Since she had taken research courses in both her graduate and undergraduate social work programs, she has to decide whether to use a scientific approach to research or a conventional approach.

Important Points about Research

- Research is a way of finding answers to questions.
- Most people conduct research for personal, professional, or educational purposes or for all of these reasons.
- Social workers who conduct research are in a position to provide more effective services to clients, be accountable, and be intelligent consumers and teach clients to be intelligent consumers.

Ways of Thinking and Acquiring Knowledge

Activity 2.   As you read this section, list the ways that you ordinarily acquire knowledge. Compare your list with the class. In what ways is that definition similar or different from the scientific method described in this chapter?

The traditional procedure for finding answers to questions differs from the scientific way of thinking and acquiring knowledge. In the quest for information, you may use tradition, the media, intuition, practice wisdom, experts, logic, or a combination of these methods, as most people do. Although these are acceptable methods for accessing information, they have not been shown to be reliable for acquiring knowledge for scientific research purposes and for practice.

Conventional Methods of Acquiring Knowledge

Tradition.   One way of acquiring knowledge is from family customs, beliefs, values, and habits. Family traditions become your traditions. For example, some family traditions may include a yearly winter fishing vacation to Key West, Florida; eating collard greens, hopping john, and corn bread on New Year's Day; eating only cereal and fruit for breakfast; and participating in an annual Three Kings Day Celebration, the annual Macy's Thanksgiving Day Parade, or Saint Patrick's Day activities. Beliefs and values are also a part of tradition. Some people have grown up believing that their religion is the only true religion, that everyone can "pull themselves up by the bootstraps," or that corporal punishment should be used with children as a disciplinary method. Customs, beliefs, values, and habits are often passed down from generation to generation and are sometimes difficult to change.

The Media.   Books, television, magazines, radio, and newspapers are also common means of acquiring knowledge. For instance, opinions are sometimes formed about people from different ethnic groups according to whether television images are negative or positive. Images portrayed in the media can influence your thinking about these different groups and bias research and practice.

Intuition.   Innate knowledge, gut level feelings, or instinct are reliable methods of learning for many people, but not in scientific research.

Practice Wisdom. For experienced social workers their own experience is a way of finding answers to questions. Practice wisdom is a storehouse of information that practitioners have learned over the years and is often applied to new cases that are similar to previous cases. Although practice wisdom is useful in many practice and practice evaluation situations, it should not be used alone or as a substitute for scientific research.

Experts and Authority Figures. Individuals feel comfortable consulting experts to help solve problems. When you have persistent pain, a medical doctor, homeopathic doctor, chiropractor, or physical therapist is contacted. A lawyer is consulted to assist when you have a car accident, need a will, or buy a home.

Logic. Organized thinking, that is, the use of sound judgment, is another traditional way of acquiring knowledge. It is also a part of the scientific approach to problem resolution and finding answers to questions.

Without dismissing the conventional ways of acquiring knowledge, the scientific method is a more appropriate approach for social work research.

The Scientific Method of Acquiring Knowledge

What is science, and what is its role in social research? What do you think about when you hear or read the word *science*? Do you reflect on college courses that include both natural science courses and social science courses? Natural science courses encompass chemistry, physics, biology, zoology, and the physical sciences that deal with inanimate matter or with energy. The social science discipline includes courses such as psychology, social work, sociology, and anthropology that study people, the thoughts, feelings, and actions of people within families and in groups, and the interactions of people within the environment, including within institutions.

Science refers to a specific method for acquiring knowledge. This method is the scientific approach to research. It is empirical research because it uses a planned, organized approach in observing phenomena when searching for answers to questions. This observation of phenomena is done in a number of ways, such as by having research participants complete questionnaires or surveys, by interviewing participants directly, by observing participants from a distance, and by becoming directly involved in participants' everyday experiences. Some additional attributes of the scientific method of obtaining knowledge include:

- *Using a planned, organized approach* through all phases of the research process, from topic or problem selection through dissemination of the final report. When these steps are outlined in the publication or presentation of findings, other researchers should be able to replicate them.
- *Making vigorous attempts to obtain objectivity* while accepting that a certain amount of subjectivity by the researcher, such as allowing the researcher's own beliefs to interfere, is practically certain. Qualitative research, however, acknowledges the existence of subjectivity in findings.
- *Collecting information about the relationship between variables* from diverse sources and attempting to find causes.

- *Formulating and testing hypotheses.*
- *Using theory to guide research* and explain and predict phenomena.
- *Developing theories* in qualitative research.

Although the scientific approach takes measures, uses guidelines, and makes concerted efforts to assure that research is as objective as possible, problems can occur when the scientific approach is used. The scientific approach can be flawed by the researcher's own biases and by poor data collection methods (described later).

Important Points about Ways of Thinking and Acquiring Knowledge

- Conventional methods of acquiring knowledge are from tradition, the media, from intuition, from experts, and through logic.
- The scientific method of acquiring knowledge and finding answers to questions involves using a planned approach throughout the research process, formulating hypotheses, and testing and building theories.

Purposes of Research

> *Activity 3.* While reading this section, explain how you have used research for exploration, description, or explanation.

Research is conducted for the purposes of exploration, description, and explanation. When individual research studies are conducted for the purpose of exploring a topic, describing a topic, or explaining a topic, these studies are not necessarily independent. Exploratory studies are initiated first to gather information on topics for which little or no research is available and to generate questions for use in descriptive and explanatory studies. Descriptive and explanatory studies are often the basis for and build on results of exploratory studies in this knowledge-building continuum. In the everyday world of the researcher, these concepts are not mutually exclusive.

Research for Exploration

Exploratory research is conducted on topics for which there is little information in the literature. From the research findings, the researcher formulates theories and research questions that could be the basis for descriptive and explanatory research. Think about Ms. Wilson, in the case example, who has seen a substantial increase in the number of baby boomers caring for their aging parents and their own children. Her agency is considering a new program to address issues faced by this new clientele but wants to conduct research first to get a better understanding of the situation and the clients' needs. Ms. Wilson uses the scientific approach to research, and the supervisor suggests an exploratory research project with a group of 20 caregivers.

In this study, Ms. Wilson is interested in the adult children's experience as caregivers, their experience with stress, their financial problems, and special issues regarding parenting children while providing care for aging parents. Although exploratory research provides valuable information, it is not generalizable to the broader population from which the sample was selected. That is, this data cannot be applied to the experience of people who were not a part of the study. These studies may, however, be used as a basis for descriptive and explanatory studies and to give the researcher a deeper understanding of the experiences of the people in the sample.

Research for Description

Descriptive research often builds on the results of exploratory research efforts and attempts to answer the questions how and who. Ordinarily, the researcher knows something about the topic when descriptive research is initiated. After Ms. Wilson shares results of her exploratory research, her supervisor requests a more detailed investigation of baby boomer caregivers. She offers Ms. Wilson the opportunity to conduct a descriptive study, or she says Ms. Wilson may refer this task to the research unit if she does not have time to conduct the research herself. Ms. Wilson refers it to the research unit because of her large caseload.

In a descriptive study, relationships between variables emerge as does a description of caregiver characteristics, such as their ethnicity, income level, motivation for providing care, age, age of parents, and ages of children living in the home. To complete a descriptive study on baby boomer caregivers, the research unit randomly selects a large number of participants to complete a survey, or questionnaire. Random selection assures that the caregivers are representative of the people being studied. Representative means that the participants in the study are similar to the population from which the sample was drawn. They are similar in age, race, occupation, religion, social and economic background, or other characteristics of interest. Results from descriptive studies using random samples are generalizable, whereas exploratory study results are not. The United States *Census,* completed every ten years, is an example of a descriptive study of the United States population.

Because Ms. Wilson's supervisor is intrigued by the results of the descriptive research, more extensive data, such as explanations for some of the findings from the exploratory and descriptive studies are requested. Explanatory research strives to explain the variance in participants and find causes for behavior.

Research for Explanation

Explanatory research builds on exploratory and descriptive studies and uses hypotheses to predict the relationship between variables. A hypothesis, a tentative statement about the relationship between or among two or more variables, is explained in detail in Chapter 9. Besides explaining behavior, explanatory research attempts to determine causes of behavior, events, or situations.

This section described the three purposes for conducting research as exploration, description, and explanation. Besides the different purposes for conducting scientific research, there are also different approaches to doing research.

Important Points about Research Purposes

- Research done for the purpose of exploring a problem or topic for which little information is available is research for exploration, or exploratory research.
- Research conducted to describe a phenomenon by providing demographic information or to show relationships that exist between variables is research for description, or descriptive research.
- Research conducted for the purpose of explaining phenomenon and determining causes of behavior, events, or situations is research for explanation, or explanatory research
- Research for description and explanation often build on the results of exploratory research.

Approaches to Research

While there are specific purposes for conducting research, there are also specific research methods, quantitative and qualitative. The quantitative approach and the qualitative approach use different scientific methods.

Quantitative Research

Quantitative research methods, also known as positivist research, study a phenomenon by collecting data using surveys (questionnaires) containing closed-ended questions. There are several types of close-ended questions that provide different response choices from which participants choose. Common response categories are True or False, Multiple Choice, and Likert (Agree, Agree Somewhat, Disagree, Somewhat Disagree). While the primary source of data collection is through surveys using closed-ended questions, these questionnaires may also contain open-ended, qualitative questions. Although data collection instruments in quantitative research are usually mailed to research participants, quantitative data can be collected by telephone, in face-to-face interviews, and over the Internet. Researchers conducting quantitative studies strive for objectivity in the research process and the elimination of biases throughout the research process. Hypothesis testing, establishing causality (where one phenomenon causes another), and being able to predict and explain behavior based on research findings are also goals of quantitative research methods. Analysis of quantitative data is done using statistical data analysis procedures. Quantitative research methods differ from the qualitative methods described in the following section. Ms. Wilson's quantitative study consists of a four-page questionnaire containing Likert questions that she mails to research participants and asks be returned by a specific date. Once these questionnaires are returned, Ms. Wilson or the research unit analyzes the data using statistical data analysis methods.

Qualitative Research

Qualitative research, also known as interpretist research, relies on either in-depth, face-to-face interviews using open-ended questions, direct observation of participants, participation in the daily activities of people being studied, and the study of artifacts. Open-ended questions used in qualitative research do not have preselected responses from which participants choose. This research method acknowledges subjectivity in the research process and in research findings, while valuing objectivity. Researchers use narratives, words, documents, text, and observations in qualitative data analysis. Ms. Wilson's qualitative study of the baby boomer caregivers consists of several case studies. She uses an interview guide with one or more open-ended questions to gather information from several caregivers, using note taking and a tape recorder. She analyzes participants' stories by searching for meaning units and themes without the help of statistical methods.

Theory and Social Work Research

> *Activity 4.* While reading this chapter, share a personal theory with the class. How has this theory influenced your thinking and your behavior? How did you construct it?

> *Activity 5.* Think about your social work, sociology, and psychology classes. Select a theory (practice theory, theoretical framework) from one of these classes and share a description of the theory with your class. How does this theory compare with your personal theory?

What Is Theory?

A theory is a group of related concepts and propositions, based on facts and observations, that attempt to define, explain, and predict phenomena such as behavior, events, attitudes, and situations. Concepts, the building blocks of a theory, are ideas and thoughts translated into symbols that help people communicate. When concepts are connected, they form a relationship that is guided and organized by propositions. Propositions are statements about the relationship between concepts in a theory. Just as you use research on a personal and professional level, you use theories to guide decision-making, both personally and professionally. For example, if you are a parent who is concerned about the self-esteem of your young children, you might be interested in information from professionals who advise that positive feedback to children, among other factors, helps to foster positive, or high, self-esteem. The self-esteem theory suggests the attributes of a person with high self-esteem and predicts that children who receive positive feedback will have high self-esteem. Based on this knowledge, praise is given when appropriate.

On a professional level, you are an intern who is shadowing a child protective services investigator who relies on what theory in the literature reports as indicators of abused children and their perpetrators. These theories guide investigations of child abuse and neglect reports, help explain behavior of abused children, assist in predicting which parents are most likely to abuse their children, and characterize the behavior and physical appearance of abused children.

Earlier in this chapter, theory was defined as a group of related concepts and propositions, based on facts and observations, that attempt to define, explain, and predict phenomena such as behavior, events, attitudes, and situations. The following example provides a closer look at concepts, propositions, and theories through examples from the baby boomer case study:

Concepts from the Social Worker's Story
- Society's expectations of women
- Caregiving responsibilities for aging parents
- Stress
- Caregiving responsibilities for children

Connecting Concepts to Form Relationships
- Society's expectations of women are related to women's assumption of caregiving responsibilities.
- Caring for young children, adolescents, and aging parents is related to stress.

Forming Propositions
- Women assume more caregiving responsibilities because this is one of society's expectations of women.
- When the caregiving roles of parenting adolescents and caring for aging parents converge, stress occurs for the caregiver.

Selecting a Theory That Relates to the Issue: Systems Theory and Role Theory.   Systems theory accents reciprocal relationships within families and emphasizes that what happens in one part of the system (the family) influences all other parts of the system. Role theory, a component of systems theory, illuminates how roles assumed by individuals and expectations of people in those roles affect the individual's behavior. When people assume too many roles, role conflict and role strain can occur. Systems theory favors renegotiating roles to achieve balance in the system. Research can be conducted to test this theory, thus guiding research. Ms. Wilson tests systems theory in the quantitative study. She develops theory from knowledge acquired in the qualitative study.

In this section, theory, components of theories and how theories are used in both research and practice were explained. The next section explains how theories are applied in the quantitative and qualitative approaches to research. Theory building is done using an inductive approach, as in qualitative research, and theory testing is done using a deductive approach, as in quantitative research.

The Deductive Approach.   Theory testing involves determining whether an existing theory can be applied to the real world. This type of reasoning begins with an established theoretical framework, such as developmental theory, social learning theory, systems theory, and feminist theory, and moves from the abstract to the specific. When the deductive approach to research is used, researchers derive hypotheses, operationally define concepts, design or select existing measuring instruments, test hypotheses, and analyze interactions among variables. Deductive reasoning is used most often in quantitative research. Ms. Wilson tests several theories relevant to the quantitative investigation on baby boomer caregivers. She selects systems theory with emphasis on role theory to test the issue of role strain and its impact on family relationships.

Ms. Wilson also applies developmental theory and feminist theory to help explain how providing care for aging parents influences the caregivers' behavior. Developmental theory focuses on the accomplishment or completion of stages before the person can move successfully to the next stage. The caregivers, according to McGoldrick (1999), function in three stages: families with young children, families with adolescents, and launching children and moving on. In these stages the families are dealing with the stressors of rearing young children and adolescents and preparing adolescents to leave home. The care of aging parents is added to these responsibilities. In these different developmental cycles, caregivers are coping with dissimilar issues and assuming divergent roles that could lead to role strain.

Because women are overwhelmingly the caregivers for aging parents in most families, Gilligan's (1982) feminist theory, specifically the ethic of care, is often used to explain this phenomenon. The ethic of care relates to women's sense of relationship, interconnectedness, and integrity. In the deductive approach, then, researchers decide on a theory or theories to test and guide their research. Whereas deductive reasoning is used more often in quantitative approaches to research, inductive reasoning is used in qualitative research methods.

The Inductive Approach.   In contrast to deductive reasoning, inductive reasoning builds theories by beginning with a specific observation and moving to a general or abstract statement. Theories are built after data are collected and analyzed. The researcher begins with a general observation or abstract idea about a specific phenomenon, collects data based on that observation or idea, analyzes the data, and then develops a theory based on the results of the analysis. For instance, using the baby boomer example, Ms. Wilson observes that in her caseload of 30 families, 20 families—7 African American, 5 Puerto Rican, 5 Jamaican, and 3 Caucasian—are adult children caring for aging parents. Based on this observation, she conducts research on these clients and other people in the community who are the major caregivers for aging parents. After interviewing the caregivers using face-to-face interviews and analyzing the data, she builds a theory based on the results of her analysis. She makes assumptions, based on observations, that caregivers who assume multiple roles, without help from family, friends, or social service agencies, experience more difficulties in the caregiving role. This observation can facilitate theory building. An initial theory could be: Caregivers who receive respite care experience minimal role strain, pressure, and stress. (Respite care is the provision of temporary assistance to the caregiver that allows the caregiver a break from taking care of the parent. It includes help in or outside of the home with caregiving tasks, such as bathing, feeding, dressing, shopping, and taking to medical appointments.) Remember that in the inductive approach the researcher is interested in building theories while in the deductive approach the researcher tests theories. Establishing causality is another important part of the scientific approach to quantitative research.

Important Points about Theory and Research

- People use theories for both personal and professional reasons. Theories are used in social work practice and research to guide, facilitate understanding, explain, and predict behavior.
- Quantitative researchers test the applicability of theories to the real world by using deductive reasoning.
- Qualitative researchers build theories by using inductive reasoning.

Causal Relationships

A causal relationship is one in which the independent variable is responsible for a change in the dependent variable. An independent variable is the causal variable in a relationship, the variable that is said to influence change in the dependent variable. The dependent variable is the outcome variable in a causal relationship. It is the phenomenon that the researcher is studying that is affected by the independent variable. Scientifically, three conditions are necessary to establish a causal relationship.

Criteria for Causal Relationships

Temporal Order.   A cause must precede an effect. Changes in the independent variable, the cause, must come before or influence the dependent variable, the effect. The dependent variable does not come first. For example, adult children assumed *caregiving responsibilities* (the independent variable) before they were feeling *stress* (the dependent variable).

Association.   There must be some measure of association between the independent variable and the dependent variable before causality can be established. In other words, if a change in the dependent variable is not related to a change in the independent variable, the independent variable cannot be said to be responsible for changes in the dependent variable. For instance, was the caregiver experiencing stress before assuming responsibility for caring for the aging parent?

Eliminating Rival Hypotheses or Alternatives.   Did the causal variable influence change in the dependent variable? This condition for establishing causality means that you strive to eliminate other variables that could have caused the change in the dependent variable. You do not want a spurious relationship, which occurs when the action of a third variable makes it appear that there is a relationship between the independent and the dependent variables. For example, is a third variable such as marital problems causing the caregiver stress instead of the caregiving responsibilities? Although researchers strive to establish cause and effect relationships, establishing causality is difficult and errors can occur in the process.

Common Errors in Causal Explanations

When the researcher does not identify the unit of analysis accurately, conclusions about research findings can be deceptive, leading to errors in explaining study results (Singleton & Straits, 1999). The unit of analysis, that is, who or what the researcher is studying, is described in detail in Chapter 5. Two of the more common errors in causal explanations are ecological fallacy and reductionism.

Ecological Fallacy.   Ecological fallacy occurs when the researcher makes inferences or explains individual behavior, based on research findings, when the unit of analysis was groups. These inferences are misleading because conclusions drawn about groups, such as families, communities, and organizations, do not necessarily apply to individuals within those groups. For example, your research findings might suggest that in communities with large populations of older people there is a high incidence of automobile accidents. From these findings, however, you cannot imply that the older people cause the accidents. Your unit of analysis (what is being studied) was cities or groups, not individuals. Applying findings from aggregated data to individuals is an error in causal explanation. In other words, the researcher may be attributing the accidents to older people, which may be incorrect.

Reductionism. Reductionism occurs when the researcher makes inferences about group, or macro-level, behavior when the unit of analysis was individuals (Neuman, 1997; Schutt, 1999). The researcher uses data on individuals' behavior to explain group behavior. In a sense, it is the opposite of the ecological fallacy. For example, in your study of older drivers (people over age 70 years) in cities with a population of over 50,000, you find a significant number of these individuals had accidents. Reductionism occurs if you also conclude from this study of individuals (the unit of analysis) that all cities with populations of 50,000 plus have older drivers who cause accidents. You are using research findings that relied on individuals as the unit of analysis to explain group (cities) events.

Important Points about Causal Relationships

- One goal in quantitative research is establishing a cause and effect relationship between variables. To establish this relationship three conditions must exist: temporal order, association, and elimination of any rival hypotheses.
- Two common errors in causal explanations are ecological fallacy and reductionism. Ecological fallacy occurs when individual behavior is explained when the study's unit of analysis was groups. Reductionism results when the researcher explains group behavior when the unit of analysis was individuals.

Human Diversity Issues, Science, and Social Work Research

You must be aware of human diversity issues throughout the research process. When selecting theoretical frameworks with people from diverse and ignored populations (such as people of color, women, people with disabilities) as part of the sample, take steps to select models that are appropriate for those groups. Schriver (2001) describes some of the traditional practice theories commonly used in social work and alternative perspectives to those theories. He illustrates, for instance, both traditional and alternative developmental perspectives on individuals used to understand individual behavior and development. While acknowledging commonalities with traditional theories postulated by Freud, Erikson, Kohlberg, and Levinson, Schriver maintains that these theories do not address the diversity among people—those with disabilities, from different ethnic backgrounds, or who choose alternative lifestyles, for example. He proposes using alternative developmental paradigms that are inclusive of people ordinarily not considered in the traditional models. Such theoretical frameworks should be considered when choosing a practice theory.

Ethical Issues, Science, and Social Work Research

As you conduct research, keep the National Association of Social Worker's (NASW) Code of Ethics in mind. Standard 5.02 (see Chapter 2) describes explicitly ethical responsibilities of social workers in relation to evaluation and research. By maintaining high ethical standards in research, as in practice, social workers can maintain support among clients and in the community at large.

WRITING STRATEGY

What information do you need about clients in your field placement that may not be readily available to you? Describe the methods you usually employ to acquire such knowledge. If you were to research this issue formally, how do you think your methods might differ?

LEARNING ACTIVITY

Tips for Succeeding in a Research Course

- Organize yourself before the semester begins.
- Refer to the research course syllabus often.
- Plan when papers and exams are due by coordinating assignments for all classes.
- Start assignments during the first two or three weeks of the semester.
- Participate in class. If you are uncomfortable asking questions in class, meet with the professor during office hours.
- Participate in research study groups.
- Read assigned materials *before* class to facilitate understanding of lectures and class activities.
- Establish regular study times in a location free from distractions.
- Make and keep regular appointments with the college or university's Academic Resource Center.

INFORMATION TECHNOLOGY FOR SCIENCE AND SOCIAL WORK RESEARCH

The following Internet sites will be helpful for the research course and other courses in which you are enrolled:

The following are from Yaffee and Gotthoffer (1999):

> *University of Southern California* offers its Top Ten Internet resources for psychology, social work, mental health, government resources, family and children, and other social work areas.
>
> www.usc.edu/socialwork/
>
> *Social Research Update* is a quarterly publication by the Department of Sociology, University of Surrey, England.
>
> www.soc.surrey.ac.uk/sru/

Institute for Social Research at the University of Michigan.

www.isr.umich.edu/

Internet Resources for Institutional Research provides annotated lists to assist institutional researchers, faculty, and students.

www.airweb.org/links

Important Points from Chapter 1

- Research is a way of finding answers to questions. The scientific approach to acquiring knowledge differs from the traditional way of acquiring knowledge in that it uses a planned, organized approach that either tests theories or builds theories.
- The purposes of research are exploration, description, and explanation of phenomena. Explanatory research often builds on the findings of exploratory and descriptive research.
- Theories are important for guiding and facilitating understanding of both research and practice. Theory is significant in both quantitative and quantitative research. Quantitative researchers test theories, and qualitative researchers usually build theories.
- An important part of quantitative scientific research is establishing causality. Three conditions must exist for causality: temporal order, association, and elimination of rival hypotheses.
- Two common errors in causal explanations are ecological fallacy and reductionism. Ecological fallacy occurs when individual behavior is explained when the study's unit of analysis was groups. Reductionism results when the researcher explains group behavior when the unit of analysis was individuals.

REFERENCES

Gilligan, C. (1982). *In a different voice: Psychological theory and women's development.* Cambridge, MA: Harvard University Press.

McGoldrick, M. (1999). History, genograms, and the family life cycle: Freud in context. In B. Carter & M. McGoldrick (Eds.), *The expanded family life model* (3rd ed., pp. 47–68). Boston: Allyn & Bacon.

McManus, P. (2000, Fall). Persistence pays off. *ARC Newsletter, 1,* 1.

Neuman, W. L. (1997). *Social research methods: Qualitative and quantitative approaches* (3rd ed.). Boston: Allyn & Bacon.

Schriver, J. M. (2001). *Human behavior and the social environment: Shifting paradigms in essential knowledge for social work practice.* Boston: Allyn & Bacon.

Schutt, R. K. (1999). *Investigating the social world* (2nd ed.). Thousand Oaks, CA: Pine Forge Press.

Singleton, R. A., & Straits, B. C. (1999). *Approaches to social research* (3rd ed.). New York: Oxford University Press.

Yaffe, J., & Gotthoffer, D. (1999). *Quick guide to the Internet for social work.* Boston: Allyn & Bacon.

CHAPTER

2 **Ethical Issues and Biases in Social Work Research**

When preparing for class, I had to consider my full-time job plus school full-time (laugh) plus my internship. So it was difficult. After each lecture, I would go home and read my lecture notes, read the book, and check the assignments. It was helpful for me to study when these things were fresh in my mind

—Nontraditional research student

CHAPTER GOALS

Your major goals upon completion of this chapter are to:

- Understand the rationale for having ethical guidelines in research.
- Understand efforts to prevent unethical practices in research globally, nationally, and in the social work profession.
- Be familiar with the NASW Code of Ethics in relation to evaluation and research.
- Apply ethical standards in evaluation and research with individuals, families, groups, and organizations.
- Recognize and avoid unethical evaluation and research practices.

Introduction

Ethical social work practice issues and biases are introduced early in the social work program through lectures, assigned readings and class discussions. Many professions, such as medicine, psychology, and social work, have ethical codes that provide guidance for their members on how to behave when carrying out their professional duties. The National Association of Social Workers (NASW) Code of Ethics (located at www.naswdc.org/pubs/code/code.asp). Standard 5.02 outlines the ethical responsibilities of social workers engaged in evaluation and research (NASW, 1999).

Which behavior is right? Which behavior is unacceptable when conducting evaluation and research? A case example illustrates these issues. This chapter also provides an historical perspective on the basis for and the development of ethical guidelines in research. It then presents social workers' obligations in evaluation and research as outlined in the NASW's Standard 5.02, on unethical research practices, such as deception, fraud, and biases in research.

Generalist Case Study: Letter of Informed Consent

As part of his work assignment, Mr. Bissell has been facilitating a group of parents from his caseload who lost an adult child suddenly through illness or accident. Because of this experience, he decides to conduct a qualitative research study to gain a broader understanding of the issues facing these families and how they cope with their loss. Before beginning the investigation, Mr. Bissell refers to the literature for guidance on working with the families, consults with his supervisor and experts, and uses a single system design evaluation mechanism for monitoring his work with the grieving parents. Mr. Bissell sends the following letter of informed consent to several clients in his caseload and in the caseloads of his colleagues.

Department of Social Services, Aging Division
3793 Grand Avenue
Coconut Grove, Florida

RE: Research on the "Effects of Sudden Death of an Adult Child on Parents"

Dear _____:

We request your assistance with a study about parents who lost an adult child, ages 25–45, from sudden death through illness or an accident within the past three years. Before agreeing to participate in the study, please read this letter carefully to understand your part in the research and be able to ask questions about the research project.

(Sponsors and Investigators) The Department of Social Services, Aging Division is sponsoring the research. The investigators are Mr. Timothy Bissell, BSW, a social worker with Aging Division and Ms. Imani Ashford, from the Research Division, the principal investigator.

(Purpose of the Study) The Department of Social Services is interested in how the loss of your child affected your family and how your family coped with the loss. Approximately 40 married couples that lost a child between the ages of 25 and 45 from sudden death through illness or accident in the past three years are being asked to participate in the study. Study results will provide social

(continued)

Generalist Case Study: Letter of Informed Consent   *Continued*

workers with a deeper understanding of how parents respond to the death of an adult child and how that death affects the family. This knowledge will assist social workers in being more sensitive to this group of clients and in providing more effective services to help clients cope with the loss.

(Description of the Study) You will be asked to meet with either Mr. Bissell or Ms. Imani and answer five open-ended questions concerning how the loss of your child affected your family and how you coped with the loss. Once this letter is returned to the investigators, you will be contacted to schedule a date, time, and place to meet for the interview. The interview will take from one to two hours and can take place over a period of one to two days.

(Experimental Aspects of the Study) This study does not involve experiments. There will, however, be an analysis of the information that is collected from the parents by the investigators.

(Risks and Benefits of the Study) Risks to people who participate in this study are minimal. For example, some questions about the loss of your child could evoke memories that cause emotional discomfort. Benefits from taking part in the study include the opportunity to share your story, which may influence how professionals work with families who have lost an adult child through sudden death from illness or accident. Furthermore, a copy of the study results will be sent to you.

(Confidentiality) To assure confidentiality of your identity and your responses:

- All people having access to your data or a role in collecting the data will be trained about confidentiality issues and required to sign a confidentiality statement.
- Your name will not be used in reports or publications of the results of this research. The principal investigators will assume responsibility for completed questionnaires to assure their inaccessibility to non-project members.
- When the questionnaires are no longer needed, the researchers will assume responsibility for their destruction or secure storage.

(Incentives for Participating) There is no monetary reward for people participating in this study. A copy of the study results, however, will be sent to participants.

(Voluntary Nature of the Study) Your participation in this research is completely voluntary. You may choose not to answer certain questions, and you may also withdraw from the research at any time without penalty. If you have questions about the research or the questionnaire, please feel free to call Mr. Timothy Bissell at (254) 667-2795, EXT. 2795, or Ms. Imani Ashford at (254) 667-2899, EXT. 2683. If you have questions about your rights in relation to this study, please contact the Director of the Institutional Review Board, Ms. Daisy Punch at (254) 663-1209, EXT. 7751.

Participant's Name and Signature (printed or typed)   Date
(Your signature indicates that you have read
this letter, had an opportunity to ask questions,
and agree to participate in the study.)

Principal Investigator's Signature   Date

Agency Administrator's Signature   Date

*These titles are used for illustrating the different components of the letter of informed consent and are not included in the letter.

A Historical Perspective

> ***Activity 1.***   Read the National Association of Social Workers (NASW) *Code of Ethics* Standard 5.02 and compare and contrast it with the 10-point Nuremberg Code found on the World Wide Web at www.naswdc.org/pubs/code/code.asp.

Unethical experimentation on human beings occurred in Germany during World War II. The testimony of two physicians from the United States during the trial for doctors who committed those crimes was the impetus for the Nuremberg Code (Perley, Fluss, Bankowski, & Simon, 1992), written to protect civilians and prisoners during military conflicts. The idea of institutionalizing guidelines internationally for ethical research with human beings started then. The Nuremberg Code was not the first attempt to establish ethical standards for research with human beings, but it was the first to have global influence. Some of the German crimes against humanity, committed prior to the code, were the sterilization program, the Nuremberg Race Laws of 1935, and the Nazi euthanasia program.

Crimes of World War II.   These war crimes were committed between September 1939 and April 1945.

The Sterilization Program. This program sanctioned the sterilization of approximately 350,000–400,000 people afflicted with certain illnesses, such as genetic blindness, deafness, schizophrenia, and epilepsy. The United States, which sterilized 15,000 people, mainly prisoners and people in mental health institutions, was a prototype for Germany's sterilization laws (Taylor, 1946; Proctor, 1992). The first sterilization law in the United States was enacted in 1907 in Indiana (Lombardo, n.d.). About 3,000 people had been involuntarily sterilized in America by 1924 and sterilization of people in mental health institutions continued through the mid-1970s.

The Nuremberg Race Laws.   These were public health enactments, mainly by physicians, which precluded marriages and sexual relations between Jews and Germans. German racial theorists used the United States and its miscegenation laws as a model for their Nuremberg Laws, and they believed that America's laws were even more restrictive (Proctor, 1992).

The Euthanasia, Genocide, and Experimentation Programs.   The German medical program killed many people. There were high-altitude experiments, for example, to determine how long people could live in extremes. As a result, people were tortured, and many died. Freezing experiments were used to evaluate the best way to treat people who had been severely chilled or frozen. Some people were forced to remain in a tank of ice water for as long as three hours.

The medical community was also the leader in the program to use gas to kill Jews, gay men, lesbians, communists, Gypsies, Slavs, and prisoners of war (Proctor, 1992). The sterilization program, race laws, euthanasia, genocide, and medical experimentation were unethical and created some of the most shocking and devastating crimes against humanity in world history.

Activity 2. Review issues of the *New York Times* from the past three years for articles about unethical experimentation with people in the United States. Were any legal actions taken against the people who performed the experiments?

Unethical Experimentation in the United States.   While unethical research occurred in Germany during World War II, there are also many documented accounts of unethical experiments on human beings by the United States government.

The Tuskegee Study.   This study is one of the more widely known examples of unethical medical research. The study was conducted by the United States Public Health Service (PHS) to determine how syphilis developed in Black men; yet it did not provide any treatment for the disease. It occurred in and around the county seat of Tuskegee, Alabama and involved 399 men in the late stage of syphilis and 201 men who served as the control group. Reports by the PHS indicated a higher mortality and morbidity rate for the infected men than for men in the control group.

By 1969 between 28 and 100 men had died from complications directly related to syphilis. During the investigation of this study, exposed in 1972, the Public Health Service declared that the only treatment for syphilis in 1932, the year the study began, would have done more harm than good to the research participants. Yet, when penicillin was introduced as a treatment for syphilis in the 1940s, the men were not treated. Although some in the medical profession defended the study, journalists nationwide were outraged (Jones, 1993).

The Plutonium Experiments.   In the mid-1940s 18 people were given plutonium (Guttman, 1997; Josefson, 1996; Welsome, 1999). In *The Plutonium Files,* Welsome explains that the experiments were conducted from April 1945 to July 1947 by the United States Army's Manhattan Project and began four months before Japan was bombed. Doctors participating in the project, who were responsible for the safety of staff in the facility, wanted to know the effects of radiation on the entire body, including genes, reproductive organs, and fetuses, if ingested or inhaled. Eighteen men, women, and children were injected with plutonium, a heavy silvery metal. Eleven of the patients were injected at the University of Rochester's secret research facility. There is no documentation suggesting that these patients were aware of their involvement in an experiment or of what was being injected into their bodies. Sixteen of the families received compensation through out-of-court settlements.

According to Makhijani (1997), plutonium is a carcinogen that is deposited in the soft tissues, such as the liver, on bone surfaces, and in bone marrow, other non-calcified parts of the bone, and parts of the bone that do not contain cartilage. If deposited in the bone marrow, Makhijani explains, plutonium can have adverse effects on blood formation. Although the exact quantitative effects of plutonium are not known, Makhijani asserts that it can be assumed that "several tens of micrograms of plutonium in the lung would greatly increase the risk of lung cancer."

The Radiation Experiments.   One study at the University of Cincinnati, between 1944 and 1974, exposed 88 cancer patients to levels of radiation with intensities known to be too high to be effective. The patients, 62 of whom were African American, were deceived about the likely side effects of the treatment. In another radiation study, at the Massachusetts Institute of Technology, boys with mental retardation were fed radioactive iron. The parental consent forms did not include experimentation with radioactivity (Beardsley, 1995; Buchanan, 1996; Eisenbud, 1997).

The LSD Experiments.   The United States Army used the mind-altering drug LSD to assess how soldiers carried out their responsibilities while using the drug and to determine whether LSD could be used during questioning. Annas (1992) describes how one soldier, James Stanley, without his knowledge and consent, was given LSD in 1958. Stanley had volunteered to participate in the testing of protective clothing and equipment. The drug so adversely affected Stanley in both his military and personal life that he was discharged from the army and divorced shortly after that. Stanley only realized that he had been given the drug when he was asked to participate in an LSD follow-up study 17 years later. The army denied compensation to Stanley, who then filed suit.

The World War II German atrocities and the unethical experiments on human beings in the United States influenced efforts to prevent unethical experimentation on people both globally and nationally.

Efforts to Prevent Unethical Research Practices

The Nuremberg Code

The Nuremberg Code, a 10-point document that resulted from the trial of German doctors involved in experiments on people during World War II, was one of the first attempts at specifying legitimate medical research practices. Although medical research was the focus of the Nuremberg Code, it influenced ethics codes globally by providing guidelines that others could use in devising their own plans (Taylor, 1946).

The Office for Protection from Research Risks

The Nuremberg Code and unethical experimentation on people in the United States influenced the formation of the Office of Human Research Protections (OHRP) in the Department of Health and Human Services (DHHS). The OHRP is responsible for developing and implementing policies, procedures, and regulations for protection of human beings involved in research sponsored by DHHS. The agency also enters into formal agreements with federally funded universities, hospitals, and other medical and behavioral research institutions (Code of Federal Regulations, 1991; USDHHS, July, 1999).

The National Research Act.   The National Research Act (P. L. 93-348), signed in 1974, mandated programs within the Department of Health and Human Services to provide clarification and guidance on ethical issues relating to biomedical, social, and behavioral research involving human subjects. It also required Institutional Review Boards (IRBs) in institutions, including universities and colleges, that conduct research involving human subjects if the institutions receive federal funding for any research conducted in the institution. The boards apply to all such research, not just projects directly funded by the government. Institutional Review Boards are responsible for evaluating applications for research with human beings before the research begins to assure that all ethical issues have been covered (Code of Federal Regulations, June 18, 1991).

The Office suspended research on human beings at several universities and a Veterans Administration hospital that received research funds from the National Institutes of Health and pharmaceutical companies (Andrews, 2000; Brainard, 2000). The Food and Drug Administration was involved in three suspensions. One suspension resulted from the death of a teenage patient participating in gene-therapy trials. The Office of Human Research Protections remains concerned about whether universities are doing enough to protect human participants, and it asserts that its office sees many violations about IRBs not monitoring the safety of research participants in continuing studies, and about whether institutions are providing enough support for members of their IRBs (Brainard, 2000).

On the other hand, universities maintain that OHRP, in addition to being an enforcer, should also provide more assistance to institutions. Universities further assert that OHRP's suspensions focus on administrative tasks, such as failure to document, rather than on the universities' failure to protect human participants from harm. To assure that the proper procedures are followed to protect research participants, some researchers plan to present a proposal to OHRP for institutionalizing an IRB accrediting body to accredit IRBs and researchers that work with human participants (Brainard, 2000).

While most social work practitioners do not present applications to Institutional Review Boards, it is imperative that all practitioners be aware of ethical standards and procedures when designing research that requires IRB evaluation.

So, as Figure 2.1 illustrates, there have been many influences on the development of standards for ethical research with human beings in the United States. The next section addresses ethical issues specific to social work researchers and practitioners in some detail.

Important Points about the History of Unethical Behavior

- The Nuremberg Code, a response to Nazi war crimes that involved unethical human research, was signed to prevent these unethical research practices.
- The Nuremberg Code and documented stories of unethical behavior in the United States involving research on human beings influenced the federal government to enact a law that addresses unethical experimentation with human beings.
- The National Research Act (P. L. 93-348) mandates the establishment of Institutional Review Boards at institutions, including colleges, universities, and agencies, that receive federal research funds and conduct research on people.
- Researchers must submit applications to the IRBs before initiating contact with potential research participants.

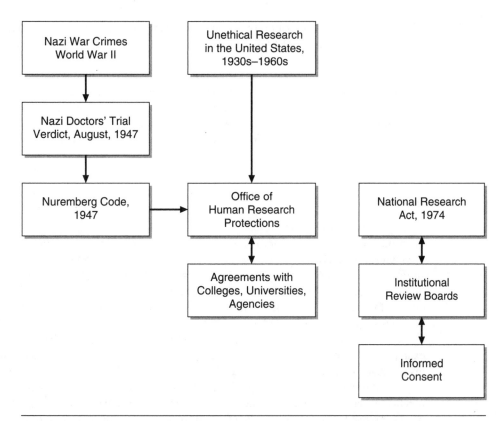

FIGURE 2.1   Influences on and the Development of Guidelines for Research with Human Beings

Social Workers and Ethical Research Responsibilities

In the previous section, you read about the brutality and inhumane treatment of research participants in Germany during World War II and of unethical research practices with people in the United States in the 1930s, 1940s, 1950s, and 1960s. These atrocities influenced global efforts to prevent unethical treatment of research participants not only in the biomedical field, but also in the social sciences. This section describes social workers' ethical obligations to research participants and to clients in both evaluation and research practice as outlined in Standard 5.02 of the National Association of Social Workers (NASW Code of Ethics, 1999).

NASW Code of Ethics Standard 5.02

After enactment of the National Research Act in 1974, many professions drew up ethical codes to guide their professionals on ethical research practices. The National Association of Social Workers, the largest social work organization in the United States, provides guidelines that cover social workers' ethical responsibilities to clients from the beginning of the social work relationship through termination of services. Standard 5.02 informs social workers of their ethical responsibilities in relation to evaluation and research. Figure 2.2 provides a copy of Standard 5.02 of the NASW Code of Ethics.

Client informed consent, confidentiality and anonymity, and protection of participants are the major issues in the NASW standards on ethical treatment of research participants. In addition, the NASW code describes ethical requirements for practice evaluation in monitoring and evaluating work with individuals, families, groups, and organizations. This section details NASW expectations of social workers with respect to scrupulous behavior when conducting research and practice evaluation.

Informed Consent

When you decide to conduct a research study and choose human beings as the unit of analysis, the participants decide whether to participate in the research. That is, their involvement must be voluntary. Permission is granted when people sign a letter of informed consent that includes sufficient information to assist potential participants in deciding whether to get involved. Getting voluntary consent can be touchy, especially if the possible participants are your clients or clients of the agency for which you work. They may believe that refusal to participate leads to penalties or punishment by the agency. Thus, attempts to attain informed consent must be handled delicately, respectfully, judiciously, and without coercion. Mr. Bissell, in the case example, will be conducting a qualitative research investigation with some clients that are in his caseload. Therefore, he must be careful about how he asks for their involvement and his response if some clients decline to participate. Participants should also be advised of their right to refuse to answer any questions and to discontinue participation in the research at any time. A parent or other guardian can provide informed consent when potential participants are unable. In the case example, Mr. Bissell states explicitly in the letter of informed consent that participation in the research is voluntary, that participants could withdraw at any time without penalty, and that they could refuse to answer any questions.

Disclosure of details about the proposed research project, such as names of research sponsors and investigators, the purpose of the research, and a description of the study are necessary. Mr. Bissell explains that the purpose of the study is to investigate how parents are affected by the loss of an adult child and how they cope with that loss. Participants in the bereaved parents group are also informed that the Department of Social Services Aging Division is sponsoring the research and that Ms. Ashford is the principal investigator. Advise participants of the nature of any planned experiments. Potential participants should know, for example, whether the project includes a control group and an experimental group. For instance, if you are attempting to determine whether parents who receive intensive family preservation services are reunited with their children (experimental group) sooner than families who do not receive services (control group), potential participants must be informed. Mr. Bissell explains that his study does not involve experiments.

Give people in your study facts about possible risks and benefits of the study. Risks to participants in social science research are usually minimal, and when they do exist, they often involve emotional risks. For example, in a study about childhood sexual abuse with adult survivors of incest, certain questions on the survey may spark memories that evoke emotional responses. In the case example, Mr. Bissell informs participants that although risks are

FIGURE 2.2   Standard 5.02 of the NASW Code of Ethics

NASW Code of Ethics

Standard 5.02 Evaluation and Research

(a) Social workers should monitor and evaluate policies, the implementation of programs, and practice interventions.

(b) Social workers should promote and facilitate evaluation and research to contribute to the development of knowledge.

(c) Social workers should critically examine and keep current with emerging knowledge relevant to social work and fully use evaluation and research evidence in their professional practice.

(d) Social workers engaged in evaluation or research should carefully consider possible consequences and should follow guidelines developed for the protection of evaluation and research participants. Appropriate institutional review boards should be consulted.

(e) Social workers engaged in evaluation or research should obtain voluntary and written informed consent from participants, when appropriate, without any implied or actual deprivation or penalty for refusal to participate; without undue inducement to participate; and with due regard for participants' well-being, privacy, and dignity. Informed consent should include information about the nature, extent, and duration of the participation requested and disclosure of the risks and benefits of participation in the research.

(f) When evaluation or research participants are incapable of giving informed consent, social workers should provide an appropriate explanation to the participants, obtain the participants' assent to the extent they are able, and obtain written consent from an appropriate proxy.

(g) Social workers should never design or conduct evaluation or research that does not use consent procedures, such as certain forms of naturalistic observation and archival research, unless rigorous and responsible review of the research has found it to be justified because of its prospective scientific, educational, or applied value and unless equally effective alternative procedures that do not involve waiver of consent are not feasible.

(h) Social workers should inform participants of their right to withdraw from evaluation and research at any time without penalty.

(i) Social workers should take appropriate steps to ensure that participants in evaluation and research have access to appropriate supportive services.

(j) Social workers engaged in evaluation or research should protect participants from unwarranted physical or mental distress, harm, danger, or deprivation.

(k) Social workers engaged in the evaluation of services should discuss collected information only for professional purposes and only with people professionally concerned with this information.

(l) Social workers engaged in evaluation or research should ensure the anonymity or confidentiality of participants and of the data obtained from them. Social workers should inform participants of any limits of confidentiality, the measures that will be taken to ensure confidentiality, and when any records containing research data will be destroyed.

(m) Social workers who report evaluation and research results should protect participants' confidentiality by omitting identifying information unless proper consent has been obtained authorizing disclosure.

(n) Social workers should report evaluation and research findings accurately. They should not fabricate or falsify results and should take steps to correct any errors later found in published data using standard publication methods.

(o) Social workers engaged in evaluation or research should be alert to and avoid conflicts of interest and dual relationships with participants, should inform participants when a real or

(continued)

FIGURE 2.2   *Continued*

NASW Code of Ethics

---

potential conflict of interest arises, and should take steps to resolve the issue in a manner that makes participants' interests primary.

(p) Social workers should educate themselves, their students, and their colleagues about responsible research practices.

---

minimal, certain questions could awaken feelings of grief about the loss of their child that they thought were diminishing.

Besides being informed about risks and benefits, ordinarily people want to know how much time they can expect to devote to the research. Inform participants of the time needed to complete a survey or do a qualitative interview(s). Mr. Bissell indicates in his letter of informed consent that interviews would take approximately one to two hours and could span one to two days. Translate letters of informed consent and questionnaires into language and terminology that participants are more comfortable with and able to understand. Consider the age, educational background, and primary language spoken and read by potential participants. These actions benefit people and facilitate the research process. In addition to making the letter user-friendly, provide names and telephone numbers of contact people in the event that participants have questions or an emergency occurs during the study. Mr. Bissell and Ms. Ashford's names are provided in the letter of informed consent for participants to contact if they wish. The name and the phone number of the director of the IRB are also included in the event that participants have questions about their rights regarding the research project.

Anonymity and Confidentiality

Confidentiality and anonymity are two different concepts used in protecting participants' identity and the information shared with the researcher. Guaranteeing anonymity means that participants are assured that no one, including people involved with the research (such as the researcher and support staff), is aware of who completed the surveys and that no one, not even the research team, can match responses to the participant completing the questionnaire. In other words, when anonymity is assured, there is no information on the survey or questionnaire, such as names, numbers, or other codes, that would identify participants. The researcher is responsible for assuring that no one, including the researcher, can identify the participant. Thus, anonymity means that the participant's identity is unknown. Assuring anonymity is much harder than assuring confidentiality of information of participants.

Guaranteeing confidentiality of data assures participants that information is not given to anyone other than people directly involved in the research process. Thus, there are limits on confidentiality, and participants should be informed of that. Limits on confidentiality mean that it may be necessary for people other than the researcher to have access to participants' data. You, the principal investigator, are obligated to protect completed questionnaires, data collected in qualitative interviews, and data stored on computers and diskettes, even though personnel other than you can access that information. Safeguarding of the participant's data can be accomplished in a number of ways:

- By destroying data after reports, presentations, training, or publications are completed.
- By training support staff about their ethical responsibilities.
- By replacing names on questionnaires with codes such as numbers.
- By locking data in file cabinets.
- By reporting findings in aggregate (without presenting information on specific individuals).
- By securing computer files with passwords.

In the case example, Mr. Bissell indicates that steps would be taken to assure confidentiality of information. Note that Mr. Bissell does not attempt to assure anonymity of information. Getting participants' informed consent and assuring confidentiality and anonymity are methods of protecting personal and other information shared with the researcher and for fully informing participants about the research project.

Office of Human Research Protections

Taking steps to protect participants from harm also strengthens the informed consent process. In social science research the harm or potential risks for harm will, more than likely, result from mental distress, such as embarrassment, fear, or loss of self-esteem or stress. Participants can feel embarrassed or feel stressed when they attempt to answer questions in a socially desirable manner. That is, they try to give answers they believe the researcher or society expects. For example, should you ask a middle-aged person who cares for his aging parents if that person physically abuses the parents, the participant would, most likely, respond no because parental abuse is unacceptable in this society. If you believe that your research has the potential for any harm to participants, explain those risks explicitly in the letter of informed consent. In the case example, Mr. Bissell explains that participants could experience some emotional discomfort during the interviews.

Practice Evaluation and Ethical Responsibilities

Activity 3.   Read the *Sanctions* section of the *NASW News,* and note the reasons why social workers have sanctions applied. Was anyone sanctioned because of unethical research practices?

The majority of social work practitioners do not conduct research for the purpose of formally advancing knowledge and disseminating information through publications in professional journals and presentations at professional conferences, seminars, and workshops. Standard 5.02, sections a and c, of the NASW Code of Ethics (1999) addresses ethical responsibilities of social workers engaged in providing services to individuals, families, groups, and organizations.

Standard 5.02, section a states that, "Social workers should monitor and evaluate policies, the implementation of programs, and practice interventions." Section c says "Social workers should critically examine and keep current with emerging knowledge relevant to social work and fully use evaluation and research evidence in their professional practice." Thus, using practice evaluation to remain informed about advances in the profession and applying that knowledge in work with clients are both employment and ethical responsibilities. Information from the literature, professional conferences, and practice wisdom prepares you for assessing client strengths, selecting and implementing interventions, and monitoring and evaluating the progress of individuals, families, groups, and organizations, additional ethical responsibilities. Mr. Bissell, in the case example, refers often to the literature and consults with his supervisor and experts on working with grieving parents in order to become better informed about the clients he is working with. Has the client's situation improved, deteriorated, or remained the same since the intervention was introduced?

Whether changes in the client's situation or behavior are due to your intervention cannot be determined unless some type of practice evaluation is used. Mr. Bissell will gain a lot of knowledge about bereaved parents as he conducts a literature review for his qualitative research (if he decides to search the literature). He will also learn about interventions that facilitate his work with bereaved families and developing theories about parents who lose an adult child and the grieving process. Besides attempting to remain current on issues affecting clients to whom he provides services, Mr. Bissell uses a single system design to evaluate his work with individual clients. Chapters 12, 13, and 14 provide more detailed information on practice evaluation methods.

Although there are national guidelines and guidelines specific to various professions for ethical research, unethical research practices still occur in social work, as in other professions that use human participants.

Important Points about the Practitioner's Ethical Responsibilities in Evaluation and Research

- The NASW Code of Ethics Standard 5.02 (1999), describes social workers' ethical responsibilities in evaluation and research.
- Social workers in organizations, universities, and colleges that receive federal funds for research are obligated to apply to an Institutional Review Board (IRB) for permission to conduct research involving human beings before starting the study.
- Institutional Review Boards assess whether the researcher has sufficient plans for fully informing the participants about all aspects of the proposed research, on obtaining participant informed consent, for protecting the participant's privacy through confidentiality or anonymity, and protecting participants from risks.
- The NASW Code of Ethics emphasizes the social work practitioner's ethical obligation to remain informed about current issues in the social work profession, to use that knowledge in work with clients, and to monitor and evaluate interventions with clients.

Unethical Research Practices

Deception in Research

Deception in research occurs when research is conducted without the knowledge of participants and when researchers are not honest with participants about its purpose. There are arguments in the social sciences, however, about what constitutes deceptive research practices. Researchers sometimes conduct investigations that are called covert, unknown, or unannounced in which the identity of the researcher is not divulged to participants. Some researchers believe that certain settings could not be entered without covert research. And, if they could be accessed with the researcher's identity exposed, the results of the research could be compromised. Participants would be aware that an investigation was occurring and could, therefore, change their behavior. Writing about covert research in open and public settings and in closed settings, Lofland and Lofland (1995) assert:

> Our view is that there are very serious, perhaps damning, ethical problems in *all* covert research *if* the presumed immorality of deception is the overriding concern. Deception is no less present in public and open-setting research than in preplanned, "deep-cover" research in closed settings. On the other hand, if other concerns are also important (for example, lack of harm to those researched, or the theoretical importance of a setting that can never be studied openly), then we can find no more justification for abolishing *all* deep-cover research, preplanned or not, than for abolishing secret research in public settings. We must admit also to the view that a portion of these adamant calls for the pristine purity of openness are just a touch naive. Among many other complexities, ethnographic researchers do not, despite the presumptions of the moralists, have complete control over "who" the researched will take them to be (1994, 34–35).

These researchers continue, saying a researcher who is informed about the problems, discussions, and the difficulties involved in covert research, about the profession's ethical code, and about other professionals' thinking on this issue is the best person to decide whether to engage in deceptive research practices.

Berg (1998) points out other issues for consideration when planning covert research, such as violation of participants' rights and being in settings that could be illegal or become threatening for the researcher. Another negative outcome of covert research is destruction of trust or diminished trust in the researcher when participants learn that research was carried out without their knowledge. When contemplating covert investigations, careful consideration should be given to balancing the possible risks against the possible gains (Berg, 1998). While acknowledging the controversy in the field over covert research, Punch (1994) argues that ". . . I would accept some moderate measure of field-related deception providing the interests of the subjects are protected" (p. 92).

According to the NASW Code of Ethics, "Social workers should never design or conduct evaluation or research that does not use consent procedures, such as certain forms of naturalistic observation and archival research, unless rigorous and responsible review of the research has found it to be justified because of its prospective scientific, educational, or applied value and unless equally effective alternative procedures that do not involve waiver of consent are not feasible" (NASW, 1999).

As a last resort, the NASW code appears to be making some exceptions to conducting research without consent. Yet, researchers are advised that when thinking about using deception in research, there must be overpowering justifications for doing so; and, even if there are compelling circumstances, using deception is strongly discouraged (Rubin & Babbie, 1997).

Fraudulent Research Practices

What constitutes fraudulent research is less controversial than questions about deception. Fraud is reporting study results when data were not collected and analyzed by the researcher or falsifying and misrepresenting data. Deception in research and fraudulent research practices can distort the study results and damage the credibility of the researcher and the researcher's colleagues.

Plagiarism, a common form of fraud, occurs when a researcher claims the work of others as his or her own by not giving credit to another's work. You must acknowledge the work of other researchers with an in-text citation and documentation on a reference list. Enclose in quotation marks verbatim statements from another author's work and give credit for paraphrased and summarized passages.

Plagiarizing is a serious ethical offense. Colleges and universities have policies relating to plagiarizing, usually covered in the school catalogue. Refer to your college or university's catalogue or student handbook for the plagiarism policy. More detailed information on citing the work of others is in Chapter 5, Research Writing.

Biases in Research

Biases can distort the research process because they negatively influence both study results and relationships with participants. A bias is a belief or an attitude that either negatively or positively influences perceptions. Biased thinking can result from experiences, culture, neighborhood norms, peer influences, and family traditions, among a host of possibilities. Biases against people often stem from preconceived ideas and stereotypes about an aspect of their lives that differs from yours—race, religion, age, sexual orientation, social and economic background, or language.

In the social work relationship, biased thinking may influence the kind of services provided to clients. For example, when biases interfere with judgment, some clients may receive services for which they are not eligible, while those who are eligible may not be approved for services they deserve. Similarly, preconceived ideas about people who are different from you can lead to erroneous study results.

Most people are unaware of their prejudices and their influence on research findings. The hope is that after reading this section, you will be more aware of your own potential biases, consider their effect on both practice evaluation and research, and take action to eliminate biased thinking. Mr. Bissell has to be aware of his own biases in working with clients. For example, is he more sensitive and responsive to the needs of clients who are more like him in terms of race, gender, and educational level? If he is more sensitive to these clients' needs and not to the needs of clients with the same or similar problems but unlike him, he could ultimately be biased in delivering services. He could exclude eligible persons from services or include the unqualified.

Gender Biases

Activity 4.   In your social work classes, you have been asked to explore biases that could interfere with the social worker and client relationship. As you read this chapter, think about how those same biases could affect you as a researcher. What steps can you take to eliminate biased thinking that would interfere with the research process and your relationship with the research participants?

> ***Activity 5.***   Read an article from a social work journal, such as *Social Work, Social Service Review,* or *Journal of Gerontological Social Work,* that includes both women and men in the sample. Are there more men or more women in the sample? If yes, is a rationale provided for this type of sampling?

One common bias is gender bias. Eichler identifies seven sexist research practices, four primary and three derived. The primary problems are summarized here.

- *Androcentricity/Gynocentricity* is perceiving the world from a male or female point of view. Consistently mentioning one sex first or validating the research instrument on one sex and then using it on both are examples of these biases.

- *Overgeneralizing* is the generalizing of findings to both sexes when only one sex was included in the research sample.

- *Gender insensitivity* occurs when the sex of participants is not stated in the results section of the report although data were collected on both men and women. Thus, the reader is unable to determine which results apply to the men and which to the women.

- *Double standard* is the application of different criteria in assessing identical behaviors or situations of male and female participants. For example, "when the same responses on a questionnaire are coded differently by sex" (p. 102).

Some of the gender bias research methods that Eichler reports are illustrated in the research of Brett, Graham, and Smythe (1995) on alcohol, drugs, and addictive behaviors in addictions-specific journals. The biases they found include:

- Journal articles that failed to explain why all or a majority of one sex was used in a study.
- No explanation for using a sex-biased sample and failure to discuss the generalizeability of results when the studies had sex-biased samples.
- Research questions using male terms, indicating inclusion of male participants and exclusion of female participants.

Gender biases were also noted in Acquired Immune Deficiency (AIDS) research (Wiebel, 1997) where women were underrepresented in some treatment programs and thus will be underrepresented in research samples. This is also a sampling bias. Although there has been tremendous improvement in eliminating sex biases in research and the literature, you should be aware of these potential problems while reading journals and conducting research.

Culture, Race, and Ethnic Group Biases

Prejudices regarding participants' cultural, racial, and ethnic background and lifestyles can also influence study results. Competence in doing research and evaluation with people from different cultures, races, and ethnic groups is as important as it is in direct practice with individuals, families, groups, and organizations. Your relationship with research participants from different racial groups, ethnic groups, and cultures, including sexual orientation, socioeconomic status, and religion, can negatively influence study results if you lack knowledge, awareness, and sensitivity about these differences. Racial, ethnic, and cultural group biases occur in research when you are oblivious to their importance in the research process or when there is awareness of the significance of these groups yet they are still excluded from the sample. Bias also occurs when people from these groups are excluded from the data analysis portion of the research, despite being part of the sample.

Exclusion of people from different ethnic, cultural, and racial backgrounds, the inclusion of an unrepresentative sample from those groups, generalizing results of a study to ethnic and racial groups that were not included in the sample represent biases in research. In the past, for example, it was common for researchers to conduct research using all White male samples and then generalize findings to different groups of people of color and to women. Read critically for cultural biases.

Age Biases

Whereas some biases are directed towards specific groups of people, age bias can be directed towards participants from any ethnic, social, economic, religious, and sexual preference group. Biomedical and behavioral research, in fact, presents few studies on ethical issues in research with older people. So, research with older people could pose ethical problems and questions. Reich (1978) provides some possible solutions to avoid biases that are relevant to biomedical, behavioral, and social science research with older people:

■ Examine how spending for anti-aging research compares with expenditures for other services that older people could take advantage of. Also, the purpose and priorities for research with older people should be explained.

■ Strive for diversity in selection of older research participants while assuring that the same participants are not chosen too frequently.

■ When appropriate, an assessment should be made of the person's ability to consent. If the person is incapable of consenting to participate, involve a legal representative or patient advocate, if possible, before the person's level of competence declines.

■ For those living in homes for people with mental health problems and in other residential facilities, assure that the facilities are accredited and limit the researcher's inclusion of people in institutions.

Although biases in research cannot be eradicated, steps can be taken to become a culturally competent researcher and to prevent bias as much as possible. Your work and your research will benefit.

Important Points about Biases in Research

■ Biased thinking can negatively influence the research process, just as it can prevent delivery of equitable and unprejudiced services to people in need of assistance.

■ Eichler (1988) identified several gender problems in research. Four of the primary problems were androcentricity/gynocentricity, perceiving the world from a male/female point of view; overgeneralizing study findings to both genders when only one gender was included in the research; and gender insensitivity, which occurs when the sex of participants is not stated in the results section of the report although data were collected on both men and women.

■ Culture, race, ethnicity, and age are additional areas of potential bias that researchers must be aware of.

Strategies for Preventing Biases in Research

Achieving cultural, ethnic, gender, age, and racial competency as a researcher is not a complex process, but it does require some effort on your part. You can begin your journey toward becoming a culturally, racially, and ethnically competent researcher by:

■ Educating yourself about people from ethnic backgrounds that are different from your own.
■ Learning about racism and oppression and its effect on the research process by reading, attending conferences, seminars, and workshops, and learning from people that you are studying can facilitate this knowledge-gathering process.
■ Being aware of attitudes toward different groups that are based on stereotypical thinking and biases.
■ Being aware of nonverbal behavior when in the presence of research participants.
■ Treating research participants with respect.
■ Including participants from different ethnic groups, who are a part of the sample, in designing of the research project.

This chapter provided the history of efforts to prevent unethical research practices globally. It described social workers' ethical responsibilities in research, including practice evaluation. It presented some specific unethical and biased research practices that might occur in social work practice. It also outlined strategies for avoiding unethical and biased research practices. Part II explains the basic research process beginning with a chapter on searching for information and concluding with a chapter on creating and evaluating research reports.

Human Diversity Issues and Social Work Research

> *Activity 6.*   After reading this section, review some of your textbooks, journal articles, and newspaper articles for language biases. Looking at specifics from the texts, what type of language biases did you observe?

Many types of human diversity issues relevant to social work research are explored in this chapter. In addition to those human diversity issues and biases described above, be aware of other human diversity issues in research, such as language biases and labeling. Language biases are often overlooked in research writing because the use of certain words, especially the masculine form of some words, has been institutionalized. Using the word *freshman,* for example, to refer to both women and men when referencing a first-year female college student or using *policeman* to refer to both men and women police officers are both language biases. Be specific in describing people. For example, if you are studying older people, state the age range—"older people, for purposes of this study, refers to people who are 70 or older."

The language that participants speak and understand should also be taken into consideration when preparing questionnaires and interview schedules. Researchers must insure that participants can read the questionnaire and understand interviewers' questions. This may call for writing questionnaires in different languages and making sure that the interviewer speaks a language that the interviewee comprehends.

Besides being specific in describing people, use names or labels that participants prefer. For instance, although African American, Black, Native American, and American Indian are all acceptable labels, let participants choose names that they prefer. When writing up the results of your study, use more personal terms to refer to people such as participants, individuals, and students instead of the impersonal term *subjects* (American Psychological Association, 2001).

WRITING STRATEGY

Think about the source or sources of your own biases. Consider gender, ethnic, physical, and personal characteristics, religious, or cultural practices that make you uncomfortable. Describe this source or sources of bias and the reaction provoked in you. How have you tried to handle this reaction in the past? Think of a research problem in which you are interested. How do you think this bias or these biases will affect you as a researcher? What might you do to overcome these biases?

LEARNING ACTIVITY

Assume a pro or con stance about entering the field to conduct research as an unknown investigator. Share your point of view with a classmate who takes the opposite perspective.

INFORMATION TECHNOLOGY FOR ETHICAL ISSUES AND BIASES IN SOCIAL WORK RESEARCH

1. Go to this Web site to read a copy of the Nuremberg Code:
   www.dallasnw.quik.com/cyberella/Anthrax/Nuremberg.htm

2. Access this Web site to read more about protecting research subjects and the role of The Office for Human Research Protections (OHRP):
   www.hhs.gov/news/press/1999pres/990708.html

3. There is an informative Web site called the Site on Scientific Misconduct by Walter W. Stewart. With Ned Feder he reports on some of their work on scientific misconduct. Among

the information included in this site are articles on scientific misconduct and ethics and material on plagiarism:

home.t-online.de/home/Bernhard.Hiller/wstewart/main.html

Important Points from Chapter 2

- World War II crimes in Germany involving unethical experimentation on human beings were the impetus for the Nuremberg Code, a global attempt to prevent unethical research.
- Documented stories of unethical behavior in the United States involving research on human beings influenced passage of the National Research Act (P.L. 93-348) which mandates the establishment of Institutional Review Boards.
- Institutions, including colleges and universities that receive federal funds and conduct research with human beings, must establish Institutional Review Boards.
- The NASW Code of Ethics (NASW, 1999), Standard 5.02 provides guidelines for social workers engaged in evaluation and research.
- Unethical practices and biases in evaluation and research can negatively affect relationships with participants and distort study results.

REFERENCES

American Psychological Association (2001). *The publication manual of the American Psychological Association* (5th ed.). Washington, DC: Author.

Andrews, L. (2000, March 10). Money is putting people at risk in biomedical research. *The Chronicle of Higher Education*, pp. B4–B5.

Annas, G. J. (1992). The Nuremberg Code in U.S. courts: Ethics versus expediency. In G. J. Annas & M. A. Grodin (Eds.), *The Nazi doctors and the Nuremberg Code* (pp. 201–222). New York: Oxford University Press.

Beardsley, T. (1995). The Cold War's dirty secrets. *Scientific American, 272*(5), 5–6. Retrieved July 23, 1999, from www.ebsco.com,

Berg, B. L. (1998). *Qualitative research methods for the social sciences* (3rd ed.). Boston: Allyn & Bacon.

Brainard, J. (2000, February 4). U.S. regulators suspend medical studies at 2 universities. *The Chronicle of Higher of Education,* p. A30.

Brainard, J. (2000, February 4). Spate of suspensions of academic research spurs questions about federal strategy. *The Chronicle of Higher Education*, pp. A29–A31.

Brett, P. A., Graham, K., & Smythe, C. (1995). An analysis of specialty journals on alcohol, drugs, and addictive behaviors for sex bias in research methods and reporting. *Journals of Studies on Alcohol, 56*(1), 24–34.

Buchanan, A. (1996). Judging the past. *Hastings Center Report, 26*(3), 25–30. Retrieved July 23, 1999, from www.ebsco.com.

Code of Federal Regulations (1991). *Federal policy for protection of human research subjects* [Basic DHHS Policy for Protection of Human Research Subjects]. (Source: 56FR 28003.) Retrieved July 19, 1999, from www.nih.gov/grants/oprr/humansubjects/45cfr46.htm

Eichler, M. (1988). *Nonsexist research methods: A practical guide*. Boston: Allen & Unwin.

Eisenbud, M. (1997). Radiation report in retrospect. *Forum for Applied Research and Public Policy, 12*, 122–126. Retrieved July 23, 1999, from Wilson Web, www.hwwilson.com.

Guttman, D. (1997). Secret human experiments test trust in government. *Forum for Applied Research and Public Policy, 12*, 109–114. Retrieved July 20, 1999 from Wilson Web, www.hwwilson. com.

Jones, J. (1993). The Tuskegee syphilis experiment: "A moral astigmatism." In S. Harding (Ed.), *"Racial" economy of science: Toward a democratic future* (pp. 275–286). Indianapolis, IN: University Press.

Josefson, D. (1996). U.S. compensate subjects of radiation experiments. *BMJ 313*, 1421–1422. Retrieved July 23, 1999, from www.ebsco.com.

Lofland, J., & Lofland, L. H. (1995). *Analyzing social settings* (3rd ed.). Belmont, CA: Wadsworth.

Lombardo, P. (n.d.). Eugenic sterilization laws, 1–3. Retrieved June 5, 2002 from www. eugenicsarchive. org/html/eugenics/essay8+ext.html.

Makhijani, A. (1997). Health effects of plutonium. *Institute for Energy and Environmental Research, 3*. Retrieved November 2, 2001, from www.ieer.org/ensec/no-3puhealth. html.

National Association of Social Workers (1999). *Code of Ethics*. Retrieved November 2, 2001, from: www.naswdc.org/pubs/code/code.asp.

Perley, S., Fluss, S. S., Bankowski, Z., & Simon, F. (1992). The Nuremberg Code: An international review. In G. J. Annas & M. A. Godin (Eds.), *The Nazi doctors and the Nuremberg Code* (pp. 149–173). New York: Oxford University Press.

Proctor, R. N. (1992). Nazi doctors, racial medicine, and human experimentation. In G. J. Annas & M. A. Grodin (Eds.), *The Nazi doctors and the Nuremberg Code* (pp. 17–31). New York: Oxford University Press.

Punch M. (1994). Politics and ethics in qualitative research. In N. Denzin & Y. S. Lincoln (Eds.), *Handbook of qualitative research*. Thousand Oaks, CA: Sage.

Reich, W.T. (1978). Ethical issues related to research involving elderly subjects. *The Gerontologist, 18*(4), 326–337.

Rubin, A., & Babbie, E. (1997). *Research methods for social work* (2nd ed.). Pacific Grove, CA: Brooks/Cole.

Taylor, T. (1946). The doctor's trial: The medical case of the subsequent Nuremberg proceedings. *Trials of war criminals before the Nuremberg military tribunals under control council law No. 10*. Nuremberg, October 1946–April 1949, 8–17. Washington, DC: USGPO, 1949–1953). Retrieved July 18, 1999 from www.ushmm.org/research/doctors/indiptx.htm.

U.S. Department of Health and Human Services (July 8, 1999). *Protecting research subjects* [HHS fact sheet]. Retrieved July 15, 1999, from www.hhs.gov/news/press/1999pres/990708.html.

Welsome, E. (1999). *The plutonium files*. New York: The Dial Press.

Wiebel, W. W. (1997). Sampling issues for natural history studies including intravenous drug abusers. *Substance Use & Misuse, 32*(12 & 13), 1703–1708.

PART TWO

The Basic
Research Process

3 Demystifying the Search for Information

CATHERINE POSTERARO

I was just returning to school after many years. Although at my age I thought I knew just about everything, I did not know where to look for information in the library and was intimidated by the computers as the reference librarian demonstrated how to use them in searching for information. It hurts your ego when you realize you really do not know half of what goes on.

—Junior research student

CHAPTER GOALS

Your major goals upon completion of this chapter are to:

- Learn the most effective and efficient means of gaining access to the increasingly diversified stores of information held by modern library systems.
- Be less intimidated by the library.
- Master the strategies for accessing information suggested in this chapter.
- Be able to conduct a competent review of the literature.
- Be able to locate information using various tools and from different locations.

Introduction

This chapter introduces you to methods used in searching for information about your research topic, or any other subject of interest to you. Although you may spend a significant amount of time in the library, the search for information is not bounded by place. The library catalogue, periodical indexes, and full-text sources of all types are available over the Internet any place, and any time, you have access to a computer and modem. Document delivery and interlibrary loan services are common. Networks allow librarians to encourage remote interlibrary loan book requests, database searching, and e-mail reference requests. This chapter also shares information that will broaden your knowledge about accessing information and facilitate the search process, such as getting to know the library staff and the layout and location of library resources.

Getting Acquainted with the Library Staff

> ***Activity 1.***   To maximize benefits from this chapter, when you begin your research assignment, return to this chapter and use it as a guide. Start with a problem to research and express it as clearly as possible. Put your initial ideas in the form of questions. For example, How do sibling relationships affect late-life satisfaction in women?

> ***Activity 2.***   Visit the reference department of your library and introduce yourself to the reference librarian. Share your initial research question and ask the librarian to suggest various places to start searching for material. Try your search in a couple of these places. Write a brief summary of this encounter. Does your initial topic look feasible?

The single most useful piece of advice I can give to you is to get to know the librarians, library assistants, and student assistants who work in the reference department of the library. They can help you with simple questions, directional assistance, and operational problems with the computers and printers. Librarians want to provide expert assistance in designing research strategies, locating information, judging the quality of the information, and integrating that information into a respectable finished product.

In this environment it is important that you help yourself by asking clear and specific questions in a timely manner. Imagine a student who approaches the librarian and assertively explains that he/she is just beginning a research project on the importance of sibling relationships in the lives of women aged 80 and over. "I need to do some background reading on sibling relationships across the life span, and then I hope to zero in on elderly women, life satisfaction, and sibling relationships." Now, imagine the student who hesitantly approaches the librarian after wandering around the library, flipping through journals, and scanning random book shelves, finally asking "Where is the section on sisters? I've got to get some stuff quickly, so I can write a paper tonight." Who do you think will produce the most productive research?

Students who are confused and overwhelmed by the prospect of research frequently procrastinate, making it difficult for the librarian to help. Often, procrastinating students develop negative attitudes toward research. Exploring (browsing through materials, in a timely fashion) is rewarding. This process will help you to define a topic that will be interesting for the duration of a research project. Librarians can point you toward good places to browse, but you need time and some idea of your subject.

The most crucial step in the research is defining exactly what you are looking for. You will want to learn as much as you can, so that you can place your research into historical perspective. This knowledge is important because it helps you to explain your topic. It also will help you to build a rationale for the research you are proposing. It is always a good idea to begin your research with general sources, such as the ones you may find in the reference room. Eventually, you should know enough to be able to express your ideas in a clear and concise manner. At this point, writing down the question or questions that you hope to answer will help. Now you will probably be ready to visit the reference librarian a second or third time. These focused visits will probably be most productive! Remember, research is a process; research takes time.

Important Points about Getting Acquainted with the Library Staff

- Approach the reference librarian assertively.
- Ask clear and specific questions.
- Allow enough time to gather the materials you will need.
- Know that research is a process.

Organization of the Library

> **Activity 3.**   Explore the library with a focus on the Reference Department. Find three general or statistical sources that you can use to help answer your research question or questions. Note the sources, and write summaries of the information you have found.

Ordinarily, libraries are organized into departments for various types of materials: books, periodicals, audio-visual materials, maps, rare books, and archival materials. In large libraries there are also subject divisions, such as separate social science or social work departments. The pattern of organization varies, but guides and other introductory material are usually readily available. Reference librarians who work in departments are especially trained in these disciplines. You will want to be sure to consult these subject specialists if you have access to them.

Books and sometimes periodicals and audio-visual materials are organized according to standardized systems of classification. Your library will use either the Dewey Decimal or the Library of Congress system of classification. These systems assign a unique *call number* to every book in the library based on the book's subject matter. You can easily find a book's call number by looking it up in the online catalogue. The result is that all books on the same subject are shelved together. In other words, knowing a call number can help you to browse effectively.

A caveat must be given with this advice. Many books are hard to classify because they are on more than one subject. For example, a book on poverty and older women might be found in the economics section, the sociology section, the women's studies section, or with the social gerontology books. Depending on the point of view of the cataloguer, this book fits in with any of these collections. So, books on your subject may be in several different sections of the library. The online catalogue is the only way to get an overview of all of the materials in the library on your subject. It is, therefore, imperative that you use the online library catalogue to make sure that you are finding all the books that you need.

Resources Commonly Found in Reference Rooms

Reference rooms are organized in the same manner as the rest of the library. Reference materials are catalogued in the online catalogue. Usually reference sources provide the best places to begin research because they provide overviews of topics, quick facts, definitions of terminology, and extensive bibliographies.

Encyclopedias. Encyclopedias are reference sources everyone has used. They offer concise, factual overviews of many subjects and are excellent sources for quick information. Today they are available in book as well as computerized format.

> *The Encyclopedia of Social Work (1995) with 1997 supplement* (New York: NASW Press) is a specialized encyclopedia that contains articles signed by social work experts. These articles go into great depth, contain extensive bibliographies, and make excellent starting points for research on unfamiliar subjects. Other examples of specialized encyclopedias are listed below:

- Bruno, F. J. (1989). *The Family Mental Health Encyclopedia.* New York: Wiley.
- Clark, R. E., and Clark, J. F. (1989) *The Encyclopedia of Child Abuse.* New York: Facts on File.
- DiCanio, M. (1989). *The Encyclopedia of Marriage, Divorce, and the Family.* New York: Facts on File.
- *Drug Identification Bible.* (1993). Denver, CO: Drug Identification Bible.
- *Encyclopedia of Disability and Rehabilitation.* (1995). New York: Simon & Schuster/ Macmillan.
- *Encyclopedia of Drugs and Alcohol.* (1995). Vols. 1–4. New York: Macmillan Library Reference USA and Simon & Schuster/Macmillan.

Handbooks. Handbooks function much like special encyclopedias, but they are frequently more extensive, more specific, and more focused and provide authoritative summaries of particular areas of study. Handbooks are usually edited by experts in the field who choose authorities to author individual chapters in their specialized areas of interest. They are usually updated frequently. Handbooks contain extensive references that you can use to identify books and journals in your field. Some examples of handbooks particularly useful to social workers are:

- *Handbook of Family Measurement Techniques*. (1990). Newbury Park, CA: Sage.
- *International Handbook on Alcohol and Culture*. (1995). Westport, CT: Greenwood Press.

Dictionaries.   Dictionaries provide brief authoritative definitions. You have probably used a dictionary from your earliest days in school, but you may not be familiar with specialized dictionaries. They can be found in the reference room and provide, in alphabetized format, scholarly definitions of the way language is used in your field. These dictionaries will also include terminology that may not be found in general dictionaries. Among the excellent dictionaries in the social sciences are:

- Barker, R. L. (1999). *The Social Work Dictionary*. Washington, DC: NASW Press.
- *Biographical Dictionary of Social Welfare in America*. (1986). New York: Greenwood Press.

Statistical Sources.   Statistical sources provide answers to the question *how many*. Frequently, statistics will help to validate your research. The quickest source for American statistics is the *Statistical Abstract of the United States* [Washington, DC: U.S. Government Printing Office]. Published annually, it is an extensive collection of statistics derived from government studies as well as reliable private sources. It contains current information and information from the recent past, is well indexed, and takes only minutes to consult. Notice the dates on individual tables because they will be different from the publication date of the book.

Sometimes books are the best source of numbers from past years, but you can use the Internet to update these government statistics. Almanacs and yearbooks, published annually and often with worldwide coverage, are also excellent sources of statistical information. Other recommended sources of statistical data include:

- *County and City Data Book*. (1994). Washington, DC: U.S. Government Printing Office.
- Ginsberg, L. H. (1995). *Social Work Almanac*. Washington, DC: NASW Press.
- *Kids Count Data Book*. (1991). Washington, DC: Center for the Study of Social Policy.
- *Statistical Handbook on the American Family*. (1992). Phoenix, AZ: Oryx Press.
- *Statistics on Alcohol, Drug, & Tobacco Use: A Selection of Charts, Graphs, and Tables*. (1995). Detroit, MI: Gale Research.
- U.S. Census Bureau. http://www.census.gov/main/www/access.html.

Bibliographies and Guides to the Literature.   Bibliographies and guides to the literature will help you identify books that you can consult. *Books in Print* is an annual bibliography of all books currently in print in the Unites States. If you want to buy a book, it will be helpful. *Books in Print* can be found in every academic library and many public libraries. Other helpful guides in the field include:

- Mendelsohn, H. N. (1997). *An Author's Guide to Social Work Journals*. Washington, DC: NASW Press.
- Mendelsohn, H. N. (1987). *A Guide to Information Sources for Social Work and the Human Services*. Phoenix, AZ: Oryx Press.

Important Points about Organization of the Library

- Research can be conducted in a number of locations, such as your home or your job, besides the library.
- Although the organization of libraries varies, most organize by departments.
- Libraries use either the Dewey Decimal or the Library of Congress System of Classification to organize books, periodicals, and audio-visual materials.
- Library reference rooms contain valuable information in encyclopedias, handbooks, dictionaries, and statistical guides.

Database Searching

Boolean Logic

Activity 4.   Write your research question using the Boolean commands AND and OR. Follow the example below and make a chart of your search. Find a thesaurus, and check for correct use of controlled vocabulary. Suggest ways of broadening or narrowing your research question.

The thinking process, which you must use to search all computerized databases (the online catalogue, periodical indexes and abstracts, the Internet), is called Boolean Logic. To be efficient and effective you must understand this process. It is governed by the principles of George Boole, a nineteenth-century mathematician. The computer does the math. You just need to ask it the right questions. Key concepts are linked with the command **AND.** These are ideas that must be present in a useful book or journal article. Synonyms, related concepts, or broader ideas are linked with the command **OR.** These are ideas that may be useful but are not necessary. The command **AND** narrows your findings; the command **OR** broadens them. The command **NOT** is used to eliminate irrelevant items. For example, if you want to find articles on gang violence, you might try *violence not domestic or family.*

Truncation.   Truncation is another technique that is available with most Boolean-based database searching systems. It allows you to drop the endings of words and replace them with a symbol. This symbol is usually ?, or *, or #. The result is always the same. The system gives you hits with all possible word endings. Think of the many hits you would have with the command *adoles?.* It could be adolescence, adolescent, adolescents, etc. This strategy is particularly helpful when you want to be sure to find both singular and plural forms of a word. You will need to check the system you are using to see which symbol it uses in order to utilize this powerful technique.

Parentheses.   Parentheses allow you to combine Boolean commands. When you implement this tool, you will write one long, but very specific search. Parentheses make it possible for the computer to know exactly what you are asking. Remember computers cannot think or order operations logically. They must be told exactly what to do. Usually parentheses are used to link OR commands. The command search (elderly or aged) and (siblings or brothers or sisters) and (quality of life or morale) will yield a set of articles that meet your exact criteria. These parentheses separate the parts of the search and link those words with similar meanings into a single set or unit. The computer will search the parts of the question inside the parentheses first. The three sets, which will be the results of this search, will then be combined using the AND commands. Computers can accomplish these complicated operations almost instantly.

Some computer databases do not recognize parentheses. In this case, you will need to do separate searches for each piece of your question and combine terms later. For example:

- Find: aged or elderly = Set 1
- Find: sibling? Or sister? Or brother? = Set 2
- Find: quality of life or morale = Set 3
- Find: Set 1 and Set 2 = Set 4
- Find Set 3 and Set 4 = Set 5

Set 5 should be a good answer to your question. Basic concepts in this example are siblings, elderly, and life satisfaction. If we wanted to know about women, this issue would provide a fourth category. Our categories will expand as our ideas become more focused. Perhaps you can understand these complicated relationships and the resulting search commands better if you look at Figure 3.1.

Expanding or Narrowing Your Search

The result of your search should be pinpointed materials that cover all of the concepts you are studying. If your search results in too few hits, you can add more OR commands. You could also use broader terminology, for example, substituting satisfaction for life satisfaction. If you still need to broaden the result, exclude one category by eliminating one AND command from your search. An example would be eliminating "women and" in order to look at sibling relationships more broadly.

Too many hits mean that you need to narrow the search. You might look at the OR commands and eliminate those concepts that seem overly expansive. You may also limit by date. Perhaps you will need to ask a more specific question. Add more AND commands.

Controlled Vocabulary

If you are using a database with a controlled or predetermined vocabulary, consult the thesaurus to make sure that you are using language that the computer can understand. Today, most

FIGURE 3.1 Search Commands

	AND	**AND**	**AND**	**AND**
OR	Siblings	Women	Elderly	Life Satisfaction
OR	Brothers	Females	Aged	Adjustment
OR	Sisters		Older Adults	Happiness
OR	Family Relationships			Morale

scholarly search systems can be expected to provide an online thesaurus. Manipulate these materials until you find what you need. Remember, computers really are incapable of creative or independent thought. They can only function using a predetermined set of commands.

Important Points about Database Searching

- Boolean logic, used in all computerized database searching, is based on the questions that you ask.
- Some techniques used with Boolean-based database searching include truncation, parentheses, and certain commands.
- When conducting database searches, you have the capacity to expand or narrow a search.

The Online Library Catalogue

Activity 5.   Examine the online catalogue in your library. Use your research question to run a keyword search. Review the printout of that search. Identify books that will be helpful.

Activity 6.   Identify subject headings used to describe those books. Run several other subject searches using those subject headings. Did you find additional materials? What would you do if you need to find more books?

Every book, journal title, video, CD map, etc., has a record in the online catalogue. The online catalogue is the database of the library holdings. Each record is made up of many elements, which are called fields. Each field contains an element of information and is searchable on the computer. There is usually a title field, an author field, a publisher field, a call number field, the item field, and a subject field. You may find data by knowing information about any one of these fields.

The online nature of catalogues makes it possible to search many libraries without leaving your own library, your home, or your dormitory room. In this way you can learn about relevant materials not available in your own library. These materials are often available on interlibrary loan. While the format of different libraries' online catalogues may vary, these differences are usually superficial. Follow the printed directions on the screen, and use the help screens. This strategy generally solves most problems because there are basically three ways of finding a book—by author, title, or subject.

Author or Title Searching

It is easiest to find a book when you know the author or the title. Sometimes you need to give the author's last name first (Sarton, May), but on many systems word order does not matter. With book titles it is usually a good idea to drop articles as that speeds the search. If the computer does not find what you need, check your spelling and check for word order. The computer does exactly what it is told. That can be quite exasperating!

Subject Searching

Searching by subject heading requires a very clear idea of your topic and knowledge of the exact subject heading which the library uses. The Library of Congress puts together the official list of standard acceptable subject headings. These subject headings determine the vocabulary that is used to search subject fields. These words are, in fact, an arbitrary language that you cannot intuitively know. The four-volume *Library of Congress Subject Headings* is the thesaurus that defines this controlled vocabulary. Sometimes you can determine searchable subject headings by examining the subject fields in a useful record you have already found. You can then repeat your search using the correct subject heading. Otherwise, you may have a problem using this most precise method of searching.

Keyword Searching

Computers search online catalogues using a tool called the *keyword,* which can provide incredible flexibility. A keyword is any word that appears in a computerized database. Keywords can search anywhere in a computerized record, searching keywords as single words or phrases. Any of the Boolean commands can be used to structure your searches to be as broad or narrow as you wish. In other words, you can use any bit of information that you have to find what you need. Examine the subject headings of the books that you find using keywords. Use traditional subject searches using this information to make sure you have found everything you need. Keyword searching is not precise, and it does not find every book. But, it will be helpful if it finds even one good record with useful subject headings. This flexibility is a significant advantage over the precision needed to search the old card catalogue!

Important Points about the Online Library Catalogue

- The online library catalogue is the database of the library holdings and contains a record of items such as books, journal titles, videos, and CDs.
- Searches for books can be conducted using either author, subject, title, or keyword.

Periodical Retrieval Systems

> *Activity 7.*   Find one journal article and one magazine article on your subject. In what significant ways are these articles different? Which will you use as a research tool? Why?

The most important thing you need to know about periodical retrieval systems is that they are all essentially indexes. Whether you are using the paper or computerized form of an index, the content remains the same. Both allow you to look up your subject and determine where to go to find information. If you can search the print form of *Social Work Abstracts*, you can use the computerized version. The principles of subject searching and controlled vocabulary remain the same. Only the mode of searching differs.

Journal or Magazine?

You must also remember to locate journals, not magazines. Journals tend to be highly specialized and research-oriented and contain research reports. Research reports are articles written in a formal manner, using scholarly language, in which scholars report their own research. These articles have extensive reviews of the literature or bibliography sections, which can help you to locate sources for your own research.

Magazines, for example, *Newsweek,* are secondary sources. In these magazines you will find that the author has no connection to the research being described. Magazine articles are entertaining, but they can be frustrating because they do not contain much detail. The validity of their content is hard to judge. Most professors will not accept these articles as research sources. Figure 3.2 illustrates the differences in the content of journals and magazines.

Computerized Periodical Searches

All of the principles of Boolean searching that we discussed in the previous section apply to all computerized periodical searches. Many libraries make specialized (scholarly) databases available in CD-ROM format. One CD-ROM can hold over 325,000 pages of text. Thus,

FIGURE 3.2   Differences between Journals and Magazines

	Journals	**Magazines**
Examples	*Social Work Research* *Sociological Review* *Social Service Review*	*Time* *Newsweek* *Psychology Today*
Content/Purpose	Original Research In-depth analysis Long articles Usually contain statistics	Brief, factual information Short articles Some interviews To entertain
Language	Scholarly Formal Specialized vocabulary	Usually simple Focus on ease General audience
Authors	Scholars Credentials given	Reporters
References	Bibliographies Footnotes Reviews of the literature	Usually not cited
Illustrations	Graphs, charts, tables Pictures are rare Advertising minimal	Colorful photographs and illustrations

whole shelves of indexes can fit on a single disc. Other libraries subscribe to journal indexes that are available through the World Wide Web or the Internet. These databases are a part of the Internet that is not free. Usually they are accessible by a password provided by your home library or are only accessible from particular computers on campus or in the library. The Internet format provides a currency that is better than CD-ROM formats. Both methods allow you to search any piece (or field) of information. If you structure your search correctly, it is quick and easy to find articles using these electronic tools.

Important Points about Periodical Retrieval Systems

- Periodical retrieval systems are either computerized or paper indexes.
- There are distinct differences between information contained in journals and information in magazines. Journals should be used for scientific research.
- The principles of Boolean searching apply to all computerized periodical searches.

Choosing Appropriate Indexes

> *Activity 8.*   Identify the indexes that you will need to consult to answer your research question, and run searches in each of these indexes. Analyze the results. Adjust your searches using the thesaurus that is appropriate for each individual database. If necessary, adjust your strategy to make your searches narrower or broader. Consider consulting a librarian if you have problems.

Social Work Abstracts

Social Work Abstracts is the specialized, professional database of choice for social workers. It indexes over 450 social work and related journals. It includes journals that cover the social work profession, theory, practice, areas of service, social issues, and social options. This index is a continuation of *Social Work Research and Abstracts* that split in 1993 into *Social Work Abstracts* and *Social Work Research*. It is available in electronic format from 1977 to the present. The print version starts in 1965.

Additional Useful Sources

One index is not enough. Many of the issues that social workers study are as complex and multifactorial as the nature of man. They lend themselves to interdisciplinary investigation. Points of view represented by relevant literature include psychology, sociology, education, economics, business, and the health sciences. You need to think about the nature of your research and determine which indexes will be relevant. If you do not do this, you will overlook many important findings. Some sources you might consider include:

- *Business Periodicals Index* provides indexing of 500 periodicals written from 1958 to the present in business, management, accounting, finance, and related areas.

- *Child Abuse and Neglect* is a computerized database provided by the National Center on Child Abuse and Neglect. It provides citations and abstracts of books, journals, government reports, and conference papers from 1965 to the present on a wide variety of child welfare issues. It is available in both CD-ROM and Internet formats.

■ *ERIC* (Educational Resources Information Center) indexes research reports through its *Resources in Education* and over 750 journals in *Current Index to Journals in Education.* The research reports, or ERIC Documents, date from 1975 and the journals from 1969. This is a federally funded national information system available in paper, CD-ROM, and Internet formats. It provides information on a surprisingly broad range of education-related issues.

■ *Index Medicus* (MEDLINE) gives worldwide coverage of over 3,000 biomedical journals. This is the world's largest biomedical library. It indexes the journal collection of the National Library of Medicine as well as general health information. The government has made these materials available to the general public in paper, CD-ROM, and Internet formats.

■ *Inventory of Marriage and Family Literature* (Family Resources Database) is produced by the National Council on Family Relations. It indexes journal articles on all aspects of family life. It is multiethnic and multicultural.

■ *Psychological Abstracts* (PsycLIT) or (PsycINFO) provides relatively complete international access to books and journals that may be of interest to psychologists.

■ *Social Sciences Citation Index* (SSCI) provides complete coverage of over 1,400 journals and selective coverage of another 3,300 in the social sciences. It indexes articles and provides extensive bibliographies. It can be used to answer questions, such as, Has this article ever been cited? or Who else is working in the field?

■ *Sociological Abstracts* (SA) is the primary index for literature in sociology and related disciplines. It indexes 1,200 scholarly periodicals from 1953 to the present.

The Internet

> *Activity 9.*   Think of your research topic. Select a World Wide Web site of interest. Type in its URL. Try out promising hyperlinks. What information have you found?

The Internet is a powerful tool that offers a wide variety of online resources to social workers and scholars interested in the social sciences. It has created a community of scholars who work together to share vast amounts of information in various formats.

The World Wide Web

To understand the Internet you need an appreciation for the mechanisms by which it works. The World Wide Web is now the vehicle of choice for searching the Internet. The Web is really a gigantic collection of Web sites. Every Web site has a home page. These home pages function like the table of contents of a book. They tell you what's there and serve as points from which you can begin searching.

Uniform Resource Locators

Every Web page has an address, or a URL (uniform resource locator). These generally end with a three-letter code that gives you an idea of the source of the information: "edu" means an educational institution, "com" a company or commercial organization, "org" an organization (usually nonprofit), and "gov" the government. This information can help you to evaluate sites even before you look at them. If you know the URL of the Web page you wish to search, you can just type it in and go there directly.

Hyperlinks

Many Web pages now have hyperlinks that will instantly connect you to other relevant Web pages. These function using hypertext technology. This is the concept upon which the Web has been built. A given word or phrase in an electronic document can be marked. If you click on, or choose, the marked item, you will be automatically linked to another relevant document. If you click on a marked address, you will immediately be taken to that document. To return to the original site you need only click on the Back button. These links provide a convenient method of browsing through the Web. Below are some excellent social work sites to browse. Many of these sites include excellent links to other sites of interest. Remember that URLs change frequently. If these addresses do not work, you can use a search engine to locate the new address.

World Wide Web Sites of Interest

- *The Council on Social Work Education* at www.cswe.org includes information about the council, meeting information, scholarships, current projects, and links to other social work associations and related sites.

- *The Institute for Research on Poverty* at www.ssc.wisc.edu/irp is a national center for research on the causes and consequences of poverty and social inequity in the United States. This site includes a frequently-asked-questions section, information about publications, and links to poverty-related sites.

- *The International Federation of Social Workers* at www.ifsw.org, based in Oslo, Norway, offers information on activities, publications, and links to policy papers and upcoming events.

- *The National Association of Social Workers* site at www.naswdc.org describes and discusses the activities of the NASW, the Code of Ethics, and social work practice. It offers links to sites of related interest.

- *The New Social Worker Online* at www.socialworker.com is a quarterly national magazine devoted to social work students and recent graduates. The site provides a table of contents for the current issue and selected back articles. It has an online career center, current job listings, and author's guidelines.

- *The Social Science Information Gateway* at www.sosig.ac.uk is a subject catalog of links to thousands of high-quality Internet resources relevant to social science and education research; each is selected and described by academic librarians and subject specialists.

■ *The Social Service Review* at www.journals.uchicago.edu/SSR/home.html is a quarterly journal published by the University of Chicago Press. It covers social welfare practice and an evaluation of its effects.

■ *The SocioSite* at www.pscw.uva.nl/sociosite provides global access to international information and resources relevant to social workers

■ *The Substance Abuse & Mental Health Services Administration* at www. samhsa.gov focuses on the availability of substance abuse and mental health services in the general health care system. It has links to other sites of interest to mental health professionals.

■ *The New Social Worker* at www.socialworker.com/websites.htm provides links to Web sites related to all aspects of social work.

■ *Ingenta* at www.ingenta.com is the largest global, user-friendly research site for scholarly journal articles.

■ *Grants for the Rural Environment* at www.uncp.edu/sw/rural/grant.html provides Web sites for grants related to rural social service research and projects.

Search Engines

Recent attempts to organize access to the Web have resulted in the development of increasingly powerful search engines. They are really indexes of Web sites that are electronically produced and function as giant catalogues of the Web. While there are so many that it is hard to know which to use, no single search engine covers the entire Web.

Search engines function best when you need specific information. You must develop search strategies that utilize the same logical principles, using Boolean logic, we discussed in the section on computer searching. There is so much information on the Internet that you need to be very specific. If not careful, you can wander around the Net for days. Search engines can take the concept of information overload to new heights! Conversely, you may also find nothing, which could mean that the search needs restructuring. If the subject is highly unusual, you may try several search engines before you get an appropriate hit.

Some Suggested Search Engines

AltaVista at www.altavista.com, a comprehensive tool, does full-text searching at a wide variety of sites.

Dogpile at www.dogpile.com searches all of the Web, Usenet, FTP Sites, and multiple news sources. It translates a search strategy into various syntaxes, so that it can look all across the Web effectively. Results are displayed by search site. This is a good tool to use when your search is highly specific, and all else has failed.

Google at www.google.com is an outstanding search engine that indexes 2,073,418,204 Web pages. It offers advanced search possibilities and a very well structured Web directory.

Hotbot at www.hotbot.com is a comprehensive Web index that works best with Boolean searches.

Lycos at www.lycos.com does not search the full text of documents. Its advantage is the provision of a strategy, which is wide ranging but not full text.

Yahoo at www.yahoo.com is a directory of carefully indexed sites.

Choosing from a handful of very general categories starts a search. You continue to click on increasingly specific categories until you find what you need. This technique works for very broad searches and helps when you have no idea of a keyword.

Remember: Each search engine works differently and is constantly being updated and improved. It is, therefore, important to make good use of the online Help screens.

E-Mail

The e-mail Web function is an important means of communication between researchers. This function is international, which makes it as easy to contact unknown scholars in foreign countries as it is to contact colleagues in the same department. Networking, or talking to people who are working in your area, can lead you to unknown sources. Personal networking can provide you with information from works in progress. E-mail also works to facilitate conversations with practitioners in the field who can sometimes give you powerful feedback. Never forget that knowledgeable individuals may be our most important sources of information.

Other Jewels of the Internet

The Internet provides access to thousands of online public catalogues of books. You can, therefore, easily search the best research libraries in this country as well as the national libraries of foreign countries. On the Internet there are newspaper services, magazines, journals, and indexing services. Some of these require a subscription price, while others are available at no cost.

Evaluation of Internet Sources

> *Activity 10.*   Use a search engine to locate promising information on the World Wide Web. Apply the criteria listed below to evaluate your findings. Will you use these materials as a part of your research?

Publication on the Internet is instantaneous. It is not peer reviewed. Many e-journals and e-magazines are available at no cost. Some are mounted on personal home pages; others are available on institutional homepages. Some of what you find represents the personal opinion of the author, some is propaganda advanced by institutions, and some is important scholarship. Unfortunately, much of the information on the Web is inaccurate and undocumented. The trick is distinguishing information coming from an original source, such as a federal agency, from the publication of someone with little knowledge of anything but HTML processing techniques. Some suggested evaluation criteria are authority, sponsorship, currency, and coverage.

Ask questions when attempting to establish the credibility of material published on the Internet. Who is the author, and are the author's credentials readily available? How do they relate to this research? Who is the sponsor of the site on which this piece is mounted? Is the sponsor reliable, for example, an educational institution, a government organization, or a commercial site? Do you believe that this sponsor may have a hidden agenda or a preconceived viewpoint on these issues? What is the currency of the material? When was this piece published? Has it been revised? Does it have updated hypertext links? How many have expired? Do you think this information is current enough to meet your needs?

To determine coverage of the piece, ask questions on why this piece was written—to inform, explain, persuade, sell? What topics are covered? Is this one-sided, or balanced coverage? Does the coverage seem complete, compared with other things you have read? How in depth is this material? Does this piece contradict, support, or broaden materials you have found in authoritative sources? Finally, in assessing Internet sources, determine if appropriate and adequate documentation has been provided. Is any documentation offered—sources cited, bibliography notes, or reference list? Are there links to authoritative sites that tend to support the assertions presented?

While the Internet provides a wealth of information, you need to be aware that:

- You cannot find everything on the Internet. Not yet.
- Sometimes hard copies of books and journals are faster, more in depth, and more reliable than any imaginable Internet site.
- You can only get out of a search what you put into it. Your results will be only as good as your search strategy.
- You need to select sites carefully. Some are jewels, but others are nothing but personal home pages. Many exist to advertise or spread propaganda.
- There is no peer review on the Internet. You must judge materials carefully.
- The very best use of the Net is a search for current information since the publication of books and journals is often time-consuming.

Important Points about the Internet

- The World Wide Web is a collection of Web sites; each site has a home page and an address called a Uniform Resource Locator, or URL.
- Hyperlinks on Web pages connect you to other relevant Web pages.
- Search engines, indexes of Web sites, help organize access to the Web.
- There are many search engines, such as Alta Vista, Dogpile, Excite, Hotbot, and Yahoo.
- Evaluating the credibility of information on the Internet is important. Assess material by determining the authority, sponsorship, currency, and coverage of the information.

Government Documents

Activity 11.   Go to the Web site of a federal department or agency working in the area you are studying. Examine the structure of the site. Does this site contain current statistical information on your topic? Can you find other useful information?

A government document is any publication in print, microform, or electronic format that is produced by a government agency. These publications are sources of an incredible variety of information. They cover women, children, health, education, science, transportation, housing, Social Security, the economy, laws, legislation, public policy, demographics, etc. You can look here for statistical information and articles on alcoholism, child abuse, mental health, urban problems, economic development, public welfare, and other important issues in the field of social work. Study these sources of information separately from other books and periodicals because they are organized in a unique way. Here the focus is on federal documents. State and foreign documents are usually available on local Web pages, and they each have their own unique system of organization.

The Federal Government

In order to understand federal documents you need to know the structure of the federal government. The Constitution of the United States establishes three separate branches of government: legislative, judicial, and executive. Each of these is a primary producer of documents that report on its accomplishments. The executive branch is broken down into cabinet level departments: Agriculture, Commerce, Defense, Education, Energy, Health, Interior, Justice, Labor, State, Transportation, and Treasury. Every one of these departments publishes extensively. There is an additional category of independent agencies and government corporations, such as the Social Security Administration, the Peace Corps, the CIA, etc. This complex system produces publications of every size and format imaginable. Government documents are organized and housed by department name in both print and online versions.

The Superintendent of Documents publishes the print editions of these materials at the Government Printing Office, the largest publisher in the country. This authority has designated several libraries in each state as depository libraries. These libraries receive an almost complete collection of all of the documents published at no cost. In exchange, the libraries make these publications available to the general public. The libraries must provide the reference service, basic indexes, and catalogues needed to access these materials. Your local depository library would be a good place to call or visit if you need assistance with these valuable resources.

Depository libraries organize their documents according to the Superintendent of Documents classification system. It is a system of letters and numbers. The letters refer to the issuing agency, and the numbers identify the particular item. Publications issued by the same agency are shelved together. Thus, two books issued by different agencies on the same subject will be located in different parts of the government documents department. Publications on widely different topics by the same agency will be housed together. This system is confusing and requires the use of indexes. Librarians can provide invaluable assistance.

The Monthly Catalog of United States Government Publications

The primary index of federal government publications is *The Monthly Catalog of United States Government Publications*. The Superintendent of Documents has produced it since

1895. Since 1976, it has used the same subject headings as the Library of Congress. Thus, you can look at the regular library catalogue and the *Monthly Catalog* using the same subject headings.

Each issue of the *Monthly Catalog* contains a description of the documents produced that month. These descriptions are arranged alphabetically by agency. Author, title, subject, series title, contract number, stock number, and title key words then index them. Today this powerful tool is published only in electronic format and is widely available on the Internet.

Nondepository Libraries

Nondepository libraries and individuals can purchase many federal government publications. Libraries that do not maintain separate government documents departments usually catalogue these materials into their general collections. In these libraries documents can be located where you would find any other book or journal on the topic.

The Internet

The World Wide Web is rapidly becoming the access point of choice for current government documents. Increasingly, the Internet is the only place where these materials are published. Each branch of government and every cabinet office has its own Web site. Almost all agencies maintain their own Web pages, on which you can find the most current statistical data available. News releases and many full-text documents are also available at these sites. In fact, in the future the Internet may well become the primary means of locating government data.

Searching a Specific Agency Site

URLs (universal resource locators) of the various federal agencies are usually based on the name of that agency For example the address of the Social Security Administration is www.ssa.gov. If you know the address of a likely source, you can go directly to that source. Many agencies have hot links to the Web pages of other agencies, which makes it easy to move between agencies.

Search Engines and Indexes

There are many computerized devices that will help you to locate government information on the Web. If you do not know the name of an agency or its Web address, there are services that provide hotlinks to federal government Web pages. Other sites are search engines that will help you gather particular pieces of information. These allow you to enter keywords or phrases that you want to check. Search engines automatically send out spiders, or robots, which will find occurrences of the word or phrase you request. There are also good Web indexes that operate by subject and are usually selective. Some search only state and federal sites. They save time by reducing the amount of information retrieved.

Any list of suggested sites is constantly in flux. URLs also change with surprising frequency. If a URL does not function, you can use a search engine to determine the new address of a site. The following is a sample of government-oriented sites you may find useful:

Suggested Sites

GPO Access at www.access.gpo.gov/su_docs/index.html is produced by the University of California. It is an interface to the Government Printing Office suite of databases.

U.S. Government Nonprofit Gateway to Government Information at www.nonprofit. gov is a complete and multifaceted search engine. It provides an easy-to-navigate network of links to all kinds of government information and services. It is intended to help nonprofit agencies interface with the government more effectively.

Government Info/Resources at http://usgovinfo.miningco.com searches a wide variety of government sites. It also includes commercial and educational sites that concentrate on American social issues, news, and politics. It includes everything from Supreme Court decisions to a master list of government agency sites.

Library of Congress Home Page at http://lcweb.loc.gov searches the complete catalog of Library of Congress holdings as well as finds hotlinks to many other governmental sites, both national and international.

Thomas Legislative Site at http://thomas.loc.gov contains full-text access to current bills under consideration in the U.S. House of Representatives and U.S. Senate, plus many other materials of interest to the Congress.

Government Information Location Service (GILS) at www.access.gpo.gov/su_docs/ gils.index.html is a sophisticated search engine. This database is provided by the federal government to help identify, locate, and describe publicly available federal information sources, both paper and online.

The American Factfinder at http://factfinder.census.gov is the U.S. Census Bureau site. It is useful for finding statistics and data maps and also provides information about American society, communities, and the economy.

Important Points about Government Documents

- A government document is any publication in print, microform, or electronic format that is produced by a government agency.
- *The Monthly Catalog of United States Publications* is the primary index of federal government publications.
- Nondepository libraries and individuals can purchase various federal government publications.
- Many federal government documents can be accessed through the World Wide Web.

Human Diversity Issues and Demystifying the Search for Information

When searching for information, make a conscious effort to include literature written by researchers from diverse backgrounds. For example, instead of relying exclusively on research conducted by White males, include in your search journal articles, books, reports, and other information by authors from different gender and ethnic backgrounds. In addition, select literature that includes, as research participants, representative numbers of people from groups, such as African Americans, Asians, Latinos, gay men and lesbians, older people, and people with disabilities. Many studies rely on samples from populations with a disproportionately high number of Caucasian participants. Inclusion of the views of researchers and participants from diverse backgrounds enhances your credibility as a culturally competent researcher. When research is inclusive, rather than exclusive, your knowledge base about differences in various groups and differences within groups is enhanced. It helps eliminate biases and stereotypical thinking and heightens awareness of the views of people who have different perspectives from you.

Ethical Issues and Demystifying the Search for Information

The National Association of Social Workers' Code of Ethics advises social workers to participate in the advancement of research and to critically examine and use current research that is relevant to their practice (1999). In order to abide by these standards, it is necessary to develop skills and strategies that will enable you to use traditional search methods as well as new search strategies and tools, such as computerized indexes and the World Wide Web.

WRITING STRATEGY

In Activity 7 you located one journal article and one magazine article on the problem you will study. Write two paragraphs describing explicitly the differences in those two articles. Review Figure 3.2, *Differences in Journals and Magazines,* and indicate which of those differences you were able to pinpoint.

LEARNING ACTIVITY

Choose three search engines. Read their online help pages, and run appropriate searches relevant to the problem you selected. Have you found anything that will add to your work?

INFORMATION TECHNOLOGY FOR DEMYSTIFYING THE SEARCH FOR INFORMATION

In the modern world time and energy are often the most valued commodities in the lives of students and professors, and reliable information is power. Thus, we need to harness the power of the computer whenever possible. The computer is certainly the tool of choice when the most current information is required. It can help if you need to do work in the shortest amount of time. Computers can, however, slow you down if you do not use them carefully, and the sheer volume of information produced by a computer search will quickly overwhelm the unsophisticated user. Thus, you need to select specific databases, know what types of information they contain and what subject headings (descriptors) they use, and be able to construct search strategies that employ Boolean logic. The Internet is a constantly changing tool. In the future, it will become more organized and more user friendly, making it an even more important research tool.

Important Points from Chapter 3

- The search for information is not confined to libraries but can occur in many different locations, especially when a computer with a modem is accessible.
- It is a good idea to get to know the library staff for assistance with searches inside and outside of the library.
- Awareness of a library's organization will make the search for information easier and more efficient.
- Learning and understanding Boolean logic is a key part of effective searching in a computerized database.
- There are both computerized and paper index periodical retrieval systems.
- The World Wide Web, a collection of Web sites, is a powerful search tool that contains a significant amount of current information.
- There are numerous search engines that help organize access to the Web.
- It is important to evaluate the credibility of information found on the World Wide Web.
- Many government documents can be accessed through the World Wide Web.

This chapter introduced you to methods used in searching for information on your research topic or any other subject. Refer to this chapter throughout your search for information to complete assignments for the research course. The chapter that follows introduces methods for selecting a problem for investigation, the research problem and problem statement, the development of research questions, the literature review, and the selection of a theoretical framework.

Selecting a Problem
for Investigation

I think that because I was not in my field placement when I took research, I felt somewhat at a disadvantage. Some of the other students were able to come up with topics a lot easier than I was because they were working with clients. The other thing was having my three children and not realizing the amount of time I would need to spend at the library. It is a good idea for the professor to warn students with families that they need to block off time to spend at the library.
                                                        —Sophomore research student

CHAPTER GOALS

Your major goals upon completion of this chapter are to:

- Select a problem to research.
- Write a problem statement and research questions.
- Conduct a literature review.
- Choose an appropriate practice theory to guide your research.

Introduction

Writing a research proposal or research paper as a class assignment is an opportunity for in-depth study. You may select a problem of interest to you, one you could not investigate because of lack of time or uncertainty over how to conduct research. Now you have the background information on the scientific approach to research, ethical practices in social work evaluation and research, and guidelines for accessing information. You are ready for the first step in the research process—problem selection. Development of a problem statement and research questions, defining and operationalizing variables, conducting a literature review, developing a theoretical framework, and forming an hypothesis are also presented in this chapter.

Although researchers use different methods in selecting a problem to investigate, choosing a problem takes time for experienced as well as novice researchers. Researchers choose topics for various reasons—for intellectual curiosity, for personal reasons, for field practicum or job-related concerns, funding, or for a combination of these reasons. The case example shows how one social worker developed an interest in a particular topic.

Generalist Case Study: Adolescent Drug Addiction and Parental Conflict

Clients:
Mother: Ms. Wendy Masters
Father: Mr. Phillip Masters
Children: Mindy, age 14
                    Martin, age 8

Agency Staff:
Social Worker: Ms. Nancy Bronson
Supervisor: Ms. Linda Scott

Presenting Concerns

A neighbor reported the Masters' family to Child Protective Services (CPS) alleging that teenager Mindy is out of control. According to the referral, Mindy, although only 14 years old, appears addicted to crack cocaine, is truant from school, stays out late at night, and sometimes all night, with men. The neighbor believes that Mindy may be prostituting and that one of the men that she spends a lot of time with may be her pimp. The neighbor wanted something done because the parents seem unable to control the youngster.

Background Information

The social worker's initial visit was at the family's home, located in a community with single-family, low to moderately priced homes. The majority of the homes were well maintained with manicured lawns. At the time of the visit, people were working in their yards, repairing and washing cars, and making home repairs. Others sat on steps and porches relaxing. Children were riding bicycles, playing games, and socializing. Ms. Bronson, the social worker, was a little nervous and hesitant about going inside the gate when she saw the Beware of Dog sign on the Masters's gate. Ms. Masters, who was waiting for the social worker, came to the door as Ms. Bronson was about to call out for her.

(continued)

Case Example *Continued*

Ms. Masters told Ms. Bronson that the family did not have a dog, and the sign was there to scare away solicitors and possible intruders. Ms. Bronson initiated a casual conversation with Ms. Masters while they waited for the children to come home from school and Mr. Masters to return from the store. Ms. Masters, a spontaneous, outgoing woman, said that they had lived in the neighborhood for eight years and that although it was a quiet community, lately there had been a few break-ins. The neighbors were coordinating a neighborhood watch program to deter criminal activity.

Meeting with Ms. and Mr. Masters

Ms. Bronson and the Masters discussed the current situation for about 30 minutes before Mindy and Martin arrived home from school. Mr. Masters said that they were at their "wits end," dealing with their daughter who is belligerent, comes and goes as she pleases, and is truant from school. They sense that she is addicted to drugs because she bathes infrequently, wears dirty clothes, is losing weight, has mood swings, and is stealing money from her parents and items from the home. Besides these signs, their initial suspicions were confirmed when they caught Mindy using crack cocaine. She may be working as a prostitute for money to support her addiction. They are concerned about Mindy's welfare and also about the negative influence Mindy could have on Martin. Mindy refuses to discuss the situation with her parents. She also rebuffs teachers and guidance counselors who reported that when Mindy does come to school, she sleeps or skips classes. She gets suspended, but does not seem to mind. In fact, she enjoys having days off from school.

Mindy appears angry with her parents for sending her to live with her grandparents after a neighbor sexually abused her. Her grandparents took care of her from age three years until she was eight years old. Mindy was unaware that Child Protective Services had intervened and granted temporary custody to the grandparents because the parents denied that a long-time friend and neighbor had sexually abused her. Because of this denial, Protective Services believed that the parents would not protect Mindy.

In addition, Mr. and Ms. Masters were constantly fighting, both verbally and physically. After Mindy was removed from the home, the parents separated for two years. Later, Mr. and Ms. Masters received marital counseling where they worked on issues regarding Mindy's sexual abuse and their marital problems. Mr. Masters also joined Alcoholics Anonymous. Mindy returned home when she was eight years old after her parents' relationship improved and they reunited. While living with her grandparents, Mindy and her grandmother spent time together sewing, playing basketball, and gardening. With her grandfather, she fished and cooked. Mindy had friends in the neighborhood and was a "B" student in school. She was ambivalent about reuniting with her parents due to these positive relationships. Furthermore, she was apprehensive about the kind of relationship she would have with her parents and her brother who was born four years after Mindy was removed from the home.

Mindy was elated the first five months after returning home. Later, though, Mindy began questioning her parents' motivation for "sending her" to live with her grandparents. Although her parents explained the circumstances that led to her removal from the home, Mindy's anger about the separation escalated through the years. The family received counseling periodically to deal with the anger and conflict within the family, but that was no longer helping. Mr. and Ms. Masters are afraid that Mindy will get into trouble with the law, overdose on drugs, or get pregnant. Both parents are under stress because of this situation, and Mr. Masters' blood pressure keeps going up. They want Mindy placed in a secure facility where she can get treatment for her drug addiction, for being out of control, for the overt anger directed towards her parents, and for the sexual abuse that she experienced. Both Mr. and Mrs. Masters are willing to participate in any program in which Mindy is placed. The grandparents remain involved with Mindy. They agree that she needs professional help and are willing to do whatever they can to assist Mindy in regaining control of her life.

Meeting with Mindy

Mr. and Ms. Masters informed Mindy five days ago that the social worker was coming to their home and the reason for her visit. They left the room so that Ms. Bronson could talk privately with Mindy, who had rolled her eyes and sucked her teeth when her parents greeted her. She also rolled her eyes at the social worker. Ms. Bronson attempted a casual conversation with Mindy by asking her about her day, but Mindy just rolled her eyes and looked up, ignoring the question. Ms. Bronson was thinking, She is a tough one. This is going to be difficult. At Ms. Bronson's suggestion, they walked a few blocks to a local convenience store and bought soft drinks. Mindy softened her attitude when they left for the store.

As they strolled back to the Masters' home, Mindy relaxed and told Ms. Bronson that her parents are unreasonable in their expectations and in giving her freedom. Therefore, she breaks all of their rules. She lived with her grandparents most of her life until her parents regained custody six years ago. Mindy never forgave her parents for what she refers to as "abandoning" her all those years. She believes that her parents still do not want her, and she does not feel close to them.

Mindy did not initiate a conversation about her alleged drug addiction or the sexual abuse. When questioned about it, she said that she "dabbles" in various drugs and can stop whenever she wants. She remembered the sexual abuse and stated that her parents did not believe her when she told them what was going on. When she tries to discuss the abuse with her parents or others, no one wants to listen. Ms. Bronson asked Mindy how she felt about moving out of her home for a while to work with a therapist on her drug usage, her behavior, her feelings towards her parents, and how the sexual abuse has affected her. To Ms. Bronson's surprise, Mindy said she wants to get away from her neighborhood and from her family temporarily.

Family Meeting

The family met with Ms. Bronson after her meeting with Mindy. The Masters said that they want Mindy to move out if she cannot abide by their rules and get outpatient treatment for her drug addiction. They are concerned about her welfare. Mindy said that she would continue doing as she pleases. Ms. Bronson suggested a group home that has a program for teenagers with drug addiction problems and also family therapy. Everyone agreed on the group home placement, but Mindy was not sure about the family therapy. Ms. Bronson said that the parents could start family therapy immediately and that Mindy could join after she is settled in the group home. Ms. Bronson said she would meet with her supervisor and then get back to the family.

The supervisor, Ms. Scott, agreed that in the best interest of everyone an out-of-home placement should be the first priority. It would take Ms. Bronson a few days to get Mindy into a group home that had the services she needed, so she began working on the placement immediately. She would also meet with school officials for their help in the transition. Two days after her visit, Ms. Bronson received a call from Ms. Masters informing her that Mindy had run away from home.

Ms. Bronson is intrigued at the number of families she sees with teenagers who are addicted to drugs, truant from school, and in conflictual relationships with their parents. She observes that a significant number of these adolescents were separated from their parents for two years or more when placed in foster care as infants or toddlers. Ms. Bronson notices that in many of these situations there is more than the usual amount of parent–child conflict and that a noticeable number of these adolescents abuse various kinds of drugs, from marijuana to heroin. She also observes that a significant number of the females were sexually abused prior to their drug usage. She wants to offer the most appropriate and effective interventions to these families. So, Ms. Bronson plans to conduct research on the issues facing these families and share the results with others within her agency and at regional and national conferences.

Deciding on a Problem for Investigation

> *Activity 1.*   While reading this section, think about topics of special interest that you would like to know more about. Decide if the subject that intrigues you is a personal issue, a field placement concern, a current social problem, or a combination of the three.

Rationale for Selecting a Problem

Personal Issues as Research Topics.   Researchers, including student researchers, often choose topics that relate directly to them, to a family member, or to a friend. Self-selected issues create enthusiasm, excitement, and motivation about the investigation. Sometimes, these personal matters are also relevant to clients students are working with on their jobs or field placement sites. For example, a motivating personal experience for one student was the death of her father by suicide several years before she enrolled in the research course. Through the literature review, she gained insight into the problem of suicide that left her family stymied and in a state of melancholy. Suicide by gay and lesbian adolescents was the topic of another student's research paper. This lesbian student discovered that, according to the literature, the rate of suicide among gay and lesbian adolescents was higher than that of heterosexual teenagers.

Field Practicum and Job-Related Issues as Research Topics.   Field placement or job-related topics can be relevant to the clients social workers serve, to administration and the staff they supervise, or to programs they implement. HIV/AIDS and the deaf community was a topic chosen by a student whose field practicum involved providing services for people with AIDS. This student reported that deaf people are at higher risk of infection because they are not being educated about AIDS to the extent that hearing people are. This student determined that HIV/AIDS information needs to be shared with people with hearing impairments in a different manner because of their disability. A field placement in a long-term care facility was the impetus for two students' investigation of the relationship between pet therapy and isolation of residents in long-term care facilities.

Ms. Bronson, the social worker in the case example, started her research because of a problem related to her job: Adolescent drug abuse. Adolescent drug abuse is a broad topic, thus she is using a deductive approach to research. Ms. Bronson was also stirred by the fact that some of the adolescents who abused drugs had been separated from their parents for a significant amount of time and many of the females had been sexually abused. Therefore, she decided to study the problem of adolescent drug abusers who had been separated from their parents and also those who had been sexually abused.

Social Problems as Research Topics.   Past or current social problems selected from newspapers, magazines, journals, television, or books that could have implications locally, regionally, nationally, or globally were chosen by some students as research topics. Throughout the years, for example, students have also conducted research on a variety of eating disorders—bulimia, anorexia, and overeating.

Problems selected may also encompass all these possible areas. A student's personal life, a field practicum, and current social problems can point to a particular issue. For example, the status of Latino students in the public education system is a national issue that concerned a Latina student who was also placed at a middle school with a high Latino student population. Students whose lives have been touched by alcoholism chose to study that social problem. These were both personal and field placement issues for these students.

Available Funding for Investigating a Specific Topic. Researchers may select a problem to investigate when grants are available from local, regional, state, or federal sources to carry out the research on particular topics. Private agencies interested in finding answers and possible solutions to the social problems they address also fund projects. Publicly supported community foundations that make charitable contributions, private independent foundations, and corporate foundations specifically formed to provide grants may also be funding sources. Local agencies in your community, such as child welfare and area agencies on aging, may offer research grants, usually in the form of Requests for Proposal (RFPs), for research on clients, staff, program, agency or organizationally specific issues directly related to their agencies. Many of the federal government's grants are listed in the *Federal Register,* published weekly. Graduate research assistants and doctoral and master's students sometimes use their professors' data sets and available funding to conduct research.

Regardless of the method used in deciding on a problem to investigate, researchers are more energized, motivated, and enthusiastic about their research when investigating a problem they find interesting, whether that problem originates from personal concerns, a field placement problem, a social ill, or because funds are available to conduct the research on a specific problem.

Important Points about Choosing a Topic for Investigation

- Devote adequate time to choosing a topic that interests, motivates, and excites you.
- A topic may be selected because it affects you personally, because it relates to your field practicum or job, because it is a current social problem of interest to you, or because funds are available to conduct the research.

Formulating the Research Problem and Problem Statement

Formulating the Research Problem

Formulating the research problem into a manageable research topic requires narrowing its focus, assessing the feasibility of the problem for research, assessing its relevancy to the profession, and evaluating whether the problem is ethical to research.

Narrowing the Focus.   Your research problem was probably selected using a deductive approach, that is, by starting with a broad problem and then narrowing it down to a manageable one. (An inductive approach is used by those who begin with a specific problem.) When working from a deductive approach, the broad problem that you chose must be refined. Otherwise, the study will be unwieldy, unfocused, overwhelming, and without direction. A review of the literature on the topic selected (described later in this chapter) and discussions with experts help you focus on a specific problem.

Assessing Feasibility.   When evaluating whether the problem is worth investigating, ask yourself these questions: Is the problem too large an undertaking given the available resources? Are there enough researchers, support staff, equipment, and supplies (computers, stamps, envelopes)? Are data and participants accessible to the researcher? For example, are agency case files, tracking system data, staff, or clients accessible? Some agencies are open to outside researchers, while others maintain a more closed-door and hands-off policy on accessing clients, staff, and files. Do you have enough time to devote to the project, for training interviewers, for interviewing, and for analyzing the data? Student researchers should consider class time, full- and part-time work, and family responsibilities when selecting a research problem.

Assessing Relevancy.   Another critical decision when evaluating a research problem is its pertinence to the social work profession—to clients, to the social work knowledge base, and to society. Is the problem significant to social work in terms of filling a gap in knowledge? Recommendations for further research and limitations of studies in journals and books can give you topic ideas. If, at this point, you determine that the problem is a doable one for research, proceed to evaluate whether the topic would positively influence change in the lives of individuals, families, groups, and in organizations. Determine if the problem is a pressing one in your community or your state and if investigating the problem takes precedence over other issues. For example, does the study of youth gang violence take priority over concerns about teenage mothers and fathers abandoning their newborns? The literature, experts on the topic, people affected by the problem, and agencies responding to the problem can assist you in assessing the significance of the problem.

Is the Research Ethical?   The final question you must ask is whether the problem is an ethical one to research. Can the researchers assure confidentiality or anonymity of participants and information shared by participants or the agency? When experimental designs are used, will some clients be denied services because they are part of a control group rather than the experimental group? Can the study be done with full disclosure of the purpose of the research and executed with a known investigator?

Ms. Bronson, in the case example, must narrow the focus of her topic into a manageable research problem. She will concentrate on female adolescent drug abusers placed in foster care between the ages of one year old and three years old and reunited with their families after being in care for three to six years. Ms. Bronson is also interested in adolescents with a history of childhood sexual abuse. When determining the feasibility of the project, she considered the amount of time she could devote to the project given her caseload of 40 families and the availability of funds. She concluded that she herself could not conduct the investigation.

The unit supervisor referred Ms. Bronson to the agency's research unit, which informed her that other workers had an interest in the problem. Therefore, the research unit would be responsible for conducting the investigation, with input from people interested in the issue. The research director assured Ms. Bronson that the problem is a relevant one for the social work profession. It is significant to the agency, the local community, and the country. The age of children addicted to drugs is decreasing, and the number of users increasing. Her own review of journal articles confirmed the director's assessment. Ms. Bronson then discussed with the research director whether it would be ethical to study this problem. The director said the agency could guarantee confidentiality of the participants and of their data and that the research would not involve denying services to any clients.

Like Ms. Bronson, you have narrowed the topic and determined that it is worthwhile, that it is relevant to the social work profession, and that it would be ethical to investigate. With these steps accomplished, you, and she, are prepared to develop a problem statement and research question specific to the issue being investigated. The problem statement and the research question will guide you through the research process, keeping you focused on the problem that you have chosen to investigate.

The Problem Statement

Activity 2.   Now that you have a more specific idea for a research topic, start developing a problem statement. Where did the idea for the problem statement originate? Share your problem statement with another person in your research class. Is your problem statement clear? Does your classmate have suggestions to strengthen your statement?

You have completed the first step in the research process by deciding on a problem to investigate. The next phase in the process is developing a problem statement. A problem statement is a description of the concern about which you are writing. It chronicles who is affected by the dilemma, the magnitude of the problem, and why it is a problem. In other words, it introduces the research, provides background information, and explains concisely, explicitly, and clearly why the topic that you have chosen is a problem. What you are attempting to discover about the problem, a description of the environment in which the problem occurs, and an explanation of who defines the concern as a problem are also part of the problem statement.

Following a brief review of the literature and conversations with experts in the field of adolescent drug abuse, the research director, working with Ms. Bronson, developed the following (hypothetical) problem statement:

Drug usage among both adolescent boys and girls between the ages of 15 and 18 in the United States increased to 20% from 15% during the period from 1985–1996 (Higgins, 1998). The age that adolescents first use drugs decreased from an average age of 15 years old in 1985 to an average age of 13 years old in 1999 (Johns, 2000). Higgins (1998) reports that in a national study of 2,500 adolescents who tried drugs between the ages of 14 and 19, 12% became addicted at some point during their adolescence.

Among drug-abusing youth, 30% had been separated from their parents early in life through placements in foster homes or with relatives (Rogers, 1999). In addition, 50% of the female drug abusers had been sexually abused prior to initiating their drug usage. The parent–child bonding is interrupted when children are separated from their parents at an early age for an extended period of time (Smart, 2000), and there could be difficulties forming bonds when the child is older.

The problem of adolescent drug abuse affects urban, rural, and suburban communities and White, Black, Latino, and other ethnic groups alike. Some of the consequences of adolescent drug abuse include permanent or temporary physical and mental damage or death (personal communication, May 2001). The education of these youth and their relationships with friends, family members, and teachers are often compromised. Parents, educators, health care providers, social workers, and foster parents view adolescent drug use as a community problem that needs to be addressed on both local and national levels. (References included here are hypothetical.)

Revisit the problem statement frequently as you review the literature (explained later in this chapter), and assess whether it should be revised as information from the literature accumulates. This process facilitates developing and refining the problem statement.

Developing Research Questions

> *Activity 3.* From your problem statement, write two research questions for an explanatory research study.

You have selected a problem to study and formulated a problem statement. The next step in the research process is devising a research question or questions. A research question is a query for information about one or more concepts that you investigate by collecting and analyzing empirical and theoretical information. It is a statement posed as a question that guides you through the research process and helps you remain focused on the research topic. This broad question asks for information for which you do not have the answer and cannot predict the answer.

The research question is a one sentence question, not an elaborate statement. Although the research question may change drastically as the process progresses, the initial research question, for some types of research, is the point of entry to a topic (Reid, 1989). As you delve more into the literature, the research question will become more specific. Regardless of whether an answer to the question is found, information accumulated during the search will broaden your understanding of the research problem.

Begin your research question development by brainstorming as many questions that you can think of relating to the research problem and the problem statement. Westerfelt and Dietz (1997) support developing questions that search for knowledge about client strengths, just as you focus on clients' strong points in direct practice. It is also helpful to review the operational definitions (explained in Chapter 6) of other researchers when developing the research question.

As Chapter 1 showed, the purposes of research are exploration, description, and explanation. Each purpose leads to particular types of questions.

Research Questions for Exploratory Studies

Research questions for exploratory studies are designed to examine and collect facts about a problem for which little or no information is available. Results from exploratory research are not generalizable to other people in the population experiencing problems similar to the participants in the study. Results of studies done using exploratory questions are often the basis for descriptive and explanatory research studies.

To explore problems experienced by the parents of adolescent substance abusers, Ms. Bronson or a member of the research unit could interview a group of parents who have experience with adolescents who abuse drugs. The research might ask one question, or many. For example, you could pose questions such as:

- Describe your experience as a parent of an adolescent who abuses drugs.
- As a parent of an adolescent who abuses drugs, what causes stress for you?
- In what ways has your child's abuse of drugs affected the family?

These questions could generate many different responses, as well as similar ones. For example, recurring themes could be fears that the children will be harmed or overdose, that the entire family is in danger, and that family belongings will be stolen by the drug-abusing youth. From the exploratory questions, you learned that you want to expand your knowledge on this topic by conducting a descriptive study to collect additional data about troubled adolescents and their families.

Research Questions for Descriptive Studies

After conducting an exploratory study, you choose to develop the research by conducting a descriptive study on the participants and the problem under investigation. Descriptive research studies ask questions about one aspect of the problem or about how one aspect of the problem is related to another. Ms. Bronson and the research director developed the following descriptive research questions to gather data describing phenomenon of interest to them:

- What proportion of families has adolescents who have overdosed on drugs?
- What proportion of adolescents addicted to drugs has been sexually abused?
- What is the race of families living with adolescents who are abusing drugs?
- Is childhood sexual abuse related to adolescent drug addiction?
- Is domestic violence between parents related to adolescent drug addiction?

If you want to build on data collected from your exploratory and descriptive studies, you move to explanatory questions, inquiries that will explain information gathered in the earlier studies.

Research Questions for Explanatory Studies

Data collected from explanatory research questions are the basis for hypotheses. This data provide answers that explain behavior, attitudes, or situations. For example, if Ms. Bronson found in her descriptive research that there is a correlation between childhood sexual abuse and adolescent drug abuse, she may want to continue her investigation with an explanatory study. Examples of explanatory research questions that Ms. Bronson might develop are:

- Are children who were sexually abused during childhood more likely to become adolescent drug abusers than children who were not sexually abused?
- Are children who witness domestic violence between their parents more likely to become drug abusers than children who do not?

Regardless of whether you develop an exploratory research question, a descriptive research question, or an explanatory research question your problem statement and research questions contain concepts that must be conceptualized and operationalized. Consider the explanatory research questions above. The concepts in those questions are highlighted below:

- Are *children who were sexually abused during childhood* more likely to become *adolescent drug abusers* than children who were not sexually abused?
- Are *children who witness domestic violence between their parents* more likely to become *adolescent drug abusers* than children who do not?

Conceptualization of concepts identified in your problem statement will be explained in Chapter 5.

Development of the problem statement and research question takes much effort. Ms. Bronson began with a general research question and revised both her problem statement and research questions several times before arriving at the final problem statement and research questions. A review of the literature, a major part of revising the problem statement and research questions, facilitates that process.

Formulating Research Questions and Problem Statements in Practice Evaluation

In order to select an appropriate intervention when using practice evaluation designs (discussed in detail in Chapters 12 and 13), research questions and problem statements must also be developed. Decide first whether the client or the practitioner is the target of the evaluation when developing the research question, and then determine the purpose of the research (Alter & Evens, 1990). When the purpose of the study is understanding the practitioner's use of a specific intervention, a process evaluation is done (Rosen & Proctor, cited in Alter & Evens). If the effect of the intervention on the client is the reason for the evaluation an outcome question is needed (Alter & Evens, 1990).

Process, or formative, evaluations are concerned with the effect of the intervention from implementation to termination. Outcome, or summative, evaluation focuses on the whether the intervention achieved the goal. Alter and Evens use a typology of research questions to help in deciding which type of question to pose. They contend that a research question that centers on process is needed when the practitioner is the target and wants to know if he or she is using the intervention appropriately or when the client is the target and the practitioner is interested in whether the right intervention is being used with a specific type of client. On the other hand, an outcome question is appropriate if the practitioner asks if he or she is being affected in an unexpected or unwanted manner or if the client is being affected as expected.

Important Points about Developing a Problem Statement and Research Questions

- The problem statement explains explicitly why the issue selected is a problem, guides you through the research process, and helps maintain the focus on issues relevant to the problem.
- Be prepared to revise the problem statement as you conduct a literature review.
- The type of research question depends on whether the purpose of the research is exploration, description, or explanation.

Reviewing the Literature

Activity 4. Conduct a preliminary review of the literature in search of information that assists you in clarifying, revising, and refining the problem statement and research question. How successful were you in locating relevant materials? What were some of the obstacles?

The Role of the Literature Review in the Research Process

Demystifying the Search for Information (Chapter 3), guided you through the search process by acquainting you with resources available in college and university libraries and by showing you how to access information for the literature review or other research that you will be conducting. This section describes the literature review, its significance in the research process, and its role in formulating the problem statement and research question. Chapter 5, *Creating and Evaluating Research Reports,* continues the discussion of literature reviews in the context of how to write a review and how to evaluate literature reviews and research reports of others.

The literature review, a paper's foundation, is a critical examination of materials, from mainly primary sources, both empirical and conceptual, that contain information relevant to your study. Literature includes current information and classic, or landmark, studies found in journal articles, books, government reports and documents, published and unpublished papers, such as theses and dissertations, and brochures. Primary sources consist of research on a specific subject that is published for the first time. Newspapers and popular magazines should be used critically and cautiously since the majority of their content is not from primary sources. The media, including audio-visuals, such as radio and television programs, are additional sources of information. The Internet is also a valuable resource. (Refer to Chapter 3 for suggestions for evaluating Internet sources.) A literature review helps you assess what has already been written about the problem you are investigating and determine whether additional research is needed on the topic. It informs you of the direction of current research on your problem and of the arguments surrounding the topic.

After a preliminary review of the literature you may conclude that there are gaps in the knowledge base related to your topic. Therefore, additional research is needed. Or, you may conclude that adequate research has been done on the topic. At this point, you can decide on a research strategy—exploratory, descriptive, or explanatory. If there were a dearth of information on the problem, for example, the most appropriate strategy would be exploratory. If exploratory and descriptive studies are available, the best approach may be explanatory. Besides informing you of gaps in the knowledge base and assisting in selecting a research strategy, a review of the literature helps in choosing a theoretical framework (discussed later in this chapter) and in assessing the level of theory development relative to your topic.

The literature review, which continues throughout the research process, is an ongoing evaluation that plays a major role in developing and refining the problem statement and research question. Your problem statement and research question in most instances will undergo many changes by the time the final problem statement and research question is written because of this continuous review of the literature. In fact, you may change to a similar topic or a totally different one as you delve into the literature. The hypothesis (explained in Chapter 9), which is based on the research question, the literature, and expert opinion, can be written by the time the literature review is completed.

Most likely, you will accumulate a significant amount of information during the literature search. From this information, be selective in choosing materials for your study. The analysis, selection, organizing, and synthesizing of the literature can be challenging, so start early on your project. Suggestions for organizing and synthesizing material are provided in Chapter 5, as well as in the following section.

What Shall I Do with All of This Information?

The results of a literature review can be overwhelming to even the most experienced researcher. As a fledgling researcher, your organization skills will be maximized at this point in the research process. If you are habitually unorganized, get suggestions on improving your organization skills from professors, classmates, friends, or the college or university's academic resource center. Although it is best to devise your own system for conducting research, analyzing the literature and organizing the information, the following are suggested organization techniques acquired through the years from personal trial and error and from students' recommendations:

- *Devise your own system.* Formulating your own plan for conducting research may be more effective than using a system developed by a classmate.

- *Prepare yourself for the research process.* Prepare by having adequate supplies, such as note cards, paper, color post-it notes, color pencils, and color pens, and access to a computer. Learn to access information in an efficient manner, using different methods (refer to Chapter 3).

- *Skim articles and books.* Skim initially to get a general idea of the content. After scanning the abstract and a few other parts of the article, decide if the information is relevant to your topic.

- *Be selective in choosing literature.* Use concepts in the problem statement and research question to guide the selection and keep you focused on the problem under investigation.

- *Use color codes to identify specific topics.* Your study will include major topics and subtitles within each major category. Color coding with markers can be used to identify both major topics and the subtitles. For example, in the case example, Ms. Bronson and the research unit used articles from *Social Work, Child and Adolescent Social Work,* and *Child Welfare Online,* among other works, to find information on adolescents who use drugs, domestic violence, and adolescents who were sexually abused as children. All of these concepts will be major topics in the literature review. Possible subtitles under adolescents and drug usage could be: (1) physical effects of drug addiction; (2) emotional effects of drug addiction; (3) peer pressure and drug addiction; and (4) adolescents and addictions. If you use these categories in the paper, as you read the literature and take notes, use different color markers (codes) for the different subtitles. For instance, color code text on physical effects in yellow, on emotional effects in blue, on addictions in green, and so on. Color coding makes it easier to identify different topics as you prepare to organize the information.

■ *Organize information by similar topics.* When you take notes from books, journals, and other sources, organize the notes by topic to prevent reviewing the same information repeatedly in search of specific topics. For instance, using the case example, information on adolescents with drug addiction from different sources should be organized together (perhaps in the same folder), material on domestic violence together, and information on sexually abused adolescents placed together. Group your notes based on these titles.

■ *Keep track of journal article abstracts and book printouts.* Attach the abstract printouts from books and journal articles to your notes for future reference when documenting sources in text and the reference list citations.

■ *Use only information that is relevant to the problem.* Avoid losing sight of the problem you are studying. Review the problem statement and research questions frequently.

Important Points about the Literature Review

- A review of the literature is a thorough, critical examination of journal articles, books, and other materials in search of information that is relevant to the problem you are investigating.
- A review of the literature helps you develop and refine the problem statement and research questions, and assess what has been researched on the topic.
- The majority of your literature should be recent primary sources, although the inclusion of relevant classic studies is acceptable.
- Synthesizing findings is a critical part of writing the literature review.
- Although conducting and writing a literature review can be challenging, strong organizational skills will facilitate the process.

Selecting a Theoretical Framework

> *Activity 5.* Choose a practice theory that provides insight into the problem selected and helps guide your research. Describe the theory and why you chose it.

What theories will you use to guide your research? In Chapter 1 theory was defined as a group of related hypotheses, concepts (ideas or thoughts), and variables, based on facts and observations. It attempts to explain and predict the how and why of people's behavior, of attitudes, or of situations. In social work practice and research, a variety of theories are used to facilitate your work with clients and to guide research.

Some social work practice theories are crisis intervention and task-centered models, cognitive behavioural theories, systems and ecological perspectives, social psychological and communication models, social and community development, anti-discriminatory and anti-oppressive perspectives, and empowerment and advocacy (Payne, 1997). A researcher could apply one theory or assume an eclectic approach and use multiple theories. For example, Ms. Bronson could appropriately use crisis intervention theory, communication theory, and systems theory to guide her research on families with adolescents who are addicted to drugs. These theories would help explain families in crisis, families with communication problems, how problems in one part of the system (the family) impact all family members, and how the environment impacts the family and its individual members.

There are numerous theoretical frameworks, models, and paradigms to choose from when conducting social work research. Schriver (2001), who offers a number of frameworks as alternatives to the traditional ones, emphasizes that when choosing a theoretical framework, it is necessary to be cognizant of other influences on peoples' lives, such as ethnicity and sexual orientation, that some of the traditional models fail to consider.

After selecting a practice theory that fits with the problem being investigated, complete the literature review section of the paper by stating the hypothesis, which is covered in Chapter 5.

Important Points about Practice Theories

- Practice theories help guide your research and explain the problem under investigation.
- Diverse practice theories are used in social work practice and social work research.
- When selecting a practice theory or theories, include models that acknowledge and explain diversity among human beings.

Human Diversity Issues in Selecting a Problem for Investigation

Reflect on issues that affect people other than those from vulnerable groups when deciding on a problem for investigation. People from these groups are frequently selected as research participants because of their accessibility as clients in public agencies. Thus, there could be a tendency to rely too much on poor people, people of color, and women. In contrast, White, mainstream, middle-class groups and communities are overlooked although they, too, have problems. They just may not be as visible as they are in other communities. Neglecting research in these communities is a disservice to the people there who could benefit from programs developed as a result of research efforts.

The selection of theoretical frameworks (practice theories) is another important human diversity issue. Practice theories that include people of color, gay men and lesbians, and other oppressed people should be sought when people from these groups are included in the sample.

Ethical Issues and Biases in Selecting a Problem for Investigation

It has been pointed out that conducting literature reviews can be overwhelming. A great deal of literature is available, and it is your responsibility to read these documents in their entirety so that the researchers' findings, conceptualizations, and theories are accurately reflected. Furthermore, precise documenting of in-text citations and references is a requirement in order to give credit to sources of information. Accurate documentation is also necessary so that others may find sources that you cited. Failure to credit work of others is plagiarism, as was discussed in Chapter 2.

WRITING STRATEGY

Conduct a preliminary review of the literature in search of information that assists you in clarifying, revising, and refining the problem statement. Draft a literature review. Structure your text to show:

- That you have organized the information by similar topics (perhaps a paragraph or two on each topic).
- That the topics are related.

It may be a useful strategy to begin each paragraph with a sentence that announces the topic. Show that you have integrated these topics by providing clear links to the problem. (You may repeat words or themes that derive from the problem statement.)

LEARNING ACTIVITY

Share with the class concepts in this chapter that you feel comfortable implementing. Next, describe to the class concepts that are unclear to you. Are there other students who can clarify the concepts that you do not understand?

INFORMATION TECHNOLOGY FOR SELECTING A PROBLEM FOR INVESTIGATION

Using one of the search engines introduced in Chapter 3, locate an article on the World Wide Web that relates specifically to concepts presented in this chapter. Share with your class the search engine that you used and the results of your search.

Important Points from Chapter 4

- Choose a research topic that both interests and excites you and has relevance to the social work profession.
- Topics can be derived from your personal life, your field placement or job, an interest in a current social problem or the availability of funds to conduct research on a particular problem.

- The problem statement explains explicitly why the issue that you selected is a problem and, with the research questions, guides you through the entire research process.
- A literature search helps you develop and refine the problem statement and research questions.
- Diverse practice theories, used in social work practice and social work research, help explain the problem that you are studying.

In Chapters 3 and 4 you were introduced to methods used to find information, including getting the most out of your library searches and selecting a problem to investigate. Chapter 5 describes methods for writing and critiquing research reports.

REFERENCES

Alter, C., & Evens, W. (1990). *Evaluating your practice: A guide to self-assessment.* New York: Springer.

Payne, M. (1997). *Modern social work theory* (2nd ed.). Chicago: Lyceum Books.

Reid, W. J., & Smith, A. D. (1989). *Research in social work* (2nd ed.). New York: Columbia University Press.

Schriver, J. M. (2001). *Human behavior and the social environment: Shifting paradigms in essential knowledge for social work practice.* Boston: Allyn & Bacon.

Singleton, R. A., Jr., & Straits, B. C. (1999). *Approaches to social research* (3rd ed.). New York: Oxford University Press.

Westerfelt, A., & Dietz, T. J. (1997). *Planning and conducting agency-based research.* New York: Longman.

5 Creating and Evaluating Research Reports

Since taking the research course and a statistics course, I can better under-
stand journal articles. I can figure out what the authors are talking about and
identify the most important parts. Before taking these courses, I skipped much
of the material because I knew that I could not comprehend it.

—Junior Research Student

CHAPTER GOALS

Your major goals upon completion of this chapter are to:

- Understand the importance of and rationale for disseminating research reports.
- Be familiar with the different methods for disseminating research reports.
- Know the components of a research report.
- Be capable of organizing and writing a research report for diverse audiences.
- Be able to present a research report orally.

Introduction

Research is critical to social work, just as it is to other professions. Both the small, informal studies of practicing social workers and the large, formal studies of academics help those in social work serve their clients better. Indeed, contributing to the knowledge base of the profession is a goal emphasized by the National Association of Social Workers *Code of Ethics* (1999).

Research is not done in a void. It has purpose and meaning—to improve both services and understanding. So, practicing social workers conduct research for a number of reasons. One goal of research is to find ways of helping clients make positive changes in their lives. Another goal is to help organizations develop and implement new programs for clients. A third is to evaluate existing programs. Finally, research may help educate clients, staff, and the community on social issues.

Other research, especially that by college and university faculty, helps inform practitioners and improve their skills Academic research is often on a larger scale, dealing with larger issues, and with larger funding. But it is based on the same concerns felt by front-line social workers.

Research alone, however, is not enough. It is also necessary to share research with others. The best research in the world is of little value if others in the profession have not read it or heard it. It is also of little value if poor reporting methods prevent others from understanding it. Students who want to be social workers must be able to do research and present it in a way that makes it available to others. Finding answers to questions using an organized, planned approach is an important goal of research. Your research results reflect answers to the research questions and hypotheses established early in the research process. This chapter will help you get a firm start to the research process.

Generalist Case Study: Homophobic Attitudes, Heterosexism, and Domestic Violence in Lesbian Relationships

Homophobic Attitudes, Heterosexism   1

Running Head: Homophobic Attitudes, Heterosexism

Homophobic Attitudes, Heterosexism, and

Domestic Violence in Lesbian Relationships

Delicia Heath

Saint Joseph College

Homophobic Attitudes, Heterosexism   2

Abstract

Lesbians in abusive relationships are often neglected by human service agencies because of institutionalized homophobia. Lesbians are an invisible minority, and the problems they experience are often overlooked. This paper proposes that lesbian women are more apt to stay in abusive partnerships because support systems are not available to them. Helping professionals need to be aware of lesbian issues in order to work effectively with this population. In addition, more research must be conducted to publicize the gravity of this issue.

Homophobic Attitudes, Heterosexism, and Domestic
Violence in Lesbian Relationships

The social problem of domestic violence has come to the forefront
in the past couple of decades with the advent of the Battered
Women's Movement and well-publicized legal battles. The defining
image of domestic violence, etched into the minds of many, is that
of a female being physically, emotionally, and sexually abused by
her male partner. In fact, 95% of all batterers are male (King, 1993).
This statistic, however, does not reveal the whole picture of
domestic violence. Lesbian battering, one of the most hidden forms
of domestic abuse, has been virtually overlooked by public and
human service agencies. Although no substantial research has been
done to record the extent of lesbian battering, it is estimated that
25% of all lesbians experience some form of abuse in their intimate
relationships. The percentage of heterosexual abusive relationships
is slightly higher at 27% (Carlson, 1992; Lockhart, White, Causby,
& Isaac, 1994).

The prevalence of this problem is evident. Why, then, has the
issue been ignored? Societal attitudes towards homosexuality need
to be examined in order to answer this question. Heterosexist beliefs
often prevent lesbians who are in perilous circumstances from

leaving. In addition, these same attitudes may give batterers a false sense of security that they can continue violent behavior without repercussion. Unfortunately, the lesbian community may help foster domestic violence situations. This community is characterized by closed boundaries, a necessary protection system against the oppression of the heterosexual world (Vincent, 1996; Tiemann, Kennedy, & Haga, 1997).

Statement of the Problem

It is estimated that there are 4 million to 13 million lesbians in the United States and that one-quarter are in violent relationships (Tully, 1995). Lesbians make up a small percentage of the American people; yet, proportionally, they are over-represented in this area. Why has the issue of domestic violence not been addressed in this community? Battered lesbians face a greater challenge in trying to get help due to homophobic attitudes. The stigmatism associated with being a lesbian often prevents abused women from seeking and obtaining services. There are specific issues involved in lesbian domestic violence. In order to manage them effectively, human service agents must be mindful of their perspectives on homosexuality. They also must be aware that the resources already

Homophobic Attitudes, Heterosexism 5

in place for battered heterosexual women may not achieve the same beneficial results with lesbians.

Purpose of the Study

This study examines the external and internal factors contributing to the continuance of domestic violence within the lesbian community. Agencies working with battered women have been unsuccessful in providing services to lesbians. Often lesbians do not feel welcomed in shelters for battered heterosexual women, nor do they feel their needs are met through the medical and legal systems (Swigonski, 1995). . . . Helping agents outside of the lesbian community must shed heterosexist and homophohic convictions in order to provide aid in this community.

Definition of Terms

Battering. The physical acts of slapping, kicking, punching, hitting, stomping, shoving, and sexual assault, which occur at the hands of a significant other (Loring, & Smith, 1994).

Domestic abuse. A pattern of dominating and forceful behavior that encompasses physical, emotional, psychological, economic, and sexual abuse between married, divorced, dating, cohabiting, gay men, and lesbian relationships (New York State Office for the Prevention of Domestic Violence, 1998).

Homophobia. A deep prejudice and fear of people due to their homosexuality. This prejudice can result in discrimination in various social institutions and violence towards gay men and lesbians.

Significance of the Study

Dr. Roderic H. Fabian (1998) conducted a Meta-analysis of the various sociological and psychological studies on domestic violence between December 1991 and April 1994. Through this examination, Fabian discovered that only three percent of sociological studies dealt with domestic violence of women against women, while only one percent of the psychological studies dealt with the same issue. The prevalence of this problem has been underrecognized in the research community; yet it merits examination. Furthermore, resources need to be developed and education and training provided in order to prevent domestic violence. Thus, the results of this study would be important for professionals such as social workers, domestic violence staff, physicians, and policymakers.

Homophobic Attitudes, Heterosexism   7

Research Questions

- Are homophobic attitudes by medical professionals preventing battered lesbians from seeking help?
- Does heterosexism by the judicial system prevent battered lesbians from leaving abusive relationships?

Review of Related Literature

Background Information

In order to understand domestic violence in lesbian relationships, it is important to examine the dynamics of these relationships. Lesbians are the invisible minority, often ostracized and discriminated against in a heterosexual world. DePoy and Noble (1992) conclude institutionalized homophobia, both perceived and tangible, often forces lesbian couples into closed and exclusive relationships. Furthermore, lack of support systems isolates lesbian dyads and creates additional stress. Family members, coworkers, and friends may not recognize the partnership as viable, rather perceiving it as pathological (Depoy & Noble, 1992). As a result, lesbian couples consider each other sole support systems, and they become increasingly dependent on each other as they insulate themselves from the negative reactions of society. Problems may arise in the relationship when one partner feels the other partner is trying to be independent, which a partner can construe as an attempt to leave the relationship.

Practice Theory

Empowerment is a concept developed to provide power and resources to oppressed members of society. Schriver (1998) maintains that the primary purpose of the empowerment perspective is . . . "to preserve and restore human dignity, to benefit from and celebrate the diversities of humans, and to transform ourselves and our society into one that welcomes and supports the voices, the potential, the ways of knowing, the energies of us all" (p. 27). In other words, the goal of the empowerment perspective is to allow a person to self-actualize, self-determine, and gain a voice. This theory is especially relevant to lesbians and, in particular, to battered lesbians, who are silenced in a heterosexual environment.

Empowering battered lesbians presents them with tools to make positive changes in their life situations. Swigonski (1995) asserts that encouraging lesbians to disclose their sexual orientation is empowering them. Coming out is a method of claiming personal and political power and although it poses a significant risk, Swigonski (1995) confirms it can be liberating. For battered lesbians, revealing their sexual orientation may release them in one way from their abusers, since batterers often threaten to cut their lovers.

<u>Health Care Obstacles</u>

One of the primary barriers to lesbian victims of domestic violence seeking help is their negative experience working with helping professionals (Loring & Smith, 1994; Tiemann, Kennedy, & Haga, 1997). . . . In addition to preconceived notions of a battered woman's sexual orientation, caregivers often exhibit homophobic attitudes when treating their patients (Curtis, 1997). . . .

Tiemann, Kennedy, and Haga (1997) conducted interviews with eight lesbians to explore their interactions with caregivers. One commonality of all the women in the study was that they waited to communicate their sexual orientations, citing that feeling safe in revealing such personal information was a factor. The results of this study indicated both positive and negative experiences. Some of the women described situations in which the health care workers did not address their lesbianism when told; rather, they reasoned, it did not have a role in treatment plans. However, Tiemann, Kennedy, and Haga (1997) maintain that this avoidance of the subject prevented the women from successfully working on their problems and may have been a reflection of the professionals' biases.

On the other hand, some caregivers delivered a more overt reaction to the information that their client was a lesbian. The women in the study noticed significant shifts in care after their sexual orientation was unveiled. Their lesbianism was considered pathological and was used to make inaccurate and superficial diagnoses. Although there were reports of positive experiences with caregivers, the women in this study admitted that these professionals were highly recommended in the lesbian community as offering lesbian-friendly services. . . .

Legal Obstacles

Although great strides have been made in protecting battered women in domestic violence cases, lesbians have been excluded from the judiciary rights. Nine states still do not grant restraining orders against batterers in same-sex partnerships (King, 1993). Because the law has been slow to recognize same-sex partnerships as equals to heterosexual partnerships, lesbians have few avenues for protection when they leave their attackers. . . . Law enforcement agents often have the perception that violence in lesbian relationships is merely two women having an insignificant squabble (King, 1993). King

Homophobic Attitudes, Heterosexism 11

also cites that in court proceedings lesbians are at a disadvantage because they cannot reveal their sexual orientation for fear of prejudicing the jury. Consequently, many lesbians feel the legal system will not protect them and do not report the domestic abuse.

Hypotheses

- Homophobic attitudes by medical professionals prevent battered lesbians from seeking help.
- Heterosexism by the judicial system prevents battered lesbians from leaving abusive relationships.

Method

This survey research descriptive study will select 100 people from a population of 1,000 lesbians in a large urban community using stratified random sampling. Mailed questionnaires, designed by the researcher, will be sent to participants, along with instructions and a letter of informed consent. The questionnaire contains 20 Likert-type questions with five possible responses each. Before implementing the research, a pilot study was conducted with 100 lesbians representing the population from which the sample was selected. After reviewing participants' responses, modifications were made to the instrument. Descriptive statistics using the

Statistical Package for the Social Sciences (SPSS) will be employed to organize and describe the characteristics of the data and to examine the relationship between variables.

Results

This section of the paper is completed after the proposal is accepted and the data collected and analyzed.

Summary and Discussion

The literature supports my conclusion that heterosexism and homophobia on both a personal and institutional level prevent lesbian women from leaving abusive relationships. Research on this issue is almost nonexistent, reflecting the invisibility of the lesbian community in mainstream America. Being a lesbian is taboo, and, therefore, issues concerning lesbians are not a priority. The few studies on domestic violence in lesbian relationships focused mainly on White middle class women, excluding the experiences of lesbians with different backgrounds. A larger, diverse sample of lesbians should be used to reflect accurately the population's experiences. However, it is certain that lesbians are an oppressed group and that view is shared by many researchers.

Homophobic Attitudes, Heterosexism   13

Social institutions, such as the medical and legal systems, consciously and unconsciously deny abused lesbians care that is conducive to their needs. The Advocates for Abused and Battered Lesbians (1997) warn against helping professionals presuming the sexuality of their clients. This type of behavior is detrimental to the helping process. Caregivers should be required to take special training seminars on working with gay men and lesbians. In addition, assessment and intake protocol should be examined for language that excludes lesbians.

Implications for Practice

Lesbians are confronted with many challenges concerning their sexual orientation. Social workers need to be aware of these issues and of their own internalized homophobia. Examining a lesbian client's perspective through an ecological framework will reveal many factors that oppress and hinder personal growth. Understanding systems that act against lesbians are essential in fostering a healthy relationship.

Recommendations for Further Research

Little research has been done to examine the extent of domestic violence in lesbian relationships. Although agencies that already work with this group know it is a serious problem, the issue has not reached the mainstream population. Broader scaled research should be conducted and publicized in every media outlet. The lesbian community must voice its outrage at the abuse and feel secure in doing so. Society plays a role in giving lesbians a voice by examining its own methods of oppression and discrimination towards this group.

References

Carlson, B. (1992). Questioning the party line on family violence. *Afflia, 2*(2), 94-109.

DePoy, E., & Noble, S. (1992). The structure of lesbian relationships in response to oppression. *Afflia, 7*(4), 49-64.

King, R. (1993, October 4). Not so different after all. Justice: The trials of gay domestic violence. *Newsweek, 122*, 75.

Lockhart, L., White, B., Causby, V., & Issac, A. (1994). Letting out the secret: Violence in lesbian relationships. *Journal of Interpersonal Violence, 9*, 469-513.

Note: This is a partial reference list.

Methods for Disseminating Research Findings

Activity 1. After reading this chapter, compare and contrast a research paper that you completed with a journal article and with a report to an employer or internship supervisor. Describe similarities and differences.

Research findings are disseminated through presentations in books, journals, and other types of written reports, through oral presentations at agency, community, and legislative meetings, at local, national, regional, and international conferences, and on the Internet. Because research reports are completed for different reasons, they are presented in various formats and presented to different audiences.

Student Research Reports

Your main interest at present is probably in writing a report for the research course or another course in which you are enrolled. Most professors, regardless of the discipline, require either a written or oral presentation, or both, during advanced classes. The audience for the paper is the professor, and classmates if it is an oral presentation. Campuswide student research symposia presentations may also be possible. These symposia are held at some colleges and universities, giving students an opportunity to present to the campus community and to visitors.

Writing a major research paper for the first time can be intimidating, so it is important that you ask questions in class or meet with the professor outside of class for guidance. But, remember that a certain amount of independence is required when doing research.

Student research reports include, but are not limited to, literature review results, empirical research investigations, and research proposals describing what you plan to do in a final research paper. If a proposal is requested before the final paper, writing a detailed proposal is recommended because, then, a significant amount of the work will have been completed. Students planning on attending graduate school often keep their research proposal or literature review to build on for a research project in graduate school. The final research report may even be submitted for publication.

Student research papers are tools for learning how to conduct a scientific investigation. Therefore, it is important to narrow your topic and take into consideration other school, work, and personal responsibilities, so that you are not overwhelmed.

Professors sometimes permit students to conduct group research projects. Before committing to participate in a group project, discuss with all potential members each person's responsibilities. If the group proceeds with the research, have frequent discussions about whether members are fulfilling their agreed-upon tasks.

The case example at the beginning of the chapter represents portions of a student research report. The assignment included providing an introduction, literature review, methods, and discussion of findings from the literature review sections. A report like this helps prepare you for other research assignments that you may need to do, such as reports for employers.

Reports for Employers

When you become a professional, your employer may require presentations of research that you have completed to agency staff, such as division or unit members, or to your supervisor or manager. For instance, in the paper provided above, the information would be helpful to social workers, doctors and nurses, and judicial workers providing services to lesbians. Practice evaluation results (see Chapters 12, 13, and 14) are also shared at interdisciplinary team meetings and during periodic administrative reviews. Your research results may also be presented to the community in which you work. When presenting to the community, be selective about which information to focus on because the main concern will be for strategies, services, and programs that can benefit the community. At the same time, it is imperative to briefly speak on the research process.

Presentations at Professional Conferences

There are local, regional, national, and international calls for proposals for presentations at conferences. Ordinarily, the paper must relate to a conference theme. Potential presenters are asked to submit, in a specific number of words, a proposal and a brief abstract by a certain date. Several volunteer reviewers read the proposals and recommend acceptance or rejection. Reasons for turning down the proposal accompany the rejection notice.

Major social work organizations, such as the National Association of Social Workers (NASW: www.naswdc.org/), the Council on Social Work Education (CSWE: www.cswe.org), the Association of Baccalaureate Social Work Program Directors (BPD: www.rit.edu/~694www/bpd/), the National Association of Black Social Workers (NABSW: ssw.unc.edu/professional/NABSW.html), and the Rural Social Work Caucus (www.uncp.edu/sw/rural/index.html), sponsor conferences annually or every other year in different locations throughout the United States. Some organizations periodically hold conferences internationally. Poster presentations, and more recently, electronic posters are also effective ways of disseminating research results. The researcher may present alone, with a co-presenter, or on a panel.

Practitioners and faculty are frequent presenters at professional conferences. Some conferences specifically solicit proposals from student presenters. The case example presented in this chapter could be presented at a conference after the study is implemented and results analyzed. If you do not present at a conference, attending gives you a chance to see how the process works. And it shows you why people present at a conference. Delivering research results at conferences provides opportunities for researchers to get feedback on their study from colleagues, to network with others in the field of social work, to meet job requirements for scholarship and research, and to be invigorated by your own presentation and those of other researchers.

Publication in Professional Journals

Although practitioners author a small proportion of publications in professional journals, publication in professional journals is primarily by college and university faculty. Faculty publishes alone, with other professors, with practitioners, and sometimes with students. *The New Social Worker* magazine and its electronic online companion www.socialworker.com/, written for social work students and recent graduates, accepts articles from students.

To publish in a journal, such as *The New Social Worker,* researchers submit papers to journal editors, following the format designated by the journal. The format includes the length of the paper and which style manual to follow. Most social work journals use APA style. Through a blind review process, which conceals authorship, manuscripts are read by two or three experts on the topic of the paper. After completion of the reviews, a decision is made about whether to (1) accept the paper as is, which is seldom the decision; (2) accept the paper contingent upon minor or major revisions by the author; and (3) reject the paper. Some journals include the date of initial acceptance of the journal and date of acceptance following the last revision upon publication of the article.

Disseminating Findings in Books

Books provide more in-depth information about a topic than do journal articles. The audience is of particular concern for book writers because the audience may be broader for books than for the journals. Often researchers write one or more journal articles on a particular topic and then develop that research into a book.

Important Points about Disseminating Research Findings

- A significant part of the research process is sharing findings with other researchers, practitioners, and students.
- Research findings can be shared through papers, books, journal articles, and Internet publications, and through oral presentations in classes, at meetings, and at professional conferences.
- Practitioners use their own research findings and findings of other researchers to implement new programs and services, to improve services to clients, to evaluate programs, and to assess the feasibility of continuing programs.

What to Include in the Research Report

> *Activity 2.* After reading this section, read one article from *Child Welfare, Social Work,* and *Omega: Journal of Death and Dying.* Did authors include the necessary information? Was the information stated implicitly or explicitly?

Whether the presentation of your research report is written or oral, it follows a specific format and includes certain information. The format often depends on the type of research and the audience for the report. Most reports, however, are like the case example. They have a title page, an abstract, an introduction, a literature review, a methods section, a results section, and a discussion section. This section chronicles parts of research reports and what to look for when reading them, especially those in professional journals. At the end of each of the specific segments, which describe a specific part of the report, an italicized explanation describes what to look for when evaluating these sections of journal research articles.

Title of the Article

The title of a report is the first item that catches your attention because it contains key words you are searching for. Have you ever, though, picked up an article based on the title and then discovered that the article had little relationship to the title? What a disappointment! So, the title should inform the reader what the research report is about, what the variables are, and who took part in the research study. It should not, however, state the results of the study.

Evaluating Journal Articles
- Assess whether the title indicates what the article is about, using as few words as possible.
- Assess whether the main variables are a part of the title.

Title Page

Your professor may require a specific format for your paper that differs from this suggested guideline, which follows the manuscript preparation guide from the *Publication Manual of the American Psychological Association* (2001). Include on this page the header, running head, title of the paper, author's name, and author's affiliation (such as the name of your college or university). Some professors provide a sample title page similar to the one in the case example at the beginning of the chapter.

Evaluating Journal Articles
- Determine if relevant identifying information is included in the title page.

Article Abstract

The abstract is a brief summary of the research report, ordinarily placed at the beginning of the paper, that informs the reader about the content of the report. It contains concise information about the topic, research questions, or hypotheses, the methodology, and study results. The abstract lets you know if the paper contains information that you are interested in. The computerized databases described in Chapter 3 contain abstracts that help you locate relevant articles. The example at the beginning of this chapter includes a brief abstract informing the reader that the paper is about violence in lesbian relationships and how homophobic people and helping professionals are harming these relationships.

Evaluating Journal Articles
- Evaluate whether the abstract briefly describes the paper including the purpose, research questions, or hypotheses, the methodology and the study results.

Introduction

The first major part of a research report is the introduction, which provides an opportunity to capture the interest of the readers. You chose a topic because it excites you. Your task is to stimulate readers' interest by writing a compelling opening. The introduction includes the problem statement, purpose of the study, operational definitions, significance of the study, and research questions.

Statement of the Problem

Activity 3.   After reading this section, write a hypothetical problem statement based on your knowledge about a particular social problem. After writing the statement, select three journal articles that according to the abstract are directly related to the problem. Incorporate three or four sentences into the hypothetical problem statement, along with citations.

The problem statement introduces the audience to the problem you chose to investigate. Describe the problem and justify a need for conducting a study on the topic that you chose. Limit yourself to one problem (unless the instructor requires more). Explain clearly and precisely:

- What the problem is.
- Why it is a problem.
- Who views it as a problem.
- Whether it is a local, regional, national, or global issue.

Including statistical information related to the problem, particularly the number of people affected by the problem or the number who could be affected, makes a stronger argument for conducting the research. Explain what makes this study different from similar studies. Include the concepts of interest, and show implicitly the possibility of a relationship between those concepts. Once conceptualized, those concepts become the independent and dependent variables. Although research questions can be implicit in the problem statement, avoid explicitly stated research questions here.

Citing both conceptual and empirical studies also strengthens the problem statement. In the case example, the student provided information about violence in lesbian relationships that many readers might not be aware of and supported those findings with statistically appropriate numbers. Make sure that you give credit to other researchers by including in-text citations. Finally, continually revise and refine the problem statement as you review the literature and discover more information about the issue.

Evaluating Journal Articles
- Evaluate whether the problem is described explicitly and succinctly.
- Evaluate whether there is a plausible rationale for undertaking the study.
- Evaluate whether there is sufficient documented literature including statistical data to support the assertion that the issue is a problem.

Purpose of the Study.   The purpose statement helps to orient the reader (and the researcher) to the research. It also provides an explanation for why the study is being done. Delicia Heath, the research student, wanted to know what factors, both internal and external, contribute to domestic violence in lesbian relationships.

Operational Definitions of Major Concepts.   In this section provide operational definitions of major concepts used in your study. Operational definitions, explicit descriptions of major concepts, are not to be confused with dictionary definitions. Operational definitions define concepts as used in your research investigation and specify how the concepts will be measured, thus assisting the reader in understanding the study. When operationally defining concepts, avoid using the term that is being defined in the operational definition. (See Chapter 5 for a detailed description of operationalizing concepts.) In the case example, the student used existing definitions by other researchers since they fit with her ideas. She also developed her own definitions based on her knowledge about the problem.

Evaluating Journal Articles
- Assess whether definitions of major concepts are operationally defined in a way that you understand their meaning in relationship to the study.

Significance of the Study.   Explain whether this study fills a theoretical void in the literature, tests theories, or extends existing theories. On the practice level, how is this research important to the field of social work and other professions? In the case example, the student asserts that it is important to educate professionals about the extent of domestic violence in lesbian relationships and that there is a dearth of research on this topic. With more knowledge about the problem, resources and education can be provided.

Evaluating Journal Articles
- Assess whether the researcher discusses both the theoretical and practical significance of the study.

Research Question(s).   Near the conclusion of the introductory section of the paper provide the research question(s), a simple, one-sentence statement asking a question about the relationship between concepts. After these concepts have been operationally defined, they become independent and dependent variables. (When working on your paper, remember to revisit the problem statement and research questions often to help you remain focused on the topic.) In the case example, Heath asks questions about possible relationships between the concepts "lesbians in abusive relationships seeking help," "lesbians terminating abusive relationships," and "homophobic attitudes towards lesbians."

Evaluating Journal Articles
- Evaluate whether the research questions are drawn directly from the problem statement.
- Evaluate whether the research questions ask about possible relationships between concepts identified in the problem statement.

Review of Related Literature

"The review of the literature chapter is the heart of your proposal" (Long, Convey, & Chwalek, 1985, p. 79). The review of related literature, the literature review or, informally, the "lit review," summarizes and integrates recent research that is pertinent to the problem and research questions in your study. While the majority of the literature should be recent, do incorporate classic studies.

Historical Information.   Classic studies are particularly useful when presenting background information about your problem. In fact, start the literature review section with the history of the problem, if relevant to your topic. This background information reveals whether the problem being investigated is a new or chronic social problem. In the case example, the student started her literature review with background information on the internal and external dynamics that influence lesbian relationships and impact lesbians' responses to violence in their relationships.

Theoretical Framework

Activity 4. After reading this section, conduct a literature review in search of an appropriate practice theory to guide your research. Textbooks for classes, such as *Human Behavior in the Social Environment* and *Human Development Through the Life Span,* are good sources for identifying theoretical frameworks.

After incorporating background information, describe the theoretical frameworks used to guide the research and explain why you chose that framework. In the case example, Heath chose empowerment theory as her theoretical framework because she believes it would help lesbians in domestic violence situations make positive changes in their lives.

Selecting Information for the Literature Review. Select conceptual and empirical literature directly related to the topic, especially if the literature review yields substantial information. When choosing studies, it is appropriate to include studies that contradict each other in terms of findings. Summarizing similar information from different sources and citing them together instead of separately adds to the fluidity of the paper. For example, in the case example, the student wrote, "The percentage of heterosexual abusive relationships is slightly higher at 27% (Carlson, 1992; Lockhart, White, Causby, & Isaac, 1994). Instead of citing these sources separately, she paraphrased, summarized, and synthesized findings from several articles that agreed on the percentage of heterosexual abusive relationships. Using too many direct quotations, a common student error, also interrupts the flow of the paper and denies you the opportunity to apply skills in paraphrasing and summarizing, so use them sparingly. Another mistake to avoid is listing studies, as if compiling an annotated bibliography, instead of summarizing. Of course, summarizing can be one of the most trying, hair-pulling aspects of writing a major research report.

Hypotheses. The paper's hypotheses conclude the literature review (see Chapter 9 for a discussion of hyotheses). In the case example, Heath's hypotheses are:

- Homophobic attitudes by medical professionals prevent battered lesbians from seeking help.
- Heterosexism by the judicial system prevents battered lesbians from leaving abusive relationships.

These hypotheses are, as they must be, consistent with the research questions.

Evaluating Journal Articles
- Assess whether selected studies, both recent and classic, are relevant to the topic.

- Assess if both conceptual and empirical studies are a part of the literature review.
- Assess whether the researcher focused on the topic described in the problem statement.
- Assess whether the literature review is synthesized and organized.

Method

The third major part of the paper, the methods section, describes the participants, data collection method, procedures, and data analysis methods. Describe the type of study that is planned, such as survey research, experimental, or quasi-experimental design, and the data collection methods. Describe the environment in which the research will occur. Give explicit, step-by-step descriptions, so that other researchers can replicate the study if they wish.

Participants. Describe the population from which you plan to draw the sample for the study, the planned sampling strategy, and the anticipated sample size. Explain sampling procedures, sample size, and whether the data are generalizable. In the case example, the student is conducting a descriptive study using 100 participants selected using stratified random sampling because the student was interested in including people from diverse ethnic backgrounds and age groups.

Data Collection Method. Describe the instrument and how it was selected. Is it an existing questionnaire or one developed by the researcher? Explain directions for completing the questionnaire and whether special instructions were given to certain groups of participants. For example, if the sample consists of young adolescents, was special language or wording used? What follow-up procedures will be implemented if participants do not return questionnaires by the requested date? Describe the type of questions and how the reliability and validity of the instrument will be evaluated. In the case example, the student used a self-designed, 20-item Likert questionnaire to gather information from people in the study.

Procedures. The study's procedures are an integral part of the methods section. Special instructions to participants, the letter of informed consent, and the pilot study must be described. Indicate whether changes were made in the instrument because of pilot study results.

Data Analysis. Describe statistical procedures that will be used to analyze study results. These might include measures of central tendency (mean, median, and mode) and measures of variability (range, standard deviation, and variance). You may use correlation coefficients to describe the relationship between variables. Also, indicate any inferential statistics that will be used to analyze data (t-tests, regression, and analysis of variance). The student in the case example indicated that she will use descriptive statistics to describe data and show relationships between variables.

Evaluating Journal Articles
- Evaluate whether a description of the participants including demographic information is included in the article;
- Evaluate whether the researcher used random sampling;
- Evaluate whether there is a description of the research instrument. Is it an existing, standardized instrument or a researcher-designed questionnaire?

- Evaluate if a discussion of whether study results can be generalized to a broader population is provided?
- Evaluate whether the response rate is discussed: how many people or percentage of people returned the questionnaire? Was it an adequate number?
- Evaluate whether data analysis procedures are described? How did the researcher evaluate validity and reliability of the instrument?

Results of Study

The next major part of a research paper is the results, or findings, section. It presents the results of your study after data have been collected and analyzed. Here you explain whether data are presented in aggregate or for individual participants. Provide demographic characteristics of the sample, such as a breakdown by gender, age, race, type of residence, or other information of interest to the researcher. Explain explicitly the type of data analysis methods used. With each description of the type of analysis used, indicate the dependent and independent variables, the level of significance, and the hypotheses and research questions addressed by the procedure. Presentation of results includes facts only. There is no interpretation of results. You will have an opportunity to give opinions in the discussion section of the report.

Present a narrative description of results followed by tables, graphs, and charts to summarize data. Indicate the type of data analysis software used, such as the Statistical Package for the Social Sciences (SPSS), Mini-tabs, or SAS. If you are not required to implement a research study, the methods and results sections of the report may not be required.

Summary and Discussion

The summary of the findings, whether from a literature review or a study are narrated in this section along with conclusions, implications for practice, limitations of the study, and recommendations for further research. Summaries of the literature review, sample, methodology, and results are presented first, providing an overview of the study. The summary then leads into the discussion section where the researcher relates findings to the research questions and hypotheses and the theoretical framework and describes studies that support or contradict the results. Present strong support for your interpretation of the results, and your conclusions in this part of the report. In the case example, Heath concludes from the literature that both individual and institutional homophobia are related to lesbians' inability or refusal to leave abusive relationships and she supports this with appropriate documentation from the literature. Unexpected findings and implications for practice are also presented in this section.

Limitations of the Study.   Study limitations that might affect study results, such as problems with sampling, low return rate, and measurement issues, are also a part of the results section of the report. A sense of the limitations keeps the researcher from making undue claims and leads the way to future research.

Implications for Practice.   In this section, you explain how study results can influence provision of services to people and contribute to the knowledge base of the profession, and how the findings are important to social workers, administrators, policy makers, program implementers, and clients. In the case example, the student suggests that to provide more effective services social workers must be aware of obstacles facing lesbian clients and their own internalized homophobia.

Recommendations for Further Research.   Present recommendations for additional research based on your results and on the literature, both theoretical and empirical. In the case example, while acknowledging that practitioners in battered women's shelters have first-hand experience working with lesbians who are in violent relationships, the student asserts that more research is needed on this social problem for dissemination to other practitioners and to the general public. Based on findings, recommendations can also be made for implementing, revising, or discontinuing programs or services.

References

References are a list of sources—the journal articles, books, government reports, personal communications, and other works—cited in the research paper. Exclude sources that you considered using but did not. The different style manuals guide in-text and reference documentation. Two manuscript preparation styles are the *Publication Manual of the American Psychological Association* (APA) (2001) and the *Chicago Manual of Style* (CMS) (1993), a manual for writers of term papers and dissertations. Use only the style manual required by the course professor. Do not combine styles, and make sure that you have access to the recommended style manual.

Preparing a reference list correctly can be tedious because there are different formatting styles based on the type of work being cited. A journal article and a book are cited differently. A book by one author and an edited book are cited differently. Assuring that all citations and references are entered with proper spelling of names and correct dates, volume, and issue numbers is an important step in the report writing process. The best advice is to keep the style manual by your side when working on the reference list. Style formatting software is also available to assist in formatting references.

Appendixes

The appendix, the last part of the research report, contains detailed information. It might include a copy of the questionnaire, the letter of informed consent, and detailed tables that would interrupt flow if placed in the body of the paper. For publications, the appendix gives production staff leverage in adjusting the style and layout of the paper (APA, 2001).

Important Points about What to Include in a Research Report

- What to include in a research report will vary according to the audience and type of report. For example, information for, and the format for journal articles differ from requirements for books and reports for your employer.
- Although requirements differ, most reports should include the following information: a title, title page, abstract, introduction, problem statement, purpose of the study, definitions of major terms, significance of the study, research questions, a literature review, a theoretical framework, methodology, results and summary and discussion sections.

Tips for Preparing Written and Oral Presentations of Research Findings

Organizing, synthesizing, revising, and writing a research paper can be time consuming and often overwhelming. To limit self-imposed stress and have positive results, start early. In fact, you should begin the literature review as soon as you have a general idea of your selected social problem. Zinsser (1991) says that writing is thinking on paper; it is a craft and not an art. A clear sentence is no accident, he adds. Writing is one of the most difficult things that people do. He further maintains that clarity, simplicity, brevity, and humanity are the four main ingredients for good writing.

The main goal in writing is to write with clarity. Simplicity is ridding the writing of clutter, unnecessary words, meaningless jargon, frills, and attempts to sound important. The higher people get in their jobs and the more authority they have, the more suspicious they often are of simplicity. Some believe it reflects a simple mind. Writing with simplicity is, however, the result of hard work. Brevity is merely writing with as few words, sentences, and paragraphs as possible. Humanity is being yourself, being the same person on paper that you are in person (Zinsser).

The organization of a research report affects the reader's ability to understand it. Part of the revision process is reading the paper for unity, coherence, and emphasis (Cheney, 1983). Unity means that you remain focused on your problem statement and research question, avoiding putting a lot of unrelated information in the paper. Cheney also writes of other types of unity, from unity of subject to unity of sentence and paragraph. The order in which information is presented within sentences, paragraphs, chapters, and within volumes and the factors used to show relationships between that information are referred to as coherence. Subtopics or subtitles within a paper can help you achieve coherence. For example, in the case example student research paper, some of the subtitles under the review of related literature section are *Background Information, Practice Theory, Health Care Obstacles,* and *Legal Obstacles.* With achieving unity and coherence you must also show emphasis by, "Conveying relative importance of the thoughts, ideas, and issues that bear on the subject of your writing" (p. 92). Cheney further maintains that emphasis is being accurate about the importance of thoughts, ideas, and issues that relate to the subject.

This chapter will not provide you with all the information needed to become a skillful writer. Other books, your school's Academic Resource Center, writing courses, and other strategies for enhancing your writing must be used, when needed.

Written Reports

The following tips make the writing process easier:

- *Follow Guidelines for Organizing the Report.* Use the format provided by your professor, employer, or entity requesting the information.

- *Include All Requested Information.* Failing to include requested information is a common student error. As you complete one item on the assignment sheet or guide, check it off or mark a line through it.

- *Have a Friend or Relative Read Your Paper.* Select a person who will give constructive criticism. This is not a time to let hurt feelings interfere.

- *Revise, Revise, Revise!* When accomplished writers use the word *revision,* they don't mean the sort of superficial changes implied in the old elementary school phrase: "Copy it over in ink." Revision doesn't even mean writing your paper over again. It means *reading* your draft carefully in order to make principled, effective changes in the existing text. It means stepping outside the draft you've created, assessing its strengths and weaknesses as if you were a reader seeing it for the first time, and deciding what parts of the draft need to be expanded, clarified, elaborated, illustrated, reworded, restructured, modified—or just plain cut. The kind of work you do during the revision process takes concentration, determination, and at times a ruthlessness with your prose that comes from knowing you can always find new and better words to express ideas (Anson, & Schwegler, 1997, p. 78).

Think about the above definition of revision when you modify a paper. Revising a report, an unending process, is one of the most important parts of writing a paper. A major author once said that she is still revising while on the way to deliver the manuscript to her publisher.

- *Proofread.* Check the paper for mechanical problems, including grammatical errors, correct spelling, sentence structure, and punctuation.

Oral Presentations

Most people fear sharing information either formally or informally before an audience. Students are often reluctant to present to their classmates and instructors if they have not had experience giving oral presentations. The following tips can alleviate some of those fears:

Preparation

- *Carefully Study Your Material.* Become familiar and comfortable with it. The better acquainted and more at ease with the material you are, the more relaxed you will be during the presentation.

- *Practice Your Presentation.* Give it in front of a friend or family member who will give honest comments.

- *Record Your Presentation.* Most people do not like this. But it is helpful to listen, and make adjustments in tone, enunciation, and emphasis where needed.

- *Practice.* Use the room in which the presentation will be given, if possible.

Presentation

- *Refrain from Reading.* If you have practiced and are familiar with your presentation, reading is not necessary.

- *Rely on Visual Aids.* PowerPoint presentations are popular and effective means of helping maintain interest. With a PowerPoint presentation, you can generate handouts, including handouts for conference participants to take notes on. You can also generate speakers' notes. When using PowerPoint, interact continuously with the audience and do not rely exclusively on PowerPoint to give the presentation.

■ *Monitor Your Time.* Do not exceed it. Presenters and panelists are given a set amount of time to present. Panelists divide time among themselves. If the workshop runs two hours, that time is divided among four panelists with each having 30 minutes. Cutting into the other panelists' time does not leave sufficient time for their presentations, and more than likely, will anger them.

■ *Allow Time for Interaction.* Let audience members ask questions, comment, or make suggestions.

A guide for organizing a research report is provided in Figure 5.1.

Important Points about Preparing for Written and Oral Presentations of Research Findings

■ For written presentations follow guidelines provided by your professor, employer, or others and include all requested information.
■ Continuous revising is critical to achieve clarity, simplicity, brevity, humanity, unity, coherence, and emphasis.
■ For oral presentations, try practicing before someone, recording the presentation, and becoming so well acquainted with your topic that you need not read it.

Human Diversity Issues in Creating and Evaluating Research Reports

The *Publication Manual of the American Psychological Association* (2001) outlines guidelines to reduce bias in language. Refer to that manual for detailed information. Be especially careful when discussing the participants in your study. The manual suggests that writers be specific in addressing people, for example, using gay men and lesbians instead of just gay to refer to both men and women when describing their sexual orientation. (Some women also refer to themselves as gay; use the term that people prefer). Be sensitive to labels. Rather than referring to "the schizophrenics," use "people with schizophrenia." Acknowledge participants in studies as more than subjects and samples. Avoid ambiguity in sex identity or sex role. Distinguish between sexual orientation and sexual preference. Be current on the terms preferred by various ethnic groups. Use nonhandicapping language when referring to people with disabilities or defining the age of participants.

Ethical Issues and Biases in Creating and Evaluating Research Reports

There are several ethical issues relating to research that you need to be aware of as both a student and a researcher. One of the biggest ethical obstacles facing students when writing research papers is plagiarism. Experience indicates that most students who commit plagiarism do so unknowingly by failing to give credit to researchers whose work they use. Use direct

FIGURE 5.1   Guide for Organizing a Research Report

    I. *Title Page*   (See example)
   II. *Abstract*
  III. *Introduction*
        A. Statement of the problem.
        B. Purpose of the study.
        C. Definitions of major terms used in your paper.
        D. Significance of the problem.
        E. Research question (s).
   IV. *Review of Related Literature*
        A. History of the problem or background information.
        B. Practice Theory (theoretical framework).
        C. Restate purpose of study (briefly).
        D. State the hypothesis(es).
    V. *Methods*
        A. Participants—describe the population from which the sample will be selected and anticipated sample size.
        B. Data collection method.
        C. Procedures used.
        D. Data Analysis—describe statistical procedure to be used. (Optional for students writing a literature review only.)
   VI. *Results*   (For students who implement a research project)
        A. Describe the sample using descriptive statistics.
        B. Planned Analyses—provide statistical results relating to the research questions and hypotheses.
        C. Describe unexpected results.
        D. Use narratives to describe results along with the descriptive and inferential statistics. Present statistics in tables, when appropriate, along with narratives.
  VII. *Summary and Discussion*   (Based on literature, review results for students writing proposal and literature reviews. If research project was implemented, on research study results.)
        A. Summary of findings from the literature review. (If a project was not implemented. If a research project was implemented, summarize the study.)
        B. Describe findings relative to your theoretical framework.
        C. Describe conclusions based on findings.
        D. What are the implications for practice?
        E. What are the weaknesses or limitations of the research?
        F. Present recommendations for further research.
 VIII. *References*

quotations when the exact words of another researcher are used, and indicate the page number for that source. Use an in-text citation to give credit when another person's work is paraphrased and summarized. All of this must then be followed with an accurate reference section at the end of the paper.

There are also other ethical problems facing students. The purchase of research papers to submit as their own work is now more prevalent than ever with access to the Internet. Concocting data and study results is another ethical lapse. Finally, failing to get permission to use the work of others in your research, when required, is a problem.

WRITING STRATEGY

Read a paper that you are preparing for a class and try to cut the paper by 50%, as Zinsser (1991) suggests. Try to eliminate 7 1/2 pages of a 15-page paper. Use a previous paper if you are not currently writing one.

LEARNING ACTIVITY

Ask a classmate to read the paper that you reduced, before and after the reduction, and to give you honest comments on both papers. Request specific comments about both papers regarding content, length, mechanics (such as sentence structure and grammar), and fluidity.

INFORMATION TECHNOLOGY FOR CREATING AND EVALUATING RESEARCH REPORTS

With the Internet and its electronic databases, more resources for research reports are available. Many colleges and universities offer access to some databases from students' homes. There are also databases from which students can download the full text of journal articles. Locate three journal articles from a database that provides full text articles. Refer back to Chapter 3 for more detailed information on using technology to conduct research.

Important Points from Chapter 5

- Results of your research can be shared using written or oral reports. People use research findings to improve the services they provide to clients, guide implementation of new programs, assess the viability of current programs, and evaluate programs.
- Most reports, whether written or oral, should follow specific guidelines in terms of the ordering of information and the content. Content and format requirements usually differ based on the type of report.
- Regardless of the type of report, work on achieving unity, coherence, emphasis, simplicity, clarity, brevity, and humanity by continually revising and rearranging materials.
- Careful preparation for both written and oral presentations plays a major role in your success here.

REFERENCES

American Psychological Association (2001). *Publication manual of the American Psychological Association* (5th ed.). Washington, DC: Author.

Anson, C. M., & Schwegler, R. A. (1997). *The Longman handbook for writers and readers.* New York: Longman.

Cheney, T. A. (1983). *Getting the words right: How to rewrite, edit & revise.* Cincinnati, OH: Writer's Digest Books.

Chicago Editorial Staff (1993). *The Chicago manual of style* (14th ed.). Chicago: University of Chicago Press.

Heath, D. (1999). Homophobic attitudes, heterosexism, and domestic violence in lesbian relationships. Unpublished manuscript.

National Association of Social Workers (1999). www.naswdc.org/pubs/code/code.asp *Code of Ethics.* Retrieved July 15, 1999 from www.socialworkers.org/Code/CDSTAN1.HTM.

Turabian, K. L. (1996). A manual for writers of term papers, theses, and dissertations. Chicago: University of Chicago Press.

Zinsser, W. (Speaker). (1991). *On writing well* (Cassette Recording No 1-55994-349-1). New York: Harper Audio.

Quantitative Research Methods

PART THREE

Quantitative Research Methods

6 Measurement

Since taking research, I understand the differences between quantitative and qualitative research methods. I can grasp the meaning of terms specific to these two research approaches. This makes it easier to raise questions about certain issues, for example, about the reliability and validity of quantitative studies.
—Nontraditional Junior Research Student

CHAPTER GOALS

Your major goals upon completion of this chapter are to:

- Understand the meaning of measurement in social work research.
- Understand the measurement process.
- Understand how concepts are both conceptualized and operationalized.
- Understand the role of the hypothesis in measurement.
- Understand the importance of measures and how they are evaluated in research.
- Recognize measurement errors.

Introduction

You measure phenomena everyday, using some methods that measure accurately and others that are imprecise. For example, if you are dieting, you use a scale to measure food, special cups and spoons when cooking. These instruments provide exact measures. Less exact measures are also common. For example, when you assert that a book was "too sexually explicit," that someone has a "bad attitude," or that someone is "depressed" or "stressed out," imprecise measures are used. How can you accurately determine how bad an attitude, how stressed, or how depressed a person is?

The researcher experiences similar problems in striving for measurement precision. A scientific approach in measuring can generate the preciseness that a researcher desires. Some concepts are simple to measure precisely—age, income, and educational level. Measuring others, such as depression, stress, self-esteem, and progress of clients accurately is more complex. Specific measures have to be created to assess these more complicated phenomena.

Measurement is the process of assigning numbers or labels to observable phenomena—people, situations, or events—in order to test them through a quantification process. Measurement helps you answer research questions, test hypotheses, and analyze data statistically. Chapter 6 explains how concepts are defined, both on a conceptual level and on an operational level, the development of hypotheses, levels of measurement, methods for evaluating measures, and errors in measurement.

Generalist Case Study: Incest

The Harris Family Household Members:

Mother:	Ms. Ilene Harris, age 20
Daughter:	Eva Harris, age 8
Mother's Brother:	Raymond Harris, age 17
Mother's Cousins:	Ms. Chantel Harris, age 21
	Ms. Simone Harris, age 25
Social Workers:	Mr. Richard Carlson
	Ms. Yvonne Ingram
Judge:	Honorable Melvin Scott

Presenting Problem: The Child Protective Services (CPS) office received a referral that a 17-year-old Caucasian boy, Raymond, had sexually assaulted his 7-year-old niece, Eva. Mr. Carlson and Ms. Ingram, social workers, went immediately to Eva's school to initiate a child protective services investigation.

Investigation: According to the teacher, from the time that Eva arrived at school at 8:00 A.M., she asked continuously to go to the restroom. After the child made several visits to the restroom, the teacher took Eva to the nurse's station. The nurse asked Eva what was wrong. She replied, "My uncle hurt me down there," pointing to her genital area. After asking some follow-up questions, the nurse called the police and Child Protective Services. Eva was transported by ambulance to the hospital after she, the nurse, and the teacher were briefly interviewed. Mr. Carlson followed the ambulance to the hospital, and Ms. Ingram rode with the police officer to the mother's place of employment, a grocery store, to inform her of the abuse and to take her to the hospital. The mother did not respond to the social worker when told about the abuse but continued reading a magazine.

At the hospital, the mother showed no emotion and did not talk to or touch her daughter upon seeing her in the rape crisis treatment center. In the days that followed, Ms. Harris avoided visiting with her daughter by going to the cafeteria or the waiting area. Ms. Ingram, the social worker, was concerned about this shunning and ignoring Eva while the cousins were embracing, kissing, and expressing their love for Raymond during his court appearances.

Before the first court appearance, the uncle's court-appointed attorneys informed Ms. Ingram that they would recommend that Raymond be sent home. Ms. Ingram objected to this plan because it would necessitate Eva's removal from the home, which would make her feel that she had done something wrong. Yet, the attorneys proceeded with their recommendation. Judge Scott was furious and admonished the attorneys for not taking the case seriously and failing to consider Eva's safety.

The social worker had been searching for an out-of-home placement for Eva in the event that the court agreed with the attorneys' recommendation. During this search she discovered a history of incest within the Harris family. In interviews with family members she found that the perpetrator, Raymond, had observed incestuous relationships within the family most of his life. Ms. Ilene Harris' stepfather sexually assaulted her from the time that she was 8 years old until she became pregnant at age 12. Another of Eva's uncles had raped a young girl in the presence of Raymond and other children in the family. After documenting these stories, Ms. Ingram wondered if Ms. Harris had been reliving her own experience with sexual abuse and if she felt powerless to do anything about her daughter's sexual assault.

Judge Scott refused to comply with the attorneys' request and sent Raymond to the adolescent ward of a psychiatric institution. Eva remained in the home with her mother. The entire family was placed in an intensive family preservation program and given treatment with a social worker who specialized in working with incestuous and abusive families.

Levels of Measurement

Activity 1. As you read this chapter, think about and list ways that you have measured something in your life. How did you measure that particular phenomenon? Do you believe that your measurement method was accurate? Why or why not?

Activity 2. Locate a measuring instrument (questionnaire or survey) and determine the level of measurement of each question.

There are four levels of measurement, that range, in terms of making a statistical inference, from the least powerful to the most powerful; they are nominal, ordinal, interval, and ratio. How a variable is conceptualized and the type of statistical procedure used depends on the level of measurement. Also, the preciseness with which a concept is measured is contingent on the level of measurement. Researchers want the highest possible precision based on the variables being measured and the purpose of their research.

When measuring a concept, you are providing categories for classifying the variable that you are studying. There are two criteria for constructing variable categories: that the categories be exhaustive and mutually exclusive. Exhaustive categories enable you to classify every subject in your study. Mutually exclusive categories allow you to classify every subject into one and only one category.

Nominal Level

The nominal level of measurement, sometimes called the categorical level, is the least powerful measure of the four. It categorizes variables into names or labels that can have only one category, and it allows the classifying of attributes of variables into mutually exclusive and exhaustive categories. The variables must have at least two attributes, and each participant must fit into one of the attributes. For example, the variable gender can be classified into the mutually exclusive categories of male and female (the participant cannot be both male and female), and these categories are exhaustive in that these are all of the attributes of the variable gender. There are times when the category *Other* has to be added to nominal variable attributes. For instance, using the variable *ethnicity,* the attributes could be:

- African American
- Asian
- Caucasian
- Native American

You can expand on these categories by adding more attributes or using *Other,* so that the person completing the application can list a different ethnicity.

Participants' responses to nominal level measures are given in words or names and not numbers. When numbers are used as labels for nominal variables, they have no mathematical or quantitative significance. For example, on a survey that asked for gender (a nominal level of measurement) and instructed you to circle 1 for female or 2 for male, in data analysis no statistical technique would be applied to these numbers that are used merely to identify or name the variables. Based on this information, the researcher cannot say that male (2) is more than female (1).

Ordinal Level

The ordinal level of measurement has exhaustive and mutually exclusive categories *and the categories are rank ordered, representing more or less of a variable*. For example, if you measure the degree of happiness of Eva, the sexually abused child, using ordinal levels of measurement, the attributes of happiness are:

1   not at all happy
2   unhappy
3   somewhat happy

4   happy
5   very happy

These degrees of happiness can be ranked with 1 being the lowest level of happiness and 5 being the highest level of happiness. Or they may be ranked with 1 being the highest level of happiness. You, the researcher, can establish how the numbers are used. The happiness categories are exhaustive in that they cover all the attributes of happy; they are mutually exclusive because a child cannot be "not at all happy" and "very happy" at the same time.

The attributes can be rank-ordered with the numbers representing the ranks. But the numbers 1 through 5 assigned to each attribute are not fixed, and the distance between the ratings are not said to be equal. For example, you do not know if the distance, or level of happiness or unhappiness, between ratings of 4 (happy) and 5 (very happy) are equal to the distance between 1 (not at all happy) and 2 (unhappy).

Interval Level

The interval level of measurement is the second most precise measure on the hierarchy. Interval level variables are exhaustive, mutually exclusive, rank-ordered *and the exact distance between categories of the variable is known and is equal to each other.* The categories of interval scale variables can be added and subtracted. For example, if you score 100% on an exam and your roommate scores 70%, the difference in the scores is 30% and would be the same as the difference between a score of 90% and a score of 60%. The 30% is the exact distance between the scores. Fahrenheit temperature scales are interval level variables because the difference between points on the scale is fixed. Intelligence quotient (IQ), Graduate Record Examination, and Scholastic Assessment Test scores and standardized measuring instruments generally are all examples of interval levels of measurement. While interval level variables can be treated as ordinal and nominal level variables, ordinal and nominal level variables are not all interval level. (The commonality in these levels is that the numbers are assigned values.)

In the chapter example, Raymond's psychiatric social worker ordered a battery of tests as part of his assessment. The IQ test and depression test are among the interval level standardized tests that she requested.

Ratio Level

Variables at the ratio level of measurement are exhaustive, mutually exclusive, rank-ordered, with the exact distance between categories of the variable known and equal to each other, *and the measures are based on a true or absolute zero point.* The absolute zero of the ratio level distinguishes this measure from the interval level of measurement. A person can have zero income, which means no income; or a person could have zero children, which means no children. At the ratio level, the variables that are used are the actual numbers. For instance, in gathering background information on Ms. Ilene Harris you ask for some of the following data, all of which are ratio level measures:

- Age
- Number of years of school completed

- Number of years employed at the grocery store
- Number of people living in the home
- Monthly salary

Using these variables you can compare and interpret the differences among the scores of responses of people completing a questionnaire. For instance, the salary of an employee who earns $50,000 a year is twice as much as the salary of someone who earns $25,000 a year. Ratio level data can be added, subtracted, multiplied, and divided, and statistical analyses can be performed.

Although ratio levels of measurement use the exact numbers, this is not always necessary. Instead of using ratio level measures to get respondents' ages, this data could be grouped into ordinal level measures by using the categories: ages 20–30, 31–41, 42–52 for the participant to choose from. Note that the levels of measurement build on each other because each succeeding level contains qualities of the level above it, as in Table 6.1.

Important Points about Measurement and Levels of Measurement

- Measurement is a method used to assign numbers or labels to observable phenomena and facilitates answering research questions, testing hypotheses, and analyzing data.
- From the least precise to the most precise, the levels on which variables can be measured are nominal, ordinal, interval, and ratio.
- The type of statistical procedure used depends on the level of measurement, and other factors.

Defining Concepts

Conceptualizing Terms Related to the Problem

> *Activity 3.*   After reading this section, write conceptual definitions for two of the major concepts used in your study.

Conceptualization is a procedure used to specify the meaning of the most pertinent concepts or ideas in your study. Concepts are abstract because they are not observable. However, attaching meanings or symbols to concepts will facilitate communication. Conceptual definitions are theoretical definitions found in the literature, dictionaries, and encyclopedias. Conceptual definitions can also be developed using a combination of theoretical definitions, your personal experience, and the knowledge of others. Regardless of the methods used, conceptual definitions must relate specifically to terms used in your research.

Conceptual definitions must be explicit, accurate, and consistent with the study. One reason for writing conceptual definitions clearly is to allow other researchers to replicate the research. To replicate a study a researcher needs to follow the exact steps in your study with the intention of achieving the same results. The researcher can also follow some of the steps and make changes in others in order to see if the results change. A second reason for preciseness and

TABLE 6.1 Levels of Measurement

Level	Characteristics	Examples
Nominal—qualitative data, no arithmetic operations; frequencies of number of cases in each category.	■ Exhaustive categories ■ Mutually exclusive categories	■ Ethnicity ■ Gender ■ Religion ■ Marital status
Ordinal—quantitative, can determine more or less of an attribute; no amounts are indicated; numerical data grouped into categories (income—10,000–30,000; age—20–30 and 31–40)	■ Exhaustive categories ■ Mutually exclusive categories + ■ Rank order (greater than, less than; agree, disagree)	■ Social class ■ Educational level ■ Attitude questions ■ Opinion questions
Interval—Almost all interval scales are ratio scales; no absolute zero	■ Exhaustive categories ■ Mutually exclusive categories ■ Rank order + ■ Exact distance between categories of the variable is known and equal to each other	■ Fahrenheit ■ and Celsius scales ■ IQ scores ■ SAT scores
Ratio—Measures are based on a true or absolute zero	■ Exhaustive categories ■ Mutually exclusive categories ■ Rank order ■ Exact distance between categories of the variable is known and equal to each other + ■ Measures based on a true or absolute zero	■ Age ■ Number years of school completed ■ Number of families in caseload ■ Number years employed with an agency ■ Number of training sessions participated in ■ Monthly salary

clarity in defining concepts is to provide students, researchers, and others with unambiguous definitions because concepts may be defined differently from study to study.

Using the incest case study as an example, the word *incest* and the phrase *intergenerational incest* are abstract and may have different meanings to various people. A theoretical or conceptual definition of incest is sexual "Intercourse or *sexual abuse* between close relatives—that is, people who are too closely related to be permitted by law to marry" (Barker, 1995, p. 181). A possible conceptual definition of *incest perpetrator who has observed incest* is, "A person who has lived in an environment wherein he or she observed incestuous relationships and subsequently engaged in a sexual relationship with a family member." Although these definitions are suitable for everyday discussions, your understanding of exactly what incest is and who is classified as an incest perpetrator based on this definition could differ from your friend's ideas. The term *incest* and the phrase *incest perpetrator* are not observable based on these definitions since they do not contain indicators, which move concepts from the abstract to the concrete and so facilitate the measurement process.

Operationalizing Concepts

> *Activity 4.*   After reading this section, operationally define the concepts that were conceptually defined in Activity 3. How do the operational definitions differ from conceptual definitions? Do your classmates agree with your definitions?

After developing conceptual definitions, define the major variables used in your research in measurable terms and convey those meanings to readers. Operational definitions provide for consistency and objectivity and delineate how variables will be measured, moving variables from the abstract to the concrete in quantitative studies. Operational definitions are not dictionary definitions. Therefore, they should be reliable so that other researchers, using your operational definitions in their studies, can replicate your study by measuring the concept or variable exactly as you did.

When operationally defining variables, demonstrate how the behaviors or attitudes are manifested. Consider the incest case study. As a Child Protective Services worker, you need to know the indicators of a sexually abused child as well as the indicators of a person who sexually abuses children. A researcher must also be aware of these indicators in order to have accurate measures. Therefore, an operational definition of incest partially derived from the literature review is:

> Sexual relationships between any family members including blood relatives and relatives by marriage such as fathers, stepfathers, mothers, stepmothers, siblings, aunts, uncles, nieces, and nephews. Incest includes sexual molestation, which involves noncoitus sexual contact, petting, fondling, exposing genitals, and voyeurism that results in sexual stimulation of the perpetrator. Incest also includes sexual assault involving manual, oral, or penetration of genitals of the victim, masturbatory activities, fellatio, and cunnilingus. Incest also includes forced sexual contact and rape with the penis (Mayer cited in Tower, 1993, p. 137).

Compare this definition with the conceptual definition of incest. This operational definition lists several indicators of incest, whereas the theoretical definition is general. Indicators in the operational definition can be used to develop a scale to measure a variable. A thorough review of the literature will assist you in operationalizing concepts. Concepts are thought of as variables after they have been conceptualized and operationalized.

Important Points about Conceptualizing and Operationalizing Concepts

- Conceptual definitions specify how you define terms for your study and could be dictionary definitions or a combination of dictionary definitions and knowledge from practical experience and experts.

- Operational definitions are not dictionary definitions and provide indicators of the concept of interest.
- Operational definitions specify how terms used in your study will be measured.
- A review of the literature helps you develop and refine your operational definitions.

What Is a Variable?

Activity 5. Now that you have conceptualized and operationalized major concepts in your study, identify the independent and dependent variables in your problem statement and research question. What is the difference between the two variables?

As mentioned in the previous section, once concepts are conceptualized and operationalized they are thought of as variables although the terms concepts and variables are often used interchangeably. A variable is something that has attributes, values, or characteristics that can vary from participant to participant, from research study to research study, that can change over time and be measured. A variable must have at least two attributes, which are words or phrases used to describe people, things, or situations. Attributes are not variables. For example, the variable *gender* has two attributes, female and male and the variable *income* has many attributes such as $10,000, $40,000, or $500,000. See Figure 6.1 for examples of variables and their attributes.

Variables may differ among people and over time. For instance, the variable *occupation* varies among people; some are teachers, data entry operators, and graphic artists. People may also change their occupations over time. A teacher becomes a consultant; a data entry operator becomes a computer technician, the graphic artist becomes a lawyer, and the line social worker is promoted to first-line supervisor. The two types of variables are independent and dependent:

- *The independent variable.* This variable, also called the causal variable, influences and explains changes in the dependent variable. It may also be called the predictor variable because it predicts changes in the dependent variable.

- *The dependent variable.* Also called the outcome variable, this is the phenomenon that you are studying. It is the behavior, attitude, or situation that you want to explain or be able to predict. Whether the dependent variable changes is contingent upon the independent variable. The independent variable in one student's study could be a dependent variable in a different study and vice versa. Students often confuse the definition of the two variables, so it may help to write the definition of both terms and keep them in a visible location while working on your paper, until you can differentiate between the two. The relationship between the independent and dependent variable is illustrated by:

$$X \longrightarrow Y$$

where X is the independent variable and Y is the dependent variable.

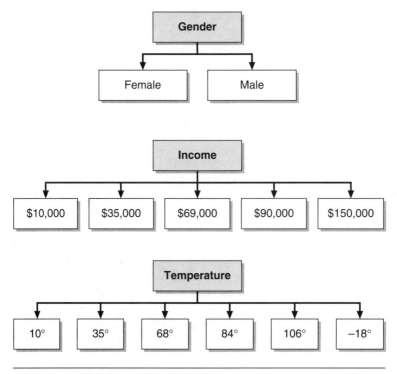

FIGURE 6.1   Variables and Their Attributes

Another important variable is the intervening variable, which may influence or cause change in the dependent variable when it appears that the independent variable, the intervention, is responsible for the change. It is also called the confounding or extraneous variable.

Table 6.2 illustrates possible independent and dependent variables derived from the incest case study. The relationship among the independent, intervening, and dependent variables is presented below:

independent variable $\longrightarrow$ **intervening variable** $\longrightarrow$ **dependent variable**

Important Points about Variables

- A variable is something that can change and be measured.
- The independent variable can cause, influence, or affect the dependent variable.
- The dependent variable is the behavior, attitude, situation, or object that you are studying.

TABLE 6.2   **Examples of Independent and Dependent Variables from Case Study**

Independent Variable	Dependent Variable
Children who have observed incest	Adolescent incest perpetrators
Family history of incest	Familial sexual abuse
Incest survivor who feels powerless	Incest survivor's inability to emotionally support her sexually abus[e] child

Stating the Hypothesis

> ***Activity 6.***   After reading this section, write a hypothesis that includes the independent and dependent variables from your study. Explain how your research question and the hypothesis differ.

A hypothesis is a statement that predicts the relationship between or among two or more variables that can be tested. Thus, it is an answer to the research question made before data are collected and analyzed. You started the literature review with a specific question directly related to the problem being examined. After reviewing the literature and defining and conceptualizing concepts, you have enough information to predict what the outcome of your research will be. With this information, reformulate the research question into a hypothesis predicting the results of the research. This prediction can be based on what you know about the topic after reviewing the literature, what you know from personal experiences and others' experiences, or a theory. There is also an element of guessing involved in predicting relationships between variables. Instead of asking if there is a relationship between concepts as you do with the research question, you state what that relationship is. Like the research question, the hypothesis is not an elaborate statement, but a one-sentence prediction. Here is an example from the incest case study.

> *Research Question:* Are children who observe incestuous relationships more likely to become adolescent incest perpetrators than children who do not observe these relationships?
>
> *Hypothesis.* Children who observe incestuous relationships are more likely to become adolescent incest perpetrators than children who do not observe these relationships.
>
> *Independent Variable.* Children who observe incestuous relationships.
>
> *Dependent Variable.* Adolescent incest perpetrators.
>
> *Theoretical Framework.* Learning Theory, applied to sexual deviancy, would contend that the sexual offender learns behavior from watching others in the environment, models that behavior, and may have also been sexually abused (Rosenberg, 2000).

In a hypothesis you can state one of several different kinds of relationships—a cause and effect, a correlation, an association, or no relationship between the variables. When a cause and effect relationship is hypothesized, the researcher is making a definite assertion that the independent variable is the cause of the change in the dependent variable. Remember from Chapter 1 that certain criteria must be met to establish causality, which is difficult to do. When the hypothesis states that a correlation exists between variables, this indicates a stronger relationship than an association but not as strong as a cause and effect relationship. A prediction that an association exists between variables in a hypothesis is a still more moderate prediction.

Types of Hypotheses

■ *Directional, or One-tailed, Hypothesis.* It predicts a relationship between variables and specifies the direction of that relationship. The direction predicts either a positive or negative relationship. Directional hypotheses are used more commonly in explanatory research.

> Example: Children that observe incestuous relationships are more likely to become adolescent sexual offenders than adolescents who did not witness incestuous relationships as children.

■ *Non-directional, or Two-tailed, Hypothesis.* It predicts a relationship between variables but does not specify the direction of that relationship. In other words, the non-directional hypothesis does not state whether the predicted relationship between the variables will be positive or negative. The problem with the non-directional hypothesis is that if the data analysis results show a direction in the relationship, the researcher cannot specify the direction of the relationship at that point. The direction of the relationship must be indicated in the hypothesis before data collection and analysis occurs.

> Example: There is a relationship between young children observing incestuous relationships and adolescent sexual offenders.

■ *Null or Statistical Hypothesis.* It can only be tested using inferential statistics and is the true workhorse of statistical testing. The null hypothesis may include relationships, prediction (estimation), association, or difference, as indicated by the type of statistical test used. The null hypothesis is discussed in detail in Chapter 9.

After the hypothesis has been stated, you can begin focusing on how the data collection instruments will be evaluated for reliability and validity.

Important Points about Hypotheses

■ The hypothesis is an answer to a research question made prior to collecting and analyzing data. It is a statement that predicts the relationships between or among two or more variables that can be tested.
■ Directional, non-directional, and null are the types of hypotheses.

Evaluating Measures

> *Activity 7.*   After reading this section, describe the differences between reliability and validity. List the different types of reliability and validity and the definitions for each.

So far, you have been informed about the scientific approach to acquiring knowledge and how that method involves, among other things, testing or building theories, establishing causal relationships, conceptualizing and operationalizing concepts, and developing hypotheses. Evaluating measures, or data collection instruments known as questionnaires or surveys, is another important part of the measurement process. The two indicators of the quality of measures are reliability and validity. Reliability evaluates whether the instrument is consistent and dependable in generating the same information each time the questionnaire is completed by a research participant. Validity assesses whether the instrument is measuring what it purports to measure by providing the correct information on the questionnaire. Reliable and valid measuring instruments generate reliable and valid data and results from your research investigation.

Reliability

When evaluating measures for reliability, you want to know if the instrument will produce the same results when administered again under similar circumstances. For example, if the adult incest survivors in your research study are given a questionnaire this week that measures their level of anger and they are given that same questionnaire next week, their anger level should be the same if their circumstances remain the same, that is, there were no interventions that changed the anger level. The measuring instrument is then said to be dependable and consistent, thus reliable. There are several different ways to test for reliability.

Test-Retest Reliability.   Test-retest reliability requires that the same group of participants complete a questionnaire at two different times to determine if the scores or results are the same. Both scores from the two tests are correlated using a measure of association with the expectation for a high degree of association—when the expected results from each test are the same, a reliable measuring tool is indicated. For example, the adult survivors of childhood incest are administered an anger test this week. The same test, in a different form, is given two weeks later. If the results or correlation are high, then the anger test is assumed to be reliable if no intervention or other change occurred that affects the adult's anger. Determining the length of time between administering the questionnaires is a problem with test-retest reliability because allowing either too much time or too little time between tests can influence participants' responses.

Alternate Form Reliability.   In the alternate, or parallel, form test for reliability, two different forms of the same test are developed that are comparable in level of difficulty, instructions, formats, content, and intent to measure the same variables. Although the tests are the same, the order of the responses to questions may be different and slight changes in wording may be made. The two different forms are administered to the same group of people. The second questionnaire can be administered shortly after the first or there can be an interim period before it is given. The Scholastic Assessment Test (SAT), Intelligence Quotients (IQ) tests, and the Graduate Record Exam (GRE) all have alternate forms. Two problems with the alternate forms test are: (1) determining how much time to allow between tests; and (2) constructing a second questionnaire or test.

Split Halves Reliability. The split halves method of checking for reliability involves randomly dividing the questionnaire or test in half and administering half of the questionnaire to half of the participants and half to the other group. The division can be made by dividing the total number of questions by two. For example, if the questionnaire consists of 100 questions, half of the participants are given the first 50 questions and the other half the last 50 questions. Or, one group may be given even numbered questions, and the other group the odd numbered questions. Reliability is present if responses from both groups correlate. The split half method estimates the internal consistency—the degree to which both halves of the measurements within an instrument correlate with each other. Some advantages of using the split halves method are that only one form of the measuring tool (questionnaire or test) is required. It is administered once, no control group is needed, and it gives the clearest indication of reliability.

Interobserver or Interrater Agreement Reliability. The aim of interobserver or interrater reliability is to have more than one trained person, using identical instruments, observe and rate the same research participants, situations, or events. As a result, the independent ratings by the raters should be similar. If the ratings agree, there is a true picture of the phenomenon being observed and minimal rater influence. For example, you, along with another student intern, are trained to use a child behavior scale to measure the behavior of kindergarten students. Using the same measuring instrument that has indicators of specific behaviors that relate to the child's interaction with peers and teachers, the two of you observe children at the same time and rate the behavior using the same measuring instrument. A correlation coefficient is computed to determine the degree of the relationship between the two ratings.

A correlation coefficient can be computed to determine if the above type of reliability exists. The correlation coefficient is a numeric descriptive statistic that indicates the relationship between two variables with a value that ranges from 0.0 to 1.00. The Pearson product-moment correlation coefficient, referred to as Pearson's *r,* is the most extensively used coefficient and will be discussed in detail in Chapter 8.

Internal Consistency Reliability. "Reliability refers to the results obtained with an evaluation instrument and not to the instrument itself. Thus, it is more appropriate to speak of the reliability of 'test scores' or the 'measurement' than of the 'test' or the 'instrument'" (Gronlund & Linn, cited in Henson, 2000). Internal consistency coefficients are theoretical estimates derived from classical test theory and are not direct measures of reliability (Henson, 2000). Cronbach's alpha, also known as coefficient alpha (α), is the favorite measure of internal consistency reliability, measuring whether all items in the questionnaire measure the same phenomenon. (This is also called item homogeneity.) Coefficient alpha is similar to the correlation coefficient with a measurement scale that also ranges from 0 to 1.00. An alpha that is closer to 1.00 indicates higher internal consistency.

Remember that reliability only indicates the measuring instrument's consistency and dependability. It is the presence of validity in a measuring instrument that indicates if the instrument measures what it was designed to measure.

Validity

A measuring instrument is valid when it measures what it purports to measure and does so accurately. There is a direct relationship between an instrument's validity and its accuracy in measuring a phenomenon. Although a reliable measuring instrument may not be valid, a valid instrument will be reliable. For example, you decide to measure the anger level of adults who were victims of incest, so a co-worker convinces you to use a test (measuring instrument) that measures depression because a stress test is not immediately available. A test-retest is done to check for the presence of reliability and you find that the incest survivors' responses are consistent. That is, their responses to the questions are the same on the second test as they were on the first. When you test for validity, however, it is clear that the tests are measuring depression and not stress. Although the instrument is reliable, it is not valid. The researcher is responsible for documenting that both existing measuring instruments and newly designed instruments are valid. Four measures of validity are used by researchers—face, content, criterion, and construct.

Face Validity.   Face validity, which is subjective, is the least accurate measure of an instrument's validity. Based on sound judgment, logic, and common sense, it is a casual review of the measuring instrument that evaluates whether the instrument asks the appropriate questions to measure the phenomenon that it intends to measure, using language that participants can understand. Anyone, including people without knowledge or expertise on the topic—your friend, partner, spouse, or classmate—can be the reviewer to help determine face, or surface, validity. Do the reviewers, including participants and the investigator, believe that the instrument is a plausible one for measuring the variable? Rubin and Babbie (2001) maintain that although face validity is essential, it is not adequate and that ". . . some researchers might argue that it is technically misleading to call it a type of validity at all" (p. 193).

Content Validity.   Content validity determines whether the measuring instrument covers all of the variable's indicators, based on the previously established definition of the variable. The researcher must first decide which attributes are a part of the variable. The literature is one frequently used source for assisting with that decision; a panel of experts on the topic may also judge whether the instrument contains all relevant components of the variable. A statistical test, such as one involving a correlation coefficient, is not a part of the process used in establishing content validity.

Researchers interested in measuring participants' learning in specific subject areas would be concerned about content validity. For example, your work unit at the Department of Children's Services attends a workshop on interviewing child sexual abuse victims. Following the end of the session, the supervisor arranges for the workshop facilitator to give a test to evaluate what or how much your unit learned about interviewing child abuse victims. The test items include only information shared in the workshop, the test is not given to other social workers who did not participate in the workshop, and the test is reviewed for inclusion of irrelevant items.

Criterion Validity.   Criterion validity, which provides a more quantitative documentation of the measuring instrument's precision and correctness in the form of a correlation coefficient, is a more objective type of validity. When results of scores on a new measuring instrument are compared to scores on an established, validated measurement (the criterion), measuring the same phenomenon, criterion validity is established. When your goal is measuring a present attribute of research participants or predicting future behavior of participants, proof of the presence of criterion validity is necessary. Hypotheses testing or additions to existing knowledge cannot use criterion validity. Predictive and concurrent are the two types of criterion validity.

Predictive validity.   It is established when a measure predicts the participant's future performance, as when a participant's test scores correlate with the participant's future behavior or performance. For example, SAT scores are often used as predictors of high school students' success in college. Students' scores on the SAT are compared with their college grade point average (GPA). In making this comparison, the researcher is looking for a high correlation between the score on the test (SAT) and the grade point average.

Concurrent validity.   It is documented when there is a high correlation between the measuring instrument and an already established, reputable measure that measures the same attribute. For example, you are measuring the self-esteem of adults who were child incest victims using an instrument that you developed based on information from caregivers, the literature, and self-esteem experts. You also use an established, validated measure known to accurately measure self-esteem, such as Rosenberg's 10-item self-esteem scale. If a correlation coefficient between scores on the two different tests is high, then your instrument is said to have concurrent validity.

Construct Validity.   Construct validity focuses on the construct being measured—the measuring instrument, hypothesizing about relationships among variables, and validating the theory upon which the instrument is based. A construct is a collection of behaviors or indicators that are not observable and cannot be measured directly. The existence of a construct, therefore, is inferred by inclusion of its indicators or behaviors in the measuring instrument. An instrument that has construct validity:

■ Identifies a research participant who has characteristics of the construct being measured. An instrument can be said not to have construct validity if there is no sign that the participant has one of the characteristics of the construct being measured.

■ Makes a distinction between participants who have and those who do not have the indicators or characteristics of the construct.

■ Demonstrates that participants with characteristics of the construct act differently from those without the characteristics.

■ Is supported by a theoretical framework.

Construct validity is established through either discriminant validity or convergent validity. To establish discriminant validity, the researcher hypothesizes that a new measuring instrument does not correlate with measures of different but related indicators. To show evidence of convergent validity the researcher hypothesizes that the new measure correlates with one or more measures of a similar indicator.

A valid measurement of a construct must include all of the main indicators of that construct. Using the child sexual abuse case study, in order to measure the concept "adult victim of childhood incest," all of the indicators or behaviors of an adult victim of incest must be included in the measuring instrument. For example, some of the indicators of an adult sexually abused as a child could include feelings of mistrust, anger, grief, depression, promiscuity, guilt, shame, alcohol and drug abuse, powerlessness, or multiple victimization (Tower, 1993). When all of the indicators are covered in the instrument, the measuring instrument should be able to identify adult survivors of childhood incest. If the instrument cannot identify these adults, it does not have construct validity. See Figure 6.2, Concept and Indicators.

Important Points about Evaluating Measures

- A reliable measuring instrument can be depended upon to consistently produce the same results when administered under similar circumstances.
- A measuring instrument is referred to as valid when it measures what it is intended to measure.
- An instrument can be reliable and not valid, but a valid instrument always has a certain amount of reliability associated with it.

Errors in Measurement

Errors occur in all measurement efforts, regardless of how much researchers strive for precision. They can range from minimal errors to significant ones. Social science research is particularly susceptible to errors because of the types of variables, such as attitudes and values, being measured. Two main types of measurement error, systematic and random, particularly need some discussion.

Systematic Errors

Systematic measurement errors are those that occur consistently, with patterns, and can be attributed to participants' responses or to the data collection methods. These errors may cause inaccurate findings. Participants' responses that can contribute to errors include social

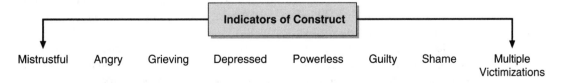

FIGURE 6.2   Construct and Indicators—Construct or Concept: Adult Survivor of Childhood Incest

desirability responses, acquiescence, and unintended errors. When a participant gives a positive picture of himself or herself to impress the interviewer or observer, this is a social desirability response. Social desirability answers often reflect what participants think the interviewer and society expect from them. For example, if an adolescent male is asked if he has ever had an incestuous relationship (after incestuous relationship is defined), there is a high probability that he would respond no. That is what he believes society expects. He may believe that a *yes* response would portray him unfavorably.

Data collection methods can also be the source of systematic errors in measurement. These errors occur when the observer's behavior indicates how participants should respond to questions. For example, a frown from the interviewer could mean that the response is not what the interviewer expects. Interviewers may also consistently give participants scores that are too high or too low.

Random Errors

In contrast with systematic errors, random errors have no consistency or patterns, can happen at any stage in the research process, and diminish the ability to accurately measure relationships between variables. With random errors the measurement results change constantly from one measurement to the other although the variables being measured do not change. These errors can lessen the exact measurement of variables. Random errors can be attributed to errors in participants' responses, observers' errors, poor training of observers, and demographic differences between the observer and the participant.

Participants' Influence on Errors.   Measurement errors occur when certain participant attributes, such as physical health, attentiveness, and interest in the research change, influencing how participants respond to questions and leading to errors in responding to questions. Also, when the measuring instrument is poorly formatted, difficult to read, hard to understand or excessively long, participants become frustrated and answer questions without much thought. So, errors occur. Participants may also make a choice that was not intended.

Observer's Influence on Errors.   Poorly trained observers, interviewers, or raters may adversely affect measurement in a number of ways. They can contribute to errors by not agreeing on what they observe. For example, if two raters are reading case files of adults, trying to identify indicators of adults who were sexually abused as children, each rater must be able to recognize those indicators or there will be disagreement.

Suppose that you, along with another social worker, are conducting a child abuse investigation to assess whether a child has been physically abused. One of you has had training in identifying signs or indicators of physical abuse, and the other has not. The trained worker, then, can distinguish between accidental injuries and nonaccidental injuries. The other worker, however, is unable to tell the difference. In this case, a disagreement over the cause of the injury can lead to measurement errors.

Measurement errors can also be attributed to the interviewer's rephrasing questions, not asking certain questions, or administering the survey in a manner other than how it was designed. The attitude of the interviewer could also create a measurement error.

Influence of Differences in Demographic Characteristics of the Interviewer or Observer and the Participant on Measurement Errors. These differences include ethnicity, age, gender, and socioeconomic status. For example, a male interviewer may be uncomfortable interviewing a female participant, or an Asian participant may be uncomfortable being interviewed by a non-Asian person. These differences and uneasiness could affect the participant's responses or how the interviewer asks questions and interprets responses.

Minimizing Measurement Error

Strategies to minimize measurement errors include properly training interviewers, developing positive relationships with participants, having experts on the topic review the instrument before it is administered, and using terminology that participants understand. Using different types of data collection methods in the same study, cleaning data before data entry occurs, and designing an instrument that is appealing and easy to use also serve to reduce measurement errors.

Important Points about Measurement Errors

- Systematic errors in measurement are consistent, patterned, and can be attributed to participants' responses or observers' errors.
- Random measurement errors have no consistency; study results change from one measurement to the next although the phenomenon being measured has not changed.
- Action can be taken to lessen measurement errors with proper planning.

Human Diversity Issues in Measurement

When the research sample includes people with different backgrounds the researcher must pay close attention to indicators or items used to measure a variable. The researcher must select indicators or measures that can accurately measure the variables across subgroups. For instance, the researcher must assess whether all items on the measuring instrument are relevant to all ethnic groups in the sample to avoid ethnocentric bias and also determine if items relevant to specific ethnic groups are included. It is often difficult to determine when specific items have been omitted. One way to avoid excluding these items is by developing measuring instruments simultaneously for the different groups using the same content validity methods and by using people representing each ethnic group in development of the instrument (Foster & Martinez, 1995). Sugland et al. (1995) in their study of the early childhood home inventory illuminate the importance of selecting indicators that accurately measure phenomena across subgroups. These authors maintain that despite the extensive use of parenting and home environment measures in child development, survey, and intervention research, minimal scientific research has been conducted to determine if the selected measures are effective in measuring variables across population subgroups. The dimensions of parenting and home environment appeared to be better predictors of child outcomes in European American than in African American and Hispanic American families.

Ethical Issues and Biases in Measurement

An ethical issue, that relates directly to a human diversity issue, is the purposeful exclusion of measures that relate to the diversity of the sample, as previously described in the Sugland example. Failure to take action to prevent errors in measurement may lead to poor research and measurement errors. For example, researchers are ethically responsible for assuring that interviewers are trained and that data collection instruments are reliable and valid.

WRITING STRATEGY

Think of a measurement instrument you have used in your field placement to measure a specific variable. Describe the way in which you measured that particular phenomenon. Do you believe your measurement was accurate? Explain why or why not. How might you make your measurement more precise or scientific?

LEARNING ACTIVITY

Using the independent and dependent variables from your study, list five indicators for each variable that would facilitate the measurement of those variables. In creating this list, consult with friends, the literature, and experts in a field that interests you.

INFORMATION TECHNOLOGY FOR MEASUREMENT

Access this site using the World Wide Web: www.unl.edu/buros. This URL takes you to the Buros Institute of Mental Measurements. Read the background information on the Buros Institute. Next, go to the Tests in Print site and then to the Subject Index link, and review the following three indexes that contain measuring instruments (tests): Personality Index, Behavior Index, and Development Index.

Important Points from Chapter 6

- Measurement is a method used to assign numbers or labels to observable phenomena.
- Nominal, ordinal, interval, and ratio are the levels on which variables can be measured.
- Concepts must be defined both conceptually and operationally before accurate measurement can occur.
- A variable is a phenomenon that can change and be measured.
- The independent variable is the causal variable that can influence the dependent variable.
- The dependent variable in a study is the behavior, attitude, situation, or object being studied.

- The hypothesis is a statement that predicts the relationship between variables that can be tested.
- Measuring instruments can be evaluated by testing for validity and reliability.
- Although steps can be taken to avoid measurement errors, no research is error free.

REFERENCES

Barker, R. L. (1995). *The social work dictionary.* Washington, DC: National Association of Social Work.

Finkelhor, D. (1984). *Child sexual abuse: New theory and research.* New York: The Free Press.

Foster, S. L., & Martinez, C. R., Jr. (1995). Ethnicity: Conceptual and methodological issues in child clinical research. *Journal of Clinical Child Psychology, 24*(2), 214–226.

Henson, R. K. (2000). Understanding internal consistency reliability estimates: A conceptual primer on coefficient alpha. *Measurement and Evaluation in Counseling and Development, 34*(3), 13.

Neuman, W. L. (1997). *Social research methods: Qualitative and quantitative approaches* (3rd ed.). Boston: Allyn & Bacon.

Newton, R. R., & Rudestam, K. E. (1999). *Your statistical consultant.* Thousand Oaks, CA: Sage.

Rosenberg, M. (2000). *Theories for sexual deviancy.* Retrieved May 29, 2000 from http://angelfire.com/mi/collateral/page2.html.

Rubin, A., & Babbie, E. (2001). *Research methods for social work* (4th ed.). Belmont, CA: Wadsworth/Thomson Learning.

Schutt, R. K. (1999) *Investigating the social world* (2nd ed.). Thousand Oaks, CA: Pine Forge Press.

Singleton, R. A., & Straits, B. C. (1999). *Approaches to social research* (3rd ed.). New York: Oxford University Press.

Sugland, B. W., Zaslow, M., Smith, J. R., Brooks-Gunn, J., Coates, D., Blumenthal, C., et al. (1995). The early childhood HOME inventory and HOME-short form in differing racial/ethnic groups: Are there differences in underlying structure, internal consistency of subscales, and patterns of prediction? *Journal of Family Issues, 16*(5), 632–663.

Tower, C. C. (1993). *Understanding child abuse and neglect* (2nd ed.). Boston: Allyn & Bacon.

7 Sampling

Since completing the research course, I have used my research skills to write a thesis for my master's degree. I knew exactly what to do and believe that I was a step ahead of students who had not taken an undergraduate research course. For my current job, I am constantly researching, in journals and books, information relative to new client situations.

—Traditional Research Student

CHAPTER GOALS

Your major goals upon completion of this chapter are to:

- Understand what sampling is.
- Understand the rationale for sampling.
- Be familiar with sampling concepts.
- Be able to differentiate between sampling techniques.
- Understand how sample size is determined.
- Recognize sampling errors in research and how to minimize them.

Introduction

You have probably engaged in sampling at some point. For example, a friend recommends a clothing store. Although the store is in an affluent neighborhood that you do not ordinarily shop in, you visit the store anyway because the friend suggests that it has good bargains. Upon entering the store, you check out the price tags on the clothing and decide after looking at the price of five or six items that the clothing is too expensive for your budget. There was no need to look at price tags on all of the clothing to make a decision about whether you could afford shopping there. Thus, you were sampling.

Although you probably sample often, in the scientific process sampling involves larger samples and different procedures. For a researcher, sampling is the process of selecting a segment or subset of a population to investigate. Once a problem to study has been selected, a research question(s) and problem statement developed, the unit of analysis determined, and major concepts conceptualized, you are ready to start selecting a sample. The people who will participate in the research, your sample, will respond to questions that you are trying to answer and provide evidence to support the hypotheses. The selection of research participants is planned and organized just as other steps are planned in the scientific approach to research. People included in the study, the sample, are chosen through a sampling procedure.

Generalist Case Study: Research with Gay, Lesbian, Bisexual, and Transgender People

Caseworker:	Mr. Walter Neil
Student Intern:	Ms. Eloise Witherspoon
Community Activists:	Mr. Ronald Gatsby and Mr. Mitchell Holmes

Ms. Witherspoon, a senior social work student, is doing her field practicum experience at a community center helping people in nontraditional families, specifically gay men, lesbians, bisexual, and transgender (GLBT) people, organize around specific issues that they are confronting in a large Southeastern community. Ronald Gatsby and Mitchell Holmes, gay partners, who are members of a national GLBT organization, approached Mr. Neil about their community's concerns. Members of the GLBT community experience both psychological and physical abuse and exclusion by homophobic heterosexual neighbors, co-workers, and their children's peers and teachers.

Discriminatory practices—refusal to accept adoption applications from the families, rejection by religious communities and the Boy Scouts, violence, refusal to accept same sex marriages (or domestic partnerships), and homophobia in the work environment—are common. Those parents who were previously in heterosexual relationships sometimes experience problems with their children, many of whom are embarrassed by their new families. Some of the older adolescents are struggling with having two same sex parents, a negative relationship between the GLBT parent and the heterosexual parent, and the ridicule by friends and teachers. The children and adolescents are uncomfortable when asked personal questions and subjected to insensitive comments about their families. They do not know how to respond to these situations. In a sense, these children and adolescents themselves often "go into the closet," as their parents come out, in an attempt to disguise and deny their nontraditional families.

(continued)

Case Example   *Continued*

The intern, Ms. Witherspoon, and her supervisor, Mr. Neil, have been facilitating a group consisting of 22 gay, lesbian, bisexual, and transgender people. This group believes strongly that the community needs education to help them overcome its homophobia. The group that Ms. Witherspoon and Mr. Neil are working with decided to take a social action approach to resolving these problems. To that end, members of the GLBT community are active participants in the organizing efforts, research, and implementation of strategies. Some residents support these efforts, while others vehemently resent the changes that this group supports.

The student, who completed an introductory research course and at present is in a community organizing class, has been assigned to work on the research and organizing efforts. She is excited about the opportunity to use knowledge from both of these classes at her field practicum, participating in community organizing activities and in research projects. The results of this research will be the foundation for strategies to work with organizations and the community in general about attitudes toward GLBT people. The field practicum supervisor and the director of research enter a partnership with a local college to collaborate on the research and possible in-service training.

Common Sampling Terms

> *Activity 1.*   After reading this section, identify and describe some of the sampling vocabulary. Discuss with a classmate terms that seem difficult to grasp.

The following definitions of sampling vocabulary will facilitate your understanding of the sampling process.

Sample

A sample is a subset, a portion, or a segment of a population. This selected portion of a population is relied upon to provide information about the problem under study. The researcher must be careful, then, about how the sample is drawn if the study results are to be valid and accurate. Why does a researcher choose to study only part of a population instead of an entire population when unbiased, valid results are sought? Ordinarily, entire populations are too large. In fact, in many situations, it is impossible to observe an entire population. Also, the researcher generally wishes to minimize costs, while attaining a high level of accuracy. So there are three overriding reasons to sample:

- *To Minimize Costs and Save Time*. Studying entire, large populations can be expensive when researchers must train and pay interviewers and data entry operators, supervise the project, and buy supplies. Furthermore, a complete sample might take so long that by the time the research is completed, the information would be outdated.

- *To Achieve a High Level of Accuracy*. It is easier to administer a project that uses a sample instead of a large population, that ultimately affects the researcher's precision in describing the population.

■ *Because It Is Often Impossible to Observe the Entire Population.* The direct observation, interviews, or surveys that the researcher uses often cannot be applied to large populations. The United States Census Bureau, for example, completes research on the entire population of the United States every 10 years. It attempts, during that time, to count everyone in the United States, Puerto Rico, and its dependents (Quaroza, 2000). Yet, even the government, with its vast resources, has problems in finding everyone.

Recently controversy erupted over whether the entire population should continue to be studied or just a segment of the population sampled in order to get a more accurate population count. Census reports have consistently undercounted people, especially children, from racial and ethnic minorities and from the poor in both rural and urban areas (Peterson, 1999).

The census 2000 plan consisted of two different methods that provided two population totals. "In the Census Bureau's approach, the traditional count is the capture phase and the survey is the recapture phase. The final population estimate would be the product of the first measure (based on counting) times the second measure (based on sampling) divided by the number of people found in both phases" (Peterson, 1999). There was discussion of how sampling errors can occur in both the traditional method of counting and the added sampling phase (Peterson, 1999). The results of the combined approaches to counting the population will be intriguing.

Population

The population is the elements, individuals, groups, organizations, or artifacts from which the sample is drawn. The population could consist of everyone in a city, state, country, or continent. The population could also include all students enrolled in your college, or all men or all women enrolled in your college, all faculty on campus, or students in a classroom.

Target Population

The target population, identified after the population has been defined, is that element from the population on which the study focuses. The definition of the target population includes specific criteria for inclusion in the sample, such as certain demographic information or other variables of interest. Using the case study at the beginning of the chapter, for instance, the researcher is interested in a community of gay, lesbian, bisexual, and transgender (GLBT) people (the population), and from that community the researcher focuses on GLBT people who meet the following criteria: (1) at least 35 years old, (2) in the same relationship for at least five years, (3) with household earnings of $40,000 a year or more, (4) attempting, for the first time, to adopt a child, and (5) have at least one biological child living in the home. Thus, people with these characteristics are the target population.

Sampling Frame

A sampling frame is a listing of all the elements (people, events, organizations, or artifacts) in a population that meet the researcher's criteria. Some sources of sampling frames are professional organization membership lists, for example, the National Association of Social Workers or the Council on Social Work Education. City and telephone directories and student rosters are also examples of sampling frames.

In the case study at the beginning of this chapter, the social work intern is asked to conduct a study to evaluate the attitude of licensed social workers in the state regarding their feelings about working with gay, lesbian, bisexual, and transgender people to assess the level of homophobia among social workers. Her sampling frame is the list of all licensed social workers in the state. Fortunately in the state in which she works, bachelor and master's level social workers employed in the field of social work must be licensed. The sample is, therefore, drawn from the licensing board's list of licensed social workers. This sampling frame does not include social workers employed outside of the field of social work or unemployed social workers who are not licensed. Findings from the study can be generalized to other licensed social workers in the state as long as it is unbiased, representing all elements in the population from which it was drawn.

The community agency in the case study is also conducting research with the gay, lesbian, bisexual, and transgender community regarding its experience with discrimination. Identifying the population and then selecting a target population and sampling frame may be complex. The researcher can, however, select specific GLBT organizations in the state to help identify a population. The researcher can also contact national organizations, such as OutProud, Children from the Shadows, the National Latina/o Lesbian, Gay, Bisexual & Transgender Organization, and the World Congress of Gay and Lesbian Jewish Organizations, for assistance in locating local chapters in the state. Researchers strive for samples that represent the population from which the sample was selected. Figure 7.1 illustrates the concepts of population, sampling frame, target population, and sample.

Representative Sample

Representative means that people in the sample mirror, in aggregate, those in the target population in characteristics of interest to the researcher, characteristics such as age, ethnicity,

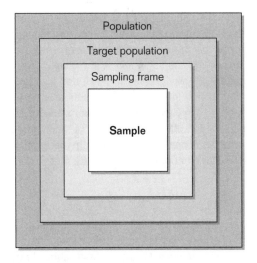

FIGURE 7.1   Population, Target Population, Sampling Frame, Sample

educational level, living environment, marital status, gender, and marital status. Research conclusions based on a representative sample can be generalized to the populations from which they were drawn. For example, in the case study in this chapter, the sampling frame consists of a list of licensed social workers in the state. To be representative of the entire population of licensed social workers, the sample should include bachelors, masters, and doctoral level social workers employed in both private and public agencies and in nonprofit and for-profit agencies and represent the age, ethnicity, and gender of all of the social workers in the targeted population. The research study can then be generalized to that entire population.

Generalizability

Generalizing findings means that the researcher can infer or apply study results, based on sample information, to the entire population from which the sample was drawn. To generalize from the sample to the entire population the researcher must assure that the differences in people in the sample adequately represent the population from which they were selected. If you assert that study results can be generalized to the target population, you must be able to confirm that the sample represents that population. For example, in the case study, if the results show that the GLBT people perceive themselves as victims of discrimination, the researcher can infer that the remainder of the gay, lesbian, bisexual, and transgender population, from which the sample was drawn, perceive themselves as being discriminated against. This is generalizing.

Element

Elements are the individuals, groups, organizations events, or artifacts that the researcher is interested in studying, collecting information on, and analyzing data on.

Parameter and Statistic

The terms parameter and statistic both relate to descriptions of variables. Parameter pertains to descriptions of distributions of variables in populations. Statistic relates to distributions of variables in samples. For example, in the case example of research with gay men, lesbians, bisexual and transgender people, calculation of the mean income for gay, lesbian, and transgender people in the sample is a statistic. This statistic is used to estimate the mean income in the population, which is a parameter.

Important Points about Sampling

- Sampling is the process of selecting a segment or subset of a population on which to conduct research.
- Samples are often studied instead of entire populations to minimize costs, save time, and achieve a higher level of accuracy and when it is impossible to study the entire population.
- In order to generalize study results to an entire population, the sample on which the study was conducted must be representative of that population.

Units of Analysis

> *Activity 2.*   Decide while reading this section what the units of analysis are for your research project.

What or who you intend to conduct research on, describe, and analyze are the units of analysis. The purpose of your study determines the units of analysis. Units of analysis can be individuals, families, groups, organizations, or social artifacts.

- *Individuals as units of analysis.* Individuals as units of analysis could be grandmothers, clients, widows, students, social workers, athletes, parents, etc.

- *Groups as units of analysis.* Examples of groups as units of analysis are families, gangs, married couples, sororities and fraternities and other social organizations, teachers, cashiers, census blocks, communities, towns, cities, geographic regions, and nations.

- *Social artifacts as units of analysis.* Books, poems, songs, periodicals, documents, paintings, buildings, cars, and scientific discoveries are examples of social artifacts.

It is important to know what your units of analysis are. Recall the discussion in Chapter 4 about how the independent variable can affect change in the dependent variable. The units of analysis also determine how a researcher measures variables. Knowing what the units of analysis are helps you avoid invalid conclusions about those relationships and thus avoid logical errors in causality. Before selecting a sample, you must know your units of analysis.

Sampling Techniques

> *Activity 3.*   After reading about the different types of sampling techniques, read two journal articles and identify the sampling method used by the researcher. Also, read a newspaper and listen to television station presentations of research findings, especially those involving polls, and determine whether sampling techniques are mentioned.

> *Activity 4.*   Think about a research project you might want to conduct in order to better serve clients. Decide whether you would use probability or nonprobability sampling, and then determine which method best suits your research. Explain the reasons behind your choice.

The two types of sampling techniques are probability and nonprobability. Each has its place in social work research.

Probability sampling methods are simple random sampling, systematic random sampling, stratified random sampling, and cluster sampling. All use some random sampling method. Probability sampling, a less subjective selection process, gives every element in the population an equal chance of being included in the sample, making the sampling process less biased and the sample more representative of the target population.

On the other hand, nonprobability sampling does not strive for an equal chance at selection. The researcher using nonprobability sampling can make direct selections of research participants without regard to random selections. This technique is appropriate for some types of research; but used in quantitative studies, nonprobability sampling can lead to sampling error due to bias in the selection of participants.

Sampling error is the degree of difference between the characteristics of variables of the sample (sample statistic) and the population (population parameter) from which the sample was drawn. Sampling error occurs when certain elements in the population are over- or underrepresented or not represented at all in the sample. Sampling errors always lead to biased samples.

For example, you are attempting to generate, from a sampling frame, a sample of gay, lesbian, bisexual, and transgender participants. If one or more of these groups is overrepresented, underrepresented, or unrepresented in the sample, then selection bias has occurred. When sampling errors occur, they are caused by chance or random errors, and the actual source of the error is unknown. For instance, your sampling frame contains sufficient numbers of people from each group of gay, lesbian, bisexual, and transgender people. Yet, one or more groups are under- or overrepresented in the sample, and the reason for this lack of representativeness is unknown. When random sampling methods are used, the researcher can assess the probable level of sampling error in an estimate using inferential statistics.

Whereas sampling error generates biased samples, *nonsampling errors* may or may not create biased samples. If an insufficient sampling frame can cause nonsampling errors, so can low response rates from participants who decline to participate or fail to complete questionnaires. The design of the questionnaire is critical; poorly worded questions and other problems can determine if sufficient participants respond. For instance, the print on the questionnaire may be hard to read, the type too small, or the space between lines is inadequate. Errors made by staff (interviewers deviating from the standard procedures they were trained to use when asking questions and recording data) are additional sources of nonsampling error.

Researchers can reduce nonsampling errors by training and supervising people who will administer the questionnaires, by giving participants tangible or intangible rewards, by paying special attention to the design of the questionnaire and its wording, and by making follow-up calls or sending postcards to remind participants to return completed questionnaires. Before questionnaires are sent, though, you must decide which sampling technique will be used.

Probability Sampling Techniques

Simple Random Sample.   In simple random sampling, every element in the population has an equal chance of being included in the sample, and every element can be selected only once, making the sample less biased and more representative of the target population. Before selection occurs, each member in the population is assigned a unique number, and then the number of elements desired for the sample is randomly selected by using a table of random numbers, if the selection is done manually, or a computer-generated list of random numbers. See Table 7.1 for a partial computer-generated list of random numbers. This table was generated from the World Wide Web site www.random.org by Mads Haahr (2000). It allows users to generate

TABLE 7.1   Partial Computer-Generated List of Random Numbers

27560	27712	23409	31403	19541	31597	22387	20802	18723	26051
12128	10357	32534	21619	36506	24534	20535	15691	24128	25550
36238	11355	16222	12664	38781	26851	13518	24356	37330	39805
21688	33104	18830	11404	26800	15470	26881	21795	19752	18850
30291	18906	11038	13700	22560	23234	37789	39857	25187	28118
11492	37769	32133	34032	22363	32518	23428	27200	35038	27028
11677	38344	31036	33561	19139	36681	34284	23406	34808	24775
35370	23121	14104	35860	16798	26123	19391	29546	34594	37832
28408	19609	38244	30527	24798	12801	25593	37719	12890	20840
35405	34083	32954	32226	28790	17737	14259	36618	20218	30110
37117	36105	14722	22151	16507	33106	33876	39583	14630	20823
14257	10544	15953	22004	35227	13485	11867	21990	11728	29947
11762	32072	38998	14612	39293	31936	26356	16667	18414	13156
24854	26826	17185	22407	27208	11135	39694	35262	12795	39757
19603	36351	26075	39221	12182	30426	33851	32315	26207	30966
28934	11758	37772	14115	17285	32493	29416	14211	35682	31434
37626	10405	10100	18283	38958	37903	32920	35792	16542	29101
39487	29209	34705	35716	37046	13891	30081	32074	34404	24337
19336	14499	22331	13697	26280	10884	30765	12492	31876	17177
28004	34608	33240	28287	15505	19285	22110	28158	15032	25550
10556	26181	24270	18146	22369	15247	30797	28316	38135	32555
38111	21816	27935	28989	23140	37563	16682	23685	24349	22863

Source: Generated from www.random.org by Mads Haahr.

their own table of random numbers. To assure that a person is selected only once, that participant number is removed from the sampling frame after being selected.

An illustration works best to show how to use a list of random numbers. Select a 20% sample, 800 social workers from the sampling frame of 4,000 licensed social workers, to participate in your study. Then, follow these steps in using a list of random numbers to make your selections:

- First, decide on the population size, which determines the number of random digits needed for selecting each element. In this case, the population of 4,000 licensed social workers is the same as the sampling frame of 4,000 for the homophobia study. Because the population size is a four-digit number, 4,000, people on the sampling frame must be assigned four-digit numbers.

- Second, assign a number to each person. In the above example, a four-digit number is assigned to each of the 4,000 social workers, starting with 0001 and ending at 4000.

- Third, determine a starting point for selecting participants by closing your eyes and arbitrarily pointing to a number on the list of random numbers to select a number. Look at the list of names; the person with the chosen number is the first participant. Using the list of random numbers in Table 7.1, say that your hand lands on the second number in the first column, 12128. Since all of the elements (social workers) in the sampling frame have been assigned four-digit numbers, the randomly selected numbers must also have four-digits. Use the first four digits of 12128, which are 1212. Thus, the social worker assigned number 1212 is the first person selected for the sample.

- Fourth, continue moving to the right selecting numbers with four digits. Starting after the last digit in the number 1212, count the next four digits moving to the right (8, 1, 0, 3 to arrive at the number 8103). This and the next two numbers could not be used (5732 and 5342) because they exceed the numbers assigned to the social workers. See the numbers in Table 7.1. The second person selected, then, will be the social worker assigned number 1619. The numbers can be randomly selected moving in different directions other than to the right, but the direction is decided before the selection process begins.

- Fifth, continue this process until 800 licensed social workers have been selected for participation in the study.

Systematic Random Sampling. In systematic random sampling every nth element is selected. Sample size is determined after the total number of elements in the sampling frame is established. Using the case example, the sampling frame for the homophobia study consists of 4,000 licensed social workers. The researcher wants a 20% sample from the sampling frame— 800 social workers. To arrive at the sampling interval, divide the sampling frame by the sample size: 4,000/800 = 5, the size of the sampling interval. The sample will include, therefore, every fifth social worker on the list. First, randomly select the first element for example by pulling numbers out of a box. If the first number is four, start with the fourth name. Thereafter, select every fifth name—0009, 0014, 0019, 0024 and so on—until 800 social workers are selected.

Of course, every sampling method has strengths and weaknesses. A problem with systematic random sampling is that the ordering of elements on the sampling frame may be done in a manner that biases the sample. For example, consider the sampling frame for the homophobia study on social workers. The sampling frame consists of 4,000 licensed social workers in the state and the sample size is 800. The sampling frame may be ordered (manner in which names are listed on the sampling frame) in such a way that each element may not have an equal chance of being selected, leading to a biased sample. In other words, if the list consists of men, women, line social workers, supervisors, and administrators, all of these diverse elements may not have an equal chance of being selected because of the manner in which the list is ordered. Fortunately, stratified sampling can prevent this error.

Stratified Random Sampling. Stratified random sampling, one way to reduce sampling error, considers certain characteristics of elements in the population that would influence study results. These characteristics are called strata, or subgroups. In order to include strata correctly, the population is divided into strata before drawing the sample; then separate random samples are drawn from each of the strata.

In the case study, you are conducting a research project on perceptions of gay, lesbian, bisexual, and transgender people on community attitudes about their sexual orientation. A stratified random sample would ensure that participants are selected from each of these groups and in correct proportions. Suppose that you want a sample of 200 from this population, which is 35% gay men, 35% lesbians, 20% bisexuals, and 10% transgender people, and you want a proportionate number included in the sample. After dividing the group into strata, 70 gay men,

70 lesbians, 40 bisexuals, and 20 transgender people are randomly selected. This is *proportionate stratified sampling,* which provides the same proportions in the sample as in the population.

With *disproportionate stratified sampling* a disproportionate number of participants are selected from one or more strata, when some subgroups are significantly smaller. This approach is used to allow for separate statistical analyses or to make statistical comparisons among subgroups. For example, in the case study, a disproportionate number of transgender people might be included in the sample because their percentage in the population is significantly smaller than that of gay men, lesbians, and bisexuals.

Cluster Sampling.   Cluster sampling, also known as multistage sampling, involves selecting elements in two or more stages, starting with large units, the clusters, instead of selecting participants individually. Smaller clusters are contained within the larger ones. Cluster sampling is often used with large populations and when sampling frames are not accessible. Clusters are selected randomly to avoid a biased sample. Using this sampling technique saves time and money, for example, by lowering travel time. As with other techniques, however, there is a disadvantage in using cluster sampling.

There is a higher chance for sampling error in cluster sampling because as the number of clusters increases, so does the chance for sampling error. On the other hand, chances for sampling errors decrease as the homogeneity of elements in the clusters increases. Both simple random sampling and stratified random sampling can be applied to cluster sampling.

Most random sampling techniques use one sampling frame to select participants. More than one sampling frame is used, however, with cluster sampling. Elements are selected from clusters, beginning with the largest cluster. This selection process continues until study participants are chosen. Consider the use of cluster sampling in the case example. You are interested in doing research on the views of GLBT students in public colleges and universities throughout the United States on their experiences with homophobic students, faculty, and staff on campus. However, there is no list of GLBT people in the United States. So, steps in cluster sampling here would involve:

- Randomly selecting a sample of clusters. The first randomly selected clusters are the states.
- Randomly selecting cities within those states.
- Randomly selecting universities within the cities.
- Randomly selecting organizations for gay, lesbian, bisexual, and transgender students within the universities.
- Randomly selecting students from the GLBT organizations to survey about their experience with homophobic students. See Figure 7.2 for an example of cluster sampling.

Nonprobability Sampling Methods

In probability sampling, the major focus is on having the sample reflect the population from which it was drawn. Some researchers, however, are interested in an in-depth understanding of the problem under study rather than in the representativeness of the sample. Nonprobability samples help deal with these concerns.

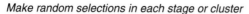

Make random selections in each stage or cluster

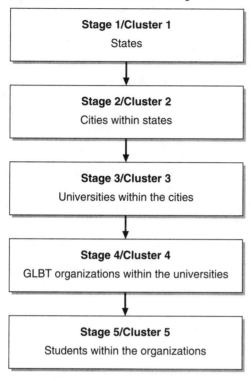

FIGURE 7.2   Cluster Sampling

Purposive Sampling.   The researcher uses her or his knowledge of and expertise on the topic and judgment when selecting participants in this nonprobability sampling method. People who meet the investigator's requirements in terms of possessing the necessary characteristics are included. Of course, attempts have to be made to locate people with experience related to the topic, to participate. If you were conducting research, for example, on people who had been sexually abused as children, you would include in the sample people who were child sexual abuse victims.

Snowball Sampling.   Snowball sampling is applied with potential participants who are difficult to identify or are easy to locate but reluctant to get involved, such as those who are crossing color lines—Black people passing for White; gay, lesbian, bisexual people who do not identify as such. If they are easily accessible, they may be hesitant about participating because of involvement in illegal activities or socially unacceptable behavior. Those involved in drug and alcohol abuse, gang activity, pedophilia, or con artist activities fall here. This method is referred to as snowball sampling because after the researcher identifies the first person that meets the criteria for participation, that participant is asked to identify others knowledgeable about the topic. Those individuals, in turn, identify other participants. This selection procedure continues until the desired sample size is attained. As participants are added, the sample "snowballs."

Quota Sampling.   Quota sampling entails describing the target population based on the variables of interest to the researcher. One goal is assuring that the sample reflects, proportionately, the population from which it was selected. In the case study cited in this chapter, for example, the target population in one instance are gay, lesbian, bisexual, and transgender people who may experience discrimination based on their sexual orientation. The following procedure would be used to conduct quota sampling on this group:

▪ Divide the population into distinct groups based on specific characteristics, that is, sexual orientation. For this population you need to know the proportion of gay, lesbian, bisexual, and transgender people. The proportion is 35% gay men, 35% lesbians, 20% bisexuals, and 10% transgendered.

▪ Establish quotas on the number of participants to be chosen from each group, based on their proportions in the population, because you are interested in individual experience with discrimination.

▪ Terminate the selection process after the specified number of quotas from each group is met.

▪ Collect data from participants in each group.

Although quota sampling is similar to proportionate stratified random sampling, it is not a random sampling procedure. This process often relies on availability of participants, rather than using random selection. To select participants to fill the set quotas, in proportionate stratified random sampling, the investigator makes random selections; in quota sampling the interviewer has discretion to choose participants as long as the participants selected meet the study criteria.

Problems with the interviewer selection process are many. For instance, the interviewer can bias the selection process by avoiding certain neighborhoods because they are isolated, in high crime areas, or too far from the interviewer's home. Interviewer bias also occurs when the interviewer selects people who are similar to the interviewer in appearance, lifestyle, race, and socioeconomic status.

The advantages of quota sampling are that it is less expensive and faster than some of the other sampling methods. Given the disadvantages associated with quota sampling, unless the researcher wants immediate response to a situation, perhaps a crime or a major disaster, quota sampling is not a recommended procedure.

Convenience Sampling.   In convenience sampling, selections are made based on convenience to the interviewer, who may choose people simply because of their availability, whether they possess the characteristics sought or not. For example, a researcher interested in getting the opinions of college students surveys students in one college classroom simply because the students are available. Or, if the researcher is in an airport during spring break, students traveling then may be selected because they are available. Common sites for convenience sampling are malls, shopping plazas, grocery stores, large bus stations, and train stations. Convenience sampling is not a scientific approach to sampling.

Sampling for Community Needs Assessment. Sampling is often a part of community needs assessments, which are conducted to evaluate whether there are gaps in services in a specific area. For example, community members may have voiced concerns about a lack of recreational facilities for teenagers, an inadequate number of grocery stores, or no mental health facilities in their community. Before attempting to fund these facilities, wise agency heads, legislators, and other funding sources would conduct, or commission, a community needs assessment.

Needs assessments, therefore, are done before a program is funded and implemented. They may use either quantitative or qualitative research methods, depending on the study. Probability sampling methods are employed when quantitative needs assessments are done, and nonprobability sampling is used for qualitative needs assessments. Questionnaires may be provided to a representative population sample in the community affected by the lack of services or to the entire population when quantitative assessments are done. People may also be recruited to participate in focus groups, a qualitative research method, to share their knowledge about the need for a specific service such as a recreational facility for adolescents. Focus group members would consist of parents of teenagers, teenagers, community leaders, teachers, and others who would know local needs relative to youths.

Important Points about Sampling Techniques

- You can expect errors in sampling to occur whether a probability or a nonprobability sampling procedure is used.
- Probability sampling methods allow each element in the population an equal chance of being selected for participation in a research study.
- A sample representative of a population is less biased, and study results can be generalized to the population from which the sample was selected.
- Nonprobability sampling techniques do not strive for representativeness in the sample; although appropriate for some types of research, they can lead to selection bias when used in quantitative research designs.

Determining Sample Size

Activity 5. Think about situations, organizations, or activities that you were involved in that used random sampling to select participants. Review two journal articles in search of the authors' description of sampling techniques. What type of sampling method was used? Was the sampling technique sufficiently explained?

The number of participants needed for a study is usually decided during the design phase. The larger the sample, the more representative it is of the population, although a large sample does not necessarily guarantee a representative sample. Some researchers maintain that a minimum of 30 participants is enough to conduct some basic statistical analysis. Others suggest at least 100 participants, and still others recommend a sample of 10% of the population as a minimum requirement. Although these suggestions are helpful for determining sample size, in each individual research project other factors must be considered—population heterogeneity and homogeneity, desired precision, available resources, and type of statistical analysis planned:

■ *Population Heterogeneity and Homogeneity.* These terms refer to how different and how similar, respectively, the population is in relation to the variable being studied. The more diverse the population, the larger the sample needs to be. On the other hand, the more similar the population, the smaller the sample.

■ *Desired Precision.* The precision the researcher is striving for is related to sample size. The greater precision desired, that is, less sampling error, the larger the sample needs to be. Thus, the larger the sample, the smaller the sampling error. A sample can be large, however, and biased, if not selected randomly.

■ *Statistical Analysis to Be Used.* The statistical test affects the size of the sample. To test research hypotheses, adequate samples are drawn based on guidelines for specific statistical analyses. Some statistical tests require small samples, while others require large ones.

■ *Available Resources.* The amount of time that the researcher has, costs of printing questionnaires, envelopes, stamps, and payment to interviewers and other support staff also affect decisions on sample size.

Two additional critical factors to be considered in discussions about sample size are *margin of error* and *confidence level.*

The precision that the researcher wants is the margin of error. For example, newspapers and television stations often report results of polls on various topics. This is done especially frequently during presidential campaigns, when polls are taken on the national, state, and local level to get people's opinion about their choices. The results are reported along with the margin of error. If 70% of the public choose candidate A, 25% candidate B, and 5% are undecided, a margin of error of 5% indicates that the results could vary as much as 5% negatively or positively. Take a closer look at candidate A, the choice 70% of the time. Allowing for a margin of error of 5%, means that the true population votes for this candidate could be anywhere from 65% to 75% (70 − 5 = 65 and 70 + 5 = 75).

The *level of confidence* refers to how often the researcher can expect to find similar results if the research were to be administered again under similar conditions, with minimal differences in study design. That is, the level of confidence indicates how often study results deviate from or fall outside the margin of error. For instance, if the above example is designed to have a 95% confidence level with a 5% margin of error, the researcher could anticipate that the findings will miss the actual values in the population by more than 5% only 5 times in 100 questionnaires. In other words, study results showing that candidate A was the choice among less than 65% or more than 75% of people polled could be expected to occur no more than 5 times in100 questionnaires. These days, some data analysis software packages offer assistance in selecting the appropriate sample size with level of confidence.

Important Points about Determining Sample Size

- Sample size is one of the most important factors to consider when attempting to attain a representative sample. Nevertheless, size is not as important as eliminating biases in sampling.
- Issues to consider when deciding on sample size include population heterogeneity and homogeneity, precision desired, statistical analysis procedure to be used, and available resources.
- Additional considerations in deciding on sample size are the margin of error and the confidence level that the researcher is aiming for and is comfortable with.

Human Diversity Issues in Sampling

When the intent of the researcher is to generalize study results to a diverse population, the sample should represent that population. That is, the sample must include people from all groups to which the researcher suggests the findings apply. If research is conducted on men only, for example, the results should not be said to apply also to women. If researchers intend to generalize research findings from studies on preschool children to all preschool children throughout the United States, then the study sample should include children from preschools throughout the United States, from different ethnic backgrounds, different social and economic classes, and rural, urban, and suburban locations. Generalizing findings to groups that are not a part of the sample is not the widespread problem it was in the past when it was common to read journal articles and other research that used, usually, White males in the sample, but generalized findings to women and people of color.

In writing "Investigating the Career Development of Gay, Lesbian, and Bisexual People: Methodological Considerations and Recommendations," Lonborg and Phillips (1996) point out that historically problems identified with sampling have prevented research on gay and lesbian people. Although writing about research on the career development of gay, lesbian, and bisexual people, the authors maintain that better sampling methods are needed to recruit larger and more diverse samples of gay, lesbian, and bisexual persons to increase the generalizeability of study results.

Ethical Issues and Biases in Sampling

Deliberately neglecting to include people from diverse backgrounds in a sample when the intent is to generalize study results to that broad population is an ethical problem. In addition, researchers should provide explanations when the sample consists of people from one sex only or when results are generalized to both males and females when only one group was included in the sample. Excluding potential participants because of interviewers' personal choices not to go into a particular neighborhood or not feeling comfortable interviewing certain people because of differences in ethnicity, gender, or sexual orientation are also ethical issues in sampling.

WRITING STRATEGY

Think about a research project you might want to conduct in order to better serve clients. From what population will you draw the sample? Explain why you chose this population and how you defined that population for the purpose of your research. What criteria did you use for inclusion in the target population? What sampling frame might you use? How does this frame represent the population from which the sample was selected?

LEARNING ACTIVITY

In this chapter, definitions are provided for several key sampling terms. Working in your study group, recall as many of the terms as possible. How many definitions does the group remember?

INFORMATION TECHNOLOGY FOR SAMPLING

Produce your own list of random numbers by going to the www.random.org Web site. You will be asked to provide specific information and will have a table generated in seconds.

Important Points from Chapter 7

- Sampling is the process of selecting a subset of a population on which to conduct research. The types of sampling techniques are random sampling and nonrandom sampling.
- Random sampling techniques generate less biased samples that are representative of the population. The goal of nonrandom sampling methods is to provide depth rather than be representative.
- Samples are often studied instead of entire populations when resources are limited, the population is not accessible, and a higher level of accuracy is desired.
- In order to generalize study results to the population from which it was selected, the sample must be representative of that population.
- Sample size and eliminating biases in sampling are two of the most important factors in assuring a representative sample.

REFERENCES

Haahr, M. (2000). www.random.org. Retrieved August 7, 2000, from www.random.org/.

Lonborg, S. D., & Phillips, J. M. (1996). Investigating the career development of gay, lesbian, and bisexual people: Methodological considerations and recommendations. *Journal of Vocational Behavior, 48*, 176–194.

Quaroza, A. (2000). Plans for Census 2000. *Government Information Quarterly, 17*(2), 12p. Retrieved July 21, 2000, from www.ebsco.com.

Peterson, I. (1999). Census *sampling* confusion. *Science News, 155*(10), 7 p. Retrieved July 21, 2000, from www.ebsco.com.

8 Designing and Using Questionnaires to Collect Data

*When I started taking this course I did not know much about research; I went
into it blindly. After the class started, I realized just how much I did not know.
I am using everything that I learned; I tell you everything that I learned.*

—Traditional Social Work Student

CHAPTER GOALS

Your major goals upon completion of this chapter are to:

- Understand the different data collection methods in quantitative research.
- Write effective survey questions.
- Design effective questionnaires to collect information.
- Understand how existing data can be used to do research.

Introduction

Collecting data is one of the most critical elements of the research process. Without data, be it primary or secondary, there is no research. Here the focus is finding data. You learn methods of collecting data by mail, in face-to-face interviews, and from telephone interviews (including computer-assisted interviewing). Development of questionnaires (also referred to as surveys) for these specific types of data collection methods is discussed. So are means of using secondary data, collected by other people for other purposes.

Surveys can be designed to collect data on most social problems if the criteria, outlined in Chapter 4, are met. Those criteria include whether the problem is manageable, feasible, relevant, and ethical in terms of its suitability as a research problem.

Researchers, of course, can use existing data for research by conducting a content analysis or accessing secondary data. A wealth of secondary data are available on most social problems and other topics of interest in the United States. On a personal level, for example, once you complete questionnaires for your doctor, school, job, and credit card companies, they have records (primary data) on you. If researchers access those files for research purposes it is then being used for reasons other than its stated purpose and is, therefore, considered secondary data. At your internship or job you are a collector of primary information instead of a giver if you ask clients to complete questionnaires, applications, or intake forms when they request services. Intake forms are standardized, so that you consistently gather the same type of information from all clients. Common standardized questions are: reasons for requesting service, demographic information, names and ages of family members, and client address. Although research is not the main reason for collecting primary data, the standardized intake forms may be used for research purposes. But, information in client records is secondary data when accessed for research purposes by someone other than the person who collected that data.

A social worker, for instance, may gather information from the questionnaires about client recidivism, patterns in child abuse and neglect cases, family risk factors for child abuse and neglect, and the average age of older clients receiving adult protective services. If the social worker that collects this data also analyzes it, the data are primary. If a different researcher analyzes that data, it is a secondary analysis. Content analysis, another way to use existing data, will also be discussed in this chapter.

Generalist Case Study: Independent Living Questionnaire

Mr. Norton, a social worker with the Department of Children and Families, works with adolescents in foster care who are preparing to live independently. Mr. Norton administered a brief survey to 60 11th- and 12th-grade students in the district in which he works to determine their perceptions about their level of preparation for independent living and career aspirations.

Independent Living Questionnaire

We are conducting a study on adolescents in foster care. One part of the study focuses on preparation of adolescents for independent living and adolescents' career goals. Independent living refers to leaving foster care and living on your own in the community, on a college campus, or in another setting where you are primarily responsible for yourself.

The information that you provide will help us improve independent living services for adolescents preparing to leave foster care and live on their own. We appreciate your answers to the following questions.

INDEPENDENT LIVING QUESTIONNAIRE

(Please do not write your name on this questionnaire)

1. Identification Number _____
   (provided by researcher)

2. I am prepared to live on my own after leaving foster care. Please circle the number to the right of your answer.

Disagree	1
Agree Somewhat	2
Agree	3

   (*Ordinal level of measurement*)*

3. Life skills training programs teach people how to budget their money, search and apply for jobs, behave appropriately on the job, dress properly for a job, and how to find and maintain housing. I am involved in a life skills training program in preparation for living on my own. Please circle the number next to the frequency of your participation in a life skills training program:

Never	1
Seldom	2
Sometimes	3
Often	4
Always	5

   (*Ordinal level of measurement*)*

4. After leaving foster care I plan on:

Going to College	1
Going to a Vocational/Technical School	2
Joining the Military	3
No Plans	4
Other	5

   (*Nominal or categorical level of measurement*)*

5. Circle the number next to your employment plans upon leaving foster care:

I plan on working full-time	1
I plan on working part-time	2
I do not plan on working	3
Undecided	4

   (*Nominal or categorical level of measurement*)*

6. In the blank below write in your most recent score on the SAT:

   My SAT Score Is _____
   (*ratio level of measurement*)*

(continued)

Case Study   *Continued*

7. In the blank below write your age at your last birthday:

   My Age Is _____
   (*ratio level of measurement*)*

8. Please circle the number that identifies your race:

African American/Black	1
Asian	2
Caucasian/White (NonLatino)	3
Latino	4
Native American	5
Other	6

   (*Nominal or categorical level of measurement*)*

9. Please circle the number next to your gender:

Male	1
Female	2

   (*Nominal or categorical level of measurement*)*

THANKS FOR YOUR HELP!

*The level of measurement of each question is included for learning purposes and would not be included on questionnaires.

Data Collection Methods

> *Activity 1.*   After reading this section, think about mailed questionnaires, telephone interviews, and in-person interviews in which you have participated recently. If possible, locate a questionnaire that you have not returned. Why were you asked to participate in these studies?

The usual means of collecting data from research participants in quantitative studies are mailed questionnaires (surveys), face-to-face interviews, and telephone interviews. While mailed surveys are the most common method for gathering this data, the other techniques have advantages in certain circumstances.

Collecting Data Using Mailed Surveys/Questionnaires

Questionnaires in quantitative research use closed-ended questions with predetermined answers provided by the researcher. Quantitative investigations, however, may include openended qualitative questions. Researchers may ask participants to share information that is used to describe, predict, or explain something about them—attributes, behavior, attitudes, frame of mind, perceptions, feelings, opinions, and knowledge about a certain topic.

Collecting data using mailed surveys is the most frequently used data collection method, although with technological advances, telephone interviews and web site interviews are becoming popular. Participants complete questionnaires designed to be self-administered and returned by a specific date in self-addressed, stamped envelopes provided by the researcher. A cover letter, instructions, and a letter of informed consent accompany the questionnaire. Mailed questionnaires for quantitative research are structured; each question is followed by a set of predetermined responses from which participants choose. For example, Mr. Norton, the social worker in the case example, used different types of closed-ended questions for collecting data from adolescents in foster care.

Some advantages of using mailed surveys are:

- A larger number of people can be reached in a given time compared to contacting people for face-to-face interviews.
- Mailed surveys are less expensive than face-to-face or telephone methods because travel and interviewer expenses are eliminated. The cost of paper, envelopes, and postage are the major expenses for mailed surveys.
- Participants can complete the questionnaire at their convenience within the timeframe set by the researcher.
- Mailed surveys can provide anonymity.
- There may be fewer social desirability responses, participants responding with answers they believe are acceptable by society, than in face-to-face and telephone interviews. While there are advantages to using mailed questionnaires there are also disadvantages.

The disadvantages of the mailed survey data collection method are:

- A low response rate. Dillman (1978) in his Total Design Method (TDM) offers suggestions for improving the response rate in mailed questionnaires. Since researchers are not available to answer questions, he suggests giving special attention to clarity, questionnaire construction, including the appearance of the questionnaire, and organization. Formatting the questionnaire like a booklet, ordering the questions with easy responses first (since they help build participants' confidence that they can answer the questions), and grouping questions with similar content are his additional recommendations.

- Late responses requiring follow-up. Sending follow-up letters or post cards when participants do not respond within the designated timeframe can increase the response rate. At some point, another copy of the questionnaire should be sent to participants who are late returning the initial questionnaire, unless responses are anonymous.

- The researcher's lack of knowledge of the participant's possible inability to read and comprehend the questionnaire.

- The researcher cannot know for sure who completed the questionnaire.

Important Points about Mailed Surveys

- Mailed surveys are used more often than telephone interviews and face-to-face interviews to collect data.
- The main advantages of mailed surveys are that they are less expensive than the alternatives and a larger number of people can be included in the study.
- The main disadvantages are the low response rate and the researcher's inability to know whether participants are competent to read and understand the questions.

Collecting Data Using Face-to-Face Interviews

Face-to-face interviews involve participants completing the questionnaire in the presence of an interviewer. The interviewer can even ask the questions and fill in the participant's answers. For quantitative research, this is the same structured questionnaire with predetermined responses used in mailed questionnaires. Face-to-face interviews are a good choice when participants need help with completing the questionnaire—if they are sick, have physical or mental disabilities, are older, or have limited reading and comprehension skills.

Some advantages of face-to-face interviews in quantitative research are:

- Immediacy and a higher response rate than the other types of data collection methods.

- Interviews can be held in different locations—the applicant's home or workplace, a park, a restaurant, or any other location that the applicant chooses.

Some disadvantages of face-to-face interviews are:

- Expenses, particularly if the sample is large, for salaries, travel costs, and interviewers training.

- Maintaining objectivity throughout the quantitative interview. The interviewer cannot ask for clarifications or probe for additional information if the participant's responses are not clear. Furthermore, the interviewer cannot get involved in any conversations with participants that could influence research results.

- Interviewer bias.

- Participants' reluctance to meet with people they do not know.

Face-to-face interviews can be held with one person or a group of people. Group interviews may be done, for example, when the researcher visits a high school or a college class and administers the instrument to each student. Group interviews save time and money and may be more convenient for the researcher.

Collecting Data Using Telephone Interviews

Telephone interviews can be a cost-effective method for collecting quantitative data. Just be sure to be selective about the time and day that you call study participants to avoid too much intrusion on people's lives. Telephone interviews can be touchy for participants. Many people resent being disturbed at home in the evenings, particularly if they are being bombarded with solicitations. Think about your own experience with calls from researchers or solicitors disrupting your life.

If telephone interviews are the choice, make the calls after dinnertime, around 8:00 or 9:00 P.M., and avoid early morning calls, before 9:00 A.M. If possible, contact participants and schedule a specific time to conduct the interview. Be organized, with the questionnaire at hand, and be prepared with responses to participants' questions about the research. Remember that participation in a research project is voluntary. Therefore, be courteous and avoid getting defensive if people choose not to become involved.

One weakness of telephone interviewing is that households without telephones and those with unlisted numbers are excluded from the sample. With the introduction of random digit dialing (RDD), however, unlisted households can now be located through random samples.

The use of computer-assisted telephone interviewing (CATI) simplifies telephone interviewing. Interviewers call participants from a central location, such as a designated room in a specific college department, ask questions, and enter the responses directly into a computer. Besides entering data into the computer instantly, responses are coded and entered in a data file. Another important part of CATI is that a different staff person, with the participant's permission, can monitor interviewers to insure consistency.

Some advantages of collecting information by telephone are:

- Immediate response.
- In the case of computer-assisted telephone interviewing, interviewers can be monitored.
- It can be less costly if expensive technology is not used.
- It is cheaper than in-person interviews.
- Interviewers can detect and perhaps deal with participant reluctance.

Some disadvantages of telephone interviews are:

- Knowing when to call people at home by telephone.
- Participants' reluctance to participate and suspicion or distrust of the interviewer.

Important Points about Face-to-Face and Telephone Interviews

- The major advantage of in-person interviews is the high response rate. Face-to-face interviews are more effective than other types of interviews when participants need assistance in completing the questionnaire.
- The main disadvantage of face-to-face interviews is the expense, which hinders large samples.
- Telephone interviews are less expensive than face-to-face interviews and are becoming more popular as a data collection method. Another advantage is immediate responses.
- The inability to contact people without telephones or with unlisted numbers has been a concern with telephone interviewing. But unlisted numbers can now be located with the use of random digit dialing.

Choosing and Designing Data Collection Instruments

Activity 2.   After reading this section, reviewing the literature, and consulting with experts on your research problem, begin constructing a questionnaire by writing five questions related to the problem.

Activity 3.   Find three journal articles in which researchers used secondary data analysis instead of using a questionnaire. What was the researcher's rationale for using secondary data?

Using Existing Questionnaires to Collect Data

You have decided on the data collection method. Now the data collection instrument (survey or questionnaire) must be selected to gather information from participants. The following sections will guide you in selecting an existing questionnaire to collect data and in developing a new questionnaire

As you review the literature, you may find that other researchers have designed or used instruments that are appropriate for your research. Earlier, it was pointed out that when creating a questionnaire, the researcher must focus on the research questions, the problem statement, hypotheses, and the participants. These guidelines also apply when selecting an existing instrument.

If a questionnaire is located that meets your needs, either the entire questionnaire or parts of the questionnaire can be used. An existing questionnaire can also be adapted or modified. Using existing surveys to collect data is less expensive and less time consuming than creating your own instrument. However, permission is required to use questionnaires designed by other researchers. Surveys can be found in journals, books, and on the World Wide Web. Sometimes the instrument, or part of it, is in a journal article. The University of Texas at Arlington's *Subject Guides* Web site (November 23, 2000) includes Helen Hough's (http://libraries. uta.edu/helen/welcome.htm) guide to locating social science research instruments. Some of the resources listed at that site are:

- Allen J. P. (Ed.). (1995). *Assessing alcohol problems: A guide for clinicians and researchers*. NIAA Treatment Handbook, Series 4. Washington, DC: National Institutes of Health.
- Beere, C. A. (1990). *Gender roles: A handbook of tests and measures*. New York: Greenwood Press.
- Brodsky, S. L., & Smitherman, O. (1983). *Handbook of scales for research in crime and delinquency*. New York: Plenum Press.
- Price, J. L., & Mueller, C. W. (1986*). Handbook of organizational measurement*. Marshfield, MA: Pitman.
- Rossetti, L. M. (1990). *Infant toddler assessment: An interdisciplinary approach*. Austin, TX: PRO-ED.
- Touliatos, J., Perlmutter, B. F., & Strauss, M. A. (Eds.). (1990*). Handbook of family measurement techniques*. Newbury Park, CA: Sage. (There is also a new, 2000 handbook. See the reference list for a complete citation.)

- Wodrich, D. L. (1984). *Children's psychological testing: A guide for nonpsychologists.* Baltimore: Brookes. (There is also a 1997 edition of this handbook. See reference list for a complete citation.)

In the hypothetical case study, Mr. Norton decided to construct his own questionnaire after reviewing several handbooks containing various measures, including Touliatos, Perlmutter, Strauss, and Holden's (2000) *Handbook of family measurement* techniques. Fischer and Corcoran have also published measures for clinical practice (2000).

Make sure that the established questionnaire that you select has been evaluated for validity and reliability and that the norming samples represent the groups you are researching. A drawback to using existing questionnaires is lack of knowledge about the instrument's validity and reliability if not explicitly stated by the investigator. The validity and reliability issues are reasons why some researchers choose to develop their own questionnaires.

Designing Questionnaires

Activity 4. Locate a questionnaire designed to gather quantitative data, and evaluate whether the researcher followed guidelines presented here for constructing questions. Rewrite questions that you believe are ineffective ones, and explain why you have rewritten them.

Creating Questions. A questionnaire consists of individual questions, or several scales. For example, one questionnaire could include three scales: a scale that measures a participant's self-esteem, one that measures happiness, and one that measures religiosity. It may include either open-ended or closed-ended questions. Open-ended questions have no prepared response choices and are used when the researcher wants in-depth understanding of a problem. There is a significant difference in using these two types of question. Here the focus is on closed-end; open-ended questions are explained later in Chapter 12.

Closed-ended questions with their predetermined responses can have several different response categories. Questions must be written before the questionnaire is constructed. Writing clear questions for a survey can, however, be challenging. Chapter 5 on research writing discussed the importance of writing with clarity, simplicity, and conciseness. Those guidelines apply especially to writing survey questions. Clarity about the problem, research questions, and hypotheses and knowledge about the characteristics of participants and the data collection method help you avoid ambiguity when writing questions. In the case example, Mr. Norton remembered from his research course that all of the participants in his study should be able to understand survey questions, regardless of the diversity among them. Clearly written questions also prevent participants from guessing the meaning of questions and becoming frustrated trying to interpret them. Complex, time-consuming questions may prevent participants from completing and returning the survey or answering all of the questions. Make sure that questions relate to the research questions and hypotheses. To write effective questions, avoid the following:

Using Jargon with which Participants Are Unfamiliar. For example, asking the question, Should Haldol be given to people diagnosed with schizophrenia? Participants are probably not familiar with the word Haldol, a psychotropic medication, and some may not know the term *schizophrenia*. If the survey were intended for medical professionals or people with schizophrenia who have been using the drug and their families, it would be an appropriate question. Know your participants.

Using Words with Multiple Meanings.   Slang, in particular, can be a problem. For example, interpret the question How many times a week do you rap with your friends? In a class discussion, several students defined *rapping* as the popular style of music, others as talking, and still others as kissing. And, the same word can have different meanings in different cultures. When participants represent diverse ethnicities, representatives from those groups should be included in the pilot study where participants give comments about the survey questions.

Using Double-Barreled Questions.   For example, when asked to respond YES or NO to the question Does attending church once a week relieve stress and reduce the divorce rate? If you answer YES to this question, are you saying that attending church relieves stress or that attending church reduces the divorce rate? Double-barreled questions ask two unrelated questions in one sentence. Therefore, the participant cannot be sure which question requires the response. To avoid the problem, pose two questions instead of one:

- Does attending church once a week relieve stress?
- Does attending church once a week reduce the divorce rate?

Using the Word NOT in Questions.   Doing this makes the question a negatively constructed one, confusing participants, who do not know whether their responses are affirmative or negative. For example, Women employees are not promoted as quickly as their male coworkers.

    AGREE   _____
    DISAGREE   _____

This negatively constructed question prevents participants from knowing whether they are agreeing or disagreeing with the above question.

Asking Questions That Could Generate Socially Desirable Responses.   Socially desirable responses cast participants in a positive light when their true response is one that society defines as negative. For example, if asked, Do you emotionally abuse your partner? The participant may respond NO although his or her true answer may be YES. After reviewing the literature, consulting experts on emotional abuse, and people who have been emotionally abused and operationally defining emotional abuse, you can ask a series of questions that would describe an emotionally abusive person.

Asking Leading Questions.   For example, Don't you agree that children should be placed in orphanages instead of in family foster homes? Phrasing a question in this manner is suggesting the answer to the participant. Instead, ask, Should children be placed in orphanages instead of in family foster care homes?

    YES   _____
    NO   _____

Asking Questions That Require Distant Memory. Don't ask for information that participants do not keep track of. For example, How many times did you withdraw cash from an Automatic Teller Machine in 1990? This question would be difficult for most people to answer unless their bank statements from 1990 were available.

Response Categories. Besides writing questions, you must decide on the type of response categories to use. Some of the response styles researchers may choose include Yes and No responses, True and False, Multiple Choice, and Likert scale responses. Yes/No responses give participants the options of choosing Yes or No as an answer. True/False provide two responses, and multiple-choice questions give participants several possible answers. The SAT, the GRE, and other similar tests that you took in high school and college are examples of standardized instruments. In the case example, questions four, five, and eight of the Independent Living Questionnaire provide multiple-choice type questions.

Likert scale responses are popular for measuring opinions, attitudes, and values. Answers along a continuum such as Satisfaction, Agreement, and Frequency are response options, illustrated in Table 8.1, that follow a statement provided by the researcher. Ordinarily, an odd number of response categories are provided that include a neutral or undecided response option. An even number of response categories is also acceptable although an odd number is used more often. In our case example questionnaire, questions two and three have Likert type responses.

The researcher assures that possible responses are exhaustive by listing all conceivable response categories for each question. For example, in question four, a multiple-choice question, Mr. Norton listed five responses for participants to choose from, including Other. Other was incorporated to give adolescents an opportunity to inform the researcher of plans besides the choices provided. Not Applicable and Don't Know are additional responses that can be added to answers.

Guidelines for Constructing Questionnaires

After questions are written, the questionnaire is constructed using a participant friendly format. The participants can then complete the questionnaire without assistance. A good self-adminis-

TABLE 8.1   Likert Type Scale Response

Agreement	Satisfaction	Frequency
Strongly Disagree	Very Dissatisfied	Never
Disagree	Dissatisfied	Seldom
Agree Somewhat	Somewhat Satisfied	Sometimes
Agree	Satisfied	Often
Strongly Agree	Very Satisfied	Always

tered questionnaire must provide clear instructions. Include all attributes of the variables in your study. Keep the questionnaire as short as possible. Be consistent in constructing the questionnaire by grouping questions with similar response formats together if there is variety in the response categories. For example, group Yes/No responses together, multiple-choice questions together, Likert scale questions together, and open-ended qualitative questions together. Look at the Independent Living Questionnaire constructed by Mr. Norton. Also, pay attention to the appearance of the questionnaire, including the formatting. Is it neat and readable with adequate spacing between questions and possible responses? Inadequate spacing between response choices makes it difficult for the researcher to determine which response was selected, as in the following example.

> I am prepared to live on my own after leaving foster care. Please circle the number to the right of your answer.
>
> Disagree $\qquad$ 1
> Agree Somewhat $\qquad$ 2
> Agree $\qquad$ 3

Which answer did the adolescent choose? It is impossible to know. Two possible responses were circled because there was insufficient space to clearly choose one.

After questions are written and the questionnaire devised, pretest a draft of the questionnaire with family and friends. They can check for whether the questions are clear, whether the questions make sense, and whether the questionnaire is easy to read. The second pretest is done on a sample of study participants (who are then excluded from the formal study). During this pretest, you are concerned about participants' comprehension of the questions, words they do not understand, and the amount of time that it takes to complete the questionnaire. Make revisions based on results of the pretests.

The questionnaire is ready for mailing to participants once revisions based on pretest results are made. Facilitate the process for participants by providing a packet containing the questionnaire, clear instructions for completing the questionnaire, the letter of informed consent, and a self-addressed, stamped envelope for returning the instrument to the researcher. Some researchers give small rewards for completion of the questionnaire, money, pencils, a copy of the study findings, and so on. It is important always to follow through with promised rewards.

This section described different ways to collect information from participants, and instruments that are used to collect the data. Besides using established questions or self-designed questionnaires to collect data, researchers are more and more using existing data as a source for research projects.

Important Points about Choosing Data Collection Instruments

- Researchers often use questionnaires with established validity and reliability developed by other researchers. These surveys can be located on the World Wide Web, in handbooks of tests and measures, and in journals.
- When a suitable questionnaire cannot be located, researchers can design their own to fit their problem statements, research questions, and hypotheses.

- Questionnaires for quantitative research consist of mainly closed-ended questions that provide several answers from which participants choose. Writing questions simply and with clarity is of the utmost importance to make the questionnaire user friendly, which contributes to a higher response rate.
- Pretest the questionnaire after it is constructed and make revisions based on comments before sending the final copy to participants.

Using Existing Data

> *Activity 5.*   As you read this section, think about ways that data are collected in your internship agency. Ask your supervisor or other staff whether employees, college and university faculty, or other researchers collect primary or existing data from the agency for research purposes.

Data collection methods discussed earlier in this chapter are ways of attaining primary, or first-hand, information directly from participants. Another method of collecting data is to use data already collected and analyzed by another researcher. Your reason for collecting and analyzing the data is different from that of the researcher who collected the primary data directly from participants using telephone or in-person interviews or mailed surveys.

Sources of secondary data, one type of existing data, are datasets, documents, case files, and client tracking systems. Practically all social service agencies use an intake system and data-gathering instruments to collect client background information for assessing clients and deciding the type of services to offer. Statistical data gathered by local, state, and federal agencies or by colleges and universities are often available to the public. Researchers also store datasets in archives for other researchers to use. Researchers can access existing data from a number of sources, and they have developed analytical tools for it. Content analysis and secondary data analysis are two methods for use with existing data.

Content Analysis

Content analysis is a research method that involves the quantitative analysis of qualitative text with the aim of identifying patterns, themes, or biases. Developing a problem statement, research questions, and sampling and measurement techniques are components of content analysis. The following are examples of text and of content:

- *Text:* Books, official records, movies/film/videotapes, letters, speeches, radio and television programs, advertisements, brochures, journals, newspapers, and magazine articles.

- *Content:* One word, body language, pictures, themes, meanings, words, phrases, sentences, paragraphs.

Social workers are well acquainted with materials that can be analyzed using content analysis—clients' written or computerized case records, child, family, and adult tracking systems, and intake forms. Although data in these materials were not collected specifically for research by social workers and other researchers, they are valuable sources of data that can be analyzed and yield useful information for the agency and the public.

Conducting a Content Analysis.   Like other types of research, content analysis uses a scientific approach, so that others wishing to conduct a content analysis can replicate the study. To that end, the following steps are taken to carry out a content analysis:

- ▪ Decide on a research problem and research questions.

- ▪ Select the type of text for the content analysis.

- ▪ Develop coding schemes and select exhaustive and mutually exclusive categories that indicate the purpose of the research based on the research questions, hypotheses, and the operational definitions to guide the coding process.

- ▪ Decide on the units of analysis—one word, words, phrases, themes, a sentence, or a paragraph. Next, decide whether the unit of analysis will be quantified by counting its presence or absence, the frequency that it occurs, the intensity of expression, or the amount of space devoted to it.

- ▪ Select a sampling procedure, using Chapter 7 as a guide. When there is a large amount of material to be analyzed, this is especially necessary, otherwise the process will be overwhelming.

- ▪ Assure reliability and validity. They affect the ability to replicate the content analysis. Reliability is the ability of a measure to produce consistent and dependable results whenever it is used. In content analysis, reliability is intercoder reliability, the ability of coders to be consistent in assigning the coding scheme constructed by the researcher so that consistent results can be attained. Intercoder reliability is of special importance in content analysis because when more than one person is rating, inconsistencies or lack of agreement among raters can make the coding system unreliable. Training of the raters and a clear coding system are ways of improving intercoder reliability.

Potocky (1993) conducted a content analysis of nine experimental studies on bereavement programs. Her five research questions related to client characteristics, practitioner characteristics, intervention characteristics, methodology characteristics, and outcome characteristics. Each of the nine studies in the content analysis was coded on the above five characteristics. Potocky concluded that her analysis provided a starting point for determining elements of successful practice with grieving people. Her study supported the importance of a continuum of care for high risk and high distress clients and using planned brief interventions that address clear goals.

Secondary Data Analysis

Secondary data analysis also uses existing documents. The difference between these two research methods, though, is that content analysis uses written or spoken communication and transforms it into quantitative data and secondary analysis uses data that have already been quantified. Some resources for accessing secondary data are listed below.

National and International Data Archives. These are located at some college and university libraries. The International Federation of Data Organizations (IFDO), for instance, has member organizations in Africa, the Americas, Asia, Australia, and Europe. Cornell University's National Data Archive on Child Abuse and Neglect (NDACAN), www.ndacan.cornell.edu/, maintains datasets on child abuse and neglect research that can be purchased for $75 per set, with a reduced rate of $25 for students. In the case example, the research unit decided to conduct a more extensive study on adolescents in foster care and independent living and purchased a dataset from NDACAN. Before purchasing a dataset, the researcher visits NDACAN'S web site and views its current holdings. Packets can be ordered with the dataset, documentation, installation instructions, and directions prepared by the Archive staff.

Federal, State, and Local Government Documents. These are collected for a specific purpose or for public use, such as the *United States Census Report* and the *Statistical Abstract of the United States.* FedStats (www.fedstats.gov) is an online source with statistics from more than 100 agencies and is maintained by the Federal Interagency Council on Statistical Policy. Social service agencies, both private and public, and any citizen may access these documents for personal use, to facilitate decision-making, or to establish policies regarding services to clients. The U.S. Census Bureau, one of the best known government agencies, collects demographic data every 10 years on the country's population. Its statistics are widely used by the public without charge. USA Statistics in Brief (www.census.gov/statab/www/brief.html), a supplement to the *Statistical Abstract of the United States,* contains national summary data and state population estimates. The U.S. Census Bureau publishes the *State and Metropolitan Area Data Book*, which presents state and metropolitan statistics on social and economic conditions, and the *County and City Data Book,* which contains official statistics on all U.S. counties and cities with 25,000 or more people.

Analyzing Secondary Data. Quantitative secondary data analysis is the same as methods used in other quantitative data analysis. Using data from The National Commission on Children, *1990 Survey of Parents and Children,* Carroll et al. (1999) conducted a study on parent–teen worry about the teen contracting AIDS. The original survey, consisting of parents and children in the same household from a national probability sample, was designed to investigate quality of relationships between parents and their children and family interactions with major institutions. The secondary data analysis focused on a subsample of 457 parent–teen pairs who responded to the "worry about AIDS" question, which was posed to children between the ages of 14 and 17. Descriptive statistics and nonparametric statistics were used to analyze the data.

Benefits of Using Existing Data

Content analysis and secondary data analysis are less expensive data collection methods since fewer resources are required to conduct the research. Research using existing data does not require a data collection instrument, permission from an Institutional Review Board, participant informed consent, or expenses for postage and staff. There is, however, a minimal cost for some datasets used for secondary data analysis.

Besides being less expensive, the researcher does not worry about whether a reasonable number of participants will choose to take part in the study. Furthermore, using existing data is less intrusive because there is no personal contact with participants who originally contributed information. Government agency and other organization's documents, records, and datasets are often more accessible. Groups will often allow access to this information rather than permit direct contact with clients and staff. Some datasets contain large samples and may consist of national or international probability samples, which would be impossible for most researchers to gather themselves. Existing data also provide opportunities for researchers to conduct longitudinal studies. Longitudinal studies occur over a period of time—months, years, or longer—and with the same or different participants.

Disadvantages to Using Existing Data

One drawback to using available data is that the current research is being conducted for a purpose which differs from the original intent of the research. Therefore, information that is needed may not be available. For instance, with content analysis, written documents may have been lost or destroyed or paper may have disintegrated over time. Similarly, in secondary data analysis, information about methods used, such as data collection methods, measurement and sampling techniques (one cannot assume that proper sampling procedures were used), and reliability and validity issues may be absent.

Important Points about Using Existing Data

- The analysis of existing data occurs when a researcher uses the work of other researchers for a different purpose. Content analysis and secondary data analysis are the main research techniques.
- Local, state, national, and international data archives, records, and datasets, case records, books, films, advertisements, journals, and newspaper and magazine articles are sources of available data.
- Research using available data requires a scientific approach—the development of a problem statement, research questions, hypotheses, and data collection methods so that others can replicate the study.
- A major benefit of using existing data is that it is less expensive than other research methods. It is also an unobtrusive approach. A larger sample can be reached; and longitudinal studies can be performed.
- Some disadvantages of using existing data are that the current research is being conducted for a different purpose than the initial study and needed information may not be available.

Human Diversity Issues in Designing and Using Questionnaires to Collect Data

When people from diverse populations are in the sample, they should be included in consultations regarding questionnaire development, so that their viewpoints and frames of reference can be considered. Furthermore, pretesting all drafts of the questionnaire informs the researcher about the different participants' understanding and interpretation of questions, which are then considered in designing the final questionnaire. In-person and telephone administration of questionnaires also require sensitivity to differences between the interviewer and interviewee. The interviewer's tone of voice, dress, and body language could be an influence, negative or positive, on participant acceptance and also on the study's outcome.

Ethical Issues and Biases in Designing and Using Questionnaires to Collect Data

It is an unethical issue to intentionally exclude from the study sample people from diverse groups in the population. Furthermore, individuals representing diverse groups of people should be involved in questionnaire design and pretests of the data collection instrument. If plans are to administer the survey to diverse populations and to generalize findings to those people, they should be represented in consultations and pretests.

WRITING STRATEGY

1. Consider your research question (s), problem statement, and hypotheses, and write a draft of five questions related to the problem you are investigating. Note the guidelines for composition outlined in this chapter. Construct the questionnaire in a friendly format, keeping in mind the guidelines for writing questions. Pretest the draft with family and friends, and revise your questions and format. Clearly label the draft and the revision.
2. Locate a questionnaire designed to gather quantitative data, and evaluate whether the research followed directions for constructing questions. Rewrite questions that you believe are ineffective, and briefly explain why each is ineffective. Be sure to turn in a copy of the original questionnaire, including careful documentation of your source.

LEARNING ACTIVITY

1. Think about what you learned in this chapter. Now relate what you learned to your own life, education, and work or internship experiences in terms of methods used to collect data. Discuss the connections with another research student.
2. Divide your study group into two debating teams, with one arguing for using existing data for research and the other against it. (It does not matter if the members are for or against their assigned side.) Discuss which team had the more logical rationale.

INFORMATION TECHNOLOGY FOR DESIGNING AND USING QUESTIONNAIRES TO COLLECT DATA

Access the *County and City Data Book* located in the U.S. Census Bureau's Uncle Sam's Reference Shelf, and research statistical information of interest to you about the county and city of your permanent residence. This site is located at www.census.gov/statab/www.

Important Points from Chapter 8

- Researchers can collect data for quantitative studies using mailed questionnaires, in-person interviews, and telephone interviews. Although mailed surveys are used more often than the others, there are advantages and disadvantages to each of these methods.
- Researchers can use an existing data collection instrument or create their own using specific guidelines to assure that a questionnaire is reliable and valid, that all participants understand, and that there is a high response rate.
- Besides administering questionnaires to gather information and conduct research, researchers can also use existing data by conducting content analysis or secondary data analysis on datasets or other documents collected by another researcher.

REFERENCES

Carroll, R. M., Shepard, M. P., Mahon, M. M., Deatrick, J. A., Orsi, A. J., Moriarty, H. J., & Feetham, S. L. (1999). Parent-teen worry about teen contracting AIDS. *Western Journal of Nursing Research, 21*(2), p. 168, 14p. Retrieved November 20, 2000, from www.ebsco.com.

Corcoran, K., & Fischer, J. (2000). *Measures for clinical practice: A sourcebook: Couples, families, and children* (3rd ed., Vol. 1). New York: Free Press.

Dillman, D. A. (1978). *Mail and telephone surveys: The total design method.* New York: John Wiley & Sons.

Edwards, J. E., Thomas, M. D., & Booth-Kewley, S. (1997). *How to conduct organizational surveys.* Thousand Oaks, CA: Sage.

Fischer, J., & Corcoran, K., (2000). *Measures for clinical practice: A sourcebook: Adults* (3rd ed., Vol. 2). New York: Free Press.

Potocky, M. (1993). Effective services for bereaved spouses: A content analysis of the empirical literature. *Health and Social Work 18*(4), 288–301.

Touliatos, J., Perlmutter, B. F., Strauss, M.A., & Holden, G. W. (Eds.). (2000). *Handbook of family measurement techniques* (Vols. 1–3). Thousand Oaks, CA: Sage.

University of Texas, Arlington (2000). *Subject Guides: Social Work.* Retrieved December 9, 2000, from www.uta.edu/library/research/rt-socialwork.html.

Wodrich, D. L. (1997). *Children's psychological testing: A guide for nonpsychologists* (3rd ed.). Baltimore: Brookes.

Taking the research course my sophomore year prepared me for future courses. For example, I took a political science course shortly after taking the research course. The professor told us to write a paper and to use journal articles related to political science. I knew exactly what he was referring to and how to search for the information. I had no problems. I was thrilled!

—Sophomore research student

CHAPTER GOALS

Your major goals upon completion of this chapter are to:

- Understand the role of statistics in the data analysis process.
- Be able to prepare data for computer analysis.
- Understand the role of descriptive statistics in the data analysis process.
- Understand the role of inferential statistics in the data analysis process.
- Interpret basic statistics reported in social work journals.

Introduction

This chapter describes data analysis methods in quantitative research once data are collected through questionnaires. Participants' responses to questions on the research instrument are raw data that must be organized, summarized, interpreted, and explained using statistical procedures, either descriptive or inferential. Although most social workers' job descriptions do not include quantitative research as a responsibility, knowledge about quantitative methods helps in understanding quantitative studies found in the literature, opinion polls, and agency reports that contain statistical data.

Statistics, a collection of techniques that assists the researcher in uncovering meaning in numerical data, play a vital role in quantitative data analysis. Descriptive statistics organize and summarize data and evaluate the extent of variation (differences) in scores or values and the degree to which different variables are associated with each other. Frequency distributions, measures of central tendency, measures of dispersion or variability, and correlation coefficients are all examples of descriptive statistical procedures. Once data are collected, summarized, and described and associations assessed, researchers may go further in their analysis by using inferential statistics.

Inferential statistics use procedures such as *t*-tests, analysis of variance, correlation, and chi-square for interpreting and explaining data and for evaluating how confident the researcher can feel about generalizing findings from a sample to the population from which the sample was drawn. In the past, data analysis and statistical computations were done by hand. Today, computer data analysis programs or packages such as Minitab, The Statistical Package for the Social Sciences (SPSS), and others are available data analysis tools.

Mr. Norton's Independent Living Questionnaire was presented as a case example in the last chapter. The case example in this chapter includes a codebook. Twenty participants' responses to that nine-question survey are also shared in this chapter. Data collected has to be coded before it is entered into a computer, and the codes assigned to the data are entered into a codebook. For example, some of the codes for race are African American/Black = 1, Asian = 2, Caucasian/White, NonLatino = 3, Latino = 4, Native American = 5, and Other = 6 for persons who do not choose any of the above races. The hypothetical data that follow illustrate statistical concepts described in this chapter.

Case Study: A Codebook

Question Number	Variable Description	Variable Name	Value Label	
1	ID Number	Participant Identification Number		As assigned by researcher
			99	Missing data
2	Preparation for independent living	PREP	1	Disagree
			2	Agree Somewhat
			3	Agree
			99	Missing data

3	Life skills training	LIFE	1	Never
			2	Seldom
			3	Sometimes
			4	Often
			5	Always
			99	Missing data
4	Immediate plans	PLANS	1	College
			2	Vocational/Technical
			3	Military
			4	No plans
			5	Other
			99	Missing data
5	Employment plans	WORK	1	Full-time
			2	Part-time
			3	No work
			4	Undecided
			99	Missing data
6	Scores on the SAT	SAT		Self-coded
			99	Missing data
7	Age at last birthday	AGE		Self-coded
			99	Missing data
8	Participant's race	RACE	1	African American/Black
			2	Asian
			3	Caucasian/White
			4	Latino
			5	Native American
			6	Other
			99	Missing data
9	Participant's gender	GENDER	1	Male
			2	Female
			99	Missing data

Preparing Data for Analysis

Once data have been collected the researcher must prepare the data for entering it into a computer for analysis. This section describes the process of coding and cleaning data prior to entering it into the computer.

Activity 1. Develop a codebook using the questionnaire developed for your research project. If you do not have a questionnaire, develop a short one to base your codebook on. Refer to the case example codebook.

Coding and Cleaning Data

Coding is a procedure for taking applicants' responses from questionnaires and translating them into language that the computer understands. Although many statistical packages accept both numeric and nonnumeric or string variables, calculations can only be done with numbers. Nominal data are assigned coding numbers. In fact, before data are even collected, a codebook is systematically developed, using the questionnaire as a guide. Mr. Norton, in the case example, reviewed the Independent Living Questionnaire beginning with the participant's identification number. He then provided codes for all possible responses to each question and developed a codebook in which the codes were entered for easy reference.

Variable descriptions, variable names, and value labels are also included. The variable description is a narrative of what the variable is and helps readers recognize the variable on the survey. The variable name usually has no more than eight characters, although it may vary by data analysis program. Value labels are the response categories for each variable and their corresponding codes. Self-coding of variables occurs when the answers to questions are the basis for the numerical codes (Newton & Rudestam, 1999), for example, SAT scores and age that participants provide about themselves. Instead of the researcher assigning a code, the information provided by participants is used as the code. Mr. Norton's codebook indicates that age and SAT scores are self-coded.

Often, codes are assigned on the data collection instrument itself. For example, in the case example, race and gender are nominal level measurements that are already coded. Instructions to participants read, Please circle the number that identifies your race:

African American/Black	1
Asian	2
Caucasian/White	3
Latino	4
Native American	5
Other	6

These same codes are used in the codebook.

Newton and Rudestam (1999) suggest the following rules when coding data:

1. *All data must be numeric.* This includes questions that yield answers in nominal data, that is, words or names.
2. *Each variable must occupy the same location for each case.* It must be in the same column or cell on a spreadsheet.
3. *All codes for a variable must be mutually exclusive and collectively exhaustive.* A participant's answer should fit only one category, that is, only be able to select one answer. For example, on the question about race on Mr. Norton's questionnaire, if Biracial or Other is not included, the participant who is biracial may feel compelled to select both Caucasian/White and Latino.
4. *Each variable should be coded to obtain maximum information.* Here the researcher attempts to define variables precisely, including as many attributes or values of the variable as possible. For example, in the case example, the variable plans (variable description, immediate plans) include the adolescents' possible plans of college, vocational/

technical school, military, no plans, and other. The variable work (variable description, employment plans) is a separate variable since it has several attributes.

Besides preparing data for analysis by coding all variables, data must be cleaned. Coding errors can cause inaccuracies in research findings. Cleaning of data for possible coding and data entry errors, which begins with a thorough review of raw data for inaccuracies, incomplete, and unclear responses and questions that could distort findings, is an important step in the data analysis process. Data are also reviewed for coding and data entry errors after being entered into the computer. Table 9.1 represents a computer printout of data for 20 of the 60 participants in Mr. Norton's study. Only after data are coded and entered into the computer, can you begin analyzing data using descriptive and inferential statistical procedures.

Important Points about Preparing Data for Analysis

- Data must be coded using symbols that represent participants' responses to questions. For example, codes are created in symbols that the computer can understand before data are entered into a computer for data analysis. These symbols are contained in codebooks.
- Organizing and cleaning data by checking for data entry and coding errors is an important part of the data analysis process and is done before data are analyzed.

TABLE 9.1 Twenty Participants' Responses to Independent Living Questionnaire

id	prep	life	plans	sat	age	race	gender	work
1	1	2	1	230	17	1	2	1
2	2	1	1	535	18	1	2	1
3	1	2	4	255	16	3	1	2
4	3	2	4	530	17	3	1	4
5	3	5	1	700	18	5	2	4
6	2	3	3	505	17	2	1	9
7	2	2	2	450	19	4	1	3
8	3	3	2	490	18	6	1	2
9	1	3	1	480	17	4	2	4
10	3	4	1	600	18	5	2	2
11	3	4	1	600	19	1	1	2
12	1	5	1	705	17	3	1	1
13	3	4	1	740	19	2	1	4
14	2	3	2	510	16	1	2	2
15	3	5	1	755	18	2	2	1
16	1	2	4	300	16	1	2	3
17	3	4	1	620	18	1	1	1
18	2	3	3	535	17	3	1	1
19	3	4	3	650	19	3	2	1
20	2	5	5	420	17	3	1	1

Descriptive Statistics

> *Activity 2.*   Identify the types of descriptive statistics used in four journal articles from your literature review. What was the researcher's purpose for applying descriptive statistics?

This section explains some common procedures for organizing and summarizing data obtained from a sample and for determining whether associations exist between variables. Information collected directly from participants by the researcher or from existing data used for secondary data analysis, explained in the previous chapter, is organized and summarized using descriptive statistics. Descriptive statistics include measures of central tendency, measures of variability, and measures of association. Descriptive statistics such as the mean, the median, and the mode, known as measures of central tendency, inform the researcher about the average scores or values in a distribution.

Measures of Central Tendency

> *Activity 3.*   Identify the types of measures of central tendency used to describe data in three journal articles. Discuss with a classmate whether the descriptions facilitated your understanding of the article.

The value that best symbolizes a total group of scores is an average. Think about the word average and how often it is used in your daily life to describe phenomena. You discuss, for example, the average age of students in your class, the average income of families, average exam scores, baseball batters' averages, or your average weight during the last year. Averages, or measures of central tendency, are the mean, the median, and the mode. These averages are computed differently and provide different information about a distribution of scores or values.

The Mode.   The mode is the most frequently occurring value in a distribution. If there is a mode, it can be used with all four levels of measurement, and is used less often than the mean and the median. The mode is appropriate for summarizing nominal data when an average is needed. Age 17 occurs more often than the other values (ages) in the age distribution in the case example and is therefore the mode.

The Mean.   The mean, used more often than either the mode or the median (described below) has mathematical properties conducive to further analyses that the mode does not have. The mean, also referred to as the arithmetic mean, is the sum of all values in a distribution, divided by the number of values in the distribution. For instance, in the case example showing participants' coded responses, to get the average age of participants, add the age of the 60 participants and divide the sum by 60:

Step 1: Add all of the values of the variable age.

17 18 16 17 18 17 19 18 17 18 19 17 19 16 18 16 18 17 19 17 17 18 18 19 20 19 18 18 17 17 16 18 18 18 19 19 17 16 18 17 17 19 18 18 17 17 18 19 17 20 17 16 18 18 17 17 19 18 17 17 = 1062

Step 2: Divide the sum of the values by the total of the values:

$$\frac{1062}{60} = 17.7$$

The mean age of adolescents who are preparing for independent living is 17.7.

One caution about the mean. It is drawn in the direction of extreme scores, which causes the mean to be higher when some scores are extremely high or lower when some scores are extremely low. Consequently, it is best to use the mean with a normal distribution and not with highly skewed distributions. Another property of the mean is that it is suitable for use only with interval and ratio levels of measurement where ranking of values is required, not with nominal and ordinal levels of measurement where codes symbolize names. The mean can also be used with more powerful statistical tests. Just remember when interpreting data that the mean is sensitive to and can be affected by extreme values in a distribution.

The Median.   The median is the middle value in the distribution when the values are listed from the highest to the lowest or from the lowest to the highest, that is, an equal number of values are smaller and an equal number are larger than the median. Using the distribution of values from the case example again, ages in ascending order are:

16 16 16 16 16 16 17 17 17 17 17 17 17 17 17 17 17 17 17 17 17 17 17 17 17 17 17 18 18 18 18 18 18 18 18 18 18 18 18 18 18 18 18 18 19 19 19 19 19 19 19 19 19 19 19 20 20

The median age of adolescents in foster care is 18 years. Because the distribution of values (ages) is an even number (60), the two middle values are the median. Therefore, there are 29 values on each side of the median. The two middle values are both 18. If these two numbers had been different, say 17 and 18, the average of these two middle scores would have been considered as the median. Table 9.2 illustrates frequency tables for the variable Age in Mr. Norton's study.

When the distribution of values, ages in the case example, is odd, the middle number is the median because there are an equal number of data values greater than and less than the median. A property of the median is that it is insensitive to the extreme scores that affect the mean. The median is appropriate for either interval or ratio level data.

Frequency distributions make it easier to get an idea of how variables are distributed, by counting the number of cases in each category.

TABLE 9.2   Age Frequencies for Adolescents in Foster Care

N Valid	Frequency	Percent	Valid Percent	Cumulative Percent
16.00	6	10.0	10.0	10.0
17.00	20	33.3	33.3	43.3
18.00	21	35.0	35.0	78.3
19.00	11	18.3	18.3	96.7
20.00	2	3.3	3.3	100.0
Total	60	100.0	100.0	

Visually Displaying and Examining Data

Activity 4.   Find additional journal articles that used tables, graphs, and charts to describe data; identify the type of visual displays and the researcher's purpose for using those methods.

Frequency Distributions.   Frequency distributions can be displayed in tables and in graphs in the form of pie charts, line graphs, bar graphs, and histograms. Graphs provide visual illustrations of a distribution of scores in a dataset and show how often particular scores appear in the distribution. Using frequency distributions, the researcher visually analyzes data, checking for errors in coding and for the shape of a distribution. Detecting errors in a distribution is part of the data cleaning process explained earlier. Frequency distributions can be used with all levels of data: nominal, ordinal, interval, and ratio. A frequency distribution, particularly a frequency polygon, provides a picture of the distribution's shape.

The shape of a distribution is important because it determines the type of analysis that can be conducted on a dataset. A bell shape, with both ends or tails tapering off equally and never touching the horizontal axis, is the property of a very special distribution called a normal distribution of scores. In this type of distribution, the three measures of central tendency have the same value or score, are all at the center of the distribution on the horizontal scale, and are below the highest point. This normal curve is used in inferential statistics explained later in this chapter. Figure 9.1 represents a normal curve.

Some data, of course, are not normally distributed and may be negatively or positively skewed. A positively skewed distribution tapers off or has a tail to the right, indicating a considerable number of low scores or values and a few extremely high scores or values. The median is less than the mean in a positively skewed distribution. Figure 9.2 represents a positively skewed distribution.

A negatively skewed distribution tapers off or has a tail to the left, illustrating many high scores and a few low scores. In a negatively skewed distribution, the mean is less than the median. Figure 9.3 represents a negatively skewed distribution.

The degree of skewness can be determined by calculating the difference between the values of the mean and the median in a distribution. The larger the difference between the two,

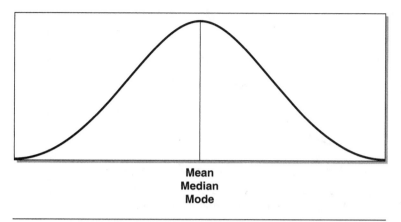

FIGURE 9.1   **A Normal Curve Showing Equal Mean, Mode, and Median**

the greater the level of skewness. An equal median and mean indicates that the distribution is not skewed. A bimodal distribution has two high points or two modes. Awareness of whether a distribution is skewed and the level or degree of skewness assists you in deciding which measure of central tendency to use to describe data. It also helps in evaluating whether the distribution is normal. Graphing is another way of summarizing and organizing data.

Graphing Data.   Two types of graphs, the *histogram* and *bar graph,* are also frequency distributions, where the frequencies are represented by bars. A histogram is like a bar graph, but the histogram's bars touch while there is space between the bars of a bar graph. Histograms are best for illustrating interval and ratio data. Figure 9.4 is a histogram based on the case example illustrating the distribution of adolescents' SAT math scores.

Bar graphs are best for displaying nominal and ordinal data. Figure 9.5 presents a bar graph showing the distribution of adolescents in foster care by race. Pie charts are for demonstrating

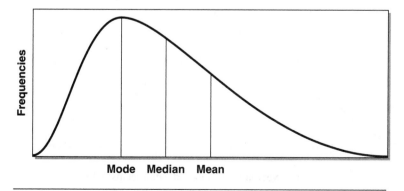

FIGURE 9.2   **A Positively Skewed Distribution Tapers to the Right**

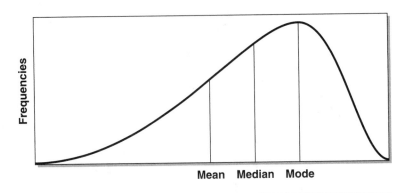

FIGURE 9.3   A Negatively Skewed Distribution Tapers to the Left

the distribution of scores of one variable and how those values add up to a whole. They are more effective in illustrating discrete variables, nominal and ordinal. Figure 9.6 represents a pie chart showing adolescents in foster care by gender.

Measures of Dispersion

Activity 5.   After reading this section, calculate the standard deviation for the SAT scores in Mr. Norton's dataset using the formula provided.

Whereas measures of central tendency illustrate the center of the distribution, or average score, measures of dispersion inform the researcher of the spread of scores, reflecting how different scores are from the mean. The researcher is attempting to determine the level of difference among participants' responses with measures of spread. When all of the values in a distribution are the same, there is zero variation. In the case example, Mr. Norton asked the adolescents to

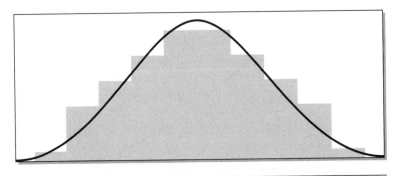

FIGURE 9.4   Histogram of Normally Distributed Adolescents' SAT Math Scores

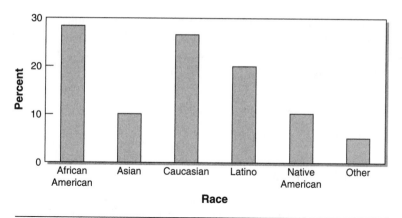

FIGURE 9.5 Bar Graph Illustrating Percentage of Adolescents in Foster Care by Race

respond on a scale from 1 (disagree) to 3 (agree) indicating their perceptions of readiness for independent living. Did the adolescents in Mr. Norton's study agree that they are prepared for independent living? Did the majority of the participants choose 1 (disagree), 2 (agree somewhat), or 3 (agree)? Ultimately, Mr. Norton wants to know how different each score in the distribution is from the mean—the variability or dispersion of scores. The range, the variance, and the standard deviation are the measures of variability described in this section. The range is used with data on the interval and ratio level while the standard deviation and the variance is more appropriate for use with interval or ratio level of data.

The Range. The range is the easiest of the three measures of dispersion to compute. Subtract the lowest score in a distribution from the highest to calculate the range. The range provides an estimate of how different the values are from each other. Mr. Norton, to compute the range of SAT scores, subtracts the lowest score from the highest: 785 – 200 = 585. The range is 585.

The Variance. The variance is the average squared distances of all the scores from the mean. Each distance and each squared distance measures how much each participants' score

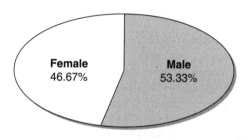

FIGURE 9.6 Pie Chart Illustrating Percentage of Adolescents in Foster Care

differs from the mean score. The larger the variance, the more participants' scores are dispersed from the mean. Like the mean, the variance is sensitive to extreme values, and there are no standard guidelines for interpreting the variance. Researchers view the variance as a significant component of various statistical tests. The formula for the variance is:

$$s^2 = \frac{\Sigma \left(X - \bar{X} \right)^2}{n - 1}$$

The Standard Deviation

The standard deviation is the most frequently used of the measures of dispersion. It is the square root of the variance; that is, it is the average distance of scores in a distribution from the mean measuring how much participants differ from the mean of their group. The larger the standard deviation, the more participants' scores are spread out; the smaller the standard deviation the less spread or dispersion there is among the scores. Like the mean, the standard deviation is sensitive to extreme scores. The standard deviation is more appropriate for use with a normal distribution or curve, and it is usually reported along with the mean. It is also more appropriate for use with interval or ratio level data. Researchers view the standard deviation as a significant component of various statistical tests. The formula for the standard deviation is:

$$s^2 = \sqrt{\frac{\Sigma \left(X - \bar{X} \right)^2}{n = 1}}$$

The translation of the formula symbols is:

s or *SD* is the standard deviation
Σ stands for sigma and informs you to sum what follows
X is each individual score
$\bar{X}$ is the mean of all scores in the data set
n is the sample size

Table 9.2 illustrates the computer printout of frequency tables for the variable age in Mr. Norton's study.

Measures of Association

Now that you have learned statistical procedures for describing, summarizing, and examining one variable (univariate statistics), you are ready to analyze whether associations or relationships exist between variables after data are described. Crosstabulation and correlation are measures of association. Measures of association are descriptive bivariate statistics. They describe relationships between two variables, analyzing how the attributes (scores, categories, or values) of one variable are associated with attributes of another variable. Different bivariate statistics are used with specific types of data and levels of measurement. Use crosstabulation for analyzing two categorical, or discrete, variables at the nominal or ordinal level. Use correlation analysis when the variables are at the interval or ratio level. If these measures indicate there is an association between the two variables, additional tests may be performed to assess whether the relationships are significant. Chi-Square, Phi, and Cramer's V are some of the significance tests for crosstabulations. T-tests are the significance tests for differences in the means of two groups. Significance tests are explained after the description of measures of association.

Crosstabulation.   Crosstabulation, often called a contingency table, is illustrated in Table 9.3. In a computer printout it is a rectangular or square array with cells containing the distribution of scores or values for two variables, which allow researchers to examine the relationship between the two variables. Rows contain categories of the dependent variable and columns contain categories of the independent variable. Squares or boxes within the tables are cells; cell frequencies are the percentages in each cell. Marginals are values in the totals column or row. Row marginals are univariate frequency distributions for the dependent variable; column marginals are univariate frequency distributions for the independent variable. The number (count) at the lower right hand corner is the total sample size excluding missing values. Table 9.3 illustrates the computer printout of crosstabulation of preparation for independent living by gender of the adolescents in Mr. Norton's study. An examination of the crosstabulation table shows a relationship between gender and perception of preparation for independent living because 61.9% (circled in the table) of the males agree that they are prepared to live on their own while only 38.1% of the females do.

TABLE 9.3   Crosstabulation of Preparation for Independent Living and Gender

PREP		*GENDER*		
		Male	**Female**	**Total**
Disagree	Count	11	12	23
	% within PREP	47.8%	52.2%	100.0%
	% within GENDER	35.5%	41.4%	38.3%
	% of Total	18.3%	20.0%	38.3%
Agree somewhat	Count	7	9	16
	% within PREP	43.8%	56.3%	100.0%
	% within GENDER	22.6%	31.0%	26.7%
	% of Total	11.7%	15.0%	26.7%
Agree	Count	13	8	21
	% within PREP	61.9%	38.1%	100.0%
	% within GENDER	41.9%	27.6%	35.0%
	% of Total	21.7%	13.3%	35.0%
Total	Count	31	29	60
	% within PREP	51.7%	48.3%	100.0%
	% within GENDER	100.0%	100.0%	100.0%
	% of Total	51.7%	48.3%	100.0%

Correlation.   The strength and the direction of the linear relationship between two variables across a group of subjects are measured using correlation, a numerical index. It is important to remember that correlation does not suggest causation, that one variable is responsible for change in the other variable. Correlation is a number between –1 and +1. The closer the correlation is to either +1.0 or –1.0, the stronger the linear relationship between the two variables; the closer the correlation is to 0.0, the weaker the correlation. A correlation of 0.0 indicates very weak or no correlation. Correlations of –1.0 and +1.0 suggest a perfect linear indirect (–1.0) or perfect direct (1.0) association between the two variables. Table 9.4 is a guide for interpreting a correlation coefficient.

A perfect linear correlation allows you to predict, with explanations for all variation between variables, what will happen with one score for one variable, if the score of the other variable is known. For more information on linear relationships, see the section on scattergrams later in this chapter.

Continuous variables can assume an infinite number of values along a continuum that can be subdivided into smaller values within the continuum and can be rank ordered. Weight, age, income, height, temperatures in degree, and test scores are examples of continuous variables. Pearson *r,* also known as Pearson correlation coefficient and the product moment-correlation coefficient, analyzes the strength of the relationship between two continuous variables at the interval or ratio.

Discrete or categorical variables are not continuous and classify values into a small number of distinct categories. Gender, race, religion, social class, and religious affiliation are examples of discrete variables. Some of the categories or attributes of race are Asian, Latino, and White/Caucasian. These attributes of the variable race have no meaning even when assigned numbers such as 1 = Asian, 2 = Latino, and 3 = White/Caucasian except to represent the category.

Data should be normally distributed for Pearson's *r*. Besides measuring the strength of the relationship between variables, Pearson's *r* also measures the direction of the relationship as indicated by the negative and positive signs. In a negative correlation, increases in values in one variable are associated with decreases in values in the other variable. For example, the higher a student's SAT score, the lower the dropout rate. A positive correlation indicates a relationship in which values in one variable increase, the values in the other variable also increase or as the values in one variable decrease, values in the other variable also decrease. For instance, if as students' grades increase, their SAT scores increase, there is a positive correlation between two variables. In this situation, if you know a student's grades, you can

TABLE 9.4   Guide for Interpreting a Correlation Coefficient

Correlation Coefficient	Explanation
.80–1.0	Very strong relationship
.60–.80	Strong relationship
.40–.60	Moderate relationship
.20–.40	Weak relationship
0.0–.20	Weak or no relationship

predict what the SAT score will be. Table 9.5 illustrates a computer printout of Pearson *r* showing no relationship between two continuous variables, the adolescents' age and SAT score. The Pearson *r* is .093 (not .93) indicating that there is not a correlation between the adolescents' age and score on the SAT test.

Scattergram. A scattergram, also called a scatterplot, is a visual representation of a correlation. It has individual frequency scores for two variables for each participant, plotted on the x and y axis, and can suggest whether there is a linear association between two interval or ratio variables. Scattergrams illustrate when relationships are positive or negative and linear or curvilinear and the strength of the relationship. Figure 9.7 illustrates scattergrams with positive (direct) and negative (indirect) linear relationships. The relationships are linear if a straight line, called a regression line, can be drawn approximately between the dots. Dots close to the line indicate strong relationships between the two variables, and dots further away from the line suggest a weaker relationship.

Important Points about Descriptive Statistics

- Descriptive statistics are used for organizing, summarizing, and interpreting data and finding associations between variables.
- Data can be displayed and described with frequency distributions, graphs, charts, and tables that provide a quick, visual view of the data.
- The mean, the median, and the mode are measures of central tendency that inform the researcher about the average values in a distribution.
- Measures of dispersion are indicators of the spread of the distribution of values, specifying how different individual values are from the mean value in the distribution.
- Measures of association are bivariate statistics that analyze relationships between two variables, evaluating how attributes of one variable are associated with attributes of another variable. Crosstabulation and correlation are the measures of association explained in this chapter.

TABLE 9.5   Correlation Between SAT Score and Age of Adolescents in Foster Care

	Correlations	**SAT**	**AGE**
SAT	Pearson Correlation	1.000	.093
	Sig. (2-tailed)	.	.481
	N	60	60
AGE	Pearson Correlation	.093	1.000
	Sig. (2-tailed)	.481	.
	N	60	60

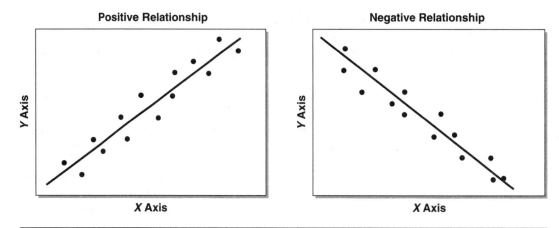

FIGURE 9.7   Scattergrams Showing Positive and Negative Correlations

Inferential Statistics

Inferential statistics, specifically significance tests, are needed to determine if differences between variables are due only to random errors produced by random sampling. Researchers use inferential statistics to test hypotheses to determine if results can be generalized from a sample to a population. When sampling does not occur, inferential statistics are not needed. For example, if the entire population of adolescents in foster care had been included in Mr. Norton's study, there could be no sampling errors because no sample was drawn. When descriptive statistics denote an association between variables, those statistics are often followed with inferential statistics to assess if a relationship exists or if the association results from random sampling errors.

Inferential statistics informs you of the probability that findings can be generalized from the sample to the population. The application of probability theory allows the researcher to calculate, with a certain degree of confidence, the likelihood that events are due to chance. The researcher tests hypotheses to determine whether these inferences can be made from the sample to the population from which the sample was selected.

Hypothesis Testing

Initial research questions are posed early in the study before the literature review is completed, although they are usually revised during the literature review. The hypothesis, developed only after completion of the literature review, is also based on the literature, other sources such as experts on the topic being studied, people experiencing the problem, the researcher's personal, professional, and educational experiences, and various documents. Weinbach and Grinnell (2001) assert that, "There are many different definitions of hypotheses, but they all suggest the same idea: A hypothesis is a tentative answer to a research question. In its simplest form, it is a statement of a proposed relationship between or among variables" (p. 83). The research question asks if a certain relationship exists between or among variables. A hypothesis, which is central to all inferential statistics, predicts whether there is a relationship or association or whether there are differences among or between variables. A hypothesis is used for bivariate and multivariate analysis.

There are two types of hypotheses—the null hypothesis and the alternative hypothesis. The null hypothesis, a negative form of a hypothesis, assumes that there is no relationship between or among variables or that there is no difference between or among variables being studied in the population and that any difference between the means of randomly selected samples is due to errors associated with random sampling. It states, then, that there is no difference or association between the means of the populations and that if differences exist, the differences occurred by chance.

The alternative to the null hypothesis, the hypothesis that the researcher wants to confirm, is called the research or alternative hypothesis. This hypothesis states that there is a relationship between sample means. There are two types of research hypotheses—directional and nondirectional. The directional, or one-tailed, hypothesis states that there is a difference between sample means or variables and states the direction of that difference. The nondirectional, or two-tailed, hypothesis, states that there is a relationship between sample means, but does not indicate the direction of that difference.

Mr. Norton in the case study devised the following research questions and possible hypotheses:

Research question: *Is there a difference in male and female adolescents in foster care in their perception of their readiness for independent living?*

After completing the literature review, Mr. Norton writes these hypotheses:

- Null hypothesis: *There is no difference in male and female adolescents in foster care in their perceptions of their readiness for independent living.*
- One-tailed hypothesis: *Male adolescents in foster care are more likely to perceive themselves as being prepared to live independently than female adolescents in foster care perceive themselves.*
- Two-tailed hypothesis: *There is a difference in adolescent males and females in foster care in their perception of their readiness for independent living.*

The crosstabulation that Mr. Norton performed using a statistical analysis package indicates that a higher percentage of males believe that they are prepared for independent living than females. The probability that the null hypothesis is true is determined by significance tests based on inferential statistics.

The Concept of Significance

Inferential significance tests for analyzing the null hypothesis also establish the probability level at which the null hypothesis could be rejected. Ordinarily, researchers do not write in journal articles that the null hypothesis is rejected. The usual way of saying that the null hypothesis is rejected is to assert that the difference is statistically significant. Findings in journal articles will state, for instance, that a difference is statistically significant at the .05 level, the most frequently used level of significance. Probability is symbolized with a lower case p. So findings that are statistically significant at the .05 level are illustrated by writing $p < .05$. This means that there is less than a 5 in 100 chance that the researcher is wrong in rejecting the null hypothesis when the null hypothesis is true. Other p values that the researcher frequently relies on are $p < .01$ (less than 1 in 100) and $p < .001$ (less than 1 in 1,000). At these levels of significance, the null hypothesis is rejected with more confidence. If the null hypothesis is rejected and it is actually correct, a Type I error occurs. Remember that the researcher is reject-ing the null hypothesis because it states that there is no difference in the variables that are being studied. A Type II error is failing to reject the null hypothesis when it is false. For example, if your alternative hypothesis states, "Male adolescents in foster care are more likely to perceive themselves as prepared to live independently after leaving the foster care system than female adolescents in foster care perceive themselves," then the null hypothesis is that there is no difference in the perception of male and female adolescents in foster care in their perception of their preparation for independent living. Mr. Norton is using significance tests to show that the null hypothesis is not true.

Significance Tests

In Chapter 8 you studied methods for collecting data and instruments used for collecting data from participants. In this chapter you have seen that after data are coded, collected, entered into the computer, and cleaned, the researcher is ready to organize, summarize, and visually exam-ine the data using descriptive statistics. The researcher can also determine if associations exist between variables using descriptive statistics. Inferential statistics are then applied to evaluate whether those associations are due to chance. Nonparametric and parametric are significant tests.

Parametric Tests.   The decision about the type of statistical test to use is made during the research design or planning phase of the research project. The type of test to apply is based on the level of measurement of the variables, methods for selecting the sample, and whether the variables are normally distributed. These considerations help you decide whether parametric or nonparametric tests of significance can be applied. Assumptions of parametric tests of sig-nificance include using variables at the interval or ratio level of measurement, using variables normally distributed in the population, and using randomly selected samples that are indepen-dent of each other.

Samples are independent of each other when one group of participants provides data for one sample and a different group of participants provide data for the other sample. The data values of one group are not affected by the data values of the other group and vice versa. In other words, when participants or a single group take the same test more than once or are interviewed more than once, the data are related, not independent (Montcalm & Royse, 2002).

The t-test is a major parametric test. There are several different types of t-tests; two are discussed here. The t-test is a bivariate analysis that compares two sample means from differ-ent groups for statistical significance using an interval or ratio level dependent variable and a nominal level, usually independent variable. The t-test analysis can be computed with less than 30 participants, which is a small number of participants. Apply the t-test for independent samples when you want to compare the means or scores of two different samples, such as men and women, social workers and psychologists, or high school graduates and people who dropped out of school. The two groups being compared are independent of each other (not related), and each group is tested once.

Use the paired samples *t*-test when there are two observations on the same single group and the goal is to determine if changes occurred within that group. The group is usually tested or measured more than once, for example with a pretest and a post-test. The researcher compares the means of the pretest and the post-test to evaluate whether participants changed. Is there a difference in the pretest and post-test scores? For example, did the group's self-esteem improve or did the group's level of depression change? Table 9.6 represents results of an independent sample *t*-test comparing SAT math score means for males and females. The first part of the printout shows group statistics (31 males with a mean score of 526 and 29 females with a mean score of 456). Another part of the independent samples *t*-test (not shown here) reflects, among other findings the *t*-test for equality of means which showed no significant differences in the mean SAT scores for males and females ($t(58) = 1.870, p > .05$). The mean of the males ($m = 526, sd = 147$) was not significantly different from the mean of the females ($m = 456, sd = 143$).

If you want to compare means of more than two groups use Analysis of Variance, referred to as ANOVA.

One-way Analysis of Variance (ANOVA), an alternate to the *t*-test, is used for testing the null hypothesis for observed differences between scores of more than two independent groups that are tested only once and the means are compared with one another. Analysis of variance uses an *F* statistic instead of a *t*. ANOVA may be chosen over a *t*-test because it has the capacity to compare more than two means. Like the *t*-test ANOVA also provides a *p* value. One-way ANOVA requires a normally distributed dependent variable at the interval or ratio levels, and an independent variable with three or more different values. Which group participants belong to is determined by the value of the independent variable.

Pearson product-moment correlation, also called Pearson's *r*, is another inferential parametric test. Pearson's *r* was described earlier in this chapter as a descriptive statistic, a measure of association. But, the correlation coefficient is versatile. In addition to its use as a descriptive statistic, it is used to evaluate the reliability of a measuring instrument—in factor analysis to help the researcher develop and understand a correlation matrix and in inferential statistics to test hypotheses. The correlation coefficient is used when the researcher plans on evaluating the relationship between two interval or two ratio level variables, and not the difference between groups. In inferential statistics, Pearson's *r* is used to test for statistical significance. See Measures of Association for more detailed information about Pearson's *r*.

TABLE 9.6   Independent Samples *t*-Test of SAT Score Means for Males and Females

Group Statistics				
Gender	**N**	**Mean**	**Std. Deviation**	**Std. Error Mean**
Male	31	526.2903	147.0939	26.4188
Female	29	456.2069	143.1636	26.5848

Nonparametric Tests.   Nonparametric tests do not require the assumptions of parametric tests, such as a normal distribution and data at the interval or ratio level. Most nonparametric tests, therefore, are not as robust as parametric tests. The researcher can, however, use smaller samples with nonparametric tests than with parametric tests. One-way and two-way chi-square analysis are nonparametric tests of use to social workers.

Two-way chi-square analysis is used to test whether a statistically significant relationship exists between two variables, but not how strong that relationship is. To make this determination, chi-square examines if values of one variable are associated with values of the other variable to the extent that the relationship is not likely to be due to sampling error. Chi-square can be used when both the dependent and independent variables are at the nominal (categorical) level of measurement when testing the association between categorical variables. Chi-square determines whether the proportion of people with a specific attribute is the same for one group (boys) as for another group (girls). Like some other nonparametric tests, chi-square can be applied when data do not conform to assumptions regarding normal distributions and large samples.

One-way chi-square categorizes randomly selected participants based on one variable. For instance, in the case example, the variable Plans (adolescents' plans for independent living, after leaving the foster care system) is categorized as College, Vocational/Technical School, Military, No Plans, and Other Plans. One-way chi-square evaluates if what the researcher observes in a distribution of frequencies is what is expected to occur by chance—the chi-square value is equal to zero if there is no difference between what we expect and what we observe. Chi-square also determines whether participants' responses are equally distributed across all levels and tests assumptions about how representative a sample is of the population from which it was drawn.

A one-way chi-square test was calculated, using data from the case example presented at the beginning of the chapter, comparing the frequency of occurrence of the values of immediate plans of adolescents after leaving foster care. It was hypothesized that each value would occur an equal number of times. No significant deviation from the hypothesized values was found (chi-square (4) = 8.6, $p > .05$). There is no significant difference between the expected and observed values or scores.

The output for the chi-square, Table 9.7, consists of two sections. The first section gives the frequencies of each value of the variable. In this example, the variable is Immediate Plans upon leaving foster care. The values of that variable and their frequencies are College (20 adolescents plan on attending), Vocational/Technical School (12 plan on attending), Military (6 plan are enlisting), No Plans (12 have no immediate plans), and Other (10 adolescents have other plans). These are the observed values, what the participants actually indicated that their plans are. The expected values are what the researcher expects to occur by chance. The expected frequencies for each category should be at least one, and a minimum of 20% of the categories should have expected frequencies of less than 5. The residual is the expected number subtracted from the observed number.

The second part of the output, labeled test statistics, provides results of the chi-square test. A significant chi-square shows that the data vary from the expected values while a test that is not significant shows data consistent with the expected values. The significance level in Table 9.7 is .070, which is greater than the .05 level of significance, set by the data analysis package or the researcher.

TABLE 9.7 **Chi-square and Adolescents' Plans for Independent Living**

Plans	Observed N	Expected N	Residual
College	20	12.0	8.0
Vocational/Technical	12	12.0	.0
Military	6	12.0	–6.0
No plans	12	12.0	.0
Other	10	12.0	–2.0
Total	60		

Test Statistics	
Chi-square	8.667
df	4
Asymp. Sig.	.070

Important Points about Inferential Statistics

- Inferential statistics determine if differences in variables are due to random sampling errors produced by random sampling.
- Inferential statistics test hypotheses to determine if results can be generalized to the population from which the sample was drawn.
- Parametric and nonparametric are the significance tests performed using inferential statistics. Parametric tests require that certain assumptions, such as a normal distribution and a large sample and variables at the interval or ratio level of measurement, are met. Nonparametric tests of significance do not require that all those assumptions are met.
- The two types of hypotheses are the null hypothesis and the alternative hypothesis, which consists of the one-tailed, directional, hypothesis and the two-tailed, nondirectional, hypothesis.

Human Diversity Issues in Analyzing Quantitative Data

Human diversity issues presented here were also discussed in Chapter 2, Ethical Issues and Biases in Social Work Research. These biases in research include consistently mentioning one sex first in research results, overgeneralizing by generalizing findings to both sexes when only one sex was included in the research sample, and failure to report gender of participants in the results section when data were reported on both men and women (Eichler, 1988). Additional human diversity issues include excluding different ethnic groups from the analysis when they were a part of the sample and generalizing findings to groups that were not a part of the sample.

Ethical Issues and Biases in Analyzing Quantitative Data

Protecting privacy of the participants and maintaining confidentiality of data continues throughout the research process. To that end, before collecting data, decisions are made about protection and destruction of data, both written and computerized, after analysis and reporting occur. Support staff, responsible for data entry and analysis, is trained about confidentiality and protection of the privacy of participants' data. Fraudulent research practices, such as reporting results when data were not collected, claiming the work of others, and falsifying data and results are also ethical issues in analyzing quantitative research. See Chapter 2 for a more detailed account of ethical issues and biases in social work research.

WRITING STRATEGY

1. Identify the type of descriptive statistics used in three journal articles from your literature review and for each explain the researcher's purpose in applying that statistic. Be sure to document properly the articles to which you refer.
2. Find three articles that used tables, graphs, and charts to describe data. Identify each visual display, and for each explain the researcher's purpose in using this display. Be sure to document properly the articles to which you refer.
3. Explain what the standard deviation tells Mr. Norton about the SAT scores he recorded.
4. Using the research question you composed for the writing assignment in Chapter 8, write a one-tailed (directional) hypothesis, a two-tailed (nondirectional) hypothesis, and a null hypothesis.

LEARNING ACTIVITY

Develop a list of questions based on class discussions, lectures, and readings relating to quantitative research. Select 10 questions from your list for an interview with a professor who conducts quantitative research. What did you learn from the interview that will help in carrying out a quantitative research study?

INFORMATION TECHNOLOGY FOR ANALYZING QUANTITATIVE DATA

Using the World Wide Web, search for information on software, such as SPSS, Minitab, Excel, or SAS, for analyzing quantitative data. Share with a classmate the type of information you located and the ease or difficulty you experienced in finding the material.

Important Points from Chapter 9

- Statistics play a vital role in the analysis of quantitative data.
- Descriptive statistics organize, summarize, reduce data, and evaluate relationships between variables by using frequencies, measures of central tendency, measures of association, and measures of dispersion.

- Inferential statistics determine whether differences in variables are due to random sampling errors produced by random sampling when testing hypotheses. Hypothesis tests also determine if results can be generalized to the population from which the sample was drawn.

REFERENCES

Eichler, M. (1988). *Nonsexist research methods: A practical guide.* Boston: Allen & Unwin.

Montcalm, D., & Royse, D. (2002). *Data analysis for social workers.* Boston: Allyn & Bacon.

Newton, R. R., & Rudestam, K. E. (1999). *Your statistical consultant.* Thousand Oaks, CA: Sage.

Weinbach, R. W., & Grinnell, R. M., Jr. (2001). *Statistics for social workers* (5th ed.). Boston: Allyn & Bacon.

PART FOUR

Qualitative Research Methods

10 Defining Qualitative Research

Since completing the research course, I have done a lot of research for my job. For instance, when I am doing the intake assessment on a client with alcoholism, we more or less go right into family history and then look for patterns of alcoholism within the family.

—Junior nontraditional research student

CHAPTER GOALS

Your major goals for this chapter are to:

- Understand qualitative research.
- Understand the similarities and differences in qualitative and quantitative research methods.
- Recognize selected qualitative research methods.
- Recognize similarities and differences between qualitative research methods and social work practice.

Introduction

Earlier in this book you learned about quantitative research—a method for finding answers to questions and acquiring knowledge and understanding about a phenomenon using numbers and narratives to translate those numbers. This chapter explores qualitative research—a means of acquiring information through interviewing, observing, and sharing in people's experiences and by examining archival materials and artifacts. Narratives of interviews and observations, rather than numbers, are analyzed in qualitative research. Interviewing and observing clients for qualitative research is similar to interviewing and observing clients conducted by social work interns and human service personnel. Narratives are written based on clients' stories detailing their perspectives of their past and present experiences, their hopes and plans.

Information gathering by social workers and qualitative researchers also have similarities. Collecting data from clients and research participants, for example, occurs in natural settings, such as their homes, a hospital, a residential facility, a rehabilitation center, a foster home, a long-term care facility or a home for people with AIDS. Social service interviews may also take place in an office or a neutral setting like a restaurant or a park. Moreover, social workers examine archival records—client case files, academic records, and court and hospital files—as part of the assessment process. Likewise, qualitative researchers evaluate these types of documents in carrying out their investigations.

This chapter defines qualitative research and describes the goals of qualitative research. It then discusses some differences and similarities between qualitative and quantitative research methods and presents selected methods for conducting qualitative research investigations. Excerpts from "Care of the Dying by Physicians-in-Training" illustrate the chapter's main concepts. This study was selected because of social workers' connection with geriatricians through their work in long-term care facilities and hospitals, because gerontological social work is an expanding field, and because of the interdisciplinary nature of social work practice.

Generalist Case Study: Excerpts from "Care of the Dying by Physicians-in-Training" (Muller, 1995)

Research Focus

This study grew out of my participation in a research project that was designed to examine how first-year residents in internal medicine learn the responsibilities of caring for dying patients as part of routine clinical instruction and to develop recommendations for instruction in terminal care (Koenig 1985). I was particularly interested in exploring four areas: (a) the professional socialization of medical trainees and how they construed their actions and made sense of their world, (b) the day-to-day practices of resident physicians with terminally ill patients and the meanings they gave to their work, (c) the process of decision making about the type and level of medical interventions to make with terminally ill patients as they neared death, and (d) the ways in which the sociocultural context of the teaching hospitals influenced the resident physicians' management and treatment of dying patients.

This study was carried out with postgraduate resident physicians who were being trained in internal medicine in an urban academic medical center. The study focused specifically on their activities while they were on the medicine services of three teaching hospitals—a tertiary care center, a public county hospital, and a Veterans Administration hospital. Although residents from each year of the three-year residency program participated in the research, the primary emphasis was on first-year residents. This year is considered to be the most stressful of training, as well as the most significant for the socialization of young physicians, because it is during this year that physicians begin to establish patterns of behaving, interacting, and thinking that are often carried with them into practice (Mumford 1970). . . . To observe the activities of residents in their natural context, I became an unofficial member of 13 teams during the research period. When I joined each team, the senior resident was asked to identify the patients being taken care of by that team who were highly likely to die within the next few months. Over the course of the research, 55 patients were so identified. I followed the care of these patients during the course of their hospitalization until their eventual death or discharge from the hospital or until I had to leave the research site. The events in the lives and deaths of these patients as circumscribed by their hospital stay, the practices and understandings of the residents regarding these patients, and the decisions made about their treatment became the focus of this research.

Why Participant Observation?

Participant observation was selected for this investigation because it appeared to be the most appropriate research strategy for exploring the areas described above. I believed there would be several advantages to using this approach in the investigation of a group of physicians. First, participant observation, by definition, refers to research that is done with members of a cultural group in their natural setting, as they go about their everyday lives. In this research, I wanted to understand the daily experiences of physicians-in-training with dying patients: their activities, decisions, perceptions, formal and informal discussions, and their interactions with other medical personnel, as well as with patients. I was interested not only in what the doctors said they did with this population of patients, but what they actually did. Submerging myself for a period of time in the participants' world appeared to be the most effective way to gain this type of intimate and grounded knowledge.

Second, I wanted to examine how the sociocultural context of the training hospital influenced the activities and decisions of the residents regarding patients highly likely to die. . . .

A third reason for selecting participant observation lay in my interest in changes over time. I was curious about the transitions between the statuses of living, dying, and death, and I wanted to see how physicians' tasks, activities, perceptions, and approaches to patients changed as patients moved toward death. . . .

Participant observation was also appealing because there was a limited amount of previous research to guide this study. In studies where relatively little is known about the topic, field research has been used effectively to identify research problems and generate hypotheses. . . .

Finally, I chose participant observation as a methodology because of its inherent flexibility (Marshall and Rossman, 1989). As with other qualitative research methods, participant observation permits the research questions to be modified and refined as the problem is clarified. At the same time, its flexibility allows for the collection of data that could not be anticipated beforehand. Because I did not fully know the nature of the problem or its boundaries, I felt that being bound to a tightly preconceived research design would be a disadvantage for both the process and product of the research endeavor.

Research Process

Entering.   . . . In the study described here, the first steps in gaining access involved getting approval from the director of the residency program and the chiefs of the medicine services of the affiliated

(continued)

Case Study   *Continued*

teaching hospitals. Once this permission was secured, it was still necessary to gain permission from the residents themselves. . . . Upon receiving their consent, I met with team members the first day of a new rotation to explain my purpose and to request approval to join the team. I explained that I would not be talking to patients or engaging in clinical work because I was not medically trained, but that I would be observing team members and asking them questions at times when it would not interfere too much with their work. . . .

While conducting the research, I encountered few barriers to joining house staff teams or to observing the many interactions and activities on the medical services. . . . I fell into an already established role category on the team—that of student. . . . Participant observers have found that one of the best ways to learn about another culture is to be a neophyte in that culture. This allows the researcher to watch, listen, ask questions that appear stupid or obvious, and try out their hunches about what they are seeing. I wanted the residents to teach me about their world. . . . So I adopted the accoutrements of a trainee—a white coat, a packet of index cards in my pocket, a busy demeanor— and blended into the mass of white-coated figures on the house staff team.

Gaining Trust.   . . . In the early days of fieldwork, my contacts with many of the house staff were relegated, for the most part, to discussions of their daily work. I had difficulty eliciting their in-depth reflections about much of anything else. At about the same time that I started being invited to team parties, however, I noticed a shift in the type and depth of information they shared. Many of the residents were more willing to discuss their perceptions of, and reactions to, events and individuals. They also became more open about their personal dilemmas, professional struggles, and the stresses caused by their training. With time, I became trustworthy in the eyes of my informants and they became more willing to reveal more of themselves. In this case, trust that emerged yielded a richer, more multilayered, and more meaningful data set.

Constructing an Ethnographic Record

Observing.   . . . In this setting, I knew I could not act as full participant because of the nature of this research, which involved analyzing the work of individuals engaged in specialized tasks in which I had no training. Beyond that, I found that the type of participant–observer role I adopted shifted with the demands and flow of the fieldwork as well as with my own degree of comfort and confidence. In the early days of fieldwork, when everything felt overwhelming and incomprehensible, I assumed a fairly passive presence on the house staff team. . . . As the environment became more familiar, people came to know and trust me, and I became more comfortable in my role as researcher in this setting— my role became more participatory. . . . For more than a year, I followed teams while they made their daily rounds; watched residents' interactions with patients, colleagues, and attending physicians; attended conferences with them; shadowed individual team members as they carried out the tasks of patient care; and spent weekends and on-call nights in the hospital with them. . . .

Interviews and Conversations.   Both semistructured and unstructured interviews were incorporated into the research design to complement observational data. Semistructured interviews, which were audiotaped and transcribed, were conducted to ascertain residents' experiences and perceptions of the dying patients they were taking care of and of other patients they had heard about. In these interviews, study participants were encouraged to respond at length to questions and to discuss events or ideas that were important to them. Unstructured interviews with members of house staff teams also occurred informally throughout a day. These were left open-ended to allow informants the opportunity to express the details of their experience as they perceived it. . . .

Recording.   . . . I took notes as unobtrusively as possible in a small notebook that could easily fit in the pocket of my lab coat. If note taking felt too obtrusive, I made mental notes, and then quickly retreated to the restroom or a quiet corner where I jotted down as much as I could remember. Fieldnotes—the expanded and permanent account of these jottings—were written as soon as possible after an observation period. These notes formed the daily record of the activities and interactions observed, conversations heard, and impressions of the field setting and its actors. . . . Following Schatzman and Strauss (1973), notes were organized into three categories: observational, theoretical, and methodological. . . .

Analysis.   Using a "grounded theory" approach in which data collection and theory-building occur simultaneously (Glaser and Strauss 1967; Strauss 1987; Strauss and Corbin 1990), I began coding the data emerging in fieldnotes and transcripts of interviews while still engaged in fieldwork. . . . Because I was interested in residents' discussions about the resuscitation status of their patients (whether they should be resuscitated in case of cardiopulmonary arrest), I initially employed the general coding category of resuscitation status. It soon became apparent, however, that there were many aspects to the phenomenon of resuscitation that concerned the residents. I then expanded the research to examine how the decisions to administer or to withhold cardiopulmonary resuscitation were made, what conflicts emerged over the decision, what type of care was given to do-not-resuscitate patients, and the meaning of resuscitation and its withholding to the physicians. As the research progressed, I was also able to observe that under certain conditions, residents sometimes negotiated intermediate steps between full resuscitation and no resuscitation. Thus "slow" codes became a core category for analysis (Muller 1992).

Leaving.   As with entering, leaving was not a one-time event. I periodically stepped out of the field to gain perspective or to catch up on fieldnotes. Because so many individuals rotated in and out of these hospital settings, the residents found my periodic absences unremarkable. After 14 months, I felt I had reached what Glaser and Strauss (1967) call the point of "theoretical saturation"—when the data become repetitive and additional observations do not yield additional insights. This is a natural time to exit the field and I, following the many observers who leave the field at this point, ended my daily visits to the hospital to conclude the analysis and write the account. . . .

References

Glaser, Barney, and Anselm Strauss. 1967. *The Discovery of Grounded Theory.* Chicago: Aldine.

Koenig, Barbara. 1985. "The Responsibility of Medical House Officers Caring for Dying Patients. A Study of Clinical Education in Terminal Illness Care." A grant proposal to Academic Senate, University of California, San Francisco.

Muller, Jessica H. 1992. "Shades of Blue: The Negotiations of Limited Codes by Medical Residents." *Social Science and Medicine* 34:885–98.

Mumford, E. (1970). *Interns: From Student to Physician.* Cambridge, MA: Harvard University Press.

Schatzman, Leonard, and Anselm Strauss. 1973. *Field Research: Strategies for a Natural Sociology.* Englewood Cliffs, NJ: Prentice-Hall.

Strauss, Anselm. 1987. *Qualitative Analysis for Social Scientists.* Cambridge, England: Cambridge University Press.

Strauss, Anselm, and Juliet Corbin. 1990. *Basics of Qualitative Research.* Thousand Oaks, CA: Sage.

Note: From "Care of the dying by physicians-in-training," by J. H. Muller, 1995, *Research on Aging, 17*(1), 65–88. Reprinted by permission of Sage Publications.

What Is Qualitative Research?

> *Activity 1.*   After reading this section, think about your experiences interviewing and observing clients. Can you relate those experiences to any qualitative research designs described in this chapter? If yes, explain the similarities and differences between them.

Qualitative research methodologies are broad, ranging from designs where interviewers use semi-structured questions constructed by the researcher, to designs that elicit all responses from the participant's experience without posing questions, to researchers participating in the lived experiences of people, to observing participants from a distance. Videotaping or analysis of written materials—stories, histories, journals, letters, documents, and books—are also methods of acquiring knowledge using qualitative research. Muller (1995), in the case example, used a combination of these methods. She was a participant–observer, although not a full participant, when she ". . . adopted the accoutrements of a trainee—a white coat, a packet of index cards in my pocket, a busy demeanor—and blended into the mass of white-coated figures on the house staff team" (p. 73). Muller also employed both semistructured and unstructured interviews to learn about residents' experiences and perceptions of the dying patients. Interviews, observations, and the sharing of participants' experiences happen in the participants' natural setting such as their homes, community, and places of employment. Data collected in interviews and through observations are recorded and analyzed using narratives and words.

Some approaches to qualitative research are case studies, ethnography, phenomenology, oral history, feminist research, hermeneutics, and focus groups. Focus groups, feminist research, oral history, and ethnography are the qualitative methods described here. Berg (2001) and Denzin and Lincoln (2000) point out that qualitative research methodologies have not been at the forefront in social science research, have met with resistance in these disciplines, and are often criticized for being nonscientific, invalid, personal, and biased, reflecting the politics involved in research. This perception of qualitative methodologies seems to be changing gradually as qualitative research gains respect and is used by more researchers and doctoral students. It is not, however, the favored research methodology among doctoral programs and grant-giving foundations.

Goals of Qualitative Research

The expected outcomes of your research, research questions, and research goals determine the type of research method that you choose, either qualitative or quantitative. Some goals of qualitative research are to:

■ Acquire in-depth information and provide detailed descriptions about a phenomenon using small or large samples.

■ Facilitate learning and understanding of how and why people behave, think, and interpret meanings in their lives. In other words, researchers strive to understand how participants interpret the significance and value of their lives from their own perspective.

■ Allow flexibility in designing research projects, which promotes understanding and new viewpoints on common questions and problems (Abel & Sankar, 1995; Ambert, Adler, Adler, & Detzner, 1995). Muller, in the case example, changed her original focus from the decision-making process relative to the treatment of terminally ill patients, because it was too narrow, to a closer examination of how and why residents determined that patients were dying.

■ Develop theories based on data collected to explain behavior, situations, or circumstances.

■ Identify relationships among themes identified in the data. In previous chapters you learned that quantitative researchers are interested in identifying relationships among variables and not relationships among themes that emerge in the data.

Qualitative and Quantitative Research Methods

Qualitative research and quantitative research methods are two different approaches to finding answers to questions, for describing people, and for understanding phenomena. Because students are often confused about differences and similarities in qualitative and quantitative research, they are explained in this section. These methods are not hierarchical, one approach is not easier than the other or superior to the other. Qualitative research methods may be used when the researcher wants to:

■ Explore a topic for which minimal or no data are available, to provide in-depth descriptions, to gain a deeper understanding, and to explain phenomena from participants' perspectives and to interpret data.
■ Capture the actual human experience from the participants' perspective.
■ Interact directly with the people being studied through interviews or observations.

Qualitative researchers rely on personal contact with participants by conducting in-depth interviews, observing participants, or sharing in their lives. They also study artifacts and written documents to arrive at an understanding of participants' worlds from their perspective. Data collected in interviews and through observations and participation are recorded and transcribed. These narratives and observations are the basis for qualitative data analysis. The qualitative researcher values equality in the researcher and participant relationship and flexible research designs. Qualitative designs are flexible because the design of the research can be changed after the study starts. Additional questions may be added or deleted after a few interviews, or the sample size may be decreased or increased. Besides having this flexibility, qualitative researchers, while valuing objectivity, accept subjectivity as part of the research process.

Both qualitative and quantitative research methods are empirical, ". . . relying on first-hand observation and data collection to guide findings and conclusions" (Padgett, 1998, pp. 3–4). Organized, planned research designs also define empirical research studies.

Some differences in qualitative and quantitative research relate to objectivity, generalizability of study results, relationships with study participants, the use of theory, and the data collection and analysis procedures. While qualitative researchers value objectivity, they recognize the subjective nature of qualitative research. On the other hand, a goal of quantitative researchers is evaluating the objectivity of data. Tutty, Rothery, and Grinnell

(1996) explain that quantitative researchers use research questions with measurable variables and standardized measuring instruments while qualitative researchers rely on more subjective data collection methods, such as participants' stories, and analysis methods to understand participants' personal experiences. In striving to maintain objectivity, quantitative researchers, who gather data using mostly mailed and telephone survey data collection methods, have minimal face-to-face contact with research participants in striving to maintain objectivity. Qualitative researchers interact with participants through in-depth personal interviews, observations, and sharing in participants' experiences, and they acknowledge their biases and values and those of the participants that may be reflected in their studies.

Quantitative researchers are interested in generalizing findings to others in the population from which the sample was drawn. While it is possible to generalize from some qualitative studies, in-depth understanding of each participant's reality, not generalizing, is the focus of qualitative research. Quantitative researchers use a deductive approach to test theories; qualitative researchers develop theories based on participants' stories, using an inductive approach. The use of numbers to describe findings in quantitative research contrasts with the words used in qualitative research. The flexibility of qualitative research designs is a significant difference with quantitative research. Figure 10.1 highlights some of the differences and similarities between qualitative and quantitative research methods.

Some researchers conduct only qualitative studies, others prefer quantitative research, and some engage in both research methodologies, often in the same study. In "Attitudes toward needle "sharing" among injection drug users: Combining qualitative and quantitative research methods," Carlson, Siegal, Wang, and Falck (1996) maintain that early in the AIDS epidemic, public health literature spread the word that intravenous drug users wanted to share needles with each other because needle sharing created special bonds among intravenous drug users. If intravenous drug users value sharing needles, then one role of prevention programs

FIGURE 10.1   Comparison of Qualitative and Quantitative Research Methods

Qualitative Methods	Quantitative Methods
An empirical research design	An empirical research design
Acknowledges that biases and values of participants and researcher exist in the study. Collects data through close personal involvement with participants.	Strives for objectivity of research findings by using, for example, representative samples, controlling for biases, and minimizing direct contact with research participants.
Focuses on attaining in-depth understanding of participants' lived experiences from participants' perspectives.	Focuses on generalizing study results to the population from which the sample was drawn and causal explanations.
Uses an inductive approach by developing theories based on participants' stories and observations.	Uses a deductive approach by testing theories.
Analyzes observations, words, written data, or narratives derived from interviews, observations, and archival data.	Analyzes numbers using mathematical and statistical procedures.

would be to devalue this sharing as a bonding experience, because needle sharing among intravenous drug users is one way that the HIV virus is transmitted.

Carlson, Siegal, Wang, and Falck first conducted an ethnographic study of needle sharing among injection drug users. The results of this study did not support information being disseminated by the public health agencies that intravenous drug users viewed needle sharing as an opportunity for developing attachments among their cohorts. Later, using quantitative research methods, the investigators reevaluated their initial qualitative findings and were able to validate the findings of their ethnographic study.

Although Carlson, Siegal, Wang, and Falck conducted two studies, a qualitative study first and then a quantitative study to confirm results of their ethnographic qualitative study, some researchers use both quantitative and qualitative approaches in the same study, as Romkens (1997) did in "Prevalence of wife abuse in the Netherlands: Combining quantitative and qualitative methods in survey research." With a representative sample of 1,016 women between the ages of 20 and 60, Romkens used semi-structured interview schedules for the qualitative portion of the study and a survey for the quantitative part. The research attempted to answer questions relating to prevalence, nature, physical and psychological consequences, help-seeking behaviors, and risk markers of wife abuse. In the article, however, Romkens focused on prevalence of wife abuse and mentions only briefly the type and severity of violence these women experienced. In both of these examples, the researchers used both qualitative and quantitative research methods to find answers to questions and to gain greater understanding.

Important Points about Qualitative Research

- Qualitative researchers focus on acquiring participants' stories about their lived experiences from their perspective.
- Data collection methods include in-depth interviews, observation, participation in people's lives in their natural settings and review and analysis of archival data.
- While they value objectivity, qualitative researchers acknowledge biases and subjectivity in their studies.
- Qualitative researchers emphasize personal contact and relationship building with participants.
- Data analysis in qualitative research studies is done using the words or narratives of participants and transcribed observations. Archival documents are also analyzed.
- There are significant differences in the qualitative and quantitative approaches to conducting research.

Selected Qualitative Research designs

Focus Groups

Activity 2.   As you read about focus groups, think about a client or a group of people in your community for whom it would be appropriate to convene as a focus group. On what topic would you want to collect data? What is the purpose for collecting the data?

Focus groups are a qualitative research method that ordinarily consist of six to eight people with similar backgrounds who are interviewed together by a trained moderator who poses preestablished, open-ended questions. The moderator, who is the facilitator, uses an interview guide to generate discussion from the group (Morgan, 1998; Greenbaum, 1998). Focus groups are used by researchers from diverse settings—academia, government and public agencies, and nonprofit and for-profit organizations. Greenbaum identifies three types of focus groups: (1) the full group consisting of 8 to 10 people, recruited because of certain similarities, and involved in a discussion lasting from 90 to 120 minutes; (2) the mini-group that consists of 4 to 6 persons, but otherwise is the same as a full group; and (3) the telephone group where participants convene for a telephone conference call for 30 to 60 minutes using a trained moderator.

There are also several appropriate uses of focus groups. Focus groups can be used for problem or goal identification, for planning to identify the most desirable way to achieve the goal, for implementation, and for assessment (Morgan, 1998). Morgan maintains that the four basic steps in a focus group project are planning, which includes anticipating major decisions; recruiting, which involves engaging participants; moderating, which incorporates presiding over the group discussions by asking questions and participating in the process; and analyzing and reporting results.

Besides illustrating one method for moderating focus groups, the following example highlights how researchers and policymakers can collaborate in the interest of clients and the public in general. In "Using qualitative data to inform public policy: Evaluating "Choose to De-Fuse," Levine and Zimmerman (1996) assert that public policies are often made without using research and research that is conducted frequently has limited value to public policy because of the questionable relationship between research and public policymaking. Levine and Zimmerman argue that evaluation can contribute to the public policy goal of finding ways to use "the media to prevent rather than promote youth violence" (p. 376).

Using focus groups as their qualitative research methodology, along with collaborative efforts, researchers and public policymakers evaluated the effectiveness of the Choose to De-Fuse media campaign designed to prevent youth violence in New York City. Focus group members consisted of 73 participants, age 8–24, who were divided into nine groups. Because of the youths' participation in the research, the evaluators had a better understanding of the youths' thinking about youth violence and the strengths and weaknesses of the media campaigns. Furthermore, the researchers created public service announcements capturing the attention of the youth that they were designed to benefit.

Marson and Powell (2000) provide another example of using focus groups to propose policy changes in their study of factors that influence welfare recidivism in a rural community. Some of the reasons that rural welfare recipients seek services again after termination are inadequate support systems, hostile attitudes and disrespect from TANF (Temporary Assistance for Needy Families) program workers and the general public, and apprehension about not being able to make it if they do not receive assistance (Marson & Powell).

Feminist Qualitative Research

There are multiple perspectives and definitions of feminist research (Esterberg, 2002; Olesen, 2000; Reinharz, 1992). Some researchers categorize feminist research as a qualitative research method (Padgett, 1998; Sherman & Reid, 1994). Other qualitative researchers classify feminist research as a method that is separate from but similar to qualitative research (Lindsey, 1997; Reinharz, 1992). Lindsey asserts that feminist research is similar to qualitative research in that both approaches emphasize experiences and voices of people and share a belief in many different realities (that there are different perspectives, beliefs, and lifestyles among diverse populations). Also, both qualitative research and feminist research acknowledge making the subjectivity of the researcher known throughout the research process and stress the significance of the researcher's responsiveness to participants (Lindsey, 1997). Feminist research methods identified by Reinharz include interview research, ethnography, survey research, experimental research, cross-cultural research, oral history, content analysis, case studies, action research, multiple methods research, and feminist research methods.

Feminist research is firmly fixed in a politics of oppression and change, with a vision for the future that eliminates privilege, hierarchy, and oppression (Davis & Srinivasan, 1994). Early feminist scholars are credited with helping change social science research, particularly traditional research's focus on White, middle-class, heterosexual women whose experiences are not necessarily representative of diversity among women, for example, women of color, lesbians, and women with disabilities (Esterberg, 2002). Thus, the increasing complexity in feminist research since the 1960s and the beginning of the second phase of the women's movement are evident in writings from women of color, gay/lesbian/queer theorists, postcolonial researchers, women with disabilities, standpoint theorists, and analysts (Olesen, 2000). According to Olesen, these writers increased the complexity of feminist research with their questioning of assumptions about the basis of and the methods of doing feminist research.

Experience, difference, and gender are additional crucial concepts that these feminist researchers illuminated. They created an imbalance in the notion of the feminist researcher as the all-knowing person capable of accessing women's lives and stories because they (the researchers) are women. These writings propelled feminist research to greater recognition and awareness of researcher characteristics, the influence of research on the researcher, and the inexcusable Whiteness in feminist research in Western industrialized societies. Furthermore, they brought to the forefront issues in globalization, such as unsafe and exploitative working conditions and the international sex trade, as topics for feminist research (Olesen, 2000). Feminist research's political agenda is about research for women that emphasizes strengths and empowerment.

The ethical issues that confronted Lindsey (1997) in her study on formerly homeless mothers were that some participants in her research were of a different race; they were African American. She recognized that Black women have had negative relationships with White women in social service agencies. She was also concerned about objectifying participants. Moreover, she writes that the women could have helped design the research, assisted in developing research questions, and provided feedback on a draft of the narrative. Besides lending credibility to her study, these actions would have given the women part ownership of the research.

Lindsey's story about conducting feminist research is significant because it deals with many of the issues you must consider when conducting qualitative research. Lindsey maintains that there were things that she could have done differently to give the women a sense of ownership of this research. This insight is important since qualitative investigators believe in equality between researcher and participant.

Oral History

Activity 3.   As you read this section, think about experiences that you have had listening to clients and writing up their stories and case histories. What kind of client histories have you written?

Oral communication was an important means of exchanging and preserving information in many societies, including those in ancient Africa. Community historians and storytellers were the keepers of this information. The African oral tradition continued during slavery in America and published accounts of some slave narratives are available.

Oral history is one area of historical research (Berg, 2000). Historical analysis generally is a method of discovering stories, descriptions, or narratives of what occurred in the past from either primary data or secondary data (Marshall & Rossman, 1999). It can be the gathering of personal historical information from people's memories by in-depth oral interviews. Data from interviews are recorded with a tape recorder or in written notes. Many of these transcripts, a rich source of history, remain unpublished in libraries (Fontana & Frey, 2000), and hundreds of audio oral history archives are available on the Internet for downloading. Oral history research respondents may have led ordinary lives or extraordinary lives; they may have experienced problematic lives or had minimal difficulties (Berg, 1998; Brown, 1997; Martin, 1995).

Social workers regularly conduct oral history interviews, and writing these interviews up into narrative form is often part of the assessment process.

Georgia Brown (1997) used oral history research to study the experiences of what some would call ordinary Black women in Louisiana. In her "Oral History: Louisiana Black Women's Memoirs," many of the Louisiana women, though initially reluctant, shared with the author their experience living in segregated communities during the Depression, the discrimination they experienced in both their personal lives and their employment, and how they coped with that discrimination. The researcher's interviews with these women educated her about the women's situation and increased her admiration for them. In qualitative research, the interviewers are the students and the participants are the teachers. Clearly, in this project, the women from Louisiana assumed the role of teacher and the researcher the role of student.

Ethnography

Activity 4.   Think about a time when you observed a client, other individuals, or a family. Also, reflect on a time when you participated in various activities as a part of your job or internship responsibilities in order to learn about another group. What was the purpose of your observations? What methods did you use to record your observations? What did you do with the data that you gathered?

Anthropologists and sociologists developed ethnography, also referred to as participant observation or field research, as a tool for understanding people from other countries. Ethnographic studies are no longer limited to the study of people from other countries; now its techniques are used by researchers from various disciplines to study people from a variety of cultures, nationally as well as globally. Interviewing, observing, and participating with people in their natural settings are goals of ethnographic researchers involved in extensive fieldwork. Living, interacting, and maintaining close contact with and observing people in their daily activities is critical to ethnography. Learning about people's lives from their own perspective or by conducting in-depth interviews develops the researcher's understanding of indigenous people and improves the researcher's ability to analyze these behaviors and actions.

Muller in the case example became an informal member of 13 teams during her 14-month research period. She observed their daily activities and interactions with other medical personnel and their decision-making. In her study, the participants' natural setting was the hospital. Her indigenous people were residents, who became her teachers.

According to Marshall and Rossman (1999), one strength of ethnographic interviewing is its concentration on learning about a culture directly from the natives' perspective. Learning from indigenous people allows for flexibility in framing a hypothesis and "avoids oversimplification of description and analysis of its rich narrative descriptions" (p.112). The researcher strives for a holistic study that encompasses both the views and interpretations of the people being studied, called the emic viewpoint, and the interpretations of the researcher, the etic perspective, which in the final project provides a holistic picture of the culture being researched (Creswell, 1998)

In the case example, Muller describes five benefits of using participant observation in her study of the experiences of postgraduate, first-year residents in internal medicine. They were "flexibility, the view of the insider, context, the quality of 'being there,' and process." These benefits allowed Muller to provide a detailed account, through narrative, of the residents' experiences caring for dying patients.

There are weaknesses to this approach, according to Marshall and Rossman (1999). They include the possible imposition of the ethnographer's values, lack of representation of people from the culture among participants leading to flawed analysis, and participants' reluctance to contribute and dishonesty endangering the study. The skill of the researcher highly influences a successful ethnographic study.

Important Points about Selected Qualitative Research Methods

- Focus groups consist of small groups of people with similar backgrounds who are convened by a facilitator to identify problems or goals for program implementation or for assessment purposes.
- Feminist qualitative research encompasses a broad spectrum of approaches to research, including ethnography, survey research, case studies, and action research.
- Oral history is a form of historical research used for discovering stories, descriptions, or narratives of what occurred in the past from primary data or secondary data (Marshall & Rossman, 1999). It involves gathering personal historical information orally via in-depth interviews about people's memories.
- Ethnography is the study of cultures using observation, participation, or in-depth interviews with a goal of understanding and interpreting the lived experiences of people in their own environment from their perspective. It analyzes these behaviors and actions through description and interpretation.

Qualitative Research and Social Work Practice

> *Activity 5.*   Now that you have been introduced to methods for conducting qualitative research, think about your work with clients at your internship or your job. Describe the practice skills you use that are similar to those applied in qualitative research designs.

Qualitative research and social work practice have much in common. As you guide in-depth interviews and observe clients in their environments, you are also improving your qualitative research skills. Qualitative research develops and refines skills utilized in direct social work practice. So, both qualitative researchers and social work practitioners use similar skills, knowledge, and activities.

Skills Needed by Practitioners and Qualitative Researchers

Effective communication skills.   Muller in the case study communicated with residents throughout the research project and with the residency program directors and the chiefs of the medicine services of affiliated teaching hospitals. She also explained the study to the senior resident and the attending physician. Social workers communicate with families, coworkers, and others in carrying out plans for working with clients.

Engagement skills.   Muller assumed various roles that helped establish rapport with the residents. One role was that of go-fer, running errands for residents; another was group historian, keeping daily notes on patients that were often shared with residents. She believed the role of "sounding board" to be the most significant (Bosk, cited in Muller). Social workers use many different engagement techniques to establish effective working relationships with clients.

Trust-building skills.   Initially, Muller had difficulty getting in-depth responses from the residents. Later, residents began inviting her to social events and sharing more intimate perceptions and responses about their lives as residents. Establishing trust in the social worker and client relationship often occurs after a successful engagement process.

Interviewing skills.   Muller engaged in both semistructured and unstructured interviews with residents. Social workers are accustomed to using diverse interviewing techniques to collect information from clients.

Activities Engaged in by Practitioners and Researchers

Information gathering using multiple sources. Interviews, observations, secondary sources (reports, letters, other documents).

Recording information. Social work practitioners record narratives in case files, logs, journals, process recordings, and in charts such as medical files. Researchers' main method of recording information is by tape recorder, but they also use logs and journals

Evaluating information. Questionnaires, reports, journal articles, books, and records, can all provide useful material.

Report writing. Practitioners write reports for case records, their supervisors, courts, administrative reviews, and multidisciplinary team meetings.

Working with and observing people in their natural settings, environments, or situations. Social workers and researchers work with people in their homes, in group homes, in foster homes, in adult facilities such as veterans hospitals, mental health facilitators and nursing homes.

Using a theoretically based foundation. Qualitative researchers develop theories based on data collected from participants, and social workers use theories to inform and guide practice.

Disseminating information. Social workers disseminate information, with client consent, to their supervisors and to other professionals who are working with the client. Researchers disseminate information at professional conferences and in journals and books.

Knowledge Required of Both Practitioners and Researchers

There are parallels in conducting qualitative research and in providing direct services to people. When interviewing clients, observing clients, writing up reports, and performing other details of social work, social workers are engaging in activities and using skills and knowledge that are excellent preparation for performing qualitative investigations. On the other hand, when researchers undertake qualitative research, they are strengthening their skills for direct service provision. To be successful as a social worker or as a researcher, it is necessary to have a:

- *Basic understanding of human behavior.*

- *Knowledge of and respect for diversity among people.*

- *Knowledge and awareness of own values, attitudes, and biases.*

Important Points about Social Work Practice and Qualitative Research

- Both social workers and qualitative researchers require communication, engagement, interviewing, and trust-building skills.
- Both social workers and qualitative researchers engage in data collection, recording, evaluating, and analyzing information, and report writing in carrying out their roles as researchers and practitioners.
- Both social workers and qualitative researchers use specific knowledge to inform practice and research.

Human Diversity Issues in Defining Qualitative Research

The diversity of participants must be taken into consideration when conducting qualitative research just as it is with quantitative research. A major difference is that with qualitative

research the researcher, in most instances, makes personal contact with participants. Therefore, the researcher must be aware, at all times, of the impression being made by verbal and
nonverbal communication, dress, and the attitude that the researcher brings to the environment
of the participant. Researchers dealing with groups that are different from them in gender,
religious preference, age, political affiliation, or sexual orientation must be aware how those
differences influence the participants and the research process. Qualitative researchers are in
key positions to strive for eliminating human oppression, helping empower people, and assisting people in enhancing their human potential.

Ethical Issues and Biases in Defining Qualitative Research

As with quantitative research, research with human subjects must be carefully considered. A
statement of informed consent (see Chapter 2) should be prepared for the signatures of participants. When the qualitative research involves working face-to-face with participants, be aware
of your nonverbal communication, biases, and attitudes. In focus group research there are
other ethical matters to bear in mind:

- Promising confidentiality on privacy issues.
- Assuring that the research sponsor protects group members' privacy.
- Preventing overdisclosure when group members already know each other.
- Dealing with stressful topics.
- Setting boundaries before the focus groups begin.
- Protecting the privacy of those sponsoring the research (Morgan, 1998).

If you have already taken the social work methods course that includes social work with
groups, you are aware that these same principles apply when you are providing client services
within a group setting. In both the research process and in group work, ethical issues should be
clarified, both verbally and in writing, prior to beginning the research.

WRITING STRATEGY

From your own experience, choose a topic or outcome you wish to explore or a perspective you wish
to understand. In a two-page paper explain:

1. Why you would use qualitative research for this topic.
2. Which qualitative research method would be the most appropriate to use and why?
3. How could you apply your research to social work practice in order to change behaviors or
   situations?

LEARNING ACTIVITY

Conduct an oral history interview with a grandparent, great grandparent, or another older person
about a topic of interest to you about which you believe the interviewee is knowledgeable.

INFORMATION TECHNOLOGY FOR DEFINING QUALITATIVE RESEARCH

1. In this chapter examples were provided on how qualitative and quantitative research methods can be used together. "Code-A Text" is software that can be used to integrate qualitative and quantitative research methods.

2. Visit these sites for more information on the use of computers with qualitative research:

   www.qualisresearch.com
   www.ualberta.ca

Important Points from Chapter 10

- Qualitative research methods focus on acquiring participants' stories about their lived experiences in their environments and from their perspective using in-depth interviews, observation, participant observation, and analysis of archival documents.
- Qualitative researchers strive for understanding the experiences of people from their perspective and analyzing those experiences using description and interpretation.
- Qualitative researchers value direct personal contact with informants where they assume the role of learner and the research participants take on the role of teachers.
- Qualitative researchers acknowledge that both subjectivity and bias may exist in their studies and that they value equality in the participant and researcher relationship.

REFERENCES

Abel, E. K., & Sankar, A. (1995). Introduction: The uses and evaluation of qualitative research. *Research on Aging, 17*(1), 3–7.

Ambert, A., Adler, P. A., Adler, P., & Detzner, D. F. (1995). Understanding and evaluating qualitative research. *Journal of Marriage and the Family, 57,* 879–893.

Berg, B. L. (2001). *Qualitative research methods for the social sciences (*4th ed.). Boston: Allyn & Bacon.

Brown, Georgia W. (1997). Oral history: Louisiana Black women's memoirs. In K. M. Vaz (Ed.) *Oral narrative research with Black women.* Thousand Oaks, CA: Sage.

Carlson, R. G., Siegal, H. A., Wang, J., & Falck, R. S. (1996). Attitudes toward needle "sharing" among injection drug users: Combining qualitative and quantitative research methods. *Human Organization, 55*(3), 361–369.

Creswell, J. W. (1998). *Qualitative inquiry and research design: Choosing among five traditions.* Thousand Oaks, CA: Sage.

Davis, L. V., & Srinivasan, M. (1994). Feminist research within a battered women's shelter. In E. Sherman & R. J. Reid (Eds.), *Qualitative research in social work.* New York: Columbia University Press.

Denzin, N. K., & Lincoln, Y. S. (Eds.). (2000). *Handbook of qualitative research* (2nd ed.). Thousand Oaks, CA: Sage.

Esterberg. K. G. (2002). *Qualitative methods in social research.* Boston: McGraw-Hill.

Fontana, A., & Frey, J. H. (2000). The interview: From structured questions to negotiated text. In N. K. Denzin & Y. S. Lincoln (Eds.), *Handbook of qualitative research* (2nd ed.). Thousand Oaks, CA: Sage.

Greenbaum, T. L. (1998). *The handbook for focus group research* (2nd ed.). Thousand Oaks, CA: Sage.

Kelle, U. (1997). Theory building in qualitative research and computer programs for the management of textual data. *Sociological Research Online, 2*, 1–19. Retrieved April 2, 1999, http://kennedy.soc. surrey.ac.uk/socresonline/2/2/1.html.

Levine, I. S., & Zimmerman, J. D. (1996). Using qualitative data to inform public policy: Evaluating "Choose to De-Fuse." *American Journal of Orthopsychiatry, 66*(3), 363–377.

Lindsey, E. W. (1997). Feminist issues in qualitative research with formerly homeless mothers. *Afflilia, 12*(1), 57–75.

Martin, R. R. (1995). *Oral history in social work: Research, assessment, and intervention.* Thousand Oaks, CA: Sage.

Marshall, C., & Rossman, G. B. (1999). *Designing qualitative research* (3rd ed.). Thousand Oaks, CA: Sage.

Morgan, D. L. (1998). *The focus group guidebook.* Thousand Oaks, CA: Sage.

Muller, J. H. (1995). Care of the dying by physicians-in-training. *Research on Aging, 17*(1), 65–88.

Olesen, V. L. (2000). Feminisms and qualitative research at and into the millennium. In N. K. Denzin & Y. S. Lincoln (Eds.) *Handbook of qualitative research* (2nd ed.). Thousand Oaks, CA: Sage.

Padgett, D. K. (1998). *Qualitative methods in social work research: Challenges and rewards.* Thousand Oaks, CA: Sage.

Reinharz, S. (1992). *Feminist methods in social research.* New York: Oxford University Press.

Romkens, R. (1997). Prevalence of wife abuse in the Netherlands: Combining qualitative methods in survey research. *Journal of Interpersonal Violence, 12*(1), 99–125.

Sherman, E., & Reid, W. (Eds.). (1994). *Qualitative research in social work.* New York: Columbia University Press.

Tutty, L. M., Rothery, M. A., & Grinnell, R. M, Jr. (1996). *Qualitative research for social workers.* Boston: Allyn & Bacon.

11 Planning, Data Collection, and Analysis in Qualitative Research

Before doing the interview I was a little nervous, even though I knew the participant. However, during the interview I was no longer nervous and was very comfortable talking with her. She also seemed very relaxed and comfortable throughout the interview although she had the same expression (a serious one) throughout the interview. Her eyes lit up a lot when she talked, and her tone of voice was one of excitement about the class and interest in the interview and seeing the results.

—Junior research student

CHAPTER GOALS

Your major goals upon completion of this chapter are to be able to

- Plan a qualitative study.
- Gain entry to settings to conduct qualitative studies.
- Collect and analyze qualitative data.
- Disseminate study findings.

Introduction

Qualitative research methods meet particular needs, so researchers have specific reasons for selecting a qualitative design. A qualitative study is the choice when there is minimal or no information on a topic, when the research question asks how or why, when there is a desire to study people in their natural environments,when theory development is a goal, and when an in-depth description of the subject being researched is desired. Creswell (1998) adds that researchers select qualitative research when they have an interest in writing in a literary style, when adequate time and resources are available to collect and analyze enormous amounts of data, when audiences accept qualitative research, and when the researcher role is that of an active learner and not an expert.

Chapter 10 defined qualitative research and described some of the diverse qualitative research models. You learned what qualitative research is, the goals of qualitative research, different models for conducting qualitative research, the differences and similarities between qualitative and quantitative research methods, and similarities between social work practice and qualitative research. This chapter familiarizes you with the steps involved in planning a qualitative study and in collecting, analyzing, and disseminating qualitative research findings. It begins with portions of a focus group–based research study by Maureen Marcenko and Linda Samost on HIV-positive mothers, which illustrates chapter concepts. It also shows how practitioners can combine research and practice and use the results of their research as a basis for direct practice with clients and to advocate for change on behalf of clients. Selecting a topic and research questions, reviewing the literature, choosing research participants, and sampling are the stages in the planning process described in this chapter. The chapter also illustrates data collection procedures, such as participant observation and intensive interviewing, and elements involved in preparing for successful interviewing. Strategies for approaching participants and gaining entry into their environments, data analysis procedures, methods for confirming credibility of the study, and for disseminating findings conclude the chapter.

Generalist Case Study: "Living with HIV/AIDS: The Voices of HIV-Positive Mothers"

The study reported here was undertaken to investigate the experiences of HIV-positive mothers with the system of services designed to help them, how they cope with the infection, particularly as it relates to parenting, and their concerns, preferences, and plans for the future care of their children. A focus group method was selected because it is well suited for this type of exploratory research. A total of 40 HIV-positive mothers participated in six different focus groups. The issues that emerged from the data analysis revealed that, using systems theory, they could be logically classified by the type or level of system in which the issue was primarily located. The three system levels were (1) individual and family, (2) organizations and providers, and (3) policy and community. Within each of these categories, issues could be further delineated by whether they provided women with resources or presented them with additional stress. Conclusions and recommendations for providers are made based on the systems framework that gave structure to the results.

Key words: focus groups; HIV/AIDS; systems theory; women; children who have lost their parents to AIDS have been referred to as "AIDS orphans" in both the popular press and professional literature (Dane & Levine, 1994; Levine & Stein, 1994; Michaels & Levine, 1992; Ritter, 1996). There is no other group of children who have been categorized as "orphans" solely on the basis of the disease from which their mothers died. For example, children whose mothers die from cancer, a disease that kills more women ages 25 to 44 annually than AIDS (Centers for Disease Control and Prevention [CDC], 1996), are not referred to as "cancer orphans." The implication of the term "AIDS orphans" is that parents with AIDS have no plan or support system to provide for the care of their children in the event of their deaths. Although this may be the case for some families, it is not known how widespread this phenomenon is or to what extent HIV-positive mothers have given thought to and planned for the future care of their children.

Participant Recruitment

An objective of the project was to survey the broadest possible representation of HIV-positive mothers. Therefore, every effort was made to recruit women into the study who were not receiving services from agencies, as well as those who were known to the services system. A total of six focus groups were held at various sites in the city of Philadelphia. Three of the groups were conducted with women who were receiving services at outpatient health centers, one was held with an ongoing support group affiliated with a church, another was conducted with women who were enrolled in an outpatient drug treatment program, and one was held at a needle exchange program.

Women who attended the focus group at the needle exchange program also were recruited from two area shelters and by word-of-mouth. This group of women was targeted because most were active in their addiction and therefore less likely to be affiliated with a formal service system.

Focus Group Procedure

At each site, researchers described the focus groups as a discussion group where mothers who were HIV positive could talk about their experiences. It was further explained that women would be asked to share their experiences since diagnosis, particularly as it related to parenting and obtaining services. In addition, participants would have an opportunity to make recommendations about how to help parents who were facing similar challenges. A focus group guide was developed based on the following research questions:

- To what extent have mothers planned for the future care of their children?
- What are mothers' experiences, preferences, and needs around parenting and future planning?
- What have been their experiences with the service system?
- What changes should be implemented in the service system to better support families affected by HIV/AIDS?

We used a chronological approach to inquiry, with the questions designed to address five topic areas: (1) diagnosis, (2) initial response to diagnosis, (3) experiences with the social services system, (4) concerns about children, parenting, and future planning, and (5) ideas about how the system could better meet the needs of families.

All of the groups were co-facilitated by a white female with experience conducting qualitative research on women's health issues and, with one exception, by an African American man trained in group process and experienced in working with chemically dependent women. The duration of each group was about two hours. Women received $25, lunch, and two transportation tokens as compensation for their time. Informed consent was obtained before the meeting, and a brief form was completed with each participant's current living situation and age; and children's living situation, age, and HIV status.

(continued)

Case Study   *Continued*

Analysis

All of the focus groups were audiotaped and the tapes transcribed. The transcriptions were analyzed by two of the focus group leaders and the lead researcher for the project. The purpose of the analysis was to identify categories or themes related to the research questions. As such, the analysis was exploratory and used an ongoing recursive process of developing codes and hypotheses and seeing how they fit the data. Categories that emerged were labeled and continually reassessed to compare the properties and clarify the relationship of the properties to the categories. The researchers performed this process independently. In the final phase of analysis, the researchers compared and discussed the coded transcripts, and the portions of the text were selected to illustrate the themes identified.

Participant Characteristics

Forty HIV-positive mothers were involved in the six focus groups. The women were mostly African American (70 percent) and Latino (10 percent). In terms of housing, 27 lived in a home or apartment, six were living in drug treatment facilities, three were renting rooms, two lived on the street, and two lived in shelters. Participants had known about their HIV status for two months to 12 years. Half had been diagnosed between four and five years earlier. The women ranged in age from 23 to 54, and the average age was 34. They had between one and eight children, and a variety of child living situations were represented: with mother, grandmother, father, or other relative, in foster care, or with adoptive parents. Ten participants had children living with HIV.

Results

The issues that emerged from the data analysis were touched on in each group, although groups gave varying degrees of emphasis to the concerns. Further examination of the issues revealed that, using systems theory, they could be logically classified by the type or level of system in which the issue was primarily located. The three system levels were (1) individual and family, (2) organizations and providers, (3) policy or community. Within each of these categories, issues could be further delineated by whether they provided women with resources or presented them with additional stress. The benefit of this conceptualization is that it accounts for the stresses HIV-positive mothers experience, as well as the personal, familial, and community strengths and resources they use to help lessen the effect of these stresses.

Individual and Family

Understandably, the issues that women discussed most frequently, both in terms of stresses and resources, were individual or family focused. The participants were most concerned about whom to disclose the diagnosis to, when and if to tell their children, how to cope with feelings of guilt and anger about a lifestyle that contributed to contraction of the infection, and general concerns about parenting and addiction.

The resources they drew on to cope with these stresses included spirituality, their own inner strength, positive thinking, and support from family and friends. Both stresses and the ability to cope were influenced by the physical and mental health of the women. The degree to which women had planned for the future care of their children varied and was dependent on a number of factors.

Disclosure. Who, when, and what to share about her diagnosis was an issue that each woman struggled with, some more than others. Some women automatically told important people in their lives. One woman said, "I reached out and asked for the help that I needed then and there, and I immediately got support groups together for myself. From my reaching out and asking others for help, it helped me and it helped others who needed it too."

Decisions to disclose were affected by the anticipated reaction, what other people had experienced, and the woman's level of acceptance of her HIV status. Many told those they felt they could trust, and some had not shared their diagnosis with anyone. One example is a woman who attended a church-based support group on Wednesday and said that Wednesday was the only day that she had AIDS. Her children did not know of her HIV status, and she lived her life "normally" the other six days. Another woman described her decision about disclosure:

> I didn't tell my family, I didn't tell anybody for real. I thought everybody would look at me all different (pushes plate away like it has germs) like that. If I wasn't going to be intimate with you I didn't see why I would have to tell you. And I carried that for three years. That was my attitude and that just made me go into my addiction more.

Future Planning

There was variation in the degree to which women had made formal plans for care of their children in the event of their death. Generally, there were four groups of planners:

1. those who had not thought about future planning;
2. those who felt that they were going to live and felt that planning for death would mark the end of life
3. those who were somewhere in the process, they had thought about it, discussed it with family members, and perhaps even contacted a lawyer
4. those who had finalized their arrangements, including a living will for themselves.

* * *

Providers and Organizations

Providers, services, and treatment regimens were a source of support and stress. Overall, women approached the social services system with a fair amount of trepidation. However, there were some experiences with providers and organizations that proved to be very helpful and supportive to women.

Diagnosis. With so much emphasis in the past decade on pre- and posttest counseling and attention to the process of testing and disclosing results, it was jarring to hear about the way in which most women learned that they were HIV positive. Women were told about their HIV status in clinics, hospitals, psychiatric wards, drug treatment facilities, prisons, and in private doctor's offices. The type of setting did not seem to affect the manner in which they were told. Largely, participants felt that they were given the news without support and compassion. When women were told by someone with whom they had a prior relationship, they felt greater compassion and caring from the provider than when the provider was not known to them:

> My story is very sad. I was in labor, and I was told as I was on the labor bed that I was HIV positive. And I feel as though, if they had waited until after I had the baby to give me some kind of pre-posttest counseling, I would not have transmitted the virus to my child. Because, when they told me, I began to push harder, and I wouldn't obey anything.

* * *

Medical Issues. Women's comments about medical providers in general indicated a lack of trust and comfort with practitioners, whom they described as disrespectful, insensitive, and unhelpful. They

(continued)

Case Study   *Continued*

recalled encounters with doctors and other providers who were abrupt, made them wait for long periods, did not answer questions, and were judgmental and confrontational about their lifestyle.

Some participants did describe exceptions to this type of experience. One woman, who attended a hospital-based medical clinic, was appreciative of the fact that all of her needs were met in one setting. Her doctor, in tandem with other clinic-based providers, met her medical needs and assisted with housing and planning for the future care of her children.

Policy or Community

There were two major systems level issues that women felt made it difficult for them to care for their children. The first was housing and the second was the way in which Children's Protective Services (CPS) functioned and the sometimes adversarial relationship they had with CPS workers. CPS is included as a systems level issue because its role and function are mandated by federal law. Both of these issues created stress in the lives of the participants, although there were some exceptions.

Children's Protective Services.   Among the women who had had experiences with CPS agencies, there were some words of appreciation, however, most women reported negative interactions. Many of the women felt that the role of CPS was to break families apart, rather than to keep them together. When considering how to plan for the care of their children in the event that they were unable, women were reluctant to rely on CPS workers, because they saw them as unreliable, inconsistent, and uncaring. As one woman put it, "If CPS is the only plan, why bother?" Others expressed similar feelings: "CPS snatched my baby. I cried for days and nights and I said whatever it takes to get my baby back." However, a few women felt that CPS had been helpful to them and their children: "I'm glad to have CPS in my life. I was doing drugs and I wasn't looking after [them]. One way or another you do neglect your children . . . but I'm blessed that I have CPS.

Recommendations

The results of this study demonstrate the need to understand the experience of living with HIV/AIDS as a complex phenomenon that is not uniform among women. The mothers who participated in the focus groups described a range of responses to living with HIV and varying types and levels of coping resources. They were also at different stages in the process of preparing for the future care of their children.

Despite the range in response to HIV/AIDS, there were some dominant themes that can provide professionals with guideline[s] when working with mothers who are HIV infected. The conclusions and recommendations flow logically from the systems framework of resources and stresses that gave structure to the findings.

Conclusion

The women in this study confront the same problems experienced by many low-income mothers in urban settings—discrimination and oppression, sometimes at the hands of well-meaning professionals, lack of access to quality health care, substance abuse, inadequate housing, and a child welfare system that often fails them. In addition to these issues, this group of mothers is living with a deadly virus that stigmatizes them and their children, a fact evidenced by the term "AIDS orphans." Despite these tremendous burdens, the women in this study were focused primarily on living their lives in a positive way rather than on dying. Furthermore, they wanted professionals to provide services in a respectful, nonjudgmental manner that helped them and their families have better lives. With improved treatment, the life expectancy of people infected with HIV has increased. The social work profession should focus its resources on improving conditions and opportunities for low-income families, while recognizing that the situation is exacerbated for families affected by HIV/AIDS.

References

Centers for Disease Control and Prevention. (1996). Update: Mortality attributable to HIV infection among persons aged 25–44 years: United State[s], 1994. *Morbidity and Mortality Weekly Report, 45*(6), 121–125.

Dane, B. O., & Levine, C. (1994). *AIDS and the new orphans: Coping with the death.* Westport, CT: Auburn House.

Levine, C., & Stein, G. L. (1994). *Orphans of the HIV epidemic: Unmet needs in six U.S. cities.* New York: Orphan Project.

Michaels, D., & Levine, C. (1992). Estimates of the number of motherless youth orphaned by AIDS in the United States. *JAMA, 268,* 3456–3461.

Ritter, J. (1996, May 7). AIDS will "orphan" 3,500 kids here by 2001, study says. *Chicago Sun-Times,* p. 12.

Maureen O. Marcenko, Ph.D., ACSW, is associate professor, School of Social Work, University of Washington, 4101 15th Avenue, Seattle, WA 98105-6299; e-mail: mmarcenk@u.washington.edu. Linda Samost, BS, is a self-employed consultant in Philadelphia. This research was funded by a Ryan White grant from the City of Philadelphia to the AIDS Law Project and the Circle of Care. The authors thank Steve Ridley and Rashidah Hassan, who assisted with the focus groups, Karen Hirschman for her assistance with the literature, and the mothers who shared their stories.

Note: From "Living with HIV/AIDS: The voices of HIV-positive mothers," by M. O. Marcenko & L. Samost, 1999, *Social Work, 44*(1), 36–45. Reprinted with permission of the National Association of Social Workers, Inc.

Planning a Qualitative Study

Choosing a Topic

Choosing a topic or issue on which you would like more detailed information is the first step in designing qualitative research. (Also, review Chapter 4, *Selecting a Problem for Investigation.*) An inductive approach is usually used with qualitative research. Recall from Chapter 1 that working inductively means that you select a topic based on observations of a specific phenomenon and that as the research progresses, you develop theories and generalizations based on the research. For example, Marcenko and Samost in the article profiled in the beginning of this chapter were interested in HIV-positive mothers' experiences with social and medical services, how the women dealt with the disease, and the impact that their health status had on their relationship with and planning for their children. Marcenko and Samost convened focus groups to answer their questions and perhaps to use study results to add to existing theories about women and HIV/AIDS. The theories that developed facilitated understanding of the phenomenon that they were studying.

When formulating ideas for a research subject, think about topics of interest to you. Through the years, students in the social research methods course have chosen topics about which they know nothing, a little, or a lot. They select problems of concern to their field practicum supervisors or to themselves, personal topics relating to their children, their parents, or other relatives, or phenomenon that arouse their curiosity. Some problems came from class discussions; others from local or national news stories; and some from the literature. Religious melancholy, child abuse, elder care, anorexia, suicide among gay and lesbian youth, rap music, and death from breast cancer are just a few of the topics students have selected. Just remember, when researchers, including student researchers, select a topic that is interesting to them, they are more committed to investigating the subject.

One student, whose mother died from breast cancer when the student was in late adolescence, was interested in the effects of a mother's death from breast cancer on surviving daughters when they enter early adulthood. How did they cope with decisions about marriage, childbearing, and their risk of breast cancer? Should they marry and have children knowing that they are at higher risk for breast cancer? She selected her topic, she began developing research questions directly related to her subject.

Developing Research Questions

You have selected a topic. Now it is time to decide on a research question or questions. (Review Chapter 4 for more information on writing research questions.) Research questions, for the most part, determine the type of research strategy to use. They pose a question about one or more ideas that you want to answer by conducting research. Because it guides you through the research process, the research question must be clearly stated. In qualitative research designs, research questions frequently begin with how or what. Marcenko and Samost's questions in the case example are "what" questions:

- To what extent have mothers planned for the future care of their children?
- What are mothers' experiences, preferences, and needs around parenting and future planning?
- What have been their experiences with the service system?
- What changes should be implemented in the service system to better support families affected by HIV/AIDS?

If you choose to review the literature before conducting interviews or observing the participants, the literature will help you clarify and refine your research question. Later, you can change the research question and the research topic if they are a poor fit or inappropriate for the study setting. Remember that in qualitative research, your question could change as you interview informants; qualitative research designs are flexible. Research questions may be theoretical, concentrated on a certain population or class of people, or site specific, that is, relating to a unique program or organization. Research on theoretical questions can be undertaken in a variety of settings and with diverse samples. Research questions that focus on a specific population or class of people can be studied in different locations (Marshall & Rossman, 1999), and unlike quantitative research questions, do not ask about relationships between variables.

The Literature Review

There is disagreement in the field about whether a literature review should be conducted for qualitative research. If the decision is made to review the literature, there is then further disagreement about whether the review should be conducted before, during, or after the interviews are completed or simply be ongoing. Some argue against reviewing the literature or reviewing it too soon because of concerns about their work being influenced by that of other researchers. In "Living with HIV/AIDS: The Voices of HIV-positive Mothers," the authors did conduct a literature review for their qualitative focus group study. Among the reasons that researchers review the literature are to assess the existing research on the topic being considered, to help develop and refine the research questions and problem statement, and to identify gaps in the literature relative to the research topic. The recommendations for further research sections of research reports can direct the researcher to topics on which little research has been done. Existing research reports can also help researchers establish a rationale for the significance of their study.

The type of qualitative approach influences the amount of literature that is used. For example in ethnographic studies, literature on a cultural concept or a critical theory is introduced early in the study design. On the other hand, in grounded theory, case studies, and phenomenological studies, the literature is used less often to introduce the study (Creswell, 1994). Creswell outlines criteria and method type for using literature in a qualitative study:

- Any type of qualitative study can use the literature in the study's introduction to frame the problem. Thus, some literature must be included.

- Studies, such as ethnographies, with compelling theory and literature background at the beginning of the study can include a literature review section, which readers knowledgeable about quantitative methods may find acceptable.

- All types of qualitative designs, but mainly grounded theory, can include the literature at the end of the study when it becomes the basis for comparing and contrasting study findings. When used in this manner, the literature assists rather than guides the researcher after patterns or categories are identified. See Chapters 4 and 5 for additional discussions on literature reviews.

Selecting Participants

Activity 1. After reading this section, locate four journal articles in social work and social work–related journals that used qualitative research designs. What methods did the researchers use in selecting participants?

Activity 2. Read the *Code of Ethics* of the National Association of Social Workers that can be found on NASW's web site. What does the section on scholarship and research require of the social worker who is engaged in scholarly inquiry?

You have chosen a research topic, decided on research questions, and conducted a literature review (if you chose to). With these tasks completed, you can start selecting study participants. The first step in this process is sampling. Sampling involves choosing people or having people self-select to share their life histories about a topic of interest to the researchers. Some researchers use documents and artifacts for analysis instead of interviewing or observing people. Snowball sampling and purposive sampling are also used, but random sampling and representativeness of participants is not a major concern in qualitative sampling.

Glesne (1999) describes seven of Patton's purposeful sampling strategies. These methods are typical case sampling, extreme or deviant case sampling, homogeneous sampling, maximum variation sampling, snowball (chain), or network sampling, and convenience sampling. Typical case sampling emphasizes the ordinary or normal; extreme or deviant case sampling goes the other way, choosing cases that deviate from the norm. Homogeneous sampling selects participants that are similar in order to make in-depth descriptions of subgroups. Maximum variation sampling selects from heterogeneous populations in search of commonalities across the diversity. Snowball (chain or network) sampling locates potential participants from people who know people with the qualifications the researcher seeks. Convenience sampling chooses participants simply because they are available, although they may not meet the qualifications the researcher is searching for in participants.

Marcenko and Samost (1999) referred to participant recruitment, not sampling, in their participant selection process. These researchers recruited informants from several different sites, including needle exchange programs and area shelters. Participants were selected from these sites by word-of-mouth (snowball sampling), staff suggestions, or flyers describing the focus group. Some respondents may self-select if recruitment is done through Web sites, newspapers, or other media, such as the flyers that Marcenko and Samost distributed. Regardless of the selection process, Luborsky and Rubinstein (1995) writing about qualitative research in gerontology express concern about the need for clarity in qualitative research sampling.

Determining sample size in qualitative research is not an easy task, and there are no established criteria. Before deciding on a sample size, the researcher needs to be clear about the direction in which the research is going, the methodology, perhaps grounded theory, oral history, or ethnography, and how much money and staff are available to conduct the research. People conducting quantitative studies face these same decisions. However, with qualitative research you can expand or limit your sample size as the research progresses.

Before selecting participants, think about whether you will reward them for taking part in the study. Rewards ranging from money to a copy of the study results may be given to participants. Be careful about appearing to be coercing potential informants with the kind of rewards that you provide, especially monetary rewards. Other rewards for participants could be the knowledge that the research will benefit other people or, if they are interested, a copy of the study results. Women in Marcenko and Samost's study were paid $25, given lunch, and two transportation tokens for their time. Most participants, however, are eager to share their stories with the researcher whether a reward is provided or not.

Important Points about Planning a Study

- When planning a study, select a topic about which you, your field placement, or your employer is interested in learning more.
- Devise clearly stated research questions that ask why and how questions and, for some types of research strategies, what questions.
- Qualitative researchers have the option of reviewing the literature before, during, or after a study or not at all.

■ Participant selection processes in qualitative studies do not focus on randomly selected representative samples, but on other methods, including purposeful and snowball sampling.

Collecting Data for Qualitative Studies

You have decided on a method for choosing informants for your study. Therefore, it is time to select a site and a data collection method. The purpose of data collection is to gather information based on the participant's frame of reference, standpoint, and perceptions of personal experiences. Participant observation and indirect observation, in-depth interviews, and review of documents are possible data collection methods in qualitative research. The decision to collect data by one of these methods depends on the kind of information you want.

Participant Observation

Participant observation is "also known as 'field observation,' 'qualitative observation,' or 'direct observation,'" (Lofland & Lofland, 1995, p. 18). In participant observation you become involved directly in the natural setting of the people being studied, taking part in all aspects of their daily activities, and experiencing their world from their perspective. Although visual observation is usually alluded to when describing participant observation, the senses of smell, hearing, feeling, and taste may also be used (Adler & Adler, 1994). During involvement as an observer, you establish and maintain a lengthy relationship with the people in their settings, meeting with participants before the study begins, deciding with them what your role will be and how it will be carried out. Before entering the field to collect data through observations, think about what could happen once you get there—will your entrance proceed smoothly or will there be barriers to overcome. Social workers also use observation as a data collection technique.

Social workers' observations of clients are recorded in case records, logs, process recordings, and journals to describe their thoughts after observing or interviewing clients. At your job or internship you observe clients' body language, their dress, and their interactions with their children. You may also be asked to observe children in the playroom as they interact with other children and their parents.

A field experience for one of my classes is attendance and participation in the services of a Black Baptist church. This visit is a new experience for the majority of the students. During the ceremony, we participate and observe. Our participation includes singing, clapping hands, praying, giving offerings, and socializing with the congregation after the service ends. Later, in class, we discuss our observations of the services. For example, we observed the congregation responding verbally to the minister as he preached. The congregation responded verbally with, "Amen," "Yes," and "Preach it brother." There was also a physical response as some members were shouting/dancing and standing, clapping their hands, and crying. Other observations were that the service lasted for about two hours, the congregation was friendly to the visitors, there was a high proportion of young adolescents and teenagers, and the service was lively with the drums, piano, and cymbals. Attending this church and participating in and observing the service is similar to participant observation in qualitative research. As a researcher conducting qualitative research, once you are prepared to enter the setting of the indigenous people, you can do so as an unknown investigator or a known investigator, as the students were (Lofland & Lofland, 1995).

Unknown Investigator.   As an unknown investigator, you disguise your identity to become a part of the group. You experience few barriers in accessing information, but you must rely only on your observations and cannot ask additional questions of the participants. Besides facing fewer obstacles as an unknown investigator, another advantage is that this approach is unobtrusive; it allows collection of data without intrusion into participants' lives. A disadvantage is that note taking is minimal, you must recall your observations when writing your notes away from the participants. Moreover, some researchers consider conducting unknown observation to be deception in research. If you decide to become an unknown observer, you should consult first with your colleagues and determine if there will be sufficient benefit to justify conducting research without disclosing your identity. Is this the only way of doing useful research? Unquestionably, the research should not be conducted if the only purpose is to deceive the participants. (See Chapter 2, *Ethical Issues in Social Research.*)

Known Investigator.   As a known observer, your identity as an investigator is revealed. You disclose to participants who you are and what you are trying to achieve and get informed consent from participants before joining them in their natural setting. Besides observing in the participants' natural setting, you may also, with the participants' consent, interview in a laboratory setting (Reid & Smith, 1989). For example, clinical social workers may observe families in therapy through a one-way window. Clients are observed but the clients cannot see the therapist. Known observers have more freedom in the setting, can ask more questions of the participants, and can also take notes. Another advantage of being a known researcher is that if you know the environment to be studied, your entry into that setting might be easier and more comfortable for you and the participants. The known observer can also be flexible in determining how much time to spend observing the participants. For example, on Saturdays the researcher may choose to observe all day and on Mondays and Thursdays only three hours.

One disadvantage of being a known observer is that the participants may be overly concerned about the research being conducted instead of interacting as they do normally. Additionally, your presence will inevitably have some effect on the participants.

Intensive Qualitative Interviews

> *Activity 3.*   As you read this chapter, think about your experiences interviewing clients. Describe the interviews that are similar to intensive qualitative interviews. What, for you, is the most difficult part of interviewing clients?

"Asking questions and getting answers is a much harder task than it may seem at first. The spoken or written word has always a residue of ambiguity, no matter how carefully we word the questions and report or code the answers. Yet, interviewing is one of the most common and most powerful ways we use to try to understand our fellow human beings" (Fontana & Frey, 1994, p. 361). There is diversity in qualitative interviews, which range from interviews with one person to group interviews to mailed interview guides to telephone interviews. Interviews can be structured, semi-structured, or unstructured and used for a variety of purposes. Some interviews are completed with one contact while others may take several contacts over time. Structured interviews are used less often in qualitative research. They are less flexible. They are also designed to have participants respond to the same questions, assume that questions are detailed enough for people to understand and to get the data the researcher is looking for (Berg, 2001).

Marcenko and Samost in their study of women living with HIV/AIDS interviewed 40 HIV-positive mothers in six different focus groups to gather data. Lofland and Lofland (1995) describe intensive interviewing as, ". . . a guided conversation whose goal is to elicit from the interviewee (usually referred to as the "informant") rich, detailed materials that can be used in qualitative analysis" (p. 18). Although you make direct personal contact with participants to conduct an in-depth interview, this type of interviewing does not involve active participation in their world. Yet, you listen to stories about their lives as they provide in-depth responses to questions.

Listening is a crucial skill for qualitative interviewers. After listening carefully to a participant's answer you can ask follow-up questions to evoke additional information or to clarify the respondent's story. Do not pretend to know informants' answers to your questions. Attempts at understanding participants' stories can be more complicated as you strive for individualizing interviews. Sufficient understanding of the interview may depend on whether the participant comprehends how the interviewer developed the questions and how participants frame their responses to these questions A certain level of understanding is achieved, though, when the interviewee and the interviewer, together, design the interview and arrive at a point where they both comprehend what is happening during the interview (Mishler, 1991). Working together, through repeated reworking of the questions, the researcher and the participant eventually arrive at mutually acceptable meanings and understandings of those meanings (Mishler), which make interviews more comfortable for the interviewer and interviewee and a more collaborative process. In-depth qualitative interviewing is similar to social worker–client interviews. Social workers use both observation and interviews in collecting data. Interviews with clients to collect data are usually held in your office, in the clients' natural environment such as their home or their place of employment, or in a neutral setting comfortable for the client.

Semi-structured Interviews. Semi-structured interviews are less formal than structured interviews but do not have as much flexibility as unstructured interviews. Semi-structured interviews use open-ended questions that are designed before the interviews take place. The researcher using semi-structured interviews poses predetermined questions as a guide to assure that specific information is gathered. There is more flexibility, for example, for probing for information, adjusting the questions as needed, and for participants' deviating from the questions than in structured interviews. All questions on the interview guide are asked of each participant although the researcher does not have a clue about what direction the responses will go after asking follow-up questions.

Unstructured Interviews. Unstructured interviews consist of open-ended questions that may be developed before the interview or as the interview evolves. The interview guide that uses open-ended questions could consist of one question or a series of questions. You enter the setting with specific ideas of the question(s) you want to ask to get participants' perceptions of their experiences; but since these questions are not set in stone, you can deviate from them or revise them, based on how the interview is proceeding. The participant here is the expert, and the investigator the learner. The researcher must be attentive and maximize listening skills during the interview. Moreover, when conducting qualitative interviews, it is important to be aware of your body language because body language often sends strong messages, either positive or negative.

Important Points about Collecting Data in Qualitative Research Designs

- Data can be collected through intensive interviews, by participating in the lived experiences of people, from existing records, and by observing people in their natural environments.
- Researchers can enter the field to collect data as known or unknown investigators, and both of these methods have advantages and disadvantages that must be considered.
- Qualitative research interviews are usually unstructured or semi-structured, with open-ended questions allowing for flexibility in asking questions and in participants' responses.

Preparing for the Qualitative Interview

Preparation before the Interview

You are ready to prepare for interviewing. You know how to plan a study, select participants, and have knowledge of different types of interviews and data collection methods. There are several activities that will help you prepare for qualitative interviews. Tutty, Rothery, and Grinnell (1996) recommend that you:

- Provide training for yourself and other interviewers to facilitate a research partnership with the interviewees.

- Keep a personal journal to record and track your thoughts, feelings, and reactions. It helps when you are sorting through raw data, and it also facilitates interpreting the interviewees' experiences.

- Get rid of your own biases and assumptions.

- Meet with experienced qualitative researchers for advice and guidance, read books, and seek out other information about qualitative interviewing.

- Pilot test the interviews, and ask yourself if this type of interview and these questions provide you with the quality and quantity of information to answer the research questions. The pilot test people will not be research participants.

- Prepare interviewees by telephone, and send a follow-up letter to request an interview. In both the telephone call and the letter explain the purpose of the interview and who is sponsoring the research. Also, identify and explain why the person is being asked to participate. Provide additional details such as what will be asked, agree on the location of the interview, and tell the approximate length and number of interviews. Ask for permission to audio- or videotape the session or to take notes. Explain how confidentiality will be protected.

■ Make sure that your tape recorder is working, that you know how to operate it, and that extra tapes and batteries are available.

Preparation for Gaining Access to Participants' Natural Environments

Gaining access to participants requires sensitivity, persistence, and knowledge about the people and setting that you plan to study. Interview people who, besides knowing something about the topic you are studying, are also living or have experienced that phenomenon. Referrals for potential participants may come from people or organizations that you know or gatekeepers, such as agency administrators, who may give permission for you to interview certain people. For example, Marcenko and Samost received assistance from the staff at one site and from a social worker at a different site when recruiting participants for the HIV-positive mother's research. When it is necessary to get agency approval to interview clients for studies, remember that clients and other participants must still volunteer to take part in the research.

Some organizations welcome researchers to their settings while others resist or refuse to get involved. Taylor and Bogdan (1984) offer suggestions to help facilitate your entry when you must go through an agency to contact participants:

■ Be candid with the agency about the purpose of the research.

■ When this approach does not work, try strategies such as having others that you know influence the administrator.

■ You can also go in "through the back door," for example, by becoming a volunteer and establishing trust with agency officials before initiating research with that agency.

Researcher and Participant Relationships

After gaining access to a setting, the researcher should work continually to preserve positive relationships with the participants. Part of developing this relationship requires resisting temptations to show the participants that you are the expert on the topic being studied. Researchers can reduce the power differential between participants and the researcher by viewing interviewees as competent observers and interviewers as reporters, a method used often by anthropologists, or by accepting interviewees as collaborators (Mishler, 1991). As collaborators, interviewees participate fully in developing the study and in analyzing and interpreting the data.

Your ability to develop and maintain trust is a critical part of relationship building with participants. Researchers who are knowledgeable about and sensitive to people who are different from the researcher and who are able to convey this to participants are more likely to engage people who will feel comfortable with the researcher during the project.

Important Points about Preparing for the Qualitative Interview

- Researchers are responsible for preparing themselves and others before accessing participants' settings. Training interviewers, ridding yourself of biases and assumptions, and pilot testing the interview schedule are among the steps that can be taken to prepare.
- Embracing participants as competent observers and collaborators and viewing yourself as reporter and learner facilitates relationship building in the field.

Analyzing Qualitative Data

You have gained access to a setting to conduct research with people who were selected for a specific purpose. Data have been collected, and now you are ready for analysis. Qualitative data analysis involves recording, transcribing, and organizing information collected from interviews, observations, documents, and audio-visual materials, in order to derive meaning from it. Data analysis also entails examining data for meaning units, categorizing, detecting patterns, connecting, synthesizing, understanding, and interpreting data.

Recording Data

> *Activity 4.*   What methods do you use to record data from client interviews? What are the advantages and disadvantages of those methods?

The data that you are collecting—using participant observation, in-depth interviews, indirect observations, or review of archival material—may be recorded during or after the interview or both during and after contact with participants. You can record participants' stories using note taking, audiotaping, videotaping, or a combination of these methods. Detailed note taking during an interview is discouraged because this could interfere with the interview. Have you ever interviewed a client while trying to take detailed notes and then discovered the client looking at your writing or realized that you were unable to listen attentively while attempting to write? Marcenko and Samost in the case example avoid these problems by audiotaping their focus group interviews.

Besides recording stories, behaviors, interactions, and perceptions of the participants, you also record your thoughts during the interview or participant observation period. If you choose to tape-record interviews, get permission from participants prior to the interview to avoid surprising them. Permission can be requested through the letter of informed consent. Review notes as soon as possible following the interview, and add your thoughts and feelings about observations during the interview.

Transcribing Data

At this point you have recorded volumes of data from your qualitative interviews and observations. The data now must be transcribed and organized. Transcribing means that your interviews or observations are written or typed using a word processor or a typewriter. You may do this yourself or hire someone. Some qualitative researchers hire research assistants to transcribe their interviews. Novice qualitative researchers may want to transcribe at least some of their own work initially to get a feel for what it is like. Listening first-hand to people's stories is both fascinating and an aid in deciding exactly how you want to handle the transcribing. Transcribing methods themselves have changed dramatically over the years. Originally transcriptions were handwritten and organized by cutting and pasting. Typewriters simplified the process some. Today, word processors and word processing packages can be used. There are even digital voice recorders that transfer spoken words to a word processor.

The great benefit of using word processing software is that it is capable of handling volumes of recorded data that can be organized on the screen without even having to print a copy. Whether you write your data using pen and paper or enter it into a word processor, the way that you format the transcript can facilitate your organizing and analysis. Double-spacing the text, numbering lines, and using large margins make this phase of qualitative research easier. Large margins provide space for coding and note taking, and facilitate finding specific text during the analysis.

Analytic Coding of Data

With the interviews recorded and transcribed, you are ready to begin coding the data. Analytic coding is a gradual process of organizing, categorizing and deriving meaning from the often massive amounts of data collected earlier in the research process. Coding begins by reading and searching each line of data for meaning units. Meaning units are statements—words, phrases, sentences or passages—that seem significant to the informants. Meaning units are then connected to themes, which are later organized into categories. For example, Marcenko and Samost identified categories or themes in their research. They ". . . compared and discussed the coded transcripts, and portions of the text were selected to illustrate the themes identified" (p. 38). Categories that emerged, identified as systems levels, were: "(1) individual and family, (2) organizations and providers, (3) policy or community" (p. 39).

As you read the transcripts and identify meaning units and themes, develop a coding scheme using abbreviations, numbers, color codes, or another method that you are comfortable with that will help you quickly locate these items. Remember that these themes should relate to research questions that you started with or revised as the project progressed. The themes facilitate building theories to assist in understanding your data. It is acceptable to change categories by adding or deleting as you read the transcripts. Glesne (1999) recommends developing a codebook soon after data collection begins to make working with your coding scheme easier. The process of looking for meaning units, connecting the meaning units to themes, and then categorizing them continues until you feel that adding new themes and categories will yield no new information. The researcher also searches for patterns in the data as meaning units and themes are identified and categorized.

Interpreting Qualitative Data

Two of the goals of qualitative research are theory development and identifying relationships between themes that emerge in the data. While some researchers end a qualitative research report with descriptions of the data, many qualitative researchers choose to add the additional step of interpreting their data. Interpretation of data facilitates identifying relationships between themes and theory development. There are many different ways to interpret qualitative data, including visual display of themes and categories using diagrams and matrices, content analysis, the use of metaphors, and a combination of these approaches.

Kvale (1996) writes about three contexts of interpretation of qualitative data and the three communities of validation that accompany the contexts of interpretation. The first context of interpretation, self-understanding, occurs when the researcher or interpreter tries to express in an abbreviated form participants' understanding of the meanings of their responses. The community of validation for the participant's interpretation is the participant. The researcher attempts to maintain an interpretation that is congruent with the interviewees' understanding.

Critical commonsense understanding is the second type of interpretation, which expands beyond the interviewees' explanation. The researcher may be critical of the interviewee's interpretation and can concentrate on either the participant or the content. The communities of validation for critical commonsense understanding are the general public in its various forms. Validity is established when a consensus is reached among the general public about whether the interpretation is documented and reasonable.

The third context of interpretation espoused by Kvale occurs when interpretation is based on theoretical understanding, which exceeds both the participant's self-understanding and the commonsense understanding. Researchers form the community of validation for this context, which evaluates the interpretation based on the validity of the theory for the discipline studied and whether the interpretation flows logically from the theory. Since the data collection, coding, and analysis phases of qualitative research are inseparable, it is at this point of immersion, when there are no new findings, understandings, or interpretations, that the researcher prepares to leave the field or setting.

Important Points about Analyzing Qualitative Data

- Recording of qualitative data can occur during the interview or observation, using note taking, audiotaping, videotaping, or a combination of these methods. After data are recorded it can be transcribed in writing or typed using a typewriter or word processing program.
- Data are coded after transcribing to organize the data, to derive meanings, and to categorize data. Meaning units could be words, phrases, sentences, or passages that appear to be important to participants.

Establishing Credibility of Qualitative Research

Throughout qualitative research projects, take steps to assure the credibility of your investigation. You can confirm credibility by remaining in the field, using triangulation, instituting peer debriefing and support groups, establishing an audit trail, or by using a combination of these approaches.

Remaining in the Field and Using Triangulation

The credibility of your research can be established when you remain in the field long enough to form trusting relationships with informants that diminish the potential for participants to withhold information, that is, the truth from the respondent's perspective (Padgett, 1998; Taylor & Bogdan, 1984). Triangulation is the use of several different viewpoints to establish credibility of qualitative data.

Employing different types of triangulation can also strengthen credibility of your investigation. Different types of triangulation are:

- Triangulation using more than one theory or perspective to interpret data.

- Triangulation using more than one research method in the same investigation. Recall Carlson, Siegal, Wang, and Falck's (1996) study of "Attitudes toward needle 'sharing' among injection drug users" in the previous chapter. These researchers used both qualitative and quantitative methods to validate their study.

- Observer triangulation uses more than one person in the field for observations and more than one person to code the same data.

- Data triangulation uses different types of data to validate or verify your observations and interview data (Carlson, Siegal, Wang, & Falck, 1996; Padgett, 1998; Denzin cited in Padgett).

Peer Debriefing and Support Groups

Support groups are used for feedback, ideas, or rejuvenation. The main reason for qualitative research support groups, however, is for debriefing and preventing bias in research. Member checking involves making contact with the participants for review of the researcher's interpretation of the data, which may or may not be congruent with the participant's interpretation (Padgett, 1998). For example, when I sent copies of my interpretations of the widows' interviews, from my study on widows and coping strategies (Salahu-Din, 1996), one widow called and told me that my interpretation of one statement was not what she meant. I changed the text to her explanation and interpretation of that conversation.

Establishing an Audit Trail

Keeping careful notes in a journal during data analysis can start an audit trail. These notes can include methods used in the study—interview transcripts, field notes, logs and memos regarding all phases of the research process—and notes on issues of credibility, decisions made during the analysis, and the rationale for those decisions (Padgett, 1998; Tutty, Rothery, & Grinnell, 1996).

Important Points about Establishing Credibility of Research Findings

- Some approaches that researchers use to establish credibility of their research findings are remaining in the field long enough to engage clients and establish rapport, using triangulation, using peer debriefing and support groups, using member checking, and establishing an audit trail.

Disseminating Qualitative Research Findings

There are numerous ways to share your research findings with other social work researchers, researchers from other disciplines, social work practitioners, and others in the human services field, such as sociologists, family studies professionals, and marriage and family therapists. International, national, state, and local professional conferences are forums for disseminating research findings. Moreover, findings may be presented to legislatures, at staff meetings, and at seminars. Publication of research findings in print and online journals, magazines, and books is one goal for some, especially academics.

Regardless of which method you choose, research reports must contain specific information, which varies depending on the audience and the dissemination method. The following is a guide outlining information to include in a research report. Some of the same components that are included in a quantitative study are also present in a qualitative study:

I. *Title Page*

II. *Abstract*   The abstract provides a brief description of the study, including the research questions, purpose of the study, the methodology, and a summary of the findings.

III. *Introduction*   The introduction includes a historical perspective, the research questions, the rationale for the questions, the purpose and goals of the study (and if they changed over time), a summary of empirical and theoretical literature related to the subject, and the significance of the study.

IV. *Methodology*   In this section describe the qualitative research design that you chose, the reason for choosing that method, and how the credibility of your study was established. Describe the setting and the informants (size of sample, number of settings, participant selection method), when the study was conducted, and study length.

V. *Results*   In this section describe participants, meaning units, themes, categories, and patterns discovered in the research. Provide examples of participants' stories, including direct statements. Include interpretations and the basis for those interpretations.

VI. *Conclusions and Discussion*   The significance of your study is included in this section, along with implications for research and practice. Include here also new theories and hypotheses developed as a result of your study. Implications for practice relates to the impact of your study on the field of social work and policy issues. Recommendations for further research are also a part of the conclusions and discussion sections.

Human Diversity Issues in Planning, Data Collection, and Analysis in Qualitative Research

Cultural sensitivity to people from whom the interviewer differs in age, race, gender, sexual orientation, religion, or social and economic backgrounds is important during data collection and analysis. Culturally competent investigators can more easily engage participants and build genuine relationships. Some researchers believe that matching the interviewer and interviewee by gender, race, and class will make entrance into the participant's setting and establishing relationships easier. Merton (1996) however, argues that participants will often openly share their stories with people that they do not know and who are different from them. Edwards (1996), on the other hand, purports that it is more difficult for outsiders to establish rapport in the interview process. Some of these difficulties can be overcome, however, Edwards argues, when "placing" occurs. In placing, interviewees search for characteristics in the researcher that are similar to those of the participant. For example, Edwards described how, "White working-class women sometimes showed a slight wariness until placing had occurred (i.e., they had asked for, or I had volunteered, information about my partner and child-rearing status) and then also talked freely. This self-disclosure lessened some of the reticence the women were exhibiting. What is interesting here is that, after an initial hesitation, the white women seemed to want to share a social similarity with me rather than to look for difference, as did the women of 'mixed' race to a certain extent" (p. 21). Besides placing and self-disclosure, showing genuine respect to participants is always a way to establish and maintain positive relationships.

Martin (1995) maintains that, "An important sign of respect, particularly in the African American community is "putting a handle on people's names," (1995, p. 53). By handles, Martin is referring to titles such as Miss, Ms., Mr., Mrs., and Dr. that are ways for you to demonstrate respect for clients and study participants. This preference for titles results from slavery when slave owners called slaves by their first names or boy or girl, refusing to address slaves with titles of respect. If, however, participants suggest that you use first names instead of titles, that request should be honored.

Cultural competency facilitates engagement and contributes to effective conversations between interviewer and interviewee. While verbal communication is important in interviewing, nonverbal communication through your appearance, body postures, silences, facial expressions, and attitudes directs and determines the mood of the interview (Fontana & Frey, 1994). Thus, being aware of your own tendency to communicate through body language is important, especially if that communication projects negative connotations. Regardless of the diversity of the participants that you interview, it is your responsibility to learn as much as possible about that community, group of people, or individual.

Ethical Issues and Biases in Planning, Data Collection, and Analysis in Qualitative Research

Ethical issues in planning a study and collecting and analyzing data include making a decision about whether to conceal your identity from research participants. Assuring confidentiality, which is central in collecting and analyzing data, is another ethical issue. Research assistants and other staff who handle confidential information should sign a confidentiality statement. When possible, refrain from using identifying information when data are handled by people other than the researcher; assign codes instead. Also, conceal identifying information in written and oral reports. Tape-recording interviews is an issue about which some participants are uncomfortable. Therefore, this issue should be addressed before the researcher enters the field.

WRITING STRATEGY

Answer these questions in paragraph form:

- On which specific phenomenon would you like to base your research?
- Why are you interested in this issue?
- Compose a research question that clearly states that issue and sufficiently narrows the issue for the purposes of your study, enabling you to conduct thorough research of the ideas or concepts interesting to you.

LEARNING ACTIVITY

Think of a topic that you and other classmates would have considerable knowledge about. Write a question to address that topic. In a 20-minute interview, pose that question to the person sitting next to you. Share results with the class.

INFORMATION TECHNOLOGY FOR PLANNING, DATA COLLECTION, AND ANALYSIS IN QUALITATIVE RESEARCH

When I began my doctoral studies, I feared computers and opted for an electronic typewriter. During the middle of the semester, after my first exams, I bought a computer. At that time, I knew little about computers and bought one that was practically outdated, although it worked well for my purposes. I decided to buy a computer because I was tired of cutting, pasting, and starting over every time I made a typographical error. That computer was a lifesaver! Since then, however, I have learned to conduct research on computers before purchasing.

Although the majority of qualitative researchers use computers to record and organize their notes, few use software packages designed for analyzing qualitative data (Richards & Richards, 1994). Several software packages, specifically for qualitative data analysis (QDA) are available. This software helps organize data. Some available qualitative data analysis programs include:

- ATLAS-ti—for data analysis, data management, and model building:

  www.atlasti.de/

- NuDist—Nonnumerical Unstructured Data—Indexing, Searching, and Theorizing:

  www.comm.cornell.edu/comm682/nudist%202.pdf

- The Ethnograph—text-based qualitative data software:

  www.qualisresearch.com

- HyperRESEARCH:

  www.researchware.com

Important Points from Chapter 11

- Choosing a topic, developing research questions, the literature review, and selecting participants are all elements in planning a qualitative study. "How" and "what" research questions are prevalent in qualitative research. Decisions about when to review the literature vary among qualitative researchers, some of whom decide not to review it. Participant selection in qualitative research does not rely on probability sampling and representativeness of samples.
- Researchers collect qualitative data through participant observation, participating in the lived experiences of people, through intensive interviews, and by reviewing various written, audio, and visual documents.
- Preparing for data collection helps set the stage for the interview and facilitates engagement and relationship building. Some ways that researchers prepare for data collection include training those responsible for collecting the data. It is also important to rid yourself of biases and assumptions about the people who will provide the data.
- A collaborative model where participants are partners and teachers, and researchers the learners is preferred in qualitative research.
- Data coding is a critical part of the data analysis process in qualitative research studies; it includes searching for meaning units, themes, and patterns, establishing categories, and interpreting data.
- To establish research credibility, remain in the field long enough to engage clients and establish rapport, use triangulation, use peer debriefing and support groups, use member checking, and establish an audit trail.
- One of your responsibilities as a researcher is to share results of your research with your agency, clients, and colleagues.
- Be aware of ethical issues, particularly confidentiality and deception in research.

REFERENCES

Adler, P. A., & Adler, P. (1994). Observational techniques. In N. K. Denzin & Y. S. Lincoln (Eds.), *Handbook of qualitative research* (pp. 377–392). Thousand Oaks, CA: Sage.

Berg, B. L. (2001). Qualitative research methods for social sciences. Boston: Allyn & Bacon.

Carlson, R. G., Siegal, H. A., Wang, J., & Falck, R. S. (1996). Attitudes toward needle "sharing" among injection drug users: Combining qualitative and quantitative research methods. *Human Organization, 55*(3), 361–369.

Creswell, J. W. (1994). *Research design: Qualitative and quantitative approaches.* Thousand Oaks, CA: Sage.

Creswell, J. W. (1998). *Qualitative inquiry and research design: Choosing among five traditions.* Thousand Oaks, CA: Sage.

Edwards, R. (1996). An education in interviewing: Placing the researcher and the research. In R. C. Monk (Ed.), *Taking sides: Clashing views on controversial issues in race and ethnicity* (2nd ed., pp. 15–25). Guilford, CT: Dushkin Publishing Group/Brown & Benchmark.

Fontana, A., & Frey, J. H. (1994). Interviewing: The art of science. In N. K. Denzin & Y. S. Lincoln (Eds.), *Handbook of qualitative research* (pp. 361–376). Thousand Oaks, CA: Sage.

Glesne, C. (1999). *Becoming qualitative researchers: An introduction* (2nd ed.). New York: Longman.

Kvale, S. (1996). *Interviews: An introduction to qualitative research interviewing.* Thousand Oaks, CA: Sage.

Lofland, J., & Lofland, L. H. (1995). *Analyzing social settings: A guide to qualitative observations and analysis* (3rd ed.). Boston: Wadsworth.

Luborsky, M., & and Rubinstein, R. L. (1995*).* Sampling in qualitative research: Rationale, issues, and methods. *Research in Aging, 17*(1), 89–113.

Marcenko, M. O., & Samost, L. (1999). Living with HIV/AIDS: The voices of HIV-positive mothers. *Social Work, 44*(1), 36–45.

Marshall, C., & Rossman, G. B. (1999). *Designing qualitative research* (3rd ed.). Thousand Oaks, CA: Sage.

Merton, R. K. (1996). Insiders and outsiders: A chapter in the sociology of knowledge. In R. C. Monk (Ed.), *Taking sides: Clashing views on controversial issues in race and ethnicity* (2nd ed., pp. 4–14). Guilford, CT: Dushkin Publishing Group/Brown & Benchmark.

Mishler, E. G. (1991). *Research interviewing: Context and narrative.* Cambridge, MA: Harvard University Press.

Padgett, D. K. (1998). *Qualitative methods in social work research.* Thousand Oaks, CA: Sage.

Reid, W. J., & Smith, A. D. (1989). *Research in social work* (2nd ed.). New York: Columbia University Press.

Richards, T. J., & Richards, L. (1994). Using computers in qualitative research. In N. K. Denzin & Y. S. Lincoln (Eds.), *Handbook of qualitative research* (pp. 445–462). Thousand Oaks, CA: Sage.

Salahu-Din, S. (1996). A comparison of coping strategies of African American and Caucasian widows. *Omega, 33*(2), 103–120.

Strauss, A., & Corbin, J. (1998). *Basics of qualitative research* (2nd ed.). Thousand Oaks, CA: Sage.

Taylor, S. J., & Bogdan, R. (1984). *Introduction to qualitative research methods.* New York: John Wiley & Sons.

Tutty, L. M., Rothery, M. A., & Grinnell, R. M., Jr. (1996). *Qualitative research for social workers.* Boston: Allyn & Bacon.

PART FIVE

Practice Evaluation Research

12 Evaluating Individual Practice

Qualitative Methods

We learned that research is a part of social work and that without studying the results of critical interventions or other types of interventions you are not going to determine whether your work was productive.

—Junior research student

CHAPTER GOALS

Your major goals upon completion of this chapter are to:

- Evaluate individual practice with clients.
- Use different qualitative individual evaluation methods.
- Understand why some practitioners do not evaluate their work.
- Evaluate your progress as a supervisor.
- Evaluate the progress of your supervisees.

Introduction

> Research that demonstrates the effectiveness of social work practice can give the profession a major boost in today's managed care–dominated world. Findings could provide answers to cost-conscious queries such as: Why bother treating a depressed welfare recipient? Why even check to see if a recipient is depressed? Or: What preventive treatment, interventions, and supports could be provided by communities and families to strengthen and protect the mental health of adults and children? And: Why do some children excel despite an impoverished background that seems to defeat others (Landers, 1999, p. 3)?

The above statement was taken from the January, 1999 issue of the National Association of Social Workers Newsletter, *NASW News*. Social workers and other helping professionals have always been interested in the impact that services have on clients. However, when I began my social work career years ago, little attention was given to formal monitoring of services, evaluating effectiveness of the social work service delivery system, accountability, or the link between practice and research. Agencies were seldom asked to submit quarterly or annual reports to the state, local, or federal funding sources. Today, practitioners must document whether interventions/treatments used with clients are contributing to positive changes in clients' behavior, situation, attitude, perceptions, or environment. In other words, practitioners need to be accountable to themselves, their clients, their employers, and their funding sources. This accountability is called evaluation research.

Practice evaluation methods are on a continuum from qualitative to quantitative. This chapter presents various qualitative methods for evaluating your practice with individual clients. In Chapter 13, quantitative methods for evaluating individual practice are presented, and in Chapter 14 methods for evaluating social service programs are described. Keep in mind that clients can be one person, a family, or an organization. If you are currently working in the human services field in a supervisory capacity, or aspiring to be a supervisor, these evaluative strategies can also be used to evaluate the performance of your employees as well as to assess your own growth and development.

Generalist Case Study: Supervising a Child, Youth, and Adult Services Unit

Agency Staff:

Supervisor: Mr. Benjamin Brothers

Social Worker: Mr. Jonathan Fife

Program Supervisor: Ms. Valerie Thomas

Presenting Concerns

Mr. Brothers, the unit supervisor, shared concerns with his supervisor, Ms. Thomas, about one of his social worker's inability to meet certain job expectations.

Background Information

Mr. Brothers, a recently promoted employee, supervises five social workers that are responsible for either children's services or adult services programs in an eight-county area. Social workers in the smaller counties are usually generalists responsible for providing adult and children and youth services. Children's services include family preservation services, family support services, child protective services investigations, foster care licensing and placement, adoption services, and daycare. Adult services include adult protective services, adult day care, homemaker services, rehabilitation services, and meals-on-wheels. Mr. Brothers is concerned about Mr. Fife, a probationary employee who is not meeting job expectations.

New Worker Orientation

Mr. Fife's previous supervisor provided six weeks of orientation for the new social worker. Mr. Fife was given a packet that included copies of his job description, local and state organizational charts, sexual harassment and discrimination policies, and the agency's client responsiveness plan. He was also provided a schedule of meeting dates, deadlines for reports, and copies of forms such as the monthly manager's report. During Mr. Fife's first week of employment, he met daily with his previous supervisor for orientation. They met three times weekly in the second and third weeks, and twice weekly in the fourth, fifth, and sixth weeks. Meetings were scheduled weekly thereafter. Unfortunately, this supervisor did not document these meetings or the status of Mr. Fife's work before leaving the agency prior to Mr. Brothers' promotion to the position.

Besides receiving orientation and supervision on a local level, Mr. Fife participated in a six-week agencywide orientation program that included job-specific training on tasks such as conducting child abuse and neglect and adult protective services investigations.

Mr. Fife's Responsibilities

Mr. Fife is a generalist practitioner responsible for 25 cases, both adult and children and youth services. He is the only social worker in a small county with a population of approximately 5,000. Child protective services investigations, foster care home studies, foster care placements, adoption studies, adoption placements, and child day care are some of Mr. Fife's child and youth services responsibilities. His adult services' obligations include homemaker services, adult day care, developmental services, and in-home services. Mr. Brothers requested that Mr. Fife bring to supervisory conferences four case records that have been updated and organized and that reflect follow-up and follow-through on case plans, that document he has informed the supervisor of pressing events as requested, and that provides evidence he meets deadlines as required.

Supervisor's Responsibilities

One of Mr. Brothers' first responsibilities as a new supervisor was to read a random selection of case records from each of the social workers in his unit. Through this review, he discovered severe problems in Mr. Fife's caseload that the previous supervisor had neglected to document. (Hence, he is no longer the supervisor.) His observations led to additional concerns about Mr. Fife's work. Mr. Brothers, along with Mr. Fife, developed a plan for addressing these issues. Mr. Brothers worked closely with Mr. Fife during the remaining four months of the six-month probationary period, discussing Mr. Fife's responsibilities and his progress on the job, the results of Mr. Brothers' case readings, and issues that Mr. Fife brought in for discussion. Weekly conferences would be held in either employee's office.

(continued)

Case Study   *Continued*

Assessment of Mr. Fife's Performance

Mr. Brothers and Mr. Fife met weekly to review the contract, the results of Mr. Brothers' case readings, and any issues that Mr. Fife brought to the conference. Mr. Brothers and Mr. Fife agreed that the following reflect Mr. Fife's current job performance:

Strengths
- Punctual and never misses work.
- Is an ideas person.
- Completes adoption home study interviews on time.
- Visits clients regularly.

Areas Needing Improvement
Caseload Management including:
- Paper work—case records are unorganized and current activity has not been recorded. As a result, worker loses track of case plans, including client goals and his designated responsibilities toward fulfilling objectives to reach goals.
- Misses deadlines.
- Fails to inform supervisor of critical events in caseload.
- Clients are losing trust in him because he does not follow through on case plans such as making referrals for eyeglasses or advocating on their behalf for services.

Although Mr. Fife agreed with this evaluation of his work, he said that he was insulted. He feels capable of doing the job, but is having family problems that are interfering with his performance. For that reason, Mr. Brothers recommended the agency's Employee Assistance Program (EAP), recognizing that he cannot mandate that Mr. Fife seek help from that program. However, since personal problems appear to be affecting his job performance, Mr. Brothers felt obligated to make the referral. After the meeting with Mr. Fife, Mr. Brothers consulted with his supervisor, Ms. Thomas, about his concerns regarding Mr. Fife and his corrective action plans. He wanted to help Mr. Fife maintain positive attributes related to his job functioning and improve weak areas. Once Mr. Brothers gathered information about the status of Mr. Fife's work, consulted with his own supervisor, and reflected on his work with Mr. Fife, an intervention was decided on. The intervention was weekly case consultations with Mr. Fife where his case files would be reviewed.

Overview of Individual Practice Evaluation

> *Activity 1.*   After reading this chapter, identify three reasons why it is important for social workers to evaluate their own practice. What kind of practice evaluation methods does your agency or employer use, and how are those methods implemented?

Rationale for Evaluating Individual Practice

There are many reasons for evaluating practice with individual clients, families, groups, and organizations as explained in this section. Practitioners evaluate their own practice in order to assess the effectiveness of interventions, enhance their knowledge base, establish accountability and credibility, and direct decision making.

Assess Effectiveness of Interventions with Clients. The main purpose of individual practice evaluation is informing practitioners if the services provided are making a difference in individual clients' and family's lives, in organizations, and in communities. Goals and objectives are examined to evaluate if the service plan is working in terms of reaching goals set by the client and you, if goals should be changed, if the client should be referred to a different agency, or if services should be terminated. In this assessment process, clients are actively involved in evaluating their progress in achieving individualized goals. Practice evaluation is also an effective means of monitoring your growth and development in a supervisory capacity as well as a way to evaluate staff performance.

Enhance Social Workers' Knowledge Base. While program effectiveness is critical, integration of practice and research requires practitioners to be competent researchers capable of making decisions based on both their research findings and the results of their practice evaluation (Rosen, 1996). Thus, social workers must consult the literature and experts on topics that they are dealing with during the process of evaluating their practice. As a new supervisor, Mr. Brothers will read scholarly journal articles and books relating to employees who are not meeting job expectations and consult with his supervisor for her expertise in handling such situations.

Establish Accountability and Credibility. The ability of organizations and social work staff within those organizations to document the effect of services in improving, changing, or maintaining positive behaviors and circumstances of people served is critical to the agency, to the clients, to the community, and to funding sources. Organizations that fund social service programs expect agencies to monitor cost effectiveness and outcomes of services that they provide. Funding agencies want to know if the amount of money being spent on programs is worth the outcomes. For example, your agency has been allocated $400,000 a year to provide parent aide services to clients. The program serves only 20 clients during a one-year period, and 10 of those clients experienced no documented changes in their parenting skills. The financial backers of this program may ask if this was a cost-effective program that benefited a sufficient number of clients. Furthermore, the funding source could argue that $400,000 is a large amount of money to spend on 20 clients with only 50% of whom attained the expected results. Besides these accountability issues, accountability and professionalism are concerns of social work as a developing profession. Its licensing laws, certification programs, recent major revisions to accreditation standards, and eligibility for third-party payments are all additional reasons for self-evaluation.

Direct Decision Making

When results of practice evaluations are available to social workers, supervisors, managers, policymakers, and funders of social service programs, they are in a position to make more informed decisions about whether services are helping to improve clients' lives and if programs should continue, receive more or less funding, be modified, or be dismantled. Despite these sound reasons for practice evaluation, some practitioners, for various reasons, are still not evaluating their practice.

Important Points about Individual Practice Evaluation

- Practice evaluation enables social workers to determine if the services they are providing to clients are making positive changes in clients' lives.
- Practice evaluation facilitates the integration of practice and research, which enables social workers to add to their general social work practice knowledge base and to select the most appropriate interventions for working with people.
- Practice evaluation assists in the documentation of service effectiveness for accountability to the agency, to clients, to the community, and to funding sources.

Practitioners' Use of Practice Evaluation

Although there are several different methods for evaluating practice, are social workers using any of these models in assessing the outcomes of their individual work with clients? A state-wide survey of licensed social workers' use of practice evaluation in Utah revealed that more than one-third of the respondents reported very strong or strong confidence in their ability to successfully complete single subject designs. Nearly 70% reported strong or very strong confidence in their ability to intuitively evaluate success of their practice interventions. While almost half of the clinical social workers described treatment in measurable terms, operationalized interventions, and monitored client progress, only a few "used empirical measures such as standardized tests and recorded measures of observable behavior" (Gerdes, Edmonds, Haslam, & McCartney, 1996, p. 34). Research shows, however, that the majority of practitioners do not evaluate their own practice consistently (Gleeson, 1990).

Making the Connection between Practice and Research

Helping students learn to integrate practice with theory in all social work courses is a major goal of social work faculty. There are many ways social workers can achieve this goal, including through practice evaluation. Practice evaluation provides workers with opportunities to select interventions from the literature that are appropriate for addressing the needs of clients.

Regardless of these opportunities to integrate practice and theory through the use of practice evaluation, practitioners may not use single case evaluations because the practice methods they use may not be fit for use with single system designs. To determine the extent of use of single system designs (described in Chapter 13) in clinical social work practice, LeCroy and Tolman (1991) conducted research with 179 practitioners in a sample consisting of 66% clinical psychologists, 8.9% social workers, and 8.9% educational psychologists and other professional behavior therapists. "The designs in question were categorized as evaluative or non-inferential (B-only, comparing pretest to post-test scores) or inferential (ABA, extended ABA, multiple baseline, other designs, e.g., changing criterion, group comparisons" (p. 50). Results of their study suggest that there is much greater use of the evaluative or non-inferential designs than of the inferential designs. Yet the majority of the participants were positive about integrating practice and research, and a significant number reported using some type of empirically based practice evaluations with most of their clients, thus facilitating the integration of practice and research.

The Value of Using Practice Evaluation

Some of the controversy in the field surrounds whether single system design research is worthwhile in social work practice, considering the low level of usage by practitioners who have been trained to use them (Millstein, Regan, & Reinherz, 1993). Mutschler (1984) provided on-the-job training on using single system designs to practitioners in a family service agency. Her follow-up survey to participating practitioners and supervisors revealed that the frequency of use of single system design evaluation depended on the relevance of the evaluation to the practitioner's job. Other factors that determined usage included utility of the evaluation, that is, whether the evaluation provided instruction for at least one phase of the intervention process, whether practitioners were involved in planning and implementing the evaluation, and whether the agency mandated some type of evaluation.

Some advantages of using individual practice evaluation research are that it is inexpensive and provides ongoing, immediate, visual feedback to the client and the practitioner. These designs give practitioners an opportunity to focus on a client, family, organization, or community rather than groups of people. The graphic display of client progress adds a different dimension that can be evaluated visually. Also, there is diversity among designs to choose from, and single system research can be conducted using a single client, instead of using large groups of clients and control groups. Single system designs are simple to design and to implement, and using single system designs contributes to a profession's empirical knowledge base and facilitates effective service delivery (Nelsen, 1994).

Limitations of Practice Evaluation

The limitations of using single system designs are that results cannot be generalized to other clients if those clients do not have similar characteristics, such as income, race, culture, and socioeconomic background. Furthermore, the designs are often used inappropriately, and there are opportunities for researcher bias. Instrumentation relating to accuracy of the researcher's observations and agreement among observers about what was observed could also be problems. Finally, practical difficulties in making the baseline and intervention periods the same length can present obstacles to using these designs.

Important Points about Practitioners' Use of Practice Evaluation

- Social workers can evaluate the outcomes of their work with people, organizations, and communities using a variety of methods, including quantitative and qualitative designs.
- Research shows that while many social workers use some form of practice evaluation, the majority of practitioners do not evaluate their practice consistently.
- Research also indicates that social workers are more inclined to use practice evaluation when it relates to their work, when they are included in the designing and implementing of the evaluation, and when evaluation is mandated by the agency.

Qualitative Methods for Evaluating Individual Practice

> *Activity 2.*   After reading this section, think about a client at your internship, a neighbor, a child, a partner, or a friend who wants to make a change in behavior. For example, if your child has problems with enuresis and wants to stop wetting the bed, design a method to help your child change the undesirable behavior.

Written Contracts

The use of contracts between clients and social workers is an established evaluation method in the social services. Contracts outline responsibilities of both the client and the social worker in concrete, measurable terms, with timeframes for achieving goals and established dates for periodic review of goal attainment. Contracts can also be used in the supervisory and worker relationship as a method for evaluating the performance of staff and for your own growth and development as a supervisor. The client and the worker write the contract before services start and build in intermittent progress review dates. Similarly, in the supervisor and the social worker relationship, the contract is written together shortly after employment begins. Figure 12.1 illustrates a contract completed for Mr. Fife, the social worker profiled at the beginning of this chapter.

Evaluating the Helping Relationship

Whereas the written contract measures the work of the client and the social worker in achieving mutually set goals, the Helping Relationship Inventory (HRI) (Poulin, 2000; Poulin & Young, 1997; Young & Poulin, 1998), evaluates the strength of the helping relationship. There is a client version, HRI: C, and a worker version, HRI: W. Each contains 10 items related to the structural component of tasks of the professional relationship and 10 items related to the interpersonal component. Structural component questions concern purposes of the professional relationship while the interpersonal part relates to the client and social worker's experience with each other. Examples of structural component questions, from the client inventory, are "How much input have you had in determining how the two of you will work together?" and "How much input have you had in determining the goals you are working on?" (Young & Poulin, 1998, p. 130). Interpersonal relationship examples, from the client inventory, are "Is your social worker's understanding of your difficulties similar to your own?" (p. 131) and "Does talking with your social worker help you believe more in yourself?" (p. 131). As a result of a trial experience with a small group of MSW social workers using the instruments with their clients, the authors concluded that the instrument is useful in diverse settings and situations in facilitating the helping process.

The B or Case Study Design

The B Design is the simplest of the single system designs. B indicates that an intervention has been initiated. There is no baseline period A, where data regarding the client's targeted

FIGURE 12.1 Conference Notes/Contract

Social Worker/Client Supervisor/Worker			Date 8/31	
Discussion of Progress/Areas	*Action Needed*		*Progress Due Dates*	*Reviews*
Strengths:				
1. Punctual and never misses work.	Continue as is			
2. Great ideas.	Continue as is			
3. Timely completion of adoption home studies.	Continue as is			
4. Regular visits to clients.	Continue as is			
Areas Needing Improvement:				
1. Paper work— unorganized case records; files are not updated which leads to failure to follow through and to follow up on case plans and goals.	**1.** Meet with supervisor each Friday morning at 9 A.M. Bring 5 case records that have been organized according to guidelines; notes showing follow-up on case plans and contacts with clients and other collaterals; develop a tickler system.		Weekly	Weekly
2. Misses deadlines for reports.	**2.** Meet deadlines 98% of the time effective 9/1.		Continuous	Weekly
3. Fails to inform supervisor of critical events in caseload.	**3.** Inform supervisor of significant incidents within 2 hours of your knowledge of emergency incidents; within one day of critical incidents. within 3 days of incidents that are not critical but that the supervisor should be aware of. Definitions of critical and emergency are based on our discussion of these factors.		Continuous	Weekly

problems are collected. There is minimal research before the intervention, and no theory. Information about the client is gathered using observations, case record information, or interviews; and in-depth narrative descriptions are provided. Harold, Mercier, and Colarossi (1997) recommend the use of eco maps in data gathering for case studies as a way to bridge the gap between practice and research. These authors found that large amounts of data could be gathered in interviews within a short timeframe and that the eco map could also be used as an assessment and intervention tool and as a tool for developing theoretical knowledge across a

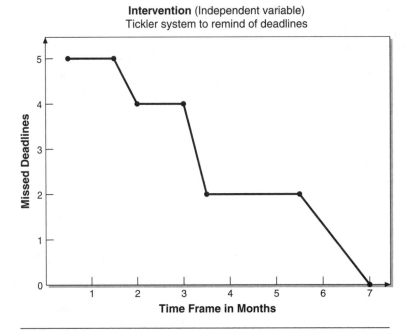

FIGURE 12.2   B or Case Study Design Used by Mr. Brothers in Supervision

large sample of clients. Among other purposes, findings from a case study could be a tentative working hypothesis (Alter & Evens, 1990).

Suppose that in the case study the new supervisor, Mr. Brothers, is aware that Mr. Fife, the social worker, has been experiencing problems completing some of his assigned tasks. Mr. Brothers does not have documentation because his predecessor did not record information about Mr. Fife's job performance. If Mr. Brothers had access to this information, it could be used as the baseline data. He is aware of problems, but does not have documented evidence, for instance, on exactly how many case records are unorganized or how many times Mr. Fife did not inform the previous supervisor of critical incidents related to his job. So, Mr. Brothers uses the B design in this situation where minimal information is available. Figure 12.2 is a copy of the B design that Mr. Brothers uses to gather in-depth information about Mr. Fife's situation. Data about the worker are collected by Mr. Brothers through a review of Mr. Fife's case records and in case conferences with Mr. Fife and with Mr. Brothers' supervisor. Based on Mr. Brothers' findings, an intervention plan is developed for working with Mr. Fife using one of the other qualitative research designs.

Target Problem Scaling

Activity 3.   After reading this section, describe the kind of clients you believe would benefit most from using target problem scaling. Explain your response.

Target problem scaling, like other forms of individual evaluation methods, requires gathering information from the client about the client's situation. The worker and the client's perceptions of the problem are recorded independently before, during, and after the intervention, and during any follow-up services, so that differences or agreements can be noted and discussed. Problems are listed on the target problem scale in order of priority to the client. This method requires a problem statement, based on targeted problems, which can be stated qualitatively or quantitatively.

An intervention is implemented although it is not necessary to specify on the data collection form what that intervention is. The degree of change in the client's situation or behavior, however, is measured repeatedly (Mutschler, 1979; Randall, cited in Alter & Evens, 1990). Target problem scaling, which concentrates on elimination of problems, is easy to use when working with clients who have difficulties sharing their stories (Alter & Evens). This evaluation methodology is also useful with clients when you can define the problem, but have difficulty determining measurable results (Hudson, cited in Alter & Evens).

Steps in Using Target Problem Scaling

- Identifying the number of persons to be included in the evaluation cohort (the target of the intervention can be one or more persons).
- Listing individual problems for each person that are the focus of the intervention.
- Rating each problem using the degree of severity scale with the client deciding on the severity of the problem. The initial rating of the degree of severity is the baseline data.
- Rank-ordering problems according to significance to the client.
- Repeating the degree of severity rating as many times as desired throughout the period of interest.
- Using the improvement scale at the end of the evaluation period to assess the amount of change across the repeated measures and as a follow-up measurement (Alter & Evens).

Figure 12.3 shows how Mr. Brothers used the target problem and goal improvement scale with Mr. Fife. This figure illustrates how the supervisor identified three problems that would be the foci of change in working with the social worker. In the column labeled Target Problem, the prioritized problems are paperwork, missed deadlines, and notifying the supervisor of critical events. The next column shows the degree of severity of the problem before the intervention (Start) and during weekly reviews in supervisory conferences: A review of the paperwork problem shows that at the start of the intervention Mr. Fife's paperwork was "extremely severe" (ES); at the first weekly review, time 1, his paperwork was "very severe" (VS); at time 2 it was "severe" (S); and at time 3 it was "not very severe" (NVS).

The next column reflects the improvement scale at the end of the intervention period and during a follow-up period: Mr. Fife's improvement scale at termination illustrates that his paperwork was "somewhat better" (4) and at follow-up it remained "somewhat better." The last column is the global improvement rating. His global improvement rating for paperwork was 4. Mr. Fife's global improvement rating for the problems of missed deadlines and notifying the supervisor were rated "a lot better" (5). In the area of paperwork, Mr. Fife was showing gradual improvement as indicated on the target problem scale.

FIGURE 12.3   Target Problem and Goal Improvement Scale

Target Problem (Rated by Mr. Brothers)	Target Problem Rating (Degree of Severity)				Target Problem Rating (Change Scale)		Global Improvement Rating
Mr. Fife	*Start*	*1 week Time 1*	*1 week Time 2*	*1 week Time 3*	*Termination*	*Follow-up*	
1. Paperwork	ES	VS	S	NVS	4	4	4
2. Missed Deadlines	S	S	NVS	NVS	5	5	5
3. Notifying Supervisor	VS	S	NVS	NVS	4	5	5

Severity Scale

NP = No Problem
NVS = Not Very Severe
S = Severe
VS = Very Severe
ES = Extremely Severe

Improvement Scale

1 = Worse
2 = No Change
3 = A Little Better
4 = Somewhat Better
5 = A Lot Better

Important Points about Target Problem Scaling

- Target problem scaling is a qualitative individual practice evaluation method that focuses on the problem statement as the basis for measuring outcomes. Perceptions of both the client and the social worker are considered independently when identifying the target problem.
- A goal statement is not needed with target problem scaling, although an intervention is required but not specified
- Target problem scaling is useful with clients when the problem can be clearly defined.

Goal Attainment Scaling

> *Activity 4.*   After reading this section, design a goal attainment scaling instrument for use with someone who wants to change a behavior or situation, such as a client, your child, your partner, a friend, your roommate, or an employee.

One of the basic ideas behind goal attainment scaling (GAS) is setting measurable goals, which social workers do often with clients. Each person participating in the intervention has his or her own goals, which must be time limited and specific for measurement purposes. Goals are established during the assessment phase of your work with clients and the outcome of those goals is evaluated when services end. Each goal is given a weight corresponding to its importance to the client The *baseline* in goal attainment scaling is the client's condition before introduction of the intervention. The *goal statement* is the focus of your work with clients or supervisees in goal attainment scaling, and it is the means for evaluating outcomes. Recall that in target problem scaling the problem statement outcomes are based on the *problem statement*.

The client's expected *level of performance* is defined using five levels of attainment or five possible outcomes so that the client knows exactly what the expectations are. The possible levels of attainment are scaled:

[+2] the best possible outcome

[+1] more than acceptable outcome

[0] the middle range, an acceptable level of outcome

[−1] less than acceptable level of outcome

[−2] the least acceptable outcome

Goal attainment scaling involves:

■ Identifying a global objective. Figure 12.4 represents a goal attainment scale set up for Mr. Fife. The global objective for Mr. Fife is to improve job performance.

■ Identifying problems that the intervention will address from the global objective, based on the client's desired areas of change in behavior. The supervisor, Mr. Fife, also had input in selecting the problems that would be the focus of the goals. For Mr. Fife, three problems were selected to focus on: failure to update case records with case activity information, failure to meet deadlines, and failure to inform supervisor of critical events.

■ Developing concise statements of a desired outcome level for each major problem area by indicating what behaviors or incidents show improvement in the designated problem areas. Expected outcome levels for each of the five points are operationalized by providing statements showing behaviors to be measured to assess change toward achieving the goal. For example, for scale #1, the least acceptable outcome for Mr. Fife is that his case records are consistently not updated within 30 days after contacts with clients or other significant persons and institutions such as schools, hospitals, and employers.

■ Developing a data collection method and designating who will collect the data. Mr. Fife collects data by completing his case records and bringing them to supervisory conferences for review by Mr. Brothers; both Mr. Fife and Mr. Brothers keep a record of deadlines that Mr. Fife meets and of his notifications of critical events to Mr. Brothers.

■ Identifying the client's current level and indicating on the scale, before the intervention starts, when the client should be rated for each goal. On scale #2 Mr. Fife's current level of functioning in regard to his case records is "misses deadlines 90% of the time."

■ Assigning a weight to each scale, indicating the importance of each goal. Scale #1 is assigned a weight of 40, scale #2 a weight of 25, and scale #3 a weight of 35.

■ Taking repeated measures (assessing client progress) during the intervention, at termination, and during follow-up.

■ Specifying which level has been attained at the end of the intervention and at follow-up. Information and formulas for scoring the GAS can be found in Alter and Evens (1990), Ottenbacher and Cusick (1989), and de Beurs, et al. (1993).

FIGURE 12.4   Goal Attainment Scale Used by Mr. Brothers

Goal Attainment Scale

Levels of Predicted Attainment	Scale #1 Updates case records in a timely manner Wt. 10	Scale #2 Meets deadlines as specified Wt. 7	Scale #3 Informs supervisor of critical events Wt. 9
Much less than the expected level of outcome (–2)	Case records consistently not updated 30 days after contact with clients and collaterals	Consistently misses deadlines	Informs supervisor 20% of the time
Somewhat less than the expected (–1)	70% of case records are updated as required	Meets deadlines 70% of the time	Informs supervisor 90% of the time
Expected level of outcome (0)	All case records are updated within two weeks after contacts	Meets deadlines 100% of the time	Informs supervisor 100% of the time one day after the incident
Somewhat more than the expected level of outcome (+1)	All case records are updated within one week after contacts	Submits reports two days before due date	Informs supervisor within 3 hours after the incident
Much more than the expected level of outcome (+2)	All case records are updated within 3 days after contacts	Submits reports one week before due date	Informs supervisor immediately after incident occurs

Adapted from Alter & Evens (1990).

Like target problem scaling, goal attainment scaling is another qualitative method for evaluating individual practice, but it can also be used as a quantitative method. When the anchor points on the scale are defined descriptively, the evaluation becomes qualitative (Unrau, Gabor & Grinnell, 2001). The anchored points are the operationalized outcomes specified for each problem on the goal attainment scale.

Important Points about Goal Attainment Scaling

- Goal attainment scaling facilitates establishing goals during the assessment phase of working with clients and acts as a means of helping the worker focus on work with clients.
- With goal attainment scaling it is not necessary to specify an intervention that centers on the goal statement as the basis for evaluating outcomes.
- Repeated measures of the dependent variable are taken when goal attainment scaling is used.

Human Diversity Issues in Evaluating Individual Practice in Qualitative Methods

There are many different types of qualitative methods for evaluating practice with individual clients (individuals, families, organizations, and communities). Some of those methods were addressed in this chapter. Diversity among clients and client problems must be considered when developing and implementing strategies to address concerns that individual clients bring to the agency. Interventions planned for clients must consider their ethnicity, language, and other differences, such as religion, age, and sexual orientation, and how these factors may positively or negatively influence the client and worker relationship in designing and carrying out an intervention. Moreover, every effort should be made to include clients in the entire evaluation process.

Ethical Issues and Biases in Evaluating Individual Practice in Qualitative Methods

Social workers are responsible for using their theoretical and empirical knowledge base, along with client input, to select the most effective intervention for addressing the client's targeted problem. As in other types of research, practitioners have an ethical responsibility to protect client confidentiality, to protect clients from harm, to get client consent before implementing these interventions, and to explain why a particular intervention is chosen and what that intervention entails. It is imperative to discuss any research involving human beings with your supervisor. Practitioners must also be careful about generalizing results of interventions from one client to another, another ethical issue.

WRITING STRATEGY

Think about your work with one person, a family, a group, or an organization. You may also consider your supervision of an employee. Write a *one-sentence* response to each of the following:

- What is the client's presenting problem?
- What is the targeted behavior?
- Describe an appropriate intervention for this targeted behavior.
- Name the evaluation design you would choose to evaluate the outcome of your work with this client, and explain why this design is particularly suited to your work with this client.

LEARNING ACTIVITY

Reflect on a client for whom you are providing services. Research a journal article that addresses a specific problem with which you are assisting this client. What interventions did the article suggest for this client? Share findings with your class.

INFORMATION TECHNOLOGY FOR EVALUATING INDIVIDUAL PRACTICE IN QUALITATIVE METHODS

 WALMYR Publishing Company provides tools to assist in evaluating practice. Some of these tools include the *Generalized Content Scale, Index of Self-esteem,* and the *Index of Marital Satisfaction.* Visit the WALMYR Web site at www.walmyr.com.

Important Points from Chapter 12

- There are both qualitative and quantitative methods for evaluating individual practice with clients.
- Practice evaluation enables social workers to determine if the services they are providing to clients are effective. It facilitates the integration of practice and research, assists in the documentation of service effectiveness for accountability to the agency, clients, community and funding sources, and helps direct decision making.
- Practice evaluation can be used in the supervisory relationship for evaluation of employees and for supervisors to evaluate their own growth and development.
- There are different methods available for social workers to evaluate the outcomes of their work with people, yet research shows that the majority of practitioners do not evaluate their practice. Most social workers, however, are positive about being able to synthesize research and practice.
- The B or case study design, contracts, conference notes, target problem scaling, and goal attainment scaling are some methods available for practitioners to evaluate their work with clients. These are also tools supervisors may use to evaluate their employees.

REFERENCES

Alter, C., & Evens, W. (1990). *Evaluating your practice: A guide to self-assessment.* New York: Springer.

de Beurs, E., Lange, A, Blonk, R. W. B., Koele, P., van Balkom, A. J. L. M., & Van Dyck, R. (1993). Goal attainment scaling: An idiosyncratic method to assess treatment effectiveness in agoraphobia. *Journal of Psychopathology and Behavioral Assessment, 15,* 357–373.

Gerdes, K. E., Edmonds, R. M., Haslam, D. R., & McCartney, T. L. (1996). A statewide survey of licensed clinical social workers' use of practice evaluation procedures. *Research on Social Work Practice, 6*(1), 27–39.

Gleeson, J. P. (1990). Engaging students in practice evaluation: Defining and monitoring critical initial interview components. *Journal of Social Work Education, 26*(3), 295–300. Retrieved September 1, 2001 from EBSCOhost.

Harold, R. D., Mercier, L. R., & Colarossi, L. G. (1997). Eco maps: A tool to bridge the practice-research gap. *Journal of Sociology and Social Welfare, 24*(4), 29–44.

Landers, S. (1999, January). Under construction: Practice research base. *NASW News*, p. 3.

LeCroy, C. W., & Tolman R. M. (1991). Single-system design use of behavior therapists: Implications for social work. *Journal of Social Service Research, 14*(1/2), 47–56.

Millstein, K. H., Regan, J. M., & Reinherz, H. Z. (1993). Practitioners' use of single system evaluation: Is the glass half full or half empty? *Smith College Studies in Social Work, 64* (1), 19–34.

Mutschler, E. (1984). Evaluating practice: A study of research utilization by practitioners. *Social Work* (July-August), 332–337.

Nelsen, J. C. (1994). Ethics, gender, and ethnicity in single-case research and evaluation. *Journal of Social Service Research, 18*(3/4), 139–152.

Ottenbacher, K. J., & Cusick, A. (1989). Goal attainment scaling as a method of clinical service evaluation. *The American Journal of Occupational Therapy, 44*, 519–525.

Poulin, J. (2000). *Collaborative social work: Strengths-based generalist practice*. Itasca, IL: F. E. Peacock.

Poulin, J., & Young, T. (1997). Development of a helping relationship inventory for social work practice. *Research on Social Work Practice, 7,* 463–489.

Rosen, A. (1996). The scientific practitioner revisited: Some obstacles and prerequisites for fuller implementation in practice. *Social Work Research, 20*(2), 105–111.

Unrau, Y. A., Gabor, P. A., & Grinnell, R. M., Jr. (2001). *Evaluation in the human services*. Itasco, IL: F. E. Peacock.

Young, T. M., & Poulin, J. E. (1998). The helping relationship inventory: A clinical appraisal. *Families in Society: The Journal of Contemporary Human Services*, March–April, 123–133.

13 Evaluating Individual Practice

Quantitative Methods

The part of the research course that really benefited me most was the material that helped me talk with my clients. I have to do a daily assessment with my clients. During these assessments I have to determine the cause and reasons for the problems. For example, if a client appears depressed during an interview, research helped me perform a more complete evaluation of the client. It helped with the interventions and with the case studies.

—Junior social work student

CHAPTER GOALS

Your major goals upon completion of this chapter are to:

- Understand concepts related to single system designs as a method for evaluating practice.
- Design single system design evaluations.
- Differentiate among various single system design models and know the appropriate use of each.
- Understand and apply ethical issues related to using single system designs.

Introduction

In Chapter 12 qualitative methods for evaluating work with individual clients (individuals, families, groups, organizations, or communities) were introduced, along with the rationale for evaluating individual practice. The reasons for using practice evaluation applying qualitative methods also relate to the implementation of quantitative approaches—assessing the effectiveness of interventions with clients, integrating practice and research, and improving accountability and credibility. This chapter presents additional methods for evaluating practice with individual clients. These methods are implemented to determine, through repeated measures, whether clients are making progress in reaching the goals agreed on between the client and social worker.

Identifying a specific behavior, situation, or circumstance, establishing a baseline, developing measurable objectives, measuring the behavior repeatedly over time and comparing the measures, and displaying data graphically are all components of quantitative practice evaluation designs. One advantage of using single system designs is the social worker's ability to individualize work with a client from problem identification, to implementing an intervention or treatment, to monitoring and evaluating progress. There can also be continuous monitoring of client progress during the intervention period, with revised interventions, if necessary. Client involvement in the plan from identifying the target problem to participating in selection of an intervention, to data collection and termination is possible. And, finally, it is inexpensive and easy to implement some designs. There are disadvantages to the single system quantitative design. Questions of external validity exist—whether results from one client situation can be applied or generalized to different clients. There is difficulty in implementing some designs. Issues of internal validity can arise. In some of the more rigorous designs other causal explanations may account for the changes in the clients' behavior, situation, or circumstances. The use of quantitative practice evaluation methods is illustrated by a case study on intensive family preservation.

Generalist Case Study: The Kodak Family, Intensive Family Preservation Case

Child Protective Services (CPS) Referral

Background Information:

Mother:	Diane Kodak, age 32
Daughter:	Carmen Kodak, age 6
Daughter:	Tara Kodak, age 3
Children's Father:	Rodney Evans, age 36

Other Significant Persons:

Social Worker:	Phyllis Davis

(continued)

Case Study   *Continued*

Teacher:	Alisa Shatner
Ms. Kodak's doctor:	Sam Jones
Ms. Kodak's neighbor:	Annie Bolton
Landlord:	Fred Means

Presenting Concerns

Carmen's teacher referred the family to Child Protective Services because Carmen comes to school every day with an offensive body and hair odor, wearing clothes with grease and food stains. Because of Carmen's physical condition, her teacher, Ms. Shatner, gives her a shower in school each day. Ms. Shatner listed her concerns about the physical neglect of Carmen and what may be happening in the home.

The social worker's first contact with the Kodak family was an unscheduled home visit. During this visit, the assessment of the client's situation began. The social worker, Ms. Davis, drove through Ms. Kodak's neighborhood, which was about five miles from her office. She observed deteriorating and abandoned buildings on a street with large apartment buildings that housed at least 100 families each. There were a few three- and four-family wood frame homes scattered throughout the neighborhood. Ms. Davis parked on the street curb in front of the Kodak home. The family lives on the second floor of a wood frame, four-family home. The multifamily dwelling was similar to other three- and four-family homes in the neighborhood. It had broken windows, rotting roof, holes in the wall, and peeling paint.

There was barely any yard, no grass, and some broken glass on the sidewalk and in the street. Ms. Davis knocked on the door. When Ms. Kodak opened the door about two minutes later, Ms. Davis introduced herself, informed Ms. Kodak that she represented the local child protective services agency, and explained that she wanted to talk to Ms. Kodak about a concern the agency had received. After hesitating a few seconds, Ms. Kodak invited Ms. Davis into her home. Upon entering the small one-bedroom apartment, the worker smelled a strong urine scent, observed clothes all over the place, and noticed that the white sheets covering a small bed were gray from dirt.

Besides observing the condition of the home, the social worker noted that Ms. Kodak had an unpleasant body odor. Ms. Davis chatted with Ms. Kodak and the children for several minutes asking about the neighborhood and asked how long she had lived there. She also inquired about the children before beginning a discussion of the child protective services referral. Ms. Davis observed the interaction between Ms. Kodak and her daughters. They appeared comfortable with their mother, who responded to them by listening to them, touching them, and speaking softly to them.

Ms. Kodak's Story

Ms. Davis explained the agency's role and her responsibilities as the investigating social worker and shared the contents of the referral with Ms. Kodak, without revealing the source of the referral. Ms. Kodak sat quietly and listened, but did not respond verbally or physically to the content of the report. Ms. Davis invited Ms. Kodak to share her story. Ms. Kodak said that she is 32 years old and has two daughters, Carmen, age six years, and Tara, age three years. She is unemployed and receives Aid to Families with Dependent Children (AFDC). Carmen, the six-year-old, is in first grade and three-year-old Tara remains home with her mother. The children's father, Mr. Rodney Evans, Ms. Kodak's former boyfriend, visits his daughters but does not live with the family. Mr. Evans pays child support to the Division of Social Services since Ms. Kodak receives Aid to Families with Dependent Children (AFDC).

Ms. Kodak's immediate concerns related to three recent incidents. Last week, she asked a neighbor to take her to the store to cash her AFDC check. After cashing the check, the neighbor stole Ms. Kodak's money and put her out of the car, leaving her stranded miles from home. In a similar incident, a friend volunteered to pick up Ms. Kodak's food stamps from the food stamp office. The friend returned from the food stamp office and informed Ms. Kodak that she had lost Ms. Kodak's identification card and, therefore, the clerk at the food stamp office refused to issue the food stamps. Ms. Kodak also shared with the worker that her electricity "was not working," and that she believed something was wrong with the wiring. Ms. Davis asked to see Ms. Kodak's electric bill and requested permission to contact the electric company.

Ms. Kodak was confronting additional problems. The landlord wanted her out of the apartment within two weeks so that he could make extensive repairs to the building, her six-year-old, Carmen, is sometimes left unsupervised and leaves the house when she is left home alone, and she, Ms. Kodak, "takes medicine for her nerves." After sharing these stories and situations with Ms. Davis, Ms. Kodak had a helpless expression on her face. Ms. Davis said, "You appear saddened by all of the things that are happening in your life. This must also be overwhelming." Ms. Kodak seemed relieved that Ms. Davis validated her feelings. She acknowledged that sometimes it is difficult to keep up with the housework and the care of the children. She was not aware that the teacher, Ms. Shatner, was bathing Carmen in school.

After listening to Ms. Kodak and asking her questions about her current situation, Ms. Davis informed Ms. Kodak that she had several concerns that she would like to help her with:

- Carmen's safety since she is left unattended at home.
- Carmen's poor hygiene and soiled clothing.
- Ms. Kodak's housing situation (order to vacate from the landlord and no electricity).
- Ms. Kodak's ability to take care of herself physically.
- Ms. Kodak's seeming inability to provide a safe environment and adequate food, clothing, and shelter for the family. (Ms. Davis referred to the stolen check and the food stamp situation.)
- Ms. Kodak's medical history and the medication she is taking.

Ms. Davis explained to Ms. Kodak that because the current living situation appeared potentially unsafe for her and the children, she would need to complete an assessment and a more in-depth investigation, followed by a report to the juvenile court about whether the children are in danger of being harmed or neglected. This report would include information about Ms. Kodak's current situation with a recommendation to remove the children immediately while a 30-day investigation is conducted, to remove them while the investigation is ongoing, or to work with the family with the children in the home. Regardless of whether the children remain with her or are removed, in 30 days, Ms. Davis explained, she would return to court with a report detailing whether Ms. Kodak's situation had changed. At that time, she would make recommendations about whether the children should remain in the home or be placed with relatives or in foster care.

Collateral Contacts

Ms. Davis received written permission from Ms. Kodak to contact her physician, Carmen's teacher, the landlord, a neighbor, and the food stamp office. The doctor confirmed that Ms. Kodak had been inconsistent in taking her haldol (psychotropic medication, for schizophrenia), as prescribed. It is his opinion that if she takes the medication and receives support, she would be capable of caring for her

(continued)

Case Study   *Continued*

children. The doctor wants Ms. Kodak to visit him the next day for a physical and to check her medication to see if a change is needed. After visiting with the doctor, Ms. Davis met with the landlord who confirmed that he wants Ms. Kodak out of the home within two weeks. If the tenants are not out so that he can make repairs on the building, the city will condemn it. He felt no obligation to assist in relocating Ms. Kodak.

Carmen's teacher stated that the other students were teasing Carmen because she came to school with grease- and dirt-stained clothing, uncombed hair, unbrushed teeth, and unbathed. She also had an unpleasant body odor. The teacher would bathe Carmen each morning in the shower in the teachers' lounge without Ms. Kodak's consent or knowledge. Ms. Davis informed Ms. Shatner that she is obliged to let Ms. Kodak know that Carmen is being bathed at school.

Mr. Evans, the children's father, acknowledged that he does not visit his children as frequently as he should. He wants the children to live with their mother and said that he would testify in court about his willingness to visit the family daily since they live close by, monitor Ms. Kodak's medication consumption, and assist with child care (bathing them and helping with their homework). A neighbor, Ms. Bolton, would also assist the family by providing transportation, helping Ms. Kodak plan and cook nutritious meals, and establishing routines for the children, such as regular mealtimes, bedtimes, and a homework schedule. The visit to the food stamp office confirmed that the friend had signed Ms. Kodak's signature card and picked up her food stamps. The food stamp office agreed to issue another set of stamps.

What Is Practice Evaluation Using Quantitative Methods?

This chapter explains quantitative practice evaluation models for practitioners' evaluation of their work with individual clients (a person, a family, a group, or an organization). These single system designs collect quantitative data instead of qualitative data during the baseline and intervention phases. Single system designs allow workers to develop, along with the client, individualized plans and interventions for addressing the targeted behavior and to monitor and evaluate client progress continuously at different points during the intervention phase and at termination of services. In quantitative designs, as with qualitative methods, clients can participate in the entire process from deciding on which behaviors to target to collecting data to taking part in decisions about termination.

Components of a Single System Design

> *Activity 1.*   At the end of this section explain the difference between the A or baseline phase of a single system design and the B or intervention phase.

A client comes to the agency with a presenting problem, which may or may not be the major issue facing that client at that time. You may choose to initiate work with the client using a single system design as an evaluative mechanism. From the presenting problem, or other issues that emerge during the assessment process, a specific behavior (or behaviors) is targeted as the focus of the working relationship and the intervention. An appropriate intervention, such as a family preservation program, a behavior modification program, a self-esteem improvement plan, a parenting program, or a stress reduction plan, that the worker and client believe will help change or maintain the targeted behavior, after a baseline is established, is selected. Baseline data are collected to evaluate the client's current situation, before the intervention is implemented. Displaying the single system design graphically is a significant part of this evaluation design. The following section describes the basic components of a single system design beginning with the A phase.

A: The Baseline Phase

The baseline phase of a single system design starts before you introduce an intervention for working with the client. Information gathered in this phase is for the purpose of assessing the current status of the client's problem. This information is used to compare the client's behavior prior to implementation of an intervention with behavior after implementation. In the baseline phase, you, along with the client:

Select a Targeted Behavior(s) from the Presenting Problem. The target behavior is the behavior or situation that the client and you select to work on reducing, increasing, eliminating, or maintaining. It is the dependent variable. For example, one of the targeted behaviors for Ms. Kodak, in the case example, is her negligence or forgetfulness in taking her psychotropic medication. You want to help her change this behavior by taking the medication as prescribed by the doctor.

Collect Data to Establish the Baseline. An assessment is made of the client's current situation before implementing an intervention by collecting data relating to the client's targeted behavior. Ms. Kodak informed the social worker that she consumes the medication once a day instead of four times a day as prescribed. You get permission from Ms. Kodak to talk with her physician about her medical status and prescribed medication. The doctor tells you that Ms. Kodak should take the medication four times a day.

This information establishes your baseline for working with Ms. Kodak about taking the proper dosage of medication. Ideally, the baseline period is the same length of time as the intervention period. Realistically, the urgency of the client's difficulties usually mandates a baseline that is shorter than the intervention period. Information that is gathered during the baseline period should be stable, allowing accurate determination of whether change is occurring during the intervention phase. A stable baseline, one that does not reflect a lot of fluctuation in behavior, indicates that there is a problem.

Develop a Theoretical Framework. A review of the literature provides theoretical perspectives and interventions to address the targeted behavior. Theories attempt to define, predict, and explain behavior or a phenomenon. Thus, your theoretical framework facilitates understanding of the client's situation and guides in selecting interventions for providing services.

Examples of formal theories are psychoanalytic theory, feminist theory, ecological theory, and developmental theory. For instance, in Ms. Kodak's situation, you could use the ecological perspective because she has many personal issues as well as environmental factors influencing her life. For example, she is attempting to cope with mental health issues that are contributing to other personal problems, such as lack of hygiene for her and her daughter.

Environmental issues include housing, medical care, and schooling for her children and the matter of support systems.

Establish How You Will Measure Change in the Client's Behavior.   In Ms. Kodak's situation, for instance, assess whether she begins taking the medication as prescribed by her physician. A friend, a relative, or the children's father can monitor and record medication intake, the intervention. This person would keep a record of the time that the medication is taken and the amount. This information is compared with the baseline data.

Establish Timeframes for Monitoring Client Progress.   A timeframe for collecting data in the A phase is determined before data collection begins. Single system designs that include a baseline phase (A) are not suitable for working with targeted behaviors that require delaying the intervention until pre-intervention data are collected. For example, you collected baseline data from Ms. Kodak's doctor and from Ms. Kodak, but you would not want to delay an intervention to collect additional data because of the seriousness of her mental health condition. You can collect the baseline data in critical or urgent situations from existing records, if there are any. When you collect data during a baseline phase, though, decide over what period of time collection will occur—a week, two weeks, or a month.

B: The Intervention Phase

Baseline data have been collected which provide you with information about the client's current behavior, and an intervention or treatment has been selected to address the problem. You are prepared to introduce the intervention, monitor the client's progress, and evaluate whether changes are occurring in the client as a result of the intervention. In this phase you:

Implement the Intervention.   The intervention is the service or treatment that the client will use or follow in an effort to change a behavior, situation, or environment. Single system designs can have one intervention or multiple interventions. The first intervention is labeled B and additional interventions are designated C, D, and E, depending on the number. In the B phase, an intervention is implemented, and the client's behavior is measured repeatedly over time. As explained earlier, the intervention for Ms. Kodak is having a friend, a relative, or the children's father monitor her medication by observing her take the medication and recording in a log the time, date, and amount of medication that was consumed. This information is then compared with information gathered from Ms. Kodak during your initial meeting when the baseline was established.

Monitor Client Progress Repeatedly and Reassess for Progress towards Established Goals.   B is the intervention phase, and the intervention is the independent variable that is chosen to effect change in the client's behavior, the dependent variable. Data for monitoring progress are collected in a variety of ways, including from client self-reports, interviews, standardized measures, observations of clients, records, journals, logs, questionnaires, and process recordings. Before starting the intervention with the client, set timeframes for reassessing progress, for example, weekly, twice a month, or monthly.

Important Points about Basic Components of a Single System Design

- The first step in beginning a single system design is identifying a client target behavior as the focus of client change efforts.
- The next step in establishing a single system design is collecting data relating to the targeted behavior to establish a baseline as a guide for evaluating client progress in relation to the intervention.
- Another step is developing a theoretical framework to guide your work with the client.
- It is also important to establish single or multiple methods to measure change in client behavior and timeframes for monitoring progress.
- The last steps in implementing the intervention are repeatedly measuring client progress and comparing that progress or lack of progress with the baseline data.

Designing Single System Design Evaluations

This section explains how to design a single system evaluation, covering the steps necessary to develop an effective program for your client. Client cooperation is essential and begins with giving consent to the process.

Getting Client Informed Consent

Activity 2.   Refresh your memory on informed consent by reviewing Chapter 2. Write a letter of informed consent to Ms. Kodak regarding working with her using a single system design evaluation.

Activity 3.   As you read this section, think about possible barriers to implementing single system designs as a generalist social worker in your work setting or internship. What suggestions do you have for overcoming those obstacles? What factors would contribute to successful implementation?

You must get informed consent when conducting single system designs with clients, just as you would with other research involving human beings (see Chapter 2). Informed consent involves explaining to clients clearly and explicitly what the research involves, and alternatives to the suggested research. Wakefield and Kirk (1997) suggest that besides informing clients of how single system design research benefits clients, practitioners should also share with clients any intervention efforts directed at attaining knowledge that benefits the field but may not directly benefit the client. Bloom, Fischer, and Orme (1999) provide a model consent form that can be used with evaluation research. They acknowledge that a separate consent form is not necessary for evaluation since it is one part of overall practice. Once you get client consent or assure that consent is already documented in the case file, begin helping the client identify the target problem.

Assisting in Problem Identification

People come to the attention of social service agencies through self-referral, referrals from other agencies such as hospitals and schools, or referrals from family, friends, or neighbors. Regardless of the referral source, clients come to the agency with a presenting problem. "Presenting problems usually are troublesome behaviors, affects, cognitions, or environmental circumstances and the attendant final goals will be that each of these change in a positive direction to the degree possible" (Nelsen, 1993, p. 71). Furthermore, presenting problems are often a sign of more serious family or environmental problems. To begin a single system design, start with the client's self-identified problem. However, when services are mandated by an agency, such as child protective services, divorce court, or adult and youth probation, that problem will be on the priority list of targeted behaviors.

Identifying Target Behaviors from the Client's Presenting Problem

A target behavior is selected as the focus of the intervention. Both the problem and the target behavior should come from the client except when providing services to involuntary clients who come to the agency with mandated services or when clients have difficulty articulating their problems. Besides mandated services, clients may present additional issues that need social service attention. The client can choose a targeted behavior, often with guidance from the social worker in articulating their concerns, in addition to concerns targeted by helping agencies such as child protective services. Blythe and Tripodi (1989) recommend using a problem hierarchy when deciding which problems to target. A problem hierarchy is a listing of the client's problems in priority order and choosing the top one or two problems as the focus of the intervention.

Targeted behaviors may relate to behaviors, situations, environments, attitudes, or perceptions and may be either positive or negative. Consider the Kodak family, for instance, for whom you can target (or select) several behaviors for focus of the intervention—poor hygiene of Ms. Kodak and her daughters and neglect of children. Regardless of the type of target behavior, it should manifest itself consistently over time during the baseline period. Target behaviors are also stated explicitly and in measurable terms. That is, the target behavior must be operationalized so that the worker and client can determine, at various intervals, whether the expected changes are occurring after introduction of the intervention.

Gathering Baseline Data

Baseline data are collected so that a comparison can be made between the behavior before the intervention and behavior after the intervention is implemented in order to assess whether change is occurring after introduction of the intervention. Baseline data may be gathered by observing the client's behavior, client self-monitoring, or by using already existing data such as school records and medical records with consent of the client. For reliable and valid data, it is best to use more than one data collection method or data collection point. For example, both

Ms. Kodak and Carmen's teacher can collect data on improvement in Carmen's hygiene by recording in a log each day and reporting the results to you.

Describing Targeted Behavior

Baseline data describes the client's current targeted behavior, the focus of the change effort, before introduction of an intervention. Collect data that illustrate how the behavior manifests itself and the frequency, intensity, or duration of the client's behavior or situation. In other words, how can you determine if the client really has this problem? Frequency measures describe how often a behavior occurs, and intensity measures illustrate the severity of a behavior. Duration measures are observations and recordings of the length of time that a behavior continues. Duration of behavior can be measured in time spans such as seconds, minutes, hours, days, months, etc.

Think about Carmen, the older daughter in the case example. One target behavior for Carmen is her poor hygiene. To describe her behavior in terms of frequency, duration, and intensity you could state:

Duration—According to Carmen's teacher she has been coming to school in this condition for three months.

Frequency—During the three months her hygiene is the same each day.

Intensity—Her teacher considers Carmen's condition extreme since her clothes have dirt and grease and they smell. Her hair is seldom shampooed and combed, and her teeth are not brushed.

After describing the targeted behavior you are prepared to operationalize terms and establish measurement goals along with the client, regarding what changes the client wants to make in behavior, situations, or environment. The changes are the focus of the intervention and the practitioner's work with the client. Establish goals that are clear, time limited, and achievable.

Operationalizing and Measuring Variables

Activity 4. Think about Carmen, Ms. Kodak's daughter in the case example. If Carmen's teacher says that Carmen's hygiene is poor, how would you operationally define poor hygiene? How did your classmates operationally define that term?

Activity 5. After reading this section, find a scale designed to measure a specific behavior in children or adults using Fischer and Corcoran's (2000) and Corcoran and Fischer's (2000) *Measures of Clinical Practice,* volumes 1 and 2, or ask the librarian for assistance in locating another book of scales.

Operationalizing terms used in your single system design study is critical in facilitating measurement of variables. Operationally defining terms is describing them in a manner that illustrates their exact meaning in your study (see Chapter 6). It is also a method of facilitating measurement of the terms. Operational definitions are not dictionary definitions. A review of the literature is an appropriate method for developing operational definitions because the literature may contain existing operational definitions that fit with terms in your study. If definitions found in the literature do not accurately reflect terms as used in your study, avoid using them.

The dependent and the independent variable are two major terms in single system design evaluations that must be operationally defined. The dependent variable is the behavior that is the focus of change. The independent variable is the intervention or service that is selected to effect change in the dependent variable. Operationally defining variables provides specificity and clarity to these variables so that the client, the social worker, and others with a vested interest in the evaluation understand their meanings. Once the independent and dependent variables and other major terms in the single system design are operationally defined, measurement of change can occur.

Measurement is the process of assigning numbers or labels to observable phenomena—people, situations, or events in order to test them scientifically through a quantification process (see Chapter 6). The purpose of measurement is to evaluate whether changes have occurred in the client's behavior, situation, or environment since services (the intervention) were started. Observing the client, assessing existing records, client self-reports, and testing are methods for measuring changes. Changes in client behavior can be measured only when before and after data are available about the behavior that is the subject of the measurement. For example, to measure change in Carmen's behavior, the social worker must have information about her behavior before and after implementation of an intervention. In this case example, behavior can be measured before and after implementation of an intervention by observing and recording Carmen's behavior using monitoring tools designed by the worker, the client, or another person in a position to observe the client. For example, Carmen's teacher can observe her behavior daily and record her observations.

Another method for measuring phenomenon is through the use of standardized instruments. Standardized instruments are measures that have been tested on a significant number of people, making them trustworthy in terms of validity and reliability. Ordinarily, clients complete these instruments themselves under the supervision of the social worker, psychologist, doctor, or another tester. Standardized instruments are administered during the baseline phase and repeatedly during the intervention phase to determine whether the client's situation has changed. One source for standardized measures is Fischer and Corcoran's *Measures for Clinical Practice* (2000). These two volumes contain copies of instruments that can be used for measuring diverse problems. There are instruments for couples, for families, for children, and for adults. Some of the instruments for couples are: "Dual Employed Coping Scales," "Index of Marital Satisfaction," "Life Distress Inventory," and the "Marital Happiness Scale." Figure 13.1, the "Self-Rating Anxiety Scale" (SAS) provides the name of the author of the scale, the purpose of the scale, and additional information that would help the social worker decide whether the scale is appropriate for use with the client. Figure 13.2 is a copy of the standardized scale, "Self-Rating Anxiety Scale (SAS)" from *Measures for Clinical Practice* (2000).

Suppose that one of the targeted behaviors for Ms. Kodak was anxiety. She could complete the anxiety scale before implementing an intervention. After the intervention is started Ms. Kodak completes the questionnaire at predetermined times to assess if her anxiety level is changing. Scales can be purchased from the authors or various companies or the author of a

FIGURE 13.1   Self-Rating Anxiety Scale (SAS)

Author: William W. K. Zung

Purpose: To assess anxiety as a clinical disorder and quantify anxiety symptoms.

Description: The SAS is a 20-item instrument consisting of the most commonly found characteristics of an anxiety disorder (5 affective and 15 somatic symptoms). Five of the items are worded symptomatically positive and 15 are worded symptomatically negative; respondents use a 4-points scale to rate how each item applied to himself or herself during the past week.

　　The author has also developed a rating scale based on the same symptoms to be used by the clinician to rate the client (Anxiety Status Inventory or ASI), thus allowing two sources of data on the same symptoms.

Norms: The initial study was carried out on 225 psychiatric patients including 152 male inpatients, and 23 male and 50 female outpatients with a mean age of 41 years. An additional 100 male and female "normal" (nonpatient) subjects were part of the study. However, little formal standardization work has been carried out on the SAS.

Scoring: The SAS is scored by summing the values on each item to produce a raw score ranging from 20 to 80. An SAS index is derived by dividing the raw score by 80, producing an index that ranges from .25 to 1.00 (higher scores equal more anxiety). A cutoff score of 50 is recommended, with scores over 50 suggesting the presence of clinically meaningful anxiety.

Reliability: Data are not available.

Validity: The SAS has fair concurrent validity, correlating significantly with the Taylor Manifest Anxiety Scale and with the clinician rating scale developed by the author (ASI). The SAS also has good known-groups validity, distinguishing between patients diagnosed as having anxiety disorders and those with other psychiatric diagnoses and between nonpatient and patient groups.

Primary Reference: Zung, W. K. (1971). A rating instrument for anxiety disorders, *Psychosomatics, 12,* 37, 1–379. Instrument reproduced by permission of W. K. Zung and *Psychosomatics,* all rights reserved.

Availability: Psykey, Inc., 7750 Daggett Street, San Diego, CA 92111.

scale may give you permission to use it free of charge. When I conducted my study on young adolescents in foster care (Salahu-Din & Bollman, 1994), permission was received directly from Morris Rosenberg (personal communication) to use the Baltimore Self-Esteem Scale (1979).

Implementing an Intervention

You have operationally defined terms specific to your client's situation, and the assessment of the client's circumstances is now complete enough for you to select an intervention. An intervention is a service, treatment, or program used to maintain, eliminate, reduce, or prevent problems that may range from simple to complex and that relate specifically to the targeted

FIGURE 13.2   The Self-Rating Anxiety Scale (SAS) Instrument

Below are twenty statements. Please rate each using the following scale:

 1 = Some or a little of the time
 2 = Some of the time
 3 = Good part of the time
 4 = Most or all of the time

Please record your rating in the space to the left of each item.

____ **1.** I feel more nervous and anxious than usual.

____ **2.** I feel afraid for no reason at all.

____ **3.** I get upset easily or feel panicky.

____ **4.** I feel like I'm falling apart and going to pieces.

____ **5.** I feel that everything is all right and nothing bad will happen.

____ **6.** My arms and legs shake and tremble.

____ **7.** I am bothered by headaches, neck and back pains.

____ **8.** I feel weak and get tired easily.

____ **9.** I feel calm and can sit still easily.

____ **10.** I can feel my heart beating fast.

____ **11.** I am bothered by dizzy spells.

____ **12.** I have fainting spells or feel like it.

____ **13.** I can breathe in and out easily.

____ **14.** I get feelings of numbness and tingling in my fingers, toes.

____ **15.** I am bothered by stomach aches or indigestion.

____ **16.** I have to empty my bladder often.

____ **17.** My hands are usually dry and warm.

____ **18.** My face gets hot and blushes.

____ **19.** I fall asleep easily and get a good night's rest.

____ **20.** I have nightmares.

Reprinted from J. Fischer and K. Corcoran, *Measures for clinical practice: A sourcebook* (3rd ed.). New York: The Free Press. © 2000 with permission from Elsevier Science.

behavior (Blythe & Tripodi, 1989). For example, one targeted behavior for Carmen, the older daughter in the case example, was her poor hygiene. Therefore, an intervention to address hygiene and no other problem, such as Carmen's intelligence, is implemented.

  If Carmen's intelligence is an issue, then a different strategy should be used to deal with that concern. You can conduct a literature review of empirical information on interventions that will work for your client's specific problem. Professional journal articles and books describe interventions that have been used successfully in addressing client issues. Also, your agency may use certain interventions to address targeted client problems. For example, agencies working with troubled adolescents may use peer mentoring as an intervention, peer group support, behavior modification, or volunteer services.

Ongoing monitoring of the clients' behavior after introduction of the intervention begins after baseline data have been collected. Depending on the type of targeted behavior, monitoring may be done through your observations, through the client self-monitoring by keeping a log, a notebook, or journals and reporting this information to you, through information in existing records, or through standardized measures. These repeated measures of the client's behavior are compared with the baseline data and each other to determine whether changes are occurring.

Visual Display of Data

The basic graph, Figure 13.3, for displaying a single system design has a horizontal line (x-axis) and a vertical line (y-axis). The left side of the horizontal axis reflects the baseline phase of the evaluation and the right side of the horizontal axis represents the intervention phase or the independent variable. Additional phases could follow the intervention phase, such as another intervention (C, D) or withdrawal of an intervention (A). Dotted lines separate different phases of a design. The independent variable is the intervention that influences change in a client's behavior and is shown along the horizontal axis. The timeframe for gathering baseline data and for implementing the intervention is also displayed along the horizontal axis. The

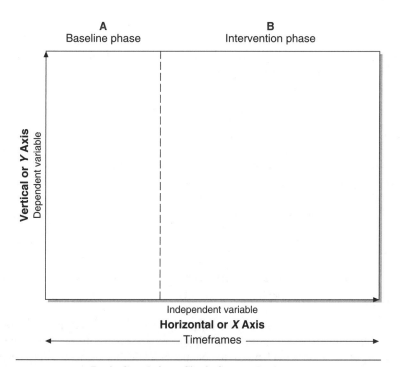

FIGURE 13.3 Basic Graph for a Single System Design

vertical axis displays the dependent variable, that is, the behavior or situation to be changed. The vertical axis also shows the duration or magnitude of the behavior or situation. A review of the graph gives the client and the social worker an instant summary of the client's progress since introduction of the intervention.

Important Points about Components of Single System Designs

- Client's informed consent for the social worker to use a single system design should be covered under the basic permission that the client provides, authorizing the agency to provide services.
- The target behavior(s) is the concern identified by the client and the social worker that will be the focus of change process. Often targeted behaviors are selected by the agency, as when a client has been identified as a child abuse perpetrator or at risk of abusing children.
- Before implementing an intervention, baseline data are gathered about the client's behavior, situation, or circumstances. The baseline information is compared with measures of the client's behavior, situation, or circumstances taken after the intervention is introduced to determine whether changes are occurring.
- The visual display of data is an important part of the single system design method for evaluating individual practice.

Single System Design Models

> *Activity 6.*   Which of the single system design models outlined below do you believe would be more suitable for implementation with clients at your job or internship? Explain your answer.

Several different types of single system designs for evaluating work with individual clients are available. Although practitioners are primarily responsible for case planning, clients can have an active role in designing single system designs, in collecting data, and in monitoring progress. The graphic display of the single system design gives both the client and the social worker an immediate visual picture of progress being made toward achieving the changes desired by the client or a referring agency.

AB Design

The AB design is the primary single system design and the most basic. It has both a baseline phase and an intervention phase.

The Baseline, A.   The client's behavior before the start of an intervention is A, the baseline. You need baseline data to measure client change over a period of time. For some clients, it would be unethical and often harmful to conduct baseline observations before beginning the intervention. Think about Ms. Kodak, for instance. Both she and her doctor acknowledged her mental health problems. It would not be prudent to delay an intervention until after monitoring her schizophrenic behaviors. Delaying the intervention could prove harmful to Ms. Kodak and others. In these situations, however, baseline data may be collected from existing information, such as the doctor's records and school files and from information that the client shares with the social worker.

The Intervention, B.   The client's behavior after an intervention or treatment has been introduced is represented by B. There is one intervention in the AB design. If the intervention phase shows that progress has been made, this does not necessarily mean that the change results from the intervention. Some other phenomenon may be the cause of the change. In other words, there may be an alternative explanation for changes in the client's behavior. Figure 13.4 represents a single system AB design that was used with Carmen, Ms. Kodak's older daughter. The

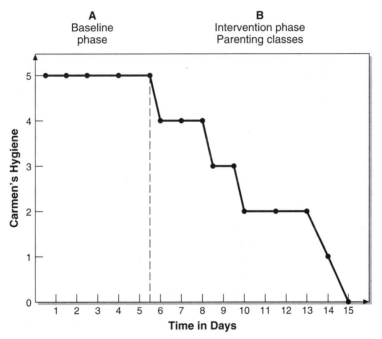

Severity of Carmen's Hygiene

5 = *Very severe*—clothes dirty and grease stained; hair smells and not combed; teeth not brushed, and face not washed; has body odor from not bathing

4 = *Somewhat severe*—clothes dirty; hair smells; took a bath, didn't brush teeth

3 = *Not severe but problematic*—clothes clean, hair still smells, took a bath, didn't brush teeth

2 = *Continued work needed*—hygiene mainly good with a few problems

1 = *No problem with hygiene*—clothes clean, hair shampooed and combed, teeth brushed

0 = *No problem with hygiene, and Carmen takes some responsibility for maintaining her hygiene*

FIGURE 13.4   AB Design

targeted behavior, Carmen's hygiene, is displayed along the vertical axis along with numbers that represent the magnitude of the hygiene problem. Data about Carmine's hygiene were collected during the baseline phase, A, and the intervention, parenting classes, was introduced during the B phase. A scale was constructed to show the magnitude of Carmine's problem with a score of 5 being the most severe and 0 indicating that hygiene is no longer a problem and that Carmen assumes responsibility for maintaining her hygiene.

ABC Design

When you use more than one intervention simultaneously with a client you are using either the ABC, ABCD, ABCDE, or another design with more than one intervention. This single system design, also called the successive intervention design, is a continuation of the AB design; however, it has multiple interventions. The C phase is the second intervention. As additional interventions are added, the designs become ABCD, ABCDE, with the additional letters representing new interventions. You can also use the C phase as a period when the client is taught to maintain desired behaviors. With multiple intervention designs, however, the practitioner cannot determine which intervention caused the change in the client's behavior. Nevertheless, this design is appealing to practitioners because the intervention is not withdrawn and because social workers usually use more than one intervention to address a client's problem. In the AB design, the intervention with Ms. Kodak was parenting classes to address Carmen's poor hygiene. Figure 13.5 illustrates the introduction of a second intervention, counseling to address the hygiene problem. The design becomes an ABC single system design.

ABA and ABAB Designs

ABA and ABAB single system designs are also called reversal designs. In the ABA design, there is a baseline phase A where data are gathered prior to implementing an intervention B. The intervention is withdrawn in the second A phase. The client is observed during a period of no intervention to determine if changes occurring in the intervention phase have stabilized or if behavior returns to the pre-intervention state. More likely than not, if the behavior returns to the pre-intervention phase, the intervention caused the change in behavior. For example, in the AB design used with Ms. Kodak, the intervention was parenting classes. Using an ABA design as demonstrated in Figure 13.6, the intervention is withdrawn after Carmen's hygiene improves. That is, Ms. Kodak is no longer required to participate in parenting classes. During this withdrawal period you monitor to see if Carmen's hygiene returns to the pre-intervention state, which was very severe.

The ABAB (reversal design) has two baseline periods and two intervention periods. This design is the same as the ABA with the introduction of the intervention a second time. The first A is the pre-intervention monitoring of the client's behavior to gather baseline information; the first B is implementation of an intervention; the second A phase is the withdrawal of the first intervention for a period of time; and the second B is the reintroduction of the intervention. Thus, Ms. Kodak begins parenting classes again with the ABAB design. Whereas with the ABA design services end during a period of no intervention, in the ABAB design services terminate during the second intervention period. Withdrawal of an intervention is not always feasible and is sometimes unethical. Figure 13.7 is an example of an ABAB

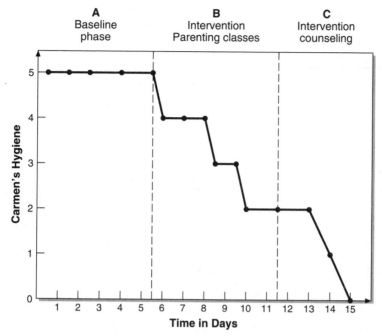

| A
Baseline
phase | B
Intervention
Parenting classes | C
Intervention
counseling |

Severity of Carmen's Hygiene

5 = *Very severe*—clothes dirty and grease stained; hair smells and not combed; teeth not brushed, and face not washed; has body odor from not bathing
4 = *Somewhat severe*—clothes dirty; hair smells; took a bath, didn't brush teeth
3 = *Not severe but problematic*—clothes clean, hair still smells, took a bath, didn't brush teeth
2 = *Continued work needed*—hygiene mainly good with a few problems
1 = *No problem with hygiene*—clothes clean, hair shampooed and combed, teeth brushed
0 = *No problem with hygiene, and Carmen takes some responsibility for maintaining her hygiene*

FIGURE 13.5   ABC Design

design, which shows that when the parenting classes (the intervention) were stopped, Carmen's hygiene became problematic, indicating that it is likely that the intervention was responsible for the change in hygiene.

Multiple Baseline Designs

The three types of multiple baseline designs are across client problems, involving one client with two or more problems in one setting, across settings, where one client has one problem shown in two or more settings, and across clients or client systems in which the social worker uses the same intervention consecutively with two or more clients demonstrating the same problems in the same settings. The intervention is not withdrawn when the multiple baseline

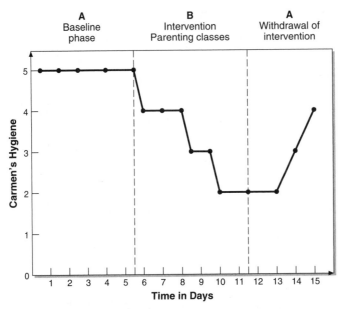

Severity of Carmen's Hygiene

5 = *Very severe*—clothes dirty and grease stained; hair smells and not combed; teeth not brushed, and face not washed; has body odor from not bathing

4 = *Somewhat severe*—clothes dirty; hair smells; took a bath, didn't brush teeth

3 = *Not severe but problematic*—clothes clean, hair still smells, took a bath, didn't brush teeth

2 = *Continued work needed*—hygiene mainly good with a few problems

1 = *No problem with hygiene*—clothes clean, hair shampooed and combed, teeth brushed

0 = *No problem with hygiene, and Carmen takes some responsibility for maintaining her hygiene*

FIGURE 13.6   ABA Design

single system design is implemented with services provided until changes occur in the targeted behavior, unless the client terminates services before goals are reached. For example, in the Kodak case study, Ms. Davis, the social worker, and Ms. Kodak delineated multiple problems that the family was experiencing, such as Carmen's leaving the house whenever she desired, her hygiene problems, and Ms. Kodak's hygiene problems, mental health problems, and inability to care for herself physically. Ms. Kodak and Ms. Davis select several of these issues to work on using one intervention.

Analyzing Single System Design Data

Three important concepts in analyzing data are practical, statistical, and theoretical significance. Practical significance is the idea that someone, especially the client, believes that purposeful change occurred from the time of the baseline measurement to measurements during the intervention.

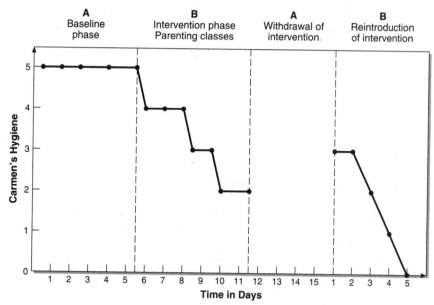

Severity of Carmen's Hygiene

5 = *Very severe*—clothes dirty and grease stained; hair smells and not combed; teeth not brushed,
     and face not washed; has body odor from not bathing
4 = *Somewhat severe*—clothes dirty; hair smells; took a bath, didn't brush teeth
3 = *Not severe but problematic*—clothes clean, hair still smells, took a bath, didn't brush teeth
2 = *Continued work needed*—hygiene mainly good with a few problems
1 = *No problem with hygiene*—clothes clean, hair shampooed and combed, teeth brushed
0 = *No problem with hygiene, and Carmen takes some responsibility for maintaining her hygiene*

FIGURE 13.7   ABAB Design

    Statistical significance in single system designs involves comparing data collected during the baseline phase with data collected during and after the intervention phase. Inferential statistics can calculate the extent to which the researcher can say with a certain amount of confidence that the intervention, the independent variable, is responsible for the change in the behavior of clients, the dependent variable. Only if the assumptions of randomization and independent observations are met, can the social worker say the change was not due to chance. One problem with achieving independent observations is autocorrelated data, which occurs when data are not independent of one another and so result in biased statistical results. Bloom, Fischer, and Orme (1999) assert that it is possible for autocorrelation to increase Type I or Type II errors, that there is controversy about the degree of autocorrelation of single system design data, and that one debate is, "... that the issue is not at all whether the autocorrelation is significant but the effect any autocorrelation has on the use of statistics" (p. 521). There are tests to detect autocorrelation as described in Bloom, Fischer, and Orme.

    Theoretical significance is based on the theoretical framework selected to help facilitate the planning of an intervention. That framework would have specific expectations for client outcomes. Single system design results can be analyzed using graphs or statistical analysis.

See Bloom, Fischer, and Orme (1999) and Alter and Evens (1990) for directions on conducting statistical analyses using different approaches, such as graphs, celeration line, proportion/frequency, and two-standard-deviation band. This section described only various single system design models and analysis of single system designs.

Important Points about Single System Designs

- Single system designs are practice evaluation models used to evaluate your practice with clients.
- Single system designs have two basic components, the baseline phase, A, and the intervention phase, B. The AB design has one baseline phase and one intervention phase. Some single system design models have more than one baseline phase and more than one intervention phase.
- Some single system design models have one baseline phase and multiple interventions. Determining which intervention caused the change in the client's behavior is difficult when this single system design method is used.
- Multiple baseline single system designs are used when one intervention addresses more than one client problem, when one client has one problem that manifests itself in two or more settings, and when more than one client in the same practitioner's caseload has the same problem in the same setting.

Validity and Reliability

Recall from Chapter 6 that a measuring instrument may be reliable and at the same time not valid. An instrument is considered valid when it measures what it purports to measure. For example, if the social worker claims to be measuring Ms. Kodak's ability to care for her children, the instrument that is used should measure that ability and not some other phenomena such as self-esteem or IQ. A reliable instrument is one that can be depended on to accurately measure a phenomenon consistently. Regarding an instrument's reliability, Bloom, Fischer, and Orme (1999) maintain that in single subject design research you may be able to examine interobserver reliability and not other types of reliability. In interobserver agreement reliability, as defined in Chapter 6, *Measurement,* two observers or raters observe the same participants at the same time, thus obtaining two measurements simultaneously. The aim of interobserver reliability is to have more than one trained person, using identical instruments, observe and rate the same research participants, situations, or events. As a result, the independent ratings by the raters should be similar. If the ratings agree, there is a true picture of the phenomenon being observed and minimal rater influence. A correlation coefficient can be computed to determine if the above types of reliability exist. Regardless, you should refer to the literature to determine if there are data that supports the reliability of the measures that you have selected. To obtain high reliability for social work–related variables you can do the following:

- *Use the same definitions and procedures of measurement.* For example, Ms. Davis asks Ms. Shatner, Carmen's teacher, to observe Carmen each day and record data about her hygiene, her clothing, her hair, her body odor, and her teeth. Since Ms. Davis will repeatedly measure Carmen's hygiene, the instructions that she gives the teacher about what to observe and record should be consistent.

- *Discuss the instrument and practice using it.*

- *Use the same information consistently to determine if changes are occurring.* Think about the teacher's monitoring of Carmen. Ms. Davis, the social worker, should have Carmen's teacher record her observations consistently and not report her observations verbally.

- *Establish a trusting relationship.* The client then believes that you will use the information being gathered to help the client.

- *Inform the client of the significance of the information.* Also, explain how it will be used (Blythe & Tripodi, 1989).

Important Points about Validity and Reliability in Single System Designs

- It is important to establish both validity and reliability of a measuring instrument. A valid instrument is one that measures what it claims to measure. For example, if you plan on measuring anxiety in a client, use an instrument that measures anxiety and not one that measures depression or stress.
- A reliable instrument is one that is consistent and dependable in measuring. The instrument can be depended on to provide accurate measurement of phenomena such as anxiety, depression, or stress.

Human Diversity Issues in Evaluating Individual Practice in Quantitative Methods

In her research with students, Nelsen (1994) found that female clients were more likely to be asked to participate in research and to respond affirmatively more frequently than male clients. She also learned that when a client is of a different ethnic background than that of the researcher, there is a tendency not to ask the client to participate in research for fear of offending that person. Avoid asking people to be participants simply because they are more agreeable or because of fear. When people are different from you, there is an obligation to become more informed about their life experiences to facilitate understanding and to improve the comfort level of researcher and client.

It is also reported that people of color, women, and low-income people are often targeted for change when environmental problems should be targeted for monitoring. This is also an ethical issue. For example, the social worker observed that Ms. Kodak lives in substandard housing that is unsafe for the family. If the social worker focuses on relocating Ms. Kodak or removing her children from the home instead of taking action to force the landlord to comply with housing codes and respond to health department warnings about the condition of his building, then Ms. Kodak is being targeted when the landlord should be targeted. In this situation, the social worker should advocate for improved housing and assist the client in relocating as an alternative, unless it is the client's choice to move instead of getting repairs made. Another human diversity issue is whether the standardized measures you are using have been tested for validity and reliability for the groups with which you are currently working (Nelsen, 1994).

Ethical Issues and Biases in Evaluating Individual Practice in Quantitative Methods

Ethical issues in single system designs include delaying the intervention for certain clients while baseline data are collected, purposely withdrawing the intervention in the ABA or ABAB designs when the intervention may have been helping the client, and delaying the intervention in multiple baseline designs for certain clients to achieve a stable baseline. Besides these ethical concerns, in certain designs, ethical issues occur when the client does not select the target behavior and the social worker attempts to monitor the client's behavior without client permission (Nelsen, 1994). For example, you are asked to monitor a client's interaction with her children, but the client thinks that you are visiting her home to help her plan nutritious meals. This is unethical.

This chapter focused on quantitative methods for evaluating individual practice with clients, a form of practice evaluation, and presented several single system design models. Figure 13.8 is a comparison of those models. Chapter 14 explains another aspect of practice evaluation, program evaluation used for evaluating programs. The experimental designs described in Chapter 14 are also applicable to single system design evaluations discussed here.

AB Designs

- Have a baseline phase
- Have an intervention phase
- Difficult to ascertain if the change results from the intervention

ABC Designs

- Have a baseline phase
- Introduces two or more interventions
- Cannot determine which intervention caused the change in the client's behavior

ABA and ABAB Designs

- Have a baseline phase
- Have an intervention phase
- In ABA design, the intervention is withdrawn while behavior is monitored
- The intervention is introduced again in the ABAB Design

Multiple Baseline Designs

- Use with clients with more than one problem and the same intervention
- Use with several clients with the same problem
- The intervention is not withdrawn

FIGURE 13.8   Comparison of Single System Design Models

WRITING STRATEGY

Think about behaviors that you want to target as the focus of your intervention with a client, a partner, a friend, a relative, or a supervisee. Write objective case notes relating to the identified problem and intervention. If your opinions are included, indicate as such in the case notes.

LEARNING ACTIVITY

Following steps outlined in the previous sections, design a single system design that is appropriate for a client that you work with. If you are not directly involved with a client, work with a supervisee, your child, a partner, a friend, or a roommate.

INFORMATION TECHNOLOGY FOR EVALUATING INDIVIDUAL PRACTICE IN QUANTITATIVE METHODS

Using a search engine of your choice, find a site on the World Wide Web that has information about single system designs. What is the source of that information? Describe the content.

Important Points from Chapter 13

- Evaluation of individual practice is necessary to determine if interventions or treatments are helping clients achieve goals related to the target behavior.
- There are several quantitative methods for evaluating individual practice with clients. These models have at least one baseline phase, A, and one intervention phase, B. In the baseline phase information is gathered about the client's problem, situation, or environment. During the intervention phase a service is provided to help the client change the problem.
- Phases in the single system design models involve targeting a problem that will be the focus of the intervention, operationalizing terms related to the target problem, establishing measurable goals, selecting a single system design, implementing an intervention, the independent variable, and repeatedly measuring the target behavior, the dependent variable.
- Data related to the targeted problem can be measured through standardized measuring instruments (testing), through observing client behavior, through client self-monitoring, and through evaluating existing records—hospital, school, and agency files.
- Measuring instruments should be tested for validity and reliability to assure that what you are measuring is what you set out to measure and to make certain that the measures are consistent and dependable.

REFERENCES

Alter, C., & Evens, W. (1990). *Evaluating your practice: A guide to self-assessment.* New York: Springer.

Bloom, M., Fischer, J., & Orme, J. G. (1999). *Evaluating practice: Guidelines for the accountable professional* (3rd ed.). Boston: Allyn & Bacon.

Blythe, B. J., & Tripodi, T. (1989). *Measurement in direct* practice. Thousand Oaks, CA.: Sage.

Corcoran, K., & Fischer, J. (2000). *Measures for clinical practice: A sourcebook* (3rd ed.). New York: The Free Press.

Nelsen, J. C. (1993). Testing practice wisdom: Another use for single system research. *Journal of Social Service Research, 18*(1/2), 65–82.

Rosenberg, M. (1979). *Conceiving the self.* New York: Basic Books.

Salahu-Din, S., & Bollman, S. (1994). Identity development and self-esteem of young adolescents in foster care. *Child and Adolescent Social Work Journal, 11*(2), 123–135.

Wakefield, J. C., & Kirk, S. A. (1997). What the practitioner knows versus what the client is told: Neglected dilemmas of informed consent in an account of single-system experimental designs. *Journal of Social Work Education, 33,* 275–291.

14 Program Evaluation Designs

*Since taking research, I feel more comfortable and less intimidated by the
subject and by journal articles. I no longer skip certain parts of the journal
articles because I understand the language now. I also know how research
relates to my other courses.*

—Junior Research Student

CHAPTER GOALS

Your major goals upon completion of this chapter are to:

- Understand what program evaluation is.
- Recognize the different types of program evaluation designs.
- Recognize program evaluation designs based on experimental designs.
- Understand the internal and external threats to validity of experimental program evaluation
  designs.

Introduction

Program evaluations assess the effectiveness of services in meeting goals relating to delivery of social services to help clients (individuals, families, groups, or organizations) change behaviors, attitudes, or situations. A social service program is a planned set of activities that outline goals, objectives, and intended outcomes. They focus on and guide social workers in empowering and assisting clients in effecting specific changes. A program may be affiliated with a governmental or nongovernmental agency or a for-profit or nonprofit agency. Child protective services, adult protective services, family preservation, Alcoholics Anonymous, adoption services, adult services, adult day care, and teenage pregnancy services are examples of programs designed to help people effect some change in their lives and to assist in empowering clients to achieve their potential. Programs are assessed periodically using program evaluations to determine the extent of program effectiveness in achieving goals set during the design of the program.

Program evaluation, also referred to as evaluation research, is one aspect of practice evaluation. The other component of practice evaluation, evaluation of individual practice using either qualitative or quantitative methods, was described in Chapters 12 and 13. Program evaluation is a systematic assessment of how social service programs or policies meet the needs of people they were designed to serve. Program evaluations assess how services have been implemented, whether programs should be modified or discontinued, and whether program goals were met and are congruent with the expectations of those with a vested interest in the program. People with a vested interest in the program, that is, stakeholders, are agency heads, program administrators, staff responsible for program implementation, policymakers, funding sources, and program participants. Program description, problem definition, planning, data collection, measurement, implementation, and reporting results are all components of program evaluation.

All those with an interest in the program use program evaluation results in their decisions about continued support, financial, political, or emotional. Agency administrators can commission an inside evaluation or hire an independent evaluator to conduct the assessment. Program processes and outcomes can be evaluated with either qualitative or quantitative evaluation research methods. One method or a combination of methods—interviews with program participants, staff, and community residents with a vested interest in the program, questionnaire administration, observations, analysis of available data including program records, statistical data and governmental reports, and experimental designs—may be used in evaluating programs.

Generalist Case Study: "The Evaluation of a Stress Management Program for Middle School Adolescents"

The amount of stress experienced by present-day adolescents and their concomitant lack of adequate coping skills have been linked to psychological and emotional disturbance (Compas, Oroson & Grant, 1993; Dise-Lewis, 1998; Gad & Johnson, 1980; Gersten, Langner, Eisenberg & Simcha-Fagan, 1977; Johnson & McCutcheon, 1980), including depression (Fredich, Reams & Jacobs, 1982;

Johnson & McCutcheon, 1980), high suicide rates (Cohen-Sandler, Berman & King, 1982; de Anda, 1995; National Center for Health Statistics, 1993), problems with regard to behavioral adjustment and academic performance (Fontana & Dovidio, 1984; Garrison, Schoenback, Schluchter & Kaplan, 1987; Vaux & Ruggiero, 1983), and a variety of health problems (De Longis, Coyne, Dakof, Folkman & Lazarus, 1982; Hotaling, Atwell & Linsky, 1978). . . .

According to the relational model proposed by Lazarus and Folkman (1984), stress is defined as: . . . A particular relationship between the person and the environment that is appraised by the person as taxing or exceeding his or her resources and endangering his or her well-being (p. 19).

In this model, the relationship between the individual and the environmental stressor is mediated by the person's appraisal of both the threat value of the stressor and the effectiveness of his/her coping strategies in dealing with the stressor. The subjective nature of the relationship implies self-evaluation of the degree of stress and the effectiveness of one's coping repertoire. In previous studies by the author with high school (de Anda et al., in press), middle school (de Anda et al., 1997), and pregnant, parenting, and substance-abusing adolescents (de Anda, Javidi, Jefford, Komorowski & Yanez, 1991; de Anda, Darroch, Davidson, Gilly, Javidi, Jefford, Komorowski, & Morejon-Schrobsdorf, 1992), one-quarter to one-third of the respondents self-reported experiencing high levels of stress on a daily and weekly basis. Moreover, they evaluated their own coping strategies to generally be low, and at best moderate, in effectiveness. Despite this, the adolescents in these studies all elected to employ positive, adaptive coping strategies (relaxation, distraction, help-seeking, cognitive control and affective release) significantly more often than maladaptive coping strategies (denial, withdrawal, confrontation, aggressive behavior, and substance abuse) in their attempts to manage stress. The consistency of these findings across the various adolescent populations led the author to hypothesize that the low to moderate success rates for the adaptive coping strategies were due to the trial and error learning process which did not provide adequate information regarding when and how to employ these skills. Furthermore, it was hypothesized that providing adolescents with instruction and practice in employing specific coping strategies via a structured stress management program would result in the development of a coping repertoire judged by the adolescents as effective in reducing the degree of stress they experience in their lives. To this end, an intervention program was designed which teaches the adolescents to employ specific cognitive coping strategies and procedures (e.g., accurate self-talk and problem-solving techniques), behavioral coping techniques (e.g., "calming actions" such as letting feelings out, exercise and use of distraction), and reduction of physiological arousal through the use of various muscle relaxation procedures.

Method

A pre-test post-test control group design was employed to determine the effectiveness of the ten-week stress management program.

Sample. Fifty-four middle school adolescents participated in this experimental study, 36 in the experimental group and 18 in the control group. The subjects ranged in age from twelve (n = 2) to fourteen (n = 3) years with 13 the median age. This distribution remained the same for both males (n = 16) and females (n = 38). Ethnic diversity was evident among the 51 students who reported their ethnicity with no differences noted by gender. . . .

All the female subjects were randomly assigned to experimental and control groups. However, due to the smaller number of male participants and the decision of half of the males to be controls, randomization was not possible for the male subjects. It is recognized that the generalizability of the findings from this sample is limited due to the small sample size and self-selection in response to the announcements used to solicit participants for the study.

(continued)

Case Study *Continued*

The Independent Variable. A cognitive-behavioral stress management program designed by the author served as the independent variable. This ten-week program is a revised and expanded version of a five-week stress management program that had been designed for, and pilot tested with, pregnant and parenting adolescents (de Anda, Darroch, Davidson, Gilly, & Morejon, 1990). . . .

The program was highly structured, employing a scripted leader's guide to assure that all three groups received the same intervention. A combination of didactic and group methods were used to instruct the adolescents in key concepts and cognitive and behavioral coping skills. The adolescents in the experimental groups were also provided with workbooks that parallel the leader's guide and audiocassette tapes containing the relaxation procedures. The workbooks were used in-session and contained instructional materials regarding concepts and skills, illustrative vignettes, practice exercises, motivational activities and written procedures for the ▼arious relaxation methods. The audio tapes were to be used to practice the relaxation exercises at home on a daily basis. . . .

Instruments. The adolescents completed two self-report measures; the Adolescent Stress and Coping Measure (ASCM); and the State-Trait Anxiety Inventory (Form Y) (Spielberger, Gorsuch, Lushene, Vagg, & Jacobs, 1983). . . .

Findings. Preintervention equivalence between the experimental and control groups was established by conducting t-tests on all the dependent variables on the pretest of the ASCM and the STAI. The two groups were found to be equivalent on all but one variable, cognitive control (t = 2.11; p ≤ .05) with the subjects in the control group employing cognitive control significantly more often (M = 5.50) than those in the experimental group (M = 4.67).

The experimental and control groups were compared with respect to the following variables: degree and duration of stress; the frequency of various manifestations of stress (physiological, behavioral, cognitive, and affective); the frequency of the use of adaptive and maladaptive coping strategies; and the perceived effectiveness of these coping strategies. T-tests were performed on the pretest–post-test gain scores. The results of these analyses follows:

As hypothesized, a significant difference was found between the experimental and control groups in the *degree* of stress they experienced. Participants in the stress management program reported a significantly lower degree of stress on both the State portion of the STAI (t = –2.38; ≤ p .05) and the ASCM (t = –1.53; p ≤ .05) than adolescents who did not participate in the program. On the STAI a decrease in scores was noted for experimentals and an increase for controls. On the ASCM, the *degree* of stress was a sum of four items providing the self-reported frequency with which they experienced stress during a typical week and a typical day. . . .

Adolescents in the experimental group reported a significant increase in the use of cognitive control (M = .82) and those in the control group, a decrease (M = –.42). This is particularly noteworthy, because at the pretest the control group had a significantly higher mean than the experimental group and the main focus of the stress management program was on the teaching of cognitive control strategies. . . . The experimental group reported a greater increase in adaptive relative to maladaptive coping strategies, whereas the control group reported an increase in maladaptive coping strategies relative to a decrease in adaptive coping strategies. . . . Adolescents in the stress management program reported a significant increase (M = 7.23) in the effectiveness of their coping strategies while the control group indicated a decrease (M = –.375) in effectiveness.

Formative evaluation procedures were also employed to determine if the relaxation skills were, in fact, successfully reducing muscle tension. Relaxation rating sheets were completed by members of the experimental group before and after every relaxation session, once a week in the group session and in home practice. The adolescents rated their subjective level of relaxation from 0 (very relaxed) to 10 (very tense) for each muscle group. Relaxation ratings were calculated by tallying the difference between "before" and "after" scores. The experimental group evidenced a 65.7 percent improvement in relaxation, demonstrating successful application of the relaxation methods.

Discussion

The final measure of the success of any stress management program is the extent to which the participants increase their ability to deal with the stress they experience in their daily lives. In this case, the participants in the stress management program reported a significant increase in the effectiveness of their coping strategies for dealing with stress, while the control subjects reported a decrease in effectiveness over the same period of time.

In sum, the stress management program appears to have been successful in increasing the participants' use of cognitive coping strategies and relaxation and the effectiveness of adaptive coping strategies in dealing with stress, as well as decreasing the degree of stress experienced by the adolescents.

Cohen-Sandler, R., Berman, A. L., & King, R. A. (1982). Life stress and symptomatology: Determinants of suicidal behavior in children. *Journal of American Academy of Child Psychiatry, 21,* 178–186.

de Anda, D. (1995). Adolescents. *Encyclopedia of Social Work,* 19th edition. Silver Spring, MD: National Association of Social Workers.

De Longis, A., Coyne, J., Dakof, G., Folkman, S., & Lazarus, R. (1982). Relationship of daily hassles, uplifts, and major life events to health status. *Health Psychology, 20,* 119–136.

Dise-Lewis, J. E. (1998). The life events and coping inventory: An assessment of stress in children. *Psychosomatic Medicine, 50,* 484–499.

Fontana, A., & Dovidio, J. F. (1984). The relationship between stressful life events and school-related performances of type A and type B adolescents *Journal of Human Stress, 10,* 50–54.

Fredich, W., Reams R., & Jacobs, J. (1982). Depression and suicidal ideation in early adolescents. *Journal of Youth and Adolescence, 11,* 403–407.

Gad, M. T., & Johnson, J. H. (1980). Correlates of adolescent life stress as related to race, SES, and levels of perceived social support. *Journal of Clinical Child Psychiatry, 9,* 13–16.

Garrison, C., Schoenback, V., Schluchter, M., & Kaplan, B. (1987). Life events in early adolescence. *Journal of the American Academy of Child and Adolescent Psychiatry, 26,* 865–872.

Gersten, J. C., Langner, T. S., Eisenberg, & Simcha-Fagan. (1977). An evaluation of the etiological role of stressful life-change events in psychological disorders. *Journal of Health and Social Behavior, 18,* 228–244.

Hotaling, G. T., Atwell, S. G., & Linsky, (1978). Adolescent life change and illness: A comparison of three models. *Journal of Youth and Adolescence, 7,* 393–403.

Johnson, J. H., & McCutcheon, S. M. (1980). Assessing life stress in older children and adolescents: Preliminary findings with the life events checklist. In I. G. Sarason & C. D. Speilberger (Eds.), *Stress and anxiety* (pp. 111–125). Washington, DC: Hemisphere.

Lazarus, R. S., & Folkman, S. (1984). *Stress, appraisal, and coping.* New York: Springer Publishing.

National Center for Health Statistics, (1993). Unpublished data. Center for Disease Control, Public Health Service, U. S. Department of Health and Human Services.

Vaux, A., & Ruggiero, M. (1983). Stressful life change and delinquent behavior. *American Journal of Community Psychology, 11,* 169–183.

Note: Excerpts from "The evaluation of a stress management program for middle school adolescents," *Child and Adolescent Social Work Journal, 15*(1), 73–85, by Diane de Anda, 1998. Reprinted with permission of Kluwer Academic/Plenum Publishers and Diane de Anda.

Why Evaluate Programs?

> *Activity 1.*   After reading this section, explain why program evaluations should be used; find
> out if program evaluations are used at your place of employment or your internship and the
> kind of evaluation that is used. Locate two journal articles that describe how program evalua-
> tion using experimental designs was implemented. Explain the purpose of the program; de-
> scribe program participants and the type of program evaluation that was applied.

Administrators, program implementers, and social workers must know how their programs are
functioning and the outcomes of those programs in terms of providing services that positively
influence clients' lives. Program evaluation is one method for gathering this information. Administrators must be cognizant of whether clients or participants are benefiting from the program, what the program strengths and weaknesses are, and whether the program is being
implemented as planned. Evaluations also determine whether program goals and objectives
have been achieved by the time the program ends. This information assists in decision making
about whether the program is operating as planned, and if it should continue, be modified,
expanded, decreased, or dismantled.

Program evaluation is also used to assure accountability to clients, to the organization, to
funding sources, and to the community by documenting that the program is making a positive
difference in clients' lives. Program evaluations benefit practitioners by informing them if the
program is helping clients. Although there are many benefits to having programs evaluated,
evaluations are not used as often as they should be. Why then, if program evaluations can be
valuable to administrators, are they not used more often? Hoefer (1994) suggests that managers
may not rely on program evaluations because negative outcomes may be uncovered that could
be damaging to the program, because more rigorous evaluations are costly and demanding, and
because many managers do not have the preparation for conducting rigorous evaluations.

Program evaluations are sometimes used for undesirable reasons (Weiss, 1998). These
justifications, according to Weiss, include the wish to postpone a decision, to avoid making a
decision while hoping that the program evaluation will make the decision, for window dressing, that is, when administrators have already made a decision when a program evaluator is
consulted, and to use program evaluation results to provide program legitimacy. Program
evaluation may also be used as a self-glorification public relations scheme to advertise positive
results to gain support for the program. Weiss acknowledges that this latter purpose is not
necessarily a negative program evaluation tactic and that it is not used as often as in the past.

Deciding what is to be evaluated and how it is to be evaluated is a must for compelling
evaluation results. In the case example, for instance, de Anda evaluated the effectiveness of a
stress management program for adolescents. Before beginning the program, she knew what
information she wanted from the program evaluation that would be completed after program
implementation. She wanted to know if the program increased the adolescents' ability to deal
with the stress they experience in their daily lives, if the program increased participants' use of
cognitive coping strategies and relaxation techniques, and if the program provided effective
adaptive coping strategies for dealing with stress. She also chose to evaluate the program using
a pretest–post-test group design and formative evaluation.

Important Points about the Purpose of Program Evaluation

- Program evaluations help administrators determine the effect of services on clients' lives.
- Program evaluations inform stakeholders of the strengths and weaknesses of programs, including whether programs should continue (with or without modifications) or if they should be discontinued.
- Some reasons that managers may resist having their programs evaluated include time and expense, fear of negative information, and prior negative experiences with program evaluations.

Types of Program Evaluations

Activity 2. After reading this section, define formative and summative evaluation and explain under what circumstances you would use these two evaluation strategies.

Formative Evaluation

Formative evaluations, also called process evaluations, use qualitative designs, quantitative designs, or both in assessing and describing the internal workings of programs or the program's process—from assessing whether a program is needed to planning and implementing programs. Observing the program activities of social workers, administrators, and support staff in the course of the delivery of services while the program is operational and tracking client participation and progress are elements of formative evaluations. Formative evaluations use descriptions and observations to provide an in-depth look at the program's daily activities. Programs can be modified to improve services to clients, the ultimate goal of formative evaluation.

Needs assessments are formative evaluations done before programs are planned, developed, and implemented, to explore whether there are unmet community services needs for individuals, families, groups, and organizations. Needs assessments prevent duplication of services, set the stage for designing programs to meet client needs, and recommend needed programs. Legislators, agency administrators, client advocates, community leaders, and client advocacy groups are among the stakeholders who may request or commission a needs assessment. Social workers are in strategic positions to identify possible gaps in services and communicate that information to their supervisors for appropriate action because of their client contact and community involvement.

Summative Evaluation

Summative program evaluations, primarily quantitative designs that evaluate causality, generalizability, and the effectiveness of treatments are concerned with program outcomes or results, not program processes. Summative evaluations apply cost-effectiveness analysis, cost-benefit analysis, and experimental designs in assessing whether the ultimate program goal was achieved. In the case study, de Anda evaluated the stress management program using an experimental design, the pretest–post-test control group design. A different type of program evaluation, cost-effectiveness analysis, calculates all program expenses—salaries of program administrators, social workers, paraprofessionals, and support staff, as well as transportation, supplies, rent, or lease costs—and divides total program costs by the number of program participants. The cost for the program may then be compared to costs of another program that serves the same purpose. For example, using the case example, is it more cost effective to provide a stress management program for a group of adolescents or to intervene with individual counseling?

Cost-effectiveness decisions are made daily in social service agencies where program managers are often given budgets for each program under their supervision. There could be a budget for homemaker services, foster care placements, and day care for adults and for children. Administrators are required to stay within their budgets and not overspend. Subsequently, they promote finding the most appropriate, cost-effective, high-quality program for clients. Whereas cost-effectiveness analysis determines total program costs, cost-benefit analysis attempts to calculate program outcomes. The main focus of this chapter is program evaluations using experimental designs.

Important Points about the Types of Program Evaluations

- Formative program evaluations occur while the programs are operating and are concerned with processes from the needs assessment point to program planning and implementation.
- Summative program evaluations differ from formative evaluations in that these evaluations are concerned with program outcomes.

Validity and Experimental Program Evaluation Designs

> *Activity 3.*   After reading this section: (1) Explain the difference between internal and external validity; (2) describe four threats to internal validity and how those threats can be controlled; (3) describe two threats to external validity.

One of the main concerns in experimental design is whether these designs have internal and external validity. A design with internal validity allows the researcher to make statements about causal relationships between the stimulus (the independent variable) and changes in program participants. External validity determines whether the researcher can generalize findings from participants to the broader population from which the participants were selected. In program evaluation, the stimulus, or independent variable, is the program in which clients are involved. In the case example, for instance, the adolescents were involved in a program that would help them learn how to cope with stress. The researcher wants the program to be responsible for the ways in which the youth handle stress in a healthy, productive manner after completing the program, and also to be able to apply results to the population from which the sample of youth participating in the program was drawn.

Internal Validity

A valid measure is one that accurately measures what it purports to measure. Internal validity in program evaluation using experimental designs refers to whether the independent variable (the program) is responsible for the effect or change it appears to have had on the dependent variable (the client participating in the program). When the researcher is unable to distinguish between the effects of the independent variable and possible effects of extraneous variables (a phenomenon other than the independent variable or the program), the effects are said to be confounded. Thus, an important validity issue in experimental designs is eliminating extraneous sources of variability so that the researcher has confidence that changes in the dependent variable (the client) were caused by the independent variable (the program). Experimental designs that control outside or extraneous variables are said to have internal validity, while uncontrolled extraneous variables are referred to as threats to internal validity.

History. The threat of history refers to events occurring in participants' environment while the experiment is taking place, not considered during the design of the research. These events are unforeseen and uncontrollable and could also affect the dependent variable sometime between the pretest and the post-test. When there is the possibility that history events changed the dependent variable, it is difficult to determine how much of a role the independent variable had in causing that change. However, a control group, which does not participate in the program, can be used to evaluate history's effect on the dependent variable (the program participant). In the case example, de Anda used a pretest–post-test control group design, which eliminates the history threat.

Maturation. Maturation alludes to the physical and psychological changes (aging, behavior, energy level, health, interest in a particular topic and ideas) occurring in participants in experimental groups over time. These physical and psychological changes in participants over time, or maturation, can affect how participants respond to tests after the pretests are administered. In the case example, the effects of maturation would be a major concern because the researcher is studying adolescents who often experience major changes, both physically and emotionally. Again, use of a control group is the best way to eliminate the maturation threat.

Testing. Threats to internal validity, caused by testing, occur when the potential exists for participants' responses on a post-test to be influenced positively or negatively by a pretest that is the same as the post-test. For instance, adolescents in the case example were tested twice using The Adolescent Stress and Coping Measure and the State-Trait Anxiety Inventory. It is conceivable that their responses and resulting scores on the post-test were influenced by the pretest. Some items on the first test may have caused participants to change their behavior in a way that lowered their stress level instead of the change occurring because of what students learned in the cognitive-behavioral stress management program. A brief timeframe between the pretest and the post-test and test items that are easy to recall seem to have more potential for affecting post-test results. Not using a pretest and assuring that there is not too little time between the times of the pretest and the post-test are two methods to control for the testing threat.

Instrumentation. The instrumentation threat to internal validity occurs when the way variables are measured changes from the time of the pretest to the time of the post-test. This change causes measurements to be done differently during the post-test. Often, these modifications result from changes in the person administering the test. That person may have become more proficient in test administration or gone through other changes that cause unwanted variation in test administration. Instrumentation also occurs when measures have not been standardized, have not been pretested, are administered incorrectly, or are influenced by the observers' biases.

Statistical Regression. Sometimes participants are placed in either experimental or control groups because of extremely high or low scores on a test. When tested again, the extremely low or extremely high scoring participants' scores will have an average score closer to the mean. In other words, the scores on the second test will be less extreme, and the score for the group improves. This is statistical regression. The score may be different for the second measurement because of a change in the participants' situation and not because of the program. Random assignment to experimental and control groups prevents statistical regression.

Selection. When participants selected for the control group and the comparison group are not equivalent, the researcher's ability to determine whether the program has caused the change in participants is harmed and selection itself becomes a threat to internal validity. One reason for the selection threat is the use of existing groups, such as support groups, students in any type of classroom, and members of an organization, to provide participants. The selection threat to internal validity illuminates the importance of random sampling (to be representative of the population from which they were selected) and random assignment to groups (to assure that the groups are equal or equivalent in significant characteristics). Findings from unrepresentative groups cannot be generalized to people other than those in the study.

Mortality. Mortality occurs when participants drop out of the experimental groups and the control groups before the program ends. People may drop out of programs for a variety of reasons—relocation, illness, death, or lack of interest. This is not a problem if the numbers leaving are not large and if the dropouts in the experimental and control groups leave in equal numbers. When a significant number of participants drop out from one group and not from another or when the dropouts from one group are different from those remaining in the other group, the post-test scores will be confounded by the group differences of those remaining.

Interaction Effect. When the interaction between two or more variables results in confounded findings, called the interaction effect, internal validity of the study is threatened. Acting together, these variables affect the outcome on the dependent measure, the client, making it appear that the effect was caused by the independent variable, the program. Interaction effects can occur between any of the threats to internal validity; however, it occurs more frequently between maturation and selection.

External Validity

While internal validity occurs when change in clients can be attributed to the program in which the client is participating, external validity is present when those findings can be generalized to the population from which the sample of program participants was drawn. The extent to which results of the program evaluation are generalizable to clients, a group, a population, a setting, or a situation other than those in the program is called external validity. In other words, are the people in the program representative of people in the broader population from which program participants were selected?

Besides being representative of the population from which the sample was drawn, there are other factors to consider when attempting to control for external validity. When more than one group is used, the groups must be equivalent in significant variables. The researcher should also be able to determine whether any other intervention, treatment, or occurrence happened at the time of the evaluation that might have modified the representative sample.

Reactive Effects of Testing. Reactive effects of testing occur when pretesting changes participants' reactions to the independent variable, the program in program evaluation, and to the post-test. That is, after taking the pretest the characteristic of the client or program participant that the program is designed to effect is changed in some way by the pretest, thus influencing results of the post-test. When the behavior of a group taking the pretest is influenced in response to the pretest not to the program, the group is no longer equivalent to the population from which it was selected.

Selection-Treatment Interaction. The selection-treatment interaction effect is a threat to external validity when probability sampling is not used, negating the opportunity for a representative sample. In these situations, the sample (the program participants) may consist of people who are volunteers or chosen using a nonprobability sampling technique such as a sample of convenience. Although the study may have internal validity, the researcher is limited in generalizing findings to a broader population other than the sample because program participants are not randomly selected.

Reactive Setting. A reactive setting is one in which clients change their usual behavior because they are aware of being in an experimental setting. The researcher may also influence results when he or she unknowingly communicates to participants what the expected changes are for program participants. Changes in the dependent variable (client) due to altered behavior because of knowledge of being in a program can threaten external validity. To avoid this effect the researcher can conduct a so-called blind program, in which participants do not know what the experimental hypothesis is or the expected outcome.

Using a double-blind method for controlling reactivity caused by the researcher can also be used. In this type of experiment, neither the clients nor the person responsible for administering the experiment know which participants are in the experimental group and which are in the control group. With this type of program, the researcher cannot communicate anticipated results to participants.

Multiple-Treatment Interference. Clients are often involved in more than one intervention or program simultaneously. They may also participate in one program after another. In either of these situations, the first intervention may affect the second intervention. If the participant benefited from the first intervention, that effect may not be apparent until after implementation of the next intervention, to which the change would be attributed. Whether the same findings would occur if only the one main intervention was applied is often dubious. Consequently, findings may be falsely attributed to only the second intervention or the effects of both interventions may be integrated.

Important Points about Validity and Experimental Program Evaluation Designs

- Validity of experimental designs is a major issue. Internal validity is needed to allow the researcher to state with a certain degree of confidence that there is a causal relationship between the program (the independent variable) and changes in program participants (the dependent variable). External validity allows the researcher to generalize findings to the population from which program participants were selected.
- There are threats to both internal and external validity for which researchers attempt to control. Threats to internal validity include history, maturation, testing, instrumentation, statistical regression, selection, mortality, and interaction effects.
- Some of the threats to external validity are reactive effects of testing, selection-treatment interaction, reactive setting, and multiple treatment interference.

Experimental Designs and Program Evaluation

Independent and dependent variables, pretesting and post-testing, experimental groups, and random assignment to comparison or control groups are important elements in experimental designs. The program is the independent variable in program evaluations based on experimental designs. The program is implemented to influence change in the dependent variable, the program goal, that is, the anticipated result or outcome of the program for participants. The researcher is looking for a cause and effect relationship between the program and the program goal's effect on participants. Random assignment is assigning people by chance to either the experimental group or the control group, so that the groups are equivalent or comparable to each other. Equivalent means that when the program is implemented both groups have the same experiences and are similar on important variables. Control group participants are not program participants. The experimental group participates in the program (the intervention). The comparison group receives a different type of intervention or an intervention that is not authentic and is not randomly assigned.

Both the comparison group and the control group are compared with the experimental group to determine if there are differences in the groups after exposure to the program. Change in program participants is attributed to the intervention if there is a difference in the experimental group and not in the control group. Experimental designs have pretests, post-tests, or both. Pretests and post-tests are the same, but are administered at different points during the experiment. Pretests are given before introduction of the intervention (the program), and the post-test is administered after the program is introduced. Preexperimental, quasi-experimental, and true experimental are the classifications of experimental designs.

Preexperimental Designs

Preexperimental designs are used when social service agencies lack resources to implement true experimental designs. Human service practitioners especially are likely to be faced with this dilemma. Random assignment to conditions and control groups are absent from preexperimental designs, thus establishing internal validity can be problematic. Preexperimental designs described in this section are the one-group post-test only design, the one-group pretest–post-test design, and the static group comparison (post-test only nonequivalent group design).

The One-Group Post-test Only Design.   A treatment group is the only group associated with this design, also called the one-shot case study design. The group participates in the program, the intervention, and is not given a pretest but is administered a post-test. It is impossible with this design to evaluate whether the program caused a change in program participants since there is no way to measure change without a pretest and without a control group for comparison. The one-group post-test only design is subject to all threats to internal validity.

The One-Group Pretest–Post-test Design.   This design consists of one experimental group that is pretested, administered a treatment or intervention, and then given a post-test. There is no control group with this design and random assignment is not necessary since there is only one group. It is conceivable with this design that the change in the dependent variable, from the time of the pretest to the post-test, was caused by something other than the independent variable. Testing, instrumentation, maturation, history, and statistical regression are threats to internal validity with this design.

The Static Group Comparison.   This design, also called the post-test only nonequivalent group design, has two groups, a post-test, a treatment or intervention, and no random assignment that would make the groups equivalent. There is no pretest. With this design, it is difficult to attribute differences in the two groups to the intervention or treatment or to differences in the groups before implementation of the intervention, since there was no randomization or pretest. Selection is the main threat to internal validity with this design.

True Experimental Program Evaluation Designs

True experimental designs are a favorite among researchers when all of the requirements of experimental designs can be met because these designs guard against threats to internal validity. True experimental designs use randomization, experimental groups, and control groups, which help in controlling threats to internal validity. Clients are randomly assigned to either the experimental or the control group. A goal of true experimental design evaluations is to establish causal relationships between the program objectives and the intervention. In other words, can change in program participants be attributed to the program, the intervention, only? True experimental designs described in this section are the pretest–post-test group design with random assignment, the Solomon four-group design, and the post-test only control group design. Among these true experimental designs, the pretest–post-test control group design, also called the classic experimental design, is the most well known.

Pretest–Post-test Control Group Design.   The evaluator's confidence that differences between experimental and control groups are due to the effect of the independent variable, the intervention, are increased with this design because random assignment to the experimental and control groups is used, eliminating threats to internal validity. The experimental group is exposed to the intervention while the control group is not. Although threats to internal validity are virtually eliminated with this design, the possibility of threats to external validity, whether results can be generalized to persons not involved in the program being evaluated, must be considered. Change in the dependent variable cannot be attributed to the independent variable, the intervention, if the same changes are occurring in both the experimental group and the control group. The researcher in the case example used a pretest–post-test control group design to evaluate the effectiveness of a stress management program for middle school adolescents. Fifty-four adolescents, 36 in the experimental group and 18 in the control group, participated in the program. Female participants were randomly assigned to the experimental and control groups. Male participants, however, were not randomized but placed in the control group. This group was smaller, and they also chose to be in the control group. The researcher acknowledges that this failure to randomize male participants affects the generalizability of the findings from the sample.

The Post-test Only Control Group Design.   The post-test only control group design randomly assigns participants to the intervention group and the control group and introduces the program to the treatment group. A pretest is not given to either group although a post-test is administered to both. Random assignment guarantees that the comparison groups are equivalent, since there are no pretests to insure equivalency. Threats to internal validity are controlled sufficiently. The likelihood of the threat to external validity by testing treatment interaction, as could occur in the pretest–post-test control group design, is small since there is no pretesting.

Solomon Four-Group Design.   The Solomon four-group design has two experimental groups and two control groups and controls the same threats to internal validity as the pretest–post-test group design. Pretests and post-tests are administered to one experimental group and one control group while only post-tests are given to the second experimental and second control group. The Solomon four-group design requires twice as many groups as some of the other designs, making it both more expensive and more time-consuming than other true experimental designs.

This design controls for the threat to external validity by informing the evaluator of whether changes in the dependent variable are due to some interaction effect between the pretest and exposure to the experimental stimulus, in this case, the program. Kvalem and Sundet (1996) used a Solomon Four-Group design to evaluate a school-based sex education program designed to prevent sexually transmitted diseases and unwanted pregnancies in youth in high schools and colleges in Norway. This design was used because it was recommended for evaluating health education programs. A stratified sample of 124 classes consisting of 2,411 students was drawn. An 80-item questionnaire was used to test the effects of the intervention. Results indicated that the intervention did not influence adolescents' use of condoms. Findings did suggest an interaction effect between the pretest and the intervention.

Quasi-Experimental Designs

The inability to assign people randomly to experimental and control groups differentiates quasi-experimental designs from true experimental designs. Failure to make random assignments eliminates the ability to establish conditions needed for experimental designs. Quasi-experimental designs are used when clients cannot be assigned randomly to experimental and control groups, which is often the case when working with clients. Quasi-experimental designs have strong possibilities for use in evaluating social service programs because the required repeated measures, such as in time-series designs, of clients' progress can be located in the documented client files that social workers are required to maintain. This data would be accessible to researchers. The time-series design and the cross-sectional design are the major quasi-experimental designs.

The Time-Series Design.   The time-series design consists of a series of measures of the dependent variable before and after introduction of the experimental condition over a long period of time and with the same participants. There is no set number of pretests and post-tests that must be administered, although the number of measures before and after the intervention should be equal and the time intervals between each measure should also be the same unless specified otherwise. This design has an experimental group, but does not require a control group. What happens immediately before the program is introduced and immediately after its introduction is important in determining whether the program produced changes in the clients. The internal validity threats of attrition, maturation, regression, testing, and instrumentation are controlled by pretesting. This design does not control for the history threat to internal validity. Catalano, Libby, Snowden, and Cuellar (2000) used an interrupted time-series design to test two propositions about the effect of capitated financing on mental health services for Medicaid-eligible children and youth in Colorado. They evaluated if capitating reduces costs and if shifting providers from fee-for-service to capitated financing would increase their efforts to prevent illness. Service providers are paid a fixed sum of money per year for care of each eligible person when capitated financing is used. The authors evaluated The Colorado Capitation Demonstrated Project using a time-series design. Two of the authors' findings are that counties with capitated services had lower costs than counties with fee-for-service financing and that secondary and tertiary prevention efforts may be enhanced when economic incentives are provided.

The Cross-Sectional Design.   The cross-sectional design has an experimental group and a control group that are matched as much as possible on characteristics pertaining to the study. The design measures both groups only once, a fault in this design. A comparison is made between the control group and the experimental group after introduction of the experimental stimulus to evaluate whether change has occurred.

Important Points about Experimental Designs in Program Evaluation

- Experimental designs are a form of summative program evaluations. These designs are categorized as preexperimental designs, true experimental designs, and quasi-experimental designs.
- Important components of experimental designs are independent and dependent variables, pretesting, post-testing, experimental groups, and random assignment to comparison or control groups.
- Preexperimental designs, which do not have random assignment to conditions and control groups, are more appropriate for use with human services agencies. Establishing internal validity of these designs, however, can create problems.
- True experimental designs use randomization, experimental groups, and control groups, which facilitate controlling for the threats to internal validity.
- Quasi-experimental designs do not randomly assign people to experimental and control groups, which distinguishes these designs from true experimental designs.

Human Diversity Issues in Program Evaluation Designs

People representing practically every country in the world reside in the United States. This fact, along with increasing emphasis on globalization efforts in most disciplines, points to the importance of culturally competent program evaluators. Regardless of where a program evaluation is done, the evaluator is bound to come in contact with people from different ethnic backgrounds, religious affiliations, genders, sexual orientation, and age groups. As in social work practice, when evaluators enter the evaluation setting, they must be aware of their own values, attitudes, behavior, and frames of reference and how they might influence the entire evaluation process, including the findings. In the next section on ethical issues, there is discussion of employees' ambivalence, apprehension, and fears of program evaluations. These feelings may be more pronounced when the evaluation involves people who are different from the evaluator in many respects. The program evaluator can either heighten these feelings or help diminish them when the evaluator is culturally aware and sensitive.

Ethical Issues and Biases in Program Evaluation Designs

Random assignment of clients is one of the main ethical issues in program evaluations that use experimental designs. Random assignment to experimental groups and assignment to comparison groups does not allow social workers the opportunity to make decisions about the type of services or intervention the client receives, which is ordinarily done based on an assessment of the client's situation and often in collaboration with the client. The denial of services to a control group is another ethical issue in program evaluation, a reason that true experimental designs are not ideal program evaluation methods for human service organizations. The denial of services due to assignment to a control group can be avoided by using clients on waiting lists as control groups.

Besides the concerns about random assignment and the use of comparison and control groups, issues relating to client informed consent also pertain to program evaluation, as they do to other types of research. Program evaluation participants must be informed that their participation in the program is voluntary, what the purpose of the program is, and how either confidentiality or anonymity will be assured. The manner in which program evaluation results are presented to stakeholders and what is provided are also ethical concerns. The behavior of staff affected by program evaluation results can be an issue if employees respond in a way that prevents the evaluator from carrying out the evaluation in as efficient a manner as proposed. Fears of the outcome of the evaluation may produce these negative or ambivalent attitudes in employees.

WRITING STRATEGY

Acquire as much information as possible about two programs in your field placement agency by reading program manuals and interviewing social workers, supervisors, and administrators about those programs. After gathering the information, write a two-page narrative explaining which program would benefit from an evaluation and the type of program you believe would be most appropriate. Share findings with your research class.

LEARNING ACTIVITY

Discuss with your internship supervisor the type of program evaluations that have been conducted on agency programs. Ask to see a copy of the evaluator's findings. Identify whether a formative or summative evaluation was done. Based on your knowledge of the program that was evaluated, do you believe that it was a fair assessment? Why or why not?

INFORMATION TECHNOLOGY FOR PROGRAM EVALUATION

The American Evaluation Association is an international professional association of evaluators devoted to applying and exploring various types of program evaluation. The American Evaluation Association's mission is to:

- Improve evaluation practices and methods.
- Increase evaluation use.
- Promote evaluation as a profession.
- Support the contribution of evaluation to the generation of theory and knowledge about effective human action.

Visit this site at www.eval.org. Review the publications and documents site, and access at least two links from this site.

Important Points from Chapter 14

- Program evaluation is essential in informing administrators of the effectiveness of their programs in making changes in clients' lives. Program evaluation also provides information about the status of programs, including their strengths and weaknesses or whether programs should continue, be reduced, expanded, or eliminated.
- The types of evaluation are summative and formative. Formative evaluations are concerned with program processes, beginning with the needs assessment to program implementation. On the other hand, summative evaluation assesses program results.
- Internal validity and external validity are two significant concepts in program evaluations using experimental designs. The presence of internal validity allows the researcher to state with a certain degree of confidence that there is a causal relationship between the program and the program goals. External validity lets the researcher generalize findings to the population from which the sample was drawn. The researcher must control for threats to both internal and external validity.
- Some program evaluations are implemented using experimental research designs, a type of summative program evaluation. These designs are categorized as preexperimental designs, true experimental designs, and quasi-experimental designs. Important components of experimental designs are independent and dependent variables, pretesting–post-testing, experimental groups, and random assignment to comparison or control groups.

REFERENCES

Catalano, R., Libby, A., Snowden, L., & Cuellar, A. E. (2000). The effect of capitated financing on mental health services for children and youth: The Colorado experience [Electronic version]. *American Journal of Public Health, 90,* 1861–1865. Retrieved June 12, 2001 from www.ebsco.com.

de Anda, D. (1998). The evaluation of a stress management program for middle school adolescents. *Child and Adolescent Social Work Journal, 15*(1), 73–85.

Hoefer, R. (1994). A good story, well told: Rules for evaluating human services programs. *Social Work, 39,* 233–236.

Kvalem, I. L., & Sundet, J. M. (1996). The effect of sex education on adolescents' use of condoms: Applying the Solomon four-group design. *Health Education Quarterly, 23*(1), p. 34, 14 pp. Retrieved June 12, 2001, from www.ebsco.com.

Weiss, C. H. (1998). *Evaluation: Methods for studying programs and policies* (2nd ed.). Upper Saddle River, NJ: Prentice Hall.

Creating Research Partnerships with Child Welfare Agencies

*Since completing the research course, I do research based on the kids that
I am working with on issues regarding adolescence and other student
issues, such as Attention Deficit Disorders. So, I have been using my
research skills, and helping the kids do research also.*
—Nontraditional research student

APPENDIX GOALS

Your major goals upon completion of this appendix are to:

- Understand the rationale for creating researcher and child welfare practitioner collaborations.
- Recognize barriers to and benefits of collaborative research relationships.
- Understand the developmental stages in forming researcher and child welfare partnerships.

Introduction

"... We were also guided by the fact that a university can do little in isolation. The best hope for impact is through partnership with individuals and agencies in the community who know the crises first-hand and who may be piloting innovations. Collaborative effort is no longer a choice—it is a necessity" (Erickson & Weinberg, 1998, p. 187). These authors were writing about the creation of the Children, Youth, and Family Consortium at the University of Minnesota to address problems in that community. There are a number of crises and potential emergencies in suburban, rural, and urban communities that could benefit from preventive services and interventions by the collaborative efforts of child welfare social work practitioners and faculty researchers. Child abuse and neglect, drug and alcohol abuse by children and adults, homeless children, poor parent and child relationships, problems in child care, and random killings by adolescents are a few of the crises that research could positively influence. Yet, the value of social work professors and social work practitioners teaming up to conduct research and to design and actualize programs has not been fully realized in social work.

There is a need for college and university social work faculty and child welfare agencies to enter collaborative relationships in carrying out research and in implementing programs to address community issues regarding children, youth, and families. This appendix outlines a rationale for entering collaborative relationships and impediments and disincentives for creating practice and research partnerships.

Generalist Case Study: A Research Partnership between the Department of Children, Youth, and Families and Grooms University

Grooms University, located in a mid-sized southeastern community, developed a research partnership with the Department of Children, Youth, and Families, a state agency responsible for child protective services, foster care (family foster care, group home and residential placements, and relative foster care). Although the university and the department had an established relationship with student interns, the research relationship began when the department issued a Request for Proposal (RFP). The agency had money for an agency or university to conduct research about interdependent living for adolescents preparing to exit the foster care system and for the development and implementation of programs for adolescents based on the research. The university was awarded funds to conduct research and develop self-sufficiency programs.

University administrators demonstrated support for the partnership by providing staff, space, and release time for faculty. Foster care staff, faculty, graduate students, foster parents, and youth in foster care collaborated on this effort. Initially all of the stakeholders were enthusiastic about working together in a different type of alliance, so assigning and selecting roles and responsibilities and establishing operating procedures went smoothly. Some of the graduate students were excited about their roles conducting literature reviews because the topics of their doctoral dissertations were similar to the issues that the group was working on. Agency social workers and supervisors were also interested in the research aspect of the project so that they could become better informed about relevant interventions for working with clients. Thus, this phase of the project proceeded without negative incidents.

While the project members appeared committed to the plan, conflict eventually occurred. Both parties believed that they were devoting more time to the research project than the other group. Researchers also complained about the difficulty in accessing the agency, its staff, and case records and about the high turnover rate among employees participating in the project. All parties agreed that in the initial planning no procedures were made for disseminating information among the group. Despite the conflicts, members decided that the project was too important to discontinue because the conflicts could be resolved. Therefore, an advisory committee was established that consisted of agency staff, researchers, community representatives, foster parents, and youth affected by the project. This committee met monthly.

Neither the researchers nor the practitioners knew exactly when they began to cooperate and function as a team. They suspect, though, that the relationship started assuming a more positive bent when they began listening to each other and valuing the strengths and knowledge that each individual brought to the team without being competitive. Furthermore, a few of the doctoral students were former employees of the child welfare agency, and their first-hand knowledge of the agency structure, its mission, its philosophy, and its goals and their established working relationships with top administrators in each geographic area and the central office also facilitated the practitioner and researcher partnership. The new attitudes, recognition of each others' specific knowledge and possible contributions to the undertaking, and respect for each other contributed to an ongoing collaborative relationship. Consequently, working together, faculty and staff conducted research on and implemented many projects. Some of the outcomes of their collaborative research efforts were:

- An area-wide three-day interdependent living conference held at the university each year for the foster care youth, agency foster care staff, and university staff involved with the research and program. The agency's central office staff also joined with local academic researchers and staff to organize a statewide youth conference.
- Support group meetings for adolescents facilitated by social work practitioners and student researchers.
- Educational groups facilitated by social work practitioners and student researchers to teach the adolescents interdependent living skills, such as career development, job searching, budgeting, socialization, and home maintenance.
- A statewide family support worker conference, researched and planned by a researcher, in-home technicians, and staff, was another research project. Student participation in research strategies, such as the interdependent living conference and the in-home family technician conference, socializes students as active participants in research with practitioners, thus decreasing obstacles to practitioners engaging in research and facilitating practitioner-researcher collaborations (Galinsky, Turnbull, Meglin, & Wilner, 1993; Hall, Jensen, Fortney, Sutter, Locher, & Cayner, 1996). While the partnership between the university and child welfare agency strengthened over time and is currently a valuable resource team in the community, the team meets periodically to review goals and to assess its continued viability, needs, and successes.

Practitioner and Researcher Collaborations

Both problems and benefits occur when researchers and child welfare practitioners attempt to form working relationships.

> *Activity 1.*   After reading this section, ask your field placement or employment supervisor about the agency's collaborative research relationships with area universities and colleges. Inquire about the purpose of the partnerships and discuss the challenges and rewards of the collaborative efforts.

For more than two decades, there has been strong encouragement from social work organizations, researchers, and practitioners for practitioners and researchers to create research partnerships in the best interest of serving children, families, and the community. Why, then, are there few of these relationships? While there are benefits, barriers do exist for agencies and researchers in collaborative research relationships.

Obstacles for Practitioners in Forming Collaborative Relationships

- *Employers' Expectations of BSW Graduates.* Employers value employees who are intelligent, can get along with people, are devoted to the organization, are articulate, have good communication skills, and have knowledge of families (Forte & Mathews, 1994; Witkin, 1998), but they place little value on inclusion of research in the BSW curriculum (Forte & Mathews).

- *Distrust of the University.* The university often uses community resources for research, but does not always share results with the community or communicate clearly with the community about the research goals; there are often physical barriers for practitioners to accessing the university, such as inadequate parking; and the university often fails to acknowledge that there are different cultures emanating from the university and the community (Erickson & Weinberg, 1998).

- *Lack of Time and Confidence.* Practitioners ordinarily do not have time to participate in large scale, quantitative research projects or the confidence or incentives from employers to do so (Hall, et al., 1996). Time restrictions result from high, often stressful caseloads and inadequate staff, leaving minimal time for practitioners to engage in research.

- *Belief That Research Is Irrelevant to Practice.*

- *Perceptions of Status Differences.* Educators are often viewed as having a higher status than practitioners because of their knowledge base and their jobs in academia (Hall, et al., 1996), which could foster animosity among practitioners towards academics.

Obstacles for Researchers in Forming Collaborative Relationships

Just as there are obstacles for practitioners to participating in research partnerships, there are barriers for researchers to creating collaborative research partnerships.

- *Educators Value Graduates Who Will Identify with the Profession.* Schools want thinkers and people who will promote the social work profession. Employers are searching for graduates who will be committed to the agency, its goals, and carrying out those goals based on the employer's expectations (Forte & Mathews, 1994).

■ *University Administration May Not Support Research Efforts.*

■ *Agency Politics That Discourage the Academic Researcher.* Courtney (1998) maintains that understanding the politics of child welfare is an important issue. Politics includes pressures facing public child welfare administrators, state–county relationships, and contrasting roles of public versus private agencies. Other common problems that often become political issues in child welfare are deaths of children, especially while in the custody of the agency, and inadequate and insufficient out-of-home placements. These problems can often influence whether agencies will open their doors to researchers from within or outside of the agency.

■ *Researchers Sometimes Confront Closed Agencies.* Some social work organizations do not value research or trust "outsiders" with their data, fearing how the information will be used.

■ *Faculty Researchers Have Insufficient Time.* Researchers need to devote extra attention to forming collaborative research efforts, which competes with teaching and community service responsibilities.

Benefits of Collaborative Research

Activity 2. After reading this section, list three benefits of forming collaborative relationships for researchers and three for practitioners. What additional benefits can you think of?

Although there are many reasons why child welfare practitioners and faculty might not be able to build research partnerships, when relationships are created, everyone involved—practitioners, faculty, children, families, and the community—profit. Accountability to clients, the community, the organization, funding sources, and other stakeholders and the integration of ideas, strategies, and knowledge from each profession generate effective methods for working with clients. Communities, therefore, emerge stronger and more involved. Research collaborators contribute to the empirical social work knowledge base by learning and applying research methods in practice, by accumulating superior studies, and by implementing the most successful interventions (Franklin, 1999). The use of empirically based research to provide a foundation for social work practice and practice wisdom advance high-quality social work practice, another contribution of research partnerships (Hall, et al., 1996).

Faculty can help practitioners review, select, and implement the most sensible and credible methods for working with diverse problems and clients. Collaborative relationships can also inspire faculty to rethink their position on and encourage the use of practice evaluation methods such as single system designs, case studies, and other quasi-experimental designs that are more appropriate for practitioners to use (Franklin, 1999). Research partnerships can also enhance a faculty's quality of teaching and improve the research skills of both practitioner and researcher.

Important Points about Obstacles to and Benefits of Collaborative Research Relationships

- Both faculty researchers and employers are often confronted with barriers to engaging in researcher and practitioner partnerships. Employers place priority on provision of services and not research. Practitioners distrust the university. Practitioners lack time and confidence. Researchers confront closed agencies and lack of support by academic administrators for research. Agency policies discourage faculty from entering research partnerships with child welfare staff.
- Practitioners and researchers that overcome obstacles to conducting research together find that there are many benefits. Integrated ideas, strategies, and knowledge from the two professions contribute to more effective client services and to the social work knowledge base. There is more accountability to stakeholders. Communities become stronger and more involved in problem resolution and prevention.

Developmental Stages in Creating Research Partnerships with Child Welfare Agencies

Most collaborative efforts between child welfare practitioners and faculty researchers do not occur overnight but through an evolutionary process. This section details the developmental stages in creating research partnerships with child welfare agencies. Christ and Siegel's (1995) phases in the development of practitioner-researcher interdependence was the impetus for developmental stages delineated in this section.

Developmental Stage I: Initiating the Partnership

There are many reasons that practitioners and researchers connect to form research partnerships. Black and Walther (1995) maintain that their practitioner-researcher partnership began casually, with no formal research agenda. Although the university and the agency that they were identified with had a long-standing relationship in MSW students' fieldwork education, a jointly administered training project, Black and Walther had no formal ties. Colleagues who were aware of their mutual interest in maternal and child health introduced them. While personal characteristics are important in creating partnerships, Black and Walther also point out the importance of institutional support. In the case study presented earlier in this appendix, the university showed support by providing administrative support, supplies, and release time for faculty.

Faculty researchers and practitioners sometimes team up to address specific issues. Galinsky, Turnbull, Meglin, and Wilner (1993) write about their experiences as a practitioner-researcher team formed to "evaluate the effectiveness of single-session groups for families of psychiatric patients" (p. 442). Their evaluation of the program illuminated problematic issues involved in developing the collaborative relationship. Practitioners and researchers may also enter collaborative relationships because of specific grants or agency-specific need. The child welfare agency and university in the case example had a dual purpose for working together.

First, there was a need for research on older adolescents who would soon be leaving the foster care system and assuming responsibility for themselves. Second, funds were available to address those issues.

Developmental Stage 2: Curiosity, Interest, and Planning

In this planning stage of the relationship, the two interests must decide on a problem to study, choose roles and responsibilities, establish protocol, set goals and objectives, and write proposals, the highlights of this period of enthusiasm. For example, Burnette and Weiner (1995) worked together as a practitioner-researcher team to develop a grant proposal to acquire information relative to delivery of mental health services to older people. To identify gaps in practice knowledge and service provision, they both reviewed the agency's mental health programs and the literature. This phase also entailed deciding on roles and responsibilities, including "relational, philosophical, organizational, and political and ethical aspects of our partnership" (p. 140).

The researcher-practitioner team described by Galinsky, Turnbull, Meglin, and Wilner (1993) developed and refined their intervention plan and evaluation measures in this stage of the relationship. In the case example, roles and responsibilities were designated, protocol established, and all members verbalized their commitment to the project.

Developmental Stage 3: Conflict and Competition

Disputes, disagreements, and discord are expected when people from different backgrounds work together. The values of practitioners and researchers are common grounds for dissension. For example, social work practitioners and administrators must respond with immediacy, select and organize resources, solve difficult problems, and make decisions, often critical ones, based on insufficient information, with limited resources, and with expectations that they will achieve unattainable results (Perkins & Wandersman, 1990; Witkin, 1998). For instance, when a child protective services worker receives a referral that a child is in immediate danger, the worker must drop everything and investigate. The worker cannot stop in the midst of the investigation and research a journal article that describes how this particular situation should be handled. Thus, while the practitioner concentrates on taking action, the researcher's primary concern is often understanding (Perkins & Wandersman, 1990; Witkin, 1998).

Christ and Siegel (1995) point out how fundraising and other support activities consumed a lot of departmental energy and time. Besides being time consuming, there was competition between the practitioners and the researchers for recognition and resources. Practitioners were also uncomfortable with and complained about some of the researchers' methods. Similarly, researchers criticized some of the practitioners' methods. An example that Christ and Siegel cite is the misunderstanding about selection of research topics. Practitioners illuminated the significance of a holistic understanding of the patient, and researchers stressed limiting the study question and the exclusion of variables to formulate a researchable question.

In the case example, researchers voiced concern about inaccessible agency staffing; and both parties were frustrated about the breakdown in communication and the amount of time they were devoting to the research. While disagreements do occur, at some point in the relationship both practitioners and researchers must move beyond that stage to a more productive one, if the partnership is to succeed.

Developmental Stage 4: The Awakening

In this stage of the research process, both the social work practitioners and the researchers realize that regardless of the excitement and interest in the joint venture, differences can occur. The key, though, is overcoming disagreements and barriers, so that the research can proceed. The research team can reassess the situation, consider alternatives to the initial plan, and network for ideas and suggestions from inside and outside of the agency. Relationships that transcend obstacles and reassess the situation can move to the cooperation stage. In the case example, team members reevaluated the project and the relationship, took steps to restore their initial enthusiasm, and took action to prevent disintegration of the group.

Developmental Stage 5: Cooperation

Acknowledgment of and respect for the practitioners' role in knowledge development is important. According to Christ and Siegel (1995), as research projects were actualized by practitioners and researchers, respect and recognition for each other's strengths and limitations and the diversity in jobs increased. Practitioners can share with faculty their complete knowledge of clients, the agency, community systems, and social support networks (Witkin, 1998). Social work practitioners should also be respected for their ability to describe what they do, including innovations in technique, practice models, programs, and policy (Hess, 1995). Showing esteem for social workers' use of practice wisdom can strengthen the bond between researchers and practitioners and positively effect cooperation. In the case example, a more harmonious, shared, reciprocal relationship emerged after researchers and faculty discussed their apprehensions and frustrations about how the project was proceeding. This openness, along with influence of doctoral students who had experience as practitioners and novice researchers, fostered a collaborative relationship.

Developmental Stage 6: Collaboration

Collaboration for Christ and Siegel (1995) occurred after respect developed among researchers and practitioners and after they began to value each other and work cooperatively. To arrive at this collaborative stage, the researcher also needs to strive for understanding of the agency's situation and position and refrain from overburdening it. Do not jump to conclusions or make assumptions about what may be going on in the agency that prevents the research from proceeding as fast as the researcher would like. Whether the agency is open or closed to outside researchers, however, could weigh heavily on the decision to participate in a research project. Some agencies welcome researchers from colleges and universities, while others prefer to have research conducted by their staff or not at all. Although the researcher may not be able to conduct research on the desired level, for example, an agencywide macro-level project, research may be done on a smaller scale with one or two individual staff people.

Important Points about Creating Collaborative Relationships

- Collaborative relationships are initiated for many different reasons, and the agency or the academic researcher may be the initiator of the relationships.
- Collaborative relationships are created over time and may be conflictual before the involved parties gain respect for differences in their respective jobs and roles.
- A goal in teamwork between academic researchers and child welfare practitioners is to cooperate with each other and move to the level of collaboration.
- Although collaborative relationships can be conflictual, ultimately the benefits outweigh the negatives.

Human Diversity Issues in Creating
Collaborative Research Relationships

People representing the community in terms of diverse ethnicity, age, disability, sexual preference, and religion should be participants in collaborative efforts of academic researchers and child welfare agencies. When the community is represented, children, adolescents, and families learn strategies that enable them to negotiate systems and become empowered to resolve problems and influence change.

Ethical Issues and Biases in Creating
Collaborative Research Relationships

One ethical issue occurs when colleges and universities fail to respond to societal changes and problems facing children, youth, and families—homelessness (children and adults), child abuse and neglect, poverty, discrimination, and homicides committed by adolescents in both urban and suburban communities. Academic researchers can answer this call by collaborating with agencies to develop programs and services for children, youth, and families. These issues need to be addressed on local, regional, national, and global levels. An ethical issue also emerges when agencies insist on excluding the community from involvement in issues that affect that community.

WRITING STRATEGY

Find a combination of three journal articles and book chapters about creating research partnerships with child welfare practitioners and faculty researchers or between faculty researchers and any public welfare staff, such as adult services. Write a two-page summary and a critical analysis of the articles. How does your critique differ from that of your research classmates?

LEARNING ACTIVITY

As a class, devise a list of questions to ask a child welfare practitioner and an academic researcher about their collaborative relationships. After completing the list, select three or four students to interview the researcher and the practitioner and report back to the class. Be sure to ask the child welfare agency if they have a research department or unit.

INFORMATION TECHNOLOGY FOR CREATING RESEARCH PARTNERSHIPS

Child Welfare Web site (www.childwelfare.com)—From the *Children and Youth Services Review* site (below), select a relevant article that addresses children's issues. Share with your class issues that you would like to see academic researchers and child welfare practitioners work together on ameliorating through collaborative research efforts:

www.childwelfare.com/kids/cysr.htm

Important Points from Appendix

- Both faculty researchers and employers are often confronted with barriers to engaging in researcher and practitioner partnerships. Practitioners and researchers that overcome obstacles to conducting research together find that there are many benefits. Integrated ideas, new strategies, and knowledge from the two professions contribute to more effective client services, contributions to the social work knowledge base, and accountability to stakeholders. Communities also become stronger and more involved in problem resolution and prevention.
- Collaborative relationships are initiated for many different reasons. Over time they may become conflictual before the involved parties gain respect for differences in their respective jobs and roles.
- Building research partnerships between faculty researchers and child welfare practitioners evolve and require understanding, respect, commitment, and cooperation from both entities. A goal of these relationships is to achieve collaboration. Although collaborative relationships can be conflictual, ultimately the benefits outweigh the negatives.

REFERENCES

Black, R. B., & Walther, V. N. (1995). The practitioner-researcher team: A case example. In P. M. Hess & E. J. Mullens (Eds.), *Practitioner-researcher partnerships: Building knowledge from, in, and for practice* (pp. 151–161). Washington, DC: NASW Press.

Burnette, D., & Weiner, A. S. (1995). Intersecting the parallel worlds of practice and research: An agency practitioner-academic researcher team. In P. M. Hess & E. J. Mullens (Eds.), *Practitioner-researcher partnerships: Building knowledge from, in, and for practice* (pp. 138–150). Washington, DC: NASW Press.

Christ, G. H., & Siegel, K. (1995). Bridging the gap between practitioners and researchers in a hospital-based social work department. In P. M. Hess & E. J. Mullens (Eds.), *Practitioner-researcher partnerships: Building knowledge from, in, and for practice* (pp. 206–226). Washington, DC: NASW Press.

Courtney, M. (1998, August). *Researcher-Practitioner Collaboration*. Paper presented at the Third Annual Child Welfare Fellows Institute, Berkeley, CA.

Erickson, M. F., & Weinberg, R. A. (1998). The children, youth, and family consortium. A University of
Minnesota/community partnership. In R. M. Lerner & L. A. K. Simon (Eds.), *University-
community collaborations for the twenty-first century* (pp. 185–201). New York: Garland.

Forte, J. A., & Mathews, C. (1994). Potential employers' reviews of the ideal undergraduate social work
curriculum. *Journal of Social Work Education, 30*(2), 228–240.

Franklin, C. G. (1999). Research on practice: Better than you think? *Social Work in Education, 21*(1),
3–9.

Galinsky, M. J., Turnbull, J. E., Meglin, D. E., & Wilner, M. E. (1993). Confronting the reality of collaborative practice research: Issues of practice, design, measurement, and team development.
Social Work, 38, 440–449.

Hall, J. A., Jensen, G. V., Fortney, M. A., Sutter, J., Locher, J., & Cayner, J. J. (1996). Education of staff
and students in health care settings: Integrating practice and research. *Social Work in Health
Care, 24*(1/2), 93–113.

Hess, P. M. (1995). Reflecting in and on practice: A role for practitioners in knowledge building. In P.
M. Hess & E. J. Mullens (Eds.), *Practitioner-researcher partnerships: Building knowledge from,
in, and for practice* (pp. 56–82). Washington, DC: NASW Press.

Perkins, D. D., & Wandersman, A. (1990). "You'll have to work to overcome our suspicions." The
benefits of research with community organizations. *Community Action, 21*(1), 32–41.

Witkin, S. L. (1998). Mirror, mirror on the wall: Creative tensions, the academy, and the field. *Social
Work, 43*, 389–391.

GLOSSARY

abstract A brief summary of a research report ordinarily placed at the beginning of the paper. It includes the research question or hypotheses, the methodology, and the study results. Computerized databases contain abstracts of journal articles and books.

alternate, or parallel, forms reliability Two different forms of the same test are developed that are comparable in level of difficulty, instructions, formats, content, and intent to measure the same variables.

anonymity Anonymity for research participants means that no one, including people involved with the research, will know participants' identity.

APA manual A style manual, *The Publication Manual of the American Psychological Association,* published by the American Psychological Association, which provides guidelines for writing scholarly papers and books. It is one of numerous style manuals.

baseline phase The period in a single system design in which data are collected to evaluate the client's behavior, situation, or circumstances before an intervention is implemented.

Boolean searching A method of information retrieval that makes use of the online commands *and, or,* and *not* that allow you to expand or narrow your search and pinpoint specific information.

causal relationship A relationship in which the independent variable is responsible for a change in the dependent variable. Scientifically, three conditions—temporal order, association, and rival hypotheses—must exist to establish causality.

cluster sampling A probability sampling technique that involves selecting elements in two or more stages starting with large units, the clusters, instead of selecting participants individually.

coding A procedure for taking data from questionnaires and translating the information into language that the computer understands.

comparison group In experimental designs, the group that receives a different type of intervention or an intervention that is not authentic and is not randomly assigned.

confidentiality Participants are assured that information collected during the research process will be protected and not shared with people not directly involved with the study.

construct validity Measures the theory upon which the measuring instrument is based.

content validity Determines whether the measuring instrument covers all of the variable's indicators, based on its previously established definition.

control group In experimental designs, the group that does not receive the intervention or participate in a program and that is compared with the experimental group.

convenience sampling A nonprobability sampling method that selects participants based on the researcher's convenience, regardless of whether they possess the characteristics of interest to the researcher.

criterion validity Using a correlation coefficient to predict future behavior of participants based on scores on a new measuring instrument and scores on an established instrument.

data Information collected from research participants, documents, and artifacts.

deception in research   Research is conducted without the knowledge of participants or when the researcher is not honest with participants about the purpose of the research. This is a controversial issue for some researchers.

deductive reasoning   This type of reasoning or approach to research, used more often in quantitative research, begins with an established theoretical framework that is then tested.

dependent variable   Referred to as the outcome variable, it is the phenomenon that is being studied; the behavior, attitude, or situation that the researcher wants to explain or predict. Change in the dependent variable is contingent upon the independent variable.

descriptive research   Research that answers how and who questions; describes variables and relationships between variables. Descriptive research often builds on the results of exploratory studies.

descriptive statistics   Organize and summarize data and evaluate the extent of variation in values and the degree to which different variables are associated with each other.

directional or one-tailed hypothesis   Predicts a relationship between or among variables and specifies the direction of that relationship.

disseminating research findings   Methods of circulating and sharing research results with others via books, journals, reports, dissertations, theses, the Internet, conferences, seminars, and meetings.

ecological fallacy   An error in causal explanations that occurs when the researcher makes inferences or explains individual behavior based on research findings using groups as the unit of analysis.

ethnography   A type of qualitative research that gains understanding of people in their natural settings through in-depth interviews, observation, or by participating with people in their environments.

experimental designs   In group designs that use independent and dependent variables, pretesting and post-testing, experimental groups, and random assignment to groups.

experimental group   In program evaluation designs the group that participates in the program and receives the intervention.

explanatory research   Research that sometimes builds on results of exploratory and descriptive studies and uses hypotheses to predict the relationship between and among variables. It is concerned with causality.

exploratory research   Research conducted when there is little or no information on a topic. It often generates questions that descriptive and explanatory studies attempt to answer.

external validity   The degree to which study results can be generalized to the population from which the sample was drawn.

face validity   A casual or surface review of the measuring instrument using logic and common sense to evaluate whether the instrument asks the appropriate questions using language that participants understand.

focus groups   A form of qualitative research in which a small group of similar people are led in discussions on a particular topic.

formative evaluation   A type of program evaluation that assesses and describes the internal workings and functioning of programs.

fraudulent research   Research is fraudulent when a researcher reports results for which the researcher did not collect or analyze data. Falsifying and misrepresenting data and plagiarism are also forms of fraudulent research.

frequency distribution   A display reflecting the distribution of values among participants and how often particular values appear in the distribution.

generalize   The ability to infer or apply study results, based on sample information, to the entire population from which the sample was selected.

goal attainment scaling   A qualitative individual practice evaluation method that requires the setting of measurable goals.

hypothesis   A statement that predicts a correlation, an association, or that no relationship exists between or among variables. A hypothesis can be tested. There are different types of hypotheses.

independent variable   The causal variable that is said to influence and explain changes in the dependent variable.

inductive reasoning   This type of reasoning or approach to research builds theories by beginning with a specific observation and moving to a general or abstract statement.

inferential statistics   Computations to determine whether differences between or among variables are due to random errors produced by random sampling and whether results can be generalized from a sample to the population from which it was drawn.

informed consent   Potential research participants volunteer to take part in a study after being given details about the research project, such as the purpose of the research, possible risks to the participant, whether experiments are involved, and whether anonymity and confidentiality are guaranteed to participants.

institutional review boards   A group of people at a university or agency that evaluate applications for research with human beings before the research begins to assure that all ethical issues regarding protection of human participants have been taken into account.

internal validity   The degree to which the independent variable is responsible for change that appears in the dependent variable.

Internet   A collection of networks throughout the world that agree to communicate using specific telecommunications protocols, which makes it possible to search the World Wide Web.

interobserver, or interrater, agreement reliability   Two observers or raters observe the same participants at the same time, thus obtaining two measurements simultaneously. The independent ratings should be similar.

interval level of measurement   This is the second most precise of the four levels of measurement, with variables that are exhaustive, mutually exclusive, and rank-ordered and with the distance between categories of the variable known and equal to each other.

intervention   A service, program, or treatment, for example, family preservation, adult day care, parenting classes, and homemaker services, to help empower clients to change their behavior or circumstances.

intervention phase   The period during a single system design when an intervention is implemented. It follows the collection of baseline data.

keyword searching   A feature of a search engine or computer program that is not subject sensitive, which allows searching for every occurrence of a particular word in a database, no matter where it is located.

known investigator   A researcher whose identity is revealed to participants in a qualitative research study.

level of measurement   There are four levels of measurement that influence the amount of precision in measurement and the type of statistical analysis applied.

Library of Congress subject headings   A list of standardized subject headings that is commonly used to index materials in libraries by subject.

literature review   A careful analysis of mainly primary sources—books, journals, audiovisuals, and archival documents—in search of information that is relevant to the researcher's study.

mean   A measure of central tendency, the sum of all values in a distribution divided by the number of values in the distribution.

measures of association   Descriptive bivariate statistics that describe relationships between two variables, analyzing how the values or scores of one variable are associated with attributes of another variable.

median   A measure of central tendency, the middle value in a distribution when the values are listed from the highest to the lowest or vice versa. An equal number of values are smaller and an equal number higher than the median.

mode   A measure of central tendency, the most frequently occurring value in a distribution.

negatively skewed distribution   A distribution of values or scores that tapers off to the left.

nominal level of measurement   Also referred to as the categorical level. It is the least precise of the four levels of measurement. The nominal level categorizes variables into names or labels. The variable must have at least two attributes that are mutually exclusive and exhaustive.

non-directional, or two-tailed, hypothesis   This hypothesis predicts a relationship between or among variables, but does not specify the direction of that relationship.

nonprobability sampling   A sampling technique in which every element in the population does not have an equal chance of being selected for a study.

normal distribution   A distribution of scores or values that is bell shaped, with both ends tapering off equally and never touching the horizontal axis.

null hypothesis   States that there is no relationship between or among variables.

Office of Human Research Protections (OHRP)   Located in the Department of Health and Human Services (DHHS), this office is responsible for developing and implementing policies, procedures, and regulations for protection of human beings involved in research sponsored by DHHS.

operational definitions   Definitions of concepts that provide for consistency and objectivity and that specify how variables will be measured, moving variables from the abstract to the concrete.

oral history   One type of qualitative research for gathering personal historical information orally via in-depth interviews from people's memories or their written experiences.

ordinal level of measurement   More precise than the nominal level and less precise than the interval and ratio levels of measurement. It has exhaustive and mutually exclusive categories, and the categories are rank-ordered, representing more or less of a variable.

population   The elements, individuals, groups, organizations, or artifacts from which the sample is drawn.

positively skewed distribution   A distribution of scores or values that tapers off to the right.

practice evaluation   Methods used to assess the effectiveness of work with individual clients and of programs.

probability sampling   A sampling method that gives every element in the population an equal chance of being included in the sampling, making the sampling process less biased and the sample more representative of the target population.

problem statement An explanation or description of the topic or concern that the researcher is studying. It guides the research process.

program evaluation Also referred to as evaluation research. It is one component of practice evaluation that systematically assesses how social service programs or policies meet the needs of the people they were designed to serve.

purposive sampling A nonprobability sampling technique that selects participants based on their experience with and knowledge of the research problem.

qualitative research Also known as interpretist research. It relies mainly on personal contact with participants using in-depth interviews with open-ended questions, direct observation, or participation in the lives of people in the study. Narratives, words, documents, text, and observations are the basis for data analysis.

quantitative research Also known as positivist research. This research method collects data using surveys containing close-ended questions with predetermined response categories and analyzes data using statistical data analysis procedures.

questionnaire A tool for gathering information or data for a research project. The term is used interchangeably with survey.

quota sampling A nonprobability sampling technique that selects a sample that reflects, proportionately, the population from which it was drawn.

random assignment In experimental designs, the assigning of people by chance to the experimental group or the control group, so that the groups are equivalent or comparable to each other.

random errors in measurement Errors with no consistency or patterns that can occur at any stage in the research process. They diminish the ability to accurately measure relationships between or among variables.

range The easiest to compute of the three measures of dispersion. Subtract the lowest score in a distribution from the highest to calculate the range.

ratio level of measurement Variables at this level are exhaustive, mutually exclusive, and rank-ordered. The exact distance between categories of the variable is known and equal to each other, and the measures are based on a true or absolute point. This is the most precise of the four levels of measurement.

reductionism An error in causal explanations, which occurs when the research uses data on individuals' behavior to explain group, or macro-level units of analysis, behavior.

reference A resource used to find quick answers to questions—books, dictionaries, encyclopedias, handbooks, guides, indexes, bibliographies, and those sources on the Web that closely resemble these print formats.

reliability The degree to which a measuring instrument is consistent and can be depended on to produce the same results when administered again under similar circumstances. There are several types of reliability.

representative sample A sample that mirrors, in aggregate, those in the aggregate target population in characteristics of interest to the researcher.

research question A one-sentence inquiry about the relationship between or among concepts. It guides the research process, along with the problem statement.

sample A subset, a portion, or a segment of a population that is relied on to provide information about the population under study.

sampling error The degree of difference or variance between the characteristics of variables of the sample and the population from which the sample was drawn.

sampling frame A listing of all the elements (people, events, organizations, or artifacts) in a population that meet the researcher's criteria.

search engine A collection of programs that gather information from the World Wide Web and places it in a database so that it can be searched.

semi-structured interviews In qualitative research, interviews that use open-ended questions and are less structured and less flexible than structured interviews.

simple random sampling A probability sampling technique in which every element (person, event, situation, artifact) in the population has an equal chance of being included in the sample.

single system designs A series of quantitative methods for evaluating individual practice that require gathering baseline data before implementing an intervention.

snowball sampling A nonprobability sampling technique used to find participants who are difficult to identify or locate or who may be accessible but reluctant to get involved in the research project.

spider Sometimes called a robot, or a wanderer, this is a computer program that travels the Internet to locate sources such as Web documents, FTP archives, and Usenet articles that are indexed into a database that can be searched by a search engine.

split-halves reliability A method of checking for reliability that involves randomly dividing the questionnaire or test in half and administering half of the questionnaire to half of the participants and half to the other group.

standard deviation The average distance of scores in a distribution from the mean, measuring how much participants differ from the mean of their group.

statistics A collection of techniques that assists in uncovering meaning in numerical data in quantitative data analysis.

stratified random sampling A probability sampling technique that considers certain characteristics, called strata or subgroups, of elements in the population that would influence study results.

summative evaluation A form of program evaluation concerned with outcomes or results of programs and not with program processes.

systematic measurement errors Errors that occur consistently, with patterns, that can be attributed to participants' responses or to data collection methods.

systematic random sampling A probability sampling technique where every *n*th element in the population is selected.

target population The element from the population that the study focuses on.

target problem scaling A qualitative individual practice evaluation method.

targeted behavior The behavior of the client that the single system design intervention will address.

test-retest reliability A type of reliability in which participants are tested at two different times to determine if the scores or results are the same or correlated.

theory A group of related concepts and propositions based on facts and observations that attempt to define, explain, and predict phenomena, events, and situations.

theoretical framework A theory, framework, perspective, or paradigm that helps guide the research process. Examples of common social work theoretical frameworks include general systems theory, ecological perspective, strengths perspective, feminist theory, and empowerment theory. One study may use more than one theoretical framework.

truncation   A method of cutting off the end of a word when you are creating a search on the Web. When given such a request, a search engine will look for all possible endings to the word in addition to the root word.

units of analysis   What or whom the research is conducted on, such as individuals, groups, and social artifacts.

unknown investigator   In qualitative research, when the researcher is disguised as a member of the group being studied.

unstructured interviews   In qualitative research, the use of interview guides consisting of open-ended questions that may or may not be developed before the interview and could consist of one question or a series of questions.

URL (uniform resource locator)   The Web address of a document, service, or resource That specifies the exact method of locating an item on the Internet.

validity   A measuring instrument is valid when it accurately measures what it set out to measure.

variable   A phenomenon that has attributes, values, or characteristics that can vary from participant to participant and from research study to research study, and can change over time, and can be measured. A variable must have at least two attributes.

variance   The average squared distances of all scores from the mean.

wildcard   A character that stands in for another character or group of characters. Most search engines use an * or ? for this function. Although the wildcard is most frequently used in truncation, it can also be used in the middle of words, i.e., Wom*n.

WWW (World Wide Web)   The collection of different resources and services available via the Web.

INDEX

ABAB design model, 274–275, 277
ABA design model, 274, 276
ABC design model, 274, 275
AB design model, 272–274
Accountability, 245
Age bias, 36
Alternate form reliability, 127–128
Alternative hypothesis, 187
Alternatives, 16
Analysis of Variance (ANOVA), 189
Analysis, units of, 142
Analytic coding of data, 231
Androcentricity/gynocentricity, 35
Anonymity, 30
Article abstracts, 100
Association, 16
Audit trails, 233
Authority figures, 9
Author searching, 50–51

Bar graph, 179, 181
Baseline, 252, 272–273
    gathering data, 266–267
    of single system design, 263–264
B Design, 248–250
Bias, 34
Biases, in research
    age, 36
    culture, race, and ethnic group, 35–36
    gender, 34–35
    labeling, 37–38
    language, 37–38
    strategies for preventing, 37
Bibliographies, 47
Boolean Logic, 48–49
Business Periodicals Index, 53

Call number, 45–46
Case examples
    Adolescent Drug Addiction and Parental Conflict, 65–67
    Letter of Informed Consent, 21–23
    Research with Gay, Lesbian, Bisexual, and Transgender People, 137–138
Case studies
    Codebook, A, 172–173

"Evaluation of a Stress Management Program for Middle School Adolescents, The," 284–287
Excerpts from "Care of the Dying by Physician-in-Training" (Muller, 1995), 198–201
Incest, 116–117
Independent Living Questionnaire, 154–156
Kodak Family, Intensive Family Preservation Case, The, 259–262
"Living with HIV/AIDS: The Voices of HIV-Positive Mothers," 216–221
Research Partnership between the Department of Children, Youth, and Families and Grooms University, A, 302–303
Supervising Children, Youth, and Adult Services Unit, 242–244
Working with Baby Boomer Caregivers, 5–6
Case study design, 248–250
Causal relationships, 30–33
Causality, 12
    criteria for, 16
    errors in
        ecological fallacy, 16–17
        reductionism, 17
Child Abuse and Neglect, 53–54
Child welfare agencies. *See* Research partnerships with child welfare agencies
Chi-square analysis, 190–191
Cleaning data, 175
Closed-ended questions, 12, 161
Cluster sampling, 146
Coding data, 174–175
Collaboration. *See* Research partnerships with child welfare agencies
Community needs assessment, 149
Computer-assisted telephone interviewing (CATI), 159
Computerized periodical searches, 52–53
Conceptualization, 120–122
Concurrent validity, 130
Confidence level, 150–151
Confidentiality, 30–31
Construct validity, 130–131
Content analysis, 165–166
Content validity, 129
Contexts of interpretation, 232
Contracts, 248, 249